Regional Liberalization in International Air Transport

Regional Liberalization in International Air Transport

Towards Northeast Asian Open Skies

Jae Woon Lee

international publishing

Published, sold and distributed by Eleven International Publishing
P.O. Box 85576
2508 CG The Hague
The Netherlands
Tel.: +31 70 33 070 33
Fax: +31 70 33 070 30
e-mail: sales@elevenpub.nl
www.elevenpub.com

Sold and distributed in USA and Canada
International Specialized Book Services
920 NE 58th Avenue, Suite 300
Portland, OR 97213-3786, USA
Tel.: 1-800-944-6190 (toll-free)
Fax: +1 503 280-8832
orders@isbs.com
www.isbs.com

Eleven International Publishing is an imprint of Boom uitgevers Den Haag.

ISBN 978-94-6236-688-6
ISBN 978-94-6274-576-6 (E-book)

© 2016 Jae Woon Lee | Eleven International Publishing

Cover picture: <www.dreamstime.com/stock-photo-aviation-airplane-architecture-plane-see-hole-image55254948>.

This publication is protected by international copyright law.
All rights reserved. No part of this publication may be reproduced, stored in a retrieval system, or transmitted in any form or by any means, electronic, mechanical, photocopying, recording or otherwise, without the prior permission of the publisher.

Printed in The Netherlands

Table of Contents

Acknowledgements	xi
Foreword	xiii
Summary	xv
List of Tables	xvii
List of Figures	xix
Abbreviations	xxi

1	**Introduction to Northeast Asian Open Skies**	**1**
1.1	Overview	1
1.2	Multilateral Air Law Treaties	11
1.3	Exceptionalism in Economic Air Transport	15
1.3.1	Historical Background	15
1.3.2	ICAO or WTO: Institutional Problems?	17
1.3.3	Nationalism	18
1.4	Economic Liberalization in International Air Transport	20
1.4.1	Scope: Relaxation of "Market Access" and "Ownership and Control" Restrictions	20
1.4.2	Economic Impact of Air Transport Liberalization	24
1.4.3	General Trends of Air Transport Liberalization	25
1.5	Regional Liberalization	27
1.5.1	Definition	27
1.5.2	Rationale for the Regional Approach in International Air Transport	28
1.5.3	Progress in Regional Liberalization	32
1.5.4	Challenges to Regional Liberalization	33
1.6	Airline Alliances	34
1.6.1	Rationale for Airline Alliances	34
1.6.2	Antitrust Immunity	37
1.6.3	Metal Neutrality	40
1.7	Object and Structure of the Research	42

2	**Comparative Analysis of Regional Liberalization Models**	**45**
2.1	Overview	45
2.2	The EU Single Aviation Market Model	46
2.2.1	Overview	46
2.2.2	Main Features	50
2.2.2.1	Market Access	50
2.2.2.2	Ownership and Control	51
2.2.2.3	External Relations	52
2.2.3	Benefits of the EU Single Aviation Market	57
2.2.4	Challenges to the EU Single Aviation Market	58
2.3	The ASEAN Single Aviation Market Model	62
2.3.1	Overview	62
2.3.2	Main Features	64
2.3.2.1	Market Access	64
2.3.2.2	Ownership and Control	67
2.3.2.3	External Relations	68
2.3.3	Benefits of the ASEAN Single Aviation Market	70
2.3.4	Challenges to the ASEAN Single Aviation Market	74
2.4	Other Regional Liberalization Models	76
2.4.1	Australia-New Zealand Single Aviation Market	76
2.4.2	Asia-Pacific Economic Cooperation (APEC)'s Initiative	78
2.4.3	Regional Liberalization in the League of Arab States	80
2.4.4	Regional Liberalization in Latin America	83
2.4.5	Regional Liberalization in the Pacific Islands	88
2.4.6	Regional Liberalization in Africa	90
2.5	Regional Liberalization in Northeast Asia	92
2.5.1	History	92
2.5.2	Justifications	93
2.5.3	Barriers	96
2.5.4	Paths to Northeast Asian Open Skies	99
2.6	Conclusion	101
3	**Market Access Issues in Northeast Asia**	**103**
3.1	Market Access Restrictions in International Air Transport	103
3.1.1	Overview	103
3.1.2	Direct Market Access Issues	104
3.1.2.1	Carrier Designation	104
3.1.2.2	Route Designation	106
3.1.2.3	Capacity and Frequency	107

3.1.3	Indirect Market Access Issues	108
3.1.3.1	Airport Capacity	109
3.1.3.2	Airspace Use	110
3.1.3.3	Visa Openness	112
3.2	National Policies on Market Access in Northeast Asia	114
3.2.1	Overview	114
3.2.2	China	115
3.2.2.1	Protecting the "Big Three" Airlines	115
3.2.2.2	Promoting LCCs	118
3.2.2.3	Managing Airspace Better	120
3.2.3	Japan	126
3.2.3.1	Policy Transformation through the "Asian Gateway Initiative"	126
3.2.3.2	Increasing Airport Capacity in the Tokyo Area	127
3.2.3.3	Promoting LCCs	130
3.2.4	Korea	131
3.2.4.1	Prioritizing Northeast Asia	131
3.2.4.2	Focusing on 6th Freedom Traffic	132
3.2.4.3	Promoting LCCs	133
3.3	Bilateral Positions on Market Access	134
3.3.1	China–Japan	134
3.3.2	Japan–Korea	135
3.3.3	Korea–China	137
3.4	The Prospect of Liberalizing Trilateral Market Access	139
3.4.1	Shuttle Services among Major Cities in Northeast	140
3.4.2	The Role of LCCs	142
3.4.3	Developing a China–Japan–Korea Free Trade Agreement	144
3.5	Conclusion	146
4	**Ownership and Control Issues in Northeast Asia**	**147**
4.1	Ownership and Control Restrictions in International Air Transport	147
4.1.1	Overview	147
4.1.2	Internal (Domestic Law) Restrictions	150
4.1.3	External (Air Services Agreement) Restrictions	154
4.2	National Law and Policy on Ownership and Control Restrictions in Northeast Asia	158
4.2.1	Overview	158
4.2.2	China	161
4.2.3	Japan	164

4.2.4	Korea	167
4.3	Options for Liberalizing Ownership and Control Restrictions	169
4.3.1	The Multilateral Approach	169
4.3.2	The Regional Approach	172
4.3.3	The Bilateral Approach	174
4.3.4	The Unilateral Approach	175
4.4	Airlines' Response to Ownership and Control Restrictions	177
4.4.1	Overview (Merger vs. Alliance)	177
4.4.2	Cross-Border Merger through Holding Company	178
4.4.3	Joint Ventures	184
4.5	Conclusion	189
5	**Airline Alliances in Northeast Asia**	**191**
5.1	Conceptual Analysis of Airline Alliances	191
5.1.1	Motivating Factors for Airline Alliances	191
5.1.1.1	Circumventing Legal Barriers	191
5.1.1.2	Increasing Revenue	193
5.1.1.3	Cutting Costs	194
5.1.1.4	Reducing Competition	195
5.1.2	Spectrum of Airline Alliances	195
5.1.2.1	Equity Alliances	197
5.1.2.2	Non-equity Alliances	200
5.2	Competition Law Analysis of Airline Alliances	202
5.2.1	General Principles	202
5.2.2	Antitrust Immunity	206
5.2.2.1	Origin	206
5.2.2.2	Correlation with Open Skies Agreements	209
5.2.2.3	Challenges to Antitrust Immunity	212
5.2.3	Metal Neutrality: New Requirement for Antitrust Immunity	216
5.3	Airline Alliances and Competition Law in Northeast Asia	217
5.3.1	Airline Alliances in the Northeast Asian Market	217
5.3.2	Competition Law Regimes Relating to Airline Alliances in Northeast Asia	219
5.3.2.1	China	220
5.3.2.2	Japan	222
5.3.2.3	Korea	224
5.4	Metal Neutral Joint Ventures in the Trans-Pacific (Northeast Asia-US) Market	226
5.4.1	US Policy on Open Skies and Antitrust Immunity in Asia	226

5.4.2	American Airlines-Japan Airlines JV	229
5.4.3	United Airlines-All Nippon Airways (ANA) JV	232
5.4.4	Proposed Delta-Korean Air JV	234
5.4.5	Possibility of a JV between a Chinese Airline and a US Airline	237
5.5	Impact of Metal Neutral Joint Ventures in Northeast Asia	238
5.5.1	Analysis of US–China Aviation Market	238
5.5.1.1	Market Definition: "Relevant Market" in the Context of Competition Law	238
5.5.1.2	Relevant Market of Passenger Air Transport	240
5.5.1.3	China–US Market for Passenger Air Transport	242
5.5.2	Impact on Chinese Aviation Policy	243
5.6	Conclusion	248
6	**Towards Northeast Asian Open Skies: Liberalization by the Airline Industry and States**	**249**
6.1	Theoretical Findings	249
6.2	Ongoing Regional Liberalization in Northeast Asia	253
6.3	Action Plans for Northeast Asian Open Skies	258
6.3.1	Institutional Framework	258
6.3.2	Legal Reforms	261
6.3.2.1	Overview	261
6.3.2.2	Roadmap for Northeast Asian Open Skies by 2020	265
6.3.2.3	Roadmap for Northeast Asian Open Skies by 2025	268
6.3.2.4	Roadmap for Northeast Asian Open Skies by 2030	270
6.3.3	Policy Liberalization	272
6.4	Conclusion	274
Bibliography		**277**
Index		**327**

Acknowledgements

I am grateful to the many wonderful people whose support made this research possible. First and foremost, I am indebted to Professor Alan Khee-Jin Tan, who was the reason I came to the National University of Singapore Faculty of Law in the first place. His insightful and detailed guidance have proved that coming to NUS Law was one of the best decisions of my life. I want to thank each member of the NUS Law team who assisted my research. Special thanks go to the staff of the C J Koh Law Library, who provided a tremendous amount of support, and to Normah, who is always willing to help.

Professor Michael Milde's encouragement has been of special importance to me. He always speaks highly of me, and I have been greatly motivated to meet his high expectations. A number of academics graciously shared their views with me. They include Professors Lee Yeong Heok, Robert Beckman, Muthucumaraswamy Sornarajah, Pablo Mendes de Leon, David Timothy Duval, Umakanth Varottil, Michael Ewing-Chow, Andrew Halpin and Victor Ramraj. Some of my good friends provided important advice when I needed it. These are Alejandro Piera, George Leloudas, Jason Bonin, Hao Duy Phan and Benoit Mayer. I have benefited from fruitful discussions with industry experts and practitioners. They are Kwon Yuri, Lee Tae Wook, Kim Byeong Chang, Dr. Akira Mitsumasu, Will Horton, Ahn Yong Seok and Dr. Han Jun. David Carruth deserves recognition not only for his English editing but also his moral support. I am also grateful to Ga Bora for her editing of this work.

Finally, my gratitude and love go to my family: my parents, who raised my brother and me to the best of their ability; my wonderful wife, Park Bomi, who supported me immensely during my research; and my two sons, Lee Jun and Lee San, who have been a motivation to finish this research. Thank you all!

Foreword

"I am nova progenies caelo demittur alto..."
Publius Vergilius Maro, Bucolica, IV. 7

A new generation is coming, not necessarily from high heavens (as Virgil would have it) but from all corners of the globe. Northeast Asia (which the author defines as China, Japan and Korea) is a powerhouse rich in traditions, culture, resources and a dynamic new generation of talented scholars is coming from there. The author of this book represents a new generation rooted in Northeast Asia but absorbing the culture of all continents.

Dr. Lee, Jae Woon originates from Seoul, Republic of Korea. Many years ago he came to the McGill University's Institute of Air and Space Law in Montreal after he completed his Bachelor of Law degree at the Hankuk University in Seoul. At the Institute I was his teacher in public and private international air law and found in him instantly a "kindred spirit" motivated to engage in research and open to creative thinking. After he received his degree of the Master of Air and Space Law he spent years in the Korean Air Legal Affairs Department in Seoul and frequently went to teach air law at the Hankuk University of Foreign Studies, at the Korea University in Seoul and was gradually attracted as expert on air law subjects to the Ministry of Foreign Affairs, Republic of Korea. That included his participation in the sessions of the ICAO Legal Committee, Assembly and Diplomatic Conferences.

Some students never fade from the memory of their ageing teachers. I never lost contact with him and we kept meeting with regularity at international conferences and lectures several times in Seoul. Some of our endless discussions took place in my home in London, Ontario which he visited repeatedly. This is where he reached his decision to dedicate his future to academic work as a researcher and teacher. It was a bold decision to leave his employment and to enroll into the Doctoral program at the National University of Singapore under the guidance of Professor Alan Tan. Four years later he emerged as "Dr Lee" and a respected scholar with extensive publications and numerous scholarly presentations at international conferences. His wife Bomi and his two young sons deserve credit for inspiration and support.

The subject of this book presents an original approach to liberalization of international air transport in Northeast Asia, i.e., China, Japan and Korea. It is not an easy subject. Some 72 years ago the Chicago Conference on International Civil Aviation failed to reach an agreement that would lead to liberalization of international air transport and the discussion continues ever since. A vast network of protectionist bilateral agreements on air services kept governing the delicate balance of national interests and it took decades before some

FOREWORD

of these bilaterals between like-minded States accepted "open skies", liberalized the market access and relaxed the ownership and control limitations. This methodology was accepted in regional arrangements in some parts of the world, including the ASEAN. However, the complexity of the relations of the States in the Northeast Asia and their entrenched historic differences and memories of hostilities so far represent an impediment to speedy liberalization of air transport services. While a positive action by States is indispensable, the author sees an important role for the airlines in influencing the regulatory process leading to liberalization. The author offers a target for short-term (2020), mid-term (2025) and long term (2030) stages of liberalization by a proposed "Trilateral Agreement on Air Services". His arguments are convincing and deserve serious consideration.

May this book, written by a new generation scholar, contribute to further progress of international air services for the new generations!

Professor Dr. Michael Milde
Emeritus Director, Institute of Air and Space Law, McGill University

Summary

This research analyzes the regulations pertaining to the economic aspects of international air transport from the perspectives of law and policy. The subject of this analysis is Northeast Asia (defined in this study as China, Japan and Korea), and the focal point is a regional approach to liberalizing the international air transport market.

International air transport is currently undergoing dynamic regulatory changes. Once, the airline industry was one of the most protected industries and was strongly marked by nationalistic sentiment. Today, however, it is largely in the process of liberalization, which can be measured by the relaxation of market access and ownership and control. While bilateral air services agreements are the principal instruments for liberalizing international air transport, regional approaches have also emerged in most parts of the world.

Thus far, progress on regional liberalization has been slower in Northeast Asia than other regions, particularly Southeast Asia, where substantial progress has been achieved. Although the aero-political calculations that impede liberalization are commonplace all over the world, this impediment is more severely entrenched in Northeast Asia in addition to non-aviation-related barriers. However, there are ample arguments in favor of Northeast Asian open skies and telltale signs of positive changes. Furthermore, the airline industry itself is pushing for Northeast Asian open skies.

In essence, this research investigates the legal and policy aspects of air transport liberalization in the Northeast Asian market and prescribes solutions for Northeast Asian open skies.

LIST OF TABLES

Table 2.1	Summary of Market Access and Ownership and Control Liberalization of the EU Packages	50
Table 2.2	The ASEAN Roadmap for Integration of the Air Travel Sector	63
Table 2.3	The 2009 Multilateral Agreement on Air Services (MAAS)	64
Table 2.4	The 2010 Multilateral Agreement for the Full Liberalization of Passenger Air Services (MAFLPAS)	66
Table 2.5	The 2009 Multilateral Agreement for the Full Liberalization of Air Freight Services (MAFLAFS)	66
Table 2.6	Top 10 International LCC Routes (2014)	71
Table 2.7	The Ownership and Control Structure of ASEAN LCC Joint Ventures	72
Table 2.8	Basic ASEAN Indicators (2014)	74
Table 2.9	Guidelines for Arab Regional Liberalization	81
Table 2.10	Basic Indicators for Andean Community (2014)	83
Table 2.11	Basic Indicators for the Parties of the Fortaleza Agreement	84
Table 2.12	The Snapshot of the Pacific Islands Air Services Agreement	89
Table 2.13	Northeast Asian Legacy Carrier Profile	96
Table 3.1	Visa Status between Three Countries and Their Nationals	113
Table 3.2	Summary of Major Incumbent Chinese Airlines	118
Table 3.3	Summary of Proposed New Chinese Airlines	119
Table 3.4	Annual Slot Changes at Tokyo Haneda and Tokyo Narita Airports	129
Table 3.5	Major Domestic Routes in Korea	131
Table 3.6	China–Korea Air Transport Statistics	138
Table 3.7	Comparison of Travel Times among the Major Cities in Northeast Asia (Downtown Airports vs. Main International Airports)	141
Table 3.8	Summary of Airlines Operating Shuttle Services	141
Table 4.1	Subdivision of Ownership and Control Restrictions	148
Table 4.2	Foreign Ownership Limits in Selected Countries	152
Table 4.3	The Ownership and Cotrol Structure of AirAsia LCC Joint Ventures	159
Table 4.4	Joint Venture Airlines Whose Local Shareholders Are Not Airline Companies	185

List of Tables

Table 4.5	Joint Venture Airlines Owned by Airline Companies or Their Subsidiaries	187
Table 5.1	Global Branded Airline Alliances	195
Table 5.2	Categories of Code-sharing Agreements	205
Table 5.3	Member Airlines in Global Alliances (China, Japan and Korea)	218
Table 5.4	Airline Alliances in the China–Japan Market	218
Table 5.5	Airline Alliances in the Japan–Korea Market	219
Table 5.6	Airline Alliances in the China–Korea Market	219
Table 5.7	Competition Law Regimes Relating to Airline Alliances in Northeast Asia	220
Table 5.8	Snapshot of American Airlines and Japan Airlines	231
Table 5.9	Routes on the Metal Neutral Joint Venture between AA and JAL	232
Table 5.10	Snapshot of United Airlines and All Nippon Airways	233
Table 5.11	Routes on the Metal Neutral Joint Venture between United and ANA	233
Table 5.12	The Largest China–US O&D Markets (2015 Winter Schedule)	242
Table 5.13	Northeast Asian Airline Service to Europe Destinations	247
Table 5.14	Comparison among China–US, Japan-EU, and Korea-EU Markets	247
Table 6.1	Profiles of Northeast Asian Low-Cost Carriers	256
Table 6.2	Ratification Dates for the Protocol 5 of MAAS	262
Table 6.3	Implementing Protocols to the TAAS	264
Table 6.4	Protocol 1 to the TAAS	265
Table 6.5	Protocol 2 to the TAAS	267
Table 6.6	Protocol 3 to the TAAS	268
Table 6.7	Protocol 4 to the TAAS	269
Table 6.8	Roadmap for Northeast Asian Open Skies by 2030	270

List of Figures

Figure 1.1	The Nine Freedoms of the Air	4
Figure 1.2	Major Multilateral Air Law	12
Figure 1.3	The Economic Impact of Air Service	25
Figure 1.4	Liberalized Country Pair Routes with Non-Stop Flights	33
Figure 1.5	Types of Code-Share Operations	37
Figure 1.6	Spectrum of Alliance Cooperation	38
Figure 2.1	LCCs' Market Shares in Europe	58
Figure 2.2	LCCs' Share of Capacity within Southeast Asia	70
Figure 3.1	LCCs' Penetration in China	120
Figure 3.2	On-Time Departures at Major International Airports	122
Figure 3.3	On-time Performance of Asian Airlines	123
Figure 3.4	Location of Beijing Daxing Airport	125
Figure 3.5	Distance of Tokyo Area Airports from Downtown Tokyo	128
Figure 3.6	Aircraft movements at Haneda and Narita airports: 1970-2010	129
Figure 3.7	LCCs' Capacity Share within Northeast Asia	143
Figure 4.1	Spectrum of Airline Integration (from Merger to Alliance)	178
Figure 4.2	Corporate Structure of Air France-KLM S.A. in 2004	180
Figure 4.3	Corporate Structure of the LATAM Group	181
Figure 4.4	Corporate Structure of Avianca Holdings S.A.	183
Figure 5.1	Etihad Equity Alliance	199
Figure 5.2	Spectrum of Non-equity Airline Alliances	201
Figure 5.3	Conceptual Description of Market Change by Antitrust Immunity under a Protectionist Air Services Agreement	211
Figure 5.4	Conceptual Description of Market Change by Antitrust Immunity under an Open Skies Agreement	212
Figure 5.5	Korean Air Route Map	235
Figure 5.6	Non-stop China–US Seat Capacity Share by Carrier Nationality: 2005-2015	245
Figure 6.1	The Influence of Airlines on Liberalizing Air Services Agreements	251
Figure 6.2	Airlines' New Business Model for *De Facto* Liberalization	252
Figure 6.3	How Airline Alliances Affect Liberalization	253
Figure 6.4	Selected Northeast Asian LCCs' Operating Margin	257

Abbreviations

ACAC	The Arab Civil Aviation Commission
AEC	ASEAN Economic Community
AFCAC	The African Civil Aviation Commission
AOC	Air Operator Certificate
APEC	Asia-Pacific Economic Cooperation
ASEAN	The Association of South East Asian Nations
ATM	Air Traffic Management
BESETO	Beijing-Seoul-Tokyo
CAAC	The Civil Aviation Authority of China
CAB	The US Civil Aeronautics Board
CAPA	The Centre for Aviation
CER	The Closer Economic Relations Trade Agreement
CITEJA	The Comitè International Technique d'Experts Juridiques Aeriens
CJEU	The Court of Justice of the European Union
COMESA	The Common Market for East South Africa
DOJ	The US Department of Justice
DOT	The US Department of Transportation
EAC	The East African Community
EASA	The European Aviation Safety Agency
FTA	Free Trade Agreement
GATS	The General Agreement on Trade in Services
IATA	The International Air Transport Association
ICAO	The International Civil Aviation Organization
JFTC	The Japan Fair Trade Commission
KFTC	The Korea Fair Trade Commission
LACAC	The Latin American Civil Aviation Commission
LCCs	Low-Cost Carriers
MAAS	The 2009 Multilateral Agreement on Air Services
MAFLAFS	The 2009 Multilateral Agreement for Full Liberalization of Air Freight Services
MAFLPAS	The 2010 Multilateral Agreement for Full Liberalization of Passenger Air Services
MALIAT	The Multilateral Agreement on the Liberalization of Air Transportation

Abbreviations

MFN	Most-Favored Nation
MLIT	The Japan's Ministry of Land, Infrastructure, Transport, and Tourism
MOFCOM	The China's Ministry of Commerce
MOFTEC	The China's Ministry of Foreign Trade and Economic Cooperation
NDRC	The China's National Development and Reform Commission
O&D	Origin and Destination
PIASA	The Pacific Islands Air Services Agreement
RIATS	The Roadmap for Integration of the Air Travel Sector
SADC	The South African Development Community
SAIC	The China's State Administration for Industry and Commerce
SAM	Single Aviation Market
SES	The Single European Sky
TAAS	The Trilateral Agreement on Air Services
TCS	The Trilateral Cooperation Secretariat
TIACA	The International Air Cargo Association
TPR	Transnational Private Regulation
UNWTO	The United Nations World Tourism Organization
WTO	The World Trade Organization
WTTC	The World Travel & Tourism Council

1 INTRODUCTION TO NORTHEAST ASIAN OPEN SKIES

1.1 OVERVIEW

International air transport is currently undergoing a regulatory transformation. From its birth at the beginning of the 20th century, the airline industry was tightly regulated by governments with a strong tradition of protectionism. In the past few decades, however, protectionism in the airline industry has steadily declined, giving way to a new era of regulation. Indeed, the airline industry is largely in the process of liberalization.

Although "liberalization" can be used in various fields, *economic* liberalization is the most common application of the term and a focal area of this study. Economic liberalization generally refers to fewer government regulations on the economy, allowing for greater participation by private entities.[1] Thus, it can be measured in terms of policy changes that increase the scope of the market for allocating goods and services.[2]

Liberalization in international air transport can be measured by the level of relaxation of the two main legal hurdles: 1) market access and 2) ownership and control restrictions. Removing these two legal hurdles lies at the heart of any meaningful policy of liberalizing international air transport services.[3] Broadly, if a state embarks on market access relaxation, it would remove or reduce the hurdles that curtail the ability of other states' airlines to operate in its markets. On its part, ownership and control relaxation entails that state loosening restrictions on foreigners' participation in its airlines.

Historically, international air transport has mainly been governed by protectively written bilateral air services agreements with states stipulating mutual restrictions on market access and ownership and control. These include the designation of airlines by other states (which airlines and how many airlines may operate the agreed services),

---

1 For more detailed explanation, see Mehmet Odekon, *Encyclopedia of World Poverty* (Thousand Oaks, California: Sage Publications, 2006) at 292 (noting that "ECONOMIC LIBERLIZATION refers to the removal of both price and non-price barriers to the functioning of markets in the economy. In a liberalized economy, decisions are made in and by the markets, as dictated by free market forces, that is, supply and demand conditions. The idea behind support of economic liberalization is that in an economy where all the markets (output, input, financial, and external) are liberalized, prices set by supply and demand reflect the true resource and opportunity costs of factors of production and allocate resources in the most efficient way, providing the most effective and efficient solution to the problem of scarcity.").
2 Francesco Giavazzi & Guido Tabellini, "Economic and Political Liberalizations" (2005) 52 Journal of Monetary Economics 1297 at 1300.
3 Alan Khee-Jin Tan, "Prospects for a Single Aviation Market in Southeast Asia" (2009) 34 Ann. Air & Sp. L. 253 at 267 [Tan, "Prospects for SAM"].

nationality requirements of designated airlines (ownership and control requirements), the routes which designated airlines are entitled to fly, frequency (caps on the number of flights flown over a given time period), and capacity (predetermined limits on the amount of passengers and/or cargo carried).[4] (The details of these restrictions will be provided in Chapter 3: Market Access Issues in Northeast Asia, and Chapter 4: Ownership and Control Issues in Northeast Asia.)

Over the past few decades, however, liberalization of market access and ownership/control restrictions for international air transport has spread over most of the world, with variations in style and substance. (See below section 1.4 Economic Liberalization in International Air Transport.) Despite this, the bilateral approach between pairs of states remains dominant not only in rigidly regulated agreements but also substantially liberalized agreements. While bilateral air services agreements are the principal instruments for regulating many aspects of international air transportation, regional approaches to air transport liberalization that employ multilateral negotiation and decision-making are emerging or have already emerged in most parts of the world. (For a detailed discussion, see Chapter 2: Comparative Analysis of Regional Liberalization Models.)

Indeed, liberalized intra-regional air transport services are currently in operation in North America, Africa (divided into several sub-regions), Latin America, the states of the Arab League, islands in the Pacific, and the Caribbean states, among others, led by the most consolidated model of all, the European model.[5]

In Asia, the Association of South East Asian Nations (ASEAN) has implemented a substantial amount of regional liberalization.[6] With a high degree of community awareness in Southeast Asia, including identity-building and legal institutionalization, the regional liberalization of air services has been negotiated in the context of ASEAN's larger economic integration.

Northeast Asia, the focal area of this study, is no exception for the application of the regional approach to air transport liberalization. The leading Northeast Asian aviation powers (defined in this study as China, Japan and the Republic of Korea ["Korea" hereinafter]) entered into negotiations on regional liberalization in 2006. However, while there has been some progress since the initiative in the region, negotiations for regional liberalization have not moved forward as much as was expected, and as yet there has been no concrete discussion of a regional open skies agreement. This research primarily aims to investigate multilateral arrangements for Northeast Asian open skies.

---

4   See Isabella H.Ph. Diederiks-Verschoor, *An Introduction to Air Law*, 9th ed. revised by Pablo Mendes de Leon (Alphen aan den Rijn: Kluwer Law International, 2012) at 48.
5   This model, EU Single Aviation Market, is elaborated in section 2.2 The EU Single Aviation Market Model.
6   See section 2.3 The ASEAN Single Aviation Market Model.

There is no universally accepted definition for "open skies," the key concept in this study.[7] In a broad sense, "open skies" is a policy concept that calls for the liberalization of international air transport. In a legal context, "open skies" typically means an "open skies agreement," which is to say an air services agreement that liberalizes the rules governing international aviation markets and minimizes government intervention.[8] In a more limited sense, "Open Skies" refers to the US model of an open skies agreement, which relaxes restrictions to market access more than the typical open skies agreement. (This difference will be discussed below in section 1.4.3 General Trends of Economic Liberalization in International Air Transport.)

For the purposes of this research, I distinguish the terms "open skies" and "open skies agreement." That is, "open skies" means a policy concept that entails or promises to entail relaxing restrictions on market access and ownership and control, while "open skies agreement" means a concrete treaty between states that lays out the details of air transport liberalization. The US model of an open skies agreement will be specifically mentioned as such rather than calling it "Open Skies."

Once again, relaxing restrictions on market access and ownership and control are the key barometers of liberalization in international air transport. In order to understand market access in international air transport, it is necessary to understand the concept of "freedoms of the air." In fact, freedoms of the air (the privileges that one state accords to the carriers of other states to conduct activities over that state's sovereign airspace)[9] are frequently referred to in international air transport. The nine freedoms of the air are illustrated as follows:

---

7   Jason Bonin noted that even Brian Havel's influential book *Beyond Open Skies* does not provide a definition for "open skies." See Jason R. Bonin, *International Air Transport Liberalization in East Asia: A Regional Approach to Reform* (Ph.D Thesis, National University of Singapore, 2013) [unpublished] at 8.
8   Charles E. Schlumberger, *Open Skies for Africa Implementing the Yamoussoukro Decision* (Washington, D.C.: The World Bank, 2010) at 6.
9   Alan Khee-Jin Tan, "Liberalizing Aviation in the Asia-Pacific Region: The Impact of the EU Horizontal Mandate" (2006) 31 Air & Sp. L. 432 at 433 [Tan, "Horizontal Mandate"].

REGIONAL LIBERALIZATION IN INTERNATIONAL AIR TRANSPORT

Figure 1.1   The Nine Freedoms of the Air[10]

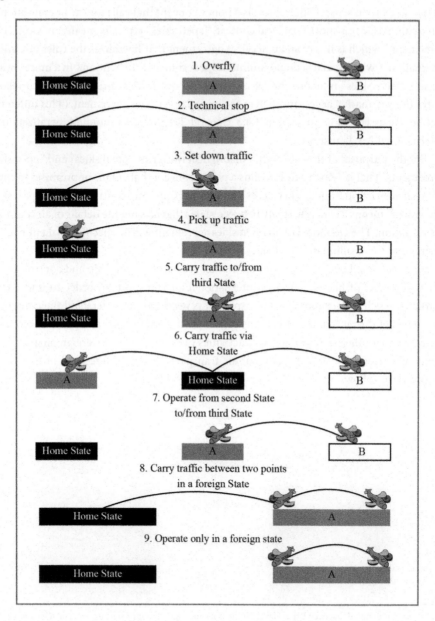

1st Freedom – For the aircraft of State A to overfly the territory of State B;

2nd Freedom – For the aircraft of State A to make technical stops in the territory of State B;

3rd Freedom – For the aircraft of State A to embark passengers and cargo in State A and disembark them in State B;

4th Freedom – For the aircraft of State A to embark passengers and cargo in State B and disembark them in State A;

5th Freedom – For the aircraft of State A, from a service originating in State A, to embark passengers and cargo in State B and disembark them in State C;

6th Freedom – For the aircraft of State A to embark passengers and cargo in State B, reroute them through State A, and disembark them in State C (this is essentially a combination of 3rd–4th freedoms);

7th Freedom – For the aircraft of State A to embark and disembark passengers and cargo between State B and State C without a stop in State A;

8th Freedom – For the aircraft of State A, from a service originating in State A, to embark passengers and cargo in State B and disembark them in another point in State B (consecutive cabotage);

9th Freedom – For the aircraft of State A, from a service originating in State B, to embark and disembark passengers and cargo between two points within State B (stand-alone cabotage).[11]

While the first five freedoms have their origins in international instruments[12] adopted at the International Civil Aviation Conference in 1944 (Chicago Conference), the rest of the freedoms (the sixth freedom to the ninth freedom) were developed outside of international instruments. Nevertheless, they are well-established concepts in practice. In 1944, a year before the end of World War II, states gathered in Chicago to discuss the principles and methods to be followed for the adoption of a new aviation convention.[13] As a consequence, the Chicago Conference of 1944 successfully adopted an overarching treaty for international

---

10 International Civil Aviation Organization (ICAO), *Manual on the Regulation of International Air Transport*, ICAO Doc. 9626 (2nd ed. 2004) at 4. [ICAO, "Regulation"]; The first five freedoms have their origins in the International Air Transport Agreement 1944 and the International Air Services Transit Agreement 1944. The rest of the freedoms (the sixth freedom to the ninth freedom) are not based in international instruments; however, they are well-established concepts in practice, and the International Civil Aviation Organization (ICAO) characterizes these freedoms as so-called.

11 Bonin, *supra* note 7 at 81-85.

12 Namely, *International Air Services Transit Agreement*, signed at Chicago, 7 December 1944; *International Air Transport Agreement*, signed at Chicago, 7 December 1944.

13 See *Proceedings of the International Conference on Civil Aviation, Chicago, 1 November – 7 December 1944* (Washington, D.C.: United States Government Printing Office, 1948) vol. I at 11-13. [U.S. Dept. of State, "Proceedings"].

air law, the Convention on International Civil Aviation (Chicago Convention), which also created the International Civil Aviation Organization (ICAO).

Nonetheless, states failed to agree on how to govern the multilateral exchange of commercial rights (i.e. the third freedom onwards) for international air transport. The most noticeable conflict of interests occurred between the US, which favored maximum flexibility and minimal regulation of air transport, and the UK, which wished to protect its vast colonial air spaces all around the globe.[14] Michael Milde notes the rationale for the difference:

> The United States developed during the war mammoth industrial capacity to build large bomber aircraft—a technology easily convertible to civilian use; the United Kingdom's industry produced efficient fighter aircraft but lagged behind in the production of large air transport equipment. The competing interests predictably influenced the competing proposals.[15]

Much of the Chicago Conference turned on the question of whether states would allow each other some or the entire first "five freedoms."[16] Not surprisingly, American negotiators called for a multilateral granting of all five freedoms without restrictions.[17] The multilateral system desired by the US, if approved, would have allowed US carriers to fly between two international points outside the US on services originating in the US with no limitations on capacity. This would provide US carriers with unlimited access to foreign carriers' most valuable traffic, which is exactly what other countries and carriers feared.[18]

Moreover, US carriers had gained control of almost 72 percent of global air commerce with their technological expertise, while British carriers only had control of about 12 percent of the market, and much of European manufacturing infrastructure had been destroyed by the war.[19] Due in large part to the frightening prospect of unrestrained competition with the dominant US carriers on international routes, participants in the Chicago Conference were unable to reach a meaningful compromise on economic regulatory issues.[20] This is illustrated by Article 6 of the Chicago Convention, which confirms that there is no

---

14 Michael Milde, *International Air Law and ICAO*, 2nd ed. (Utrecht: Eleven International Publishing, 2012) at 14-15.
15 Milde, *supra* note 14 at 14-15.
16 Anthony Sampson, *Empires of the Sky: the Politics, and Cartels of World Airlines* (London: Hodder and Stroughton, 1984) at 67.
17 Paul Stephen Dempsey, *Law and Foreign Policy in International Aviation* (Dobbs Ferry, Transnational Publishers: 1987) at 11 [Dempsey, "Foreign Policy"].
18 *Ibid.* at 12.
19 Paul Stephen Dempsey, *Public International Air Law* (Montreal: Institute of Air and Space Law, 2008) at 21-22 [Dempsey, "Air Law"].
20 *Ibid.* at 25 & 29.

universal freedom of international air transport and that "special permission or other authorization" is required for international air transport.

> Article 6 – Scheduled Air Services
> No scheduled international air service may be operated over or into the territory of a contracting State, except with the special permission or other authorization of that State, and in accordance with the terms of such permission or authorization.

Article 6 of the Chicago Convention prohibits scheduled international air service operations "over" or "into" the territory of a contracting state. This means that the Convention does not even permit the first freedom—the freedom of overflight, which does not grant any commercial rights—not to mention all the commercial rights beginning with the third freedom. Instead, the Chicago Conference adopted two instruments dealing with the exchange of traffic rights: the International Air Services Transit Agreement and the International Air Services Transport Agreement (discussed in the next section 1.2 Multilateral Air Law Treaties).

After the states attending the Chicago Conference failed to agree upon a comprehensive multilateral solution to economic regulation of the international civil aviation industry, it became clear that bilateral negotiations between individual states were the only viable option for determining route assignments, frequencies, capacities, and fares.[21] Indeed, all commercial rights for international air transport since 1944 have been negotiated largely on a bilateral basis. It is worth noting that although the bilateral method of exchange was not rooted in the Chicago Convention, one of the collateral resolutions adopted in the Chicago Conference, Resolution VIII Standard Form of Agreement for Provisional Air Routes, recommended a model bilateral agreement during a transitional period (the period immediately after the war).[22]

More importantly, the US and the UK succeeded in reaching a bilateral agreement acceptable to both in 1946 in Bermuda despite their vastly different views on economic air transport at the Chicago Conference.[23] This protectively written bilateral air services agreement between the US and the UK, the so-called Bermuda type 1 agreement, became the prototype for many bilateral air transport agreements throughout the world.[24]

In the early 1990s, a new perspective on bilateral air services agreements was introduced through the so-called open skies agreements. The pioneering agreement was concluded

---

21 *Ibid.* at 522.
22 Brian Havel, *Beyond Open Skies: A New Regime for International Aviation* (Alphen aan den Rijn, Kluwer Law International: 2009) at 109-110 [Havel, "Open Skies"].
23 Dempsey, "Air Law", *supra* note 19 at 523.
24 *Ibid.* at 524.

between the US and the Netherlands in 1992. The U.S. Department of Transportation (DOT) identified the basic elements that constitute the essential components of open skies bilateral air transport agreements. These are, inter alia, 1) open entry on all routes, 2) unrestricted capacity and frequency on all routes, and 3) unrestricted route and traffic rights, that is, the right to operate service between any points including no restrictions on intermediate and beyond points, or the right to carry fifth freedom traffic.[25] In essence, the US open skies model promised unlimited economic rights, *i.e.* the third, fourth and fifth freedoms. Since 1992, more states have started to change their aviation policies from a protectionist to a more liberalized stance, although the changes have still arisen mostly from bilateral agreements.

Along with market access liberalization, relaxation of ownership and control requirements is the other significant legal hurdle for air transport liberalization. The ownership and control restriction is the traditional requirement that an airline must be substantially owned and effectively controlled by nationals of the state which designates it for international air transport and under whose flag the airline is operated.[26] In other words, foreign ownership in an airline designated by a particular state is restricted, typically to less than 50 percent ownership (These issues are elaborated upon in Chapter 4: Ownership and Control Issues in Northeast Asia.)

While some of the more liberalized approaches have been introduced, *e.g.* the principal place of business/incorporation formula[27] and effective regulatory control,[28] traditional ownership and control restrictions are still firmly entrenched in national laws as well as in most air services agreements. One response to these rigid governmental regulations has been airline alliances, which were formed in part to maximize airlines' business opportunities. In an industry in which mergers are often difficult because of ownership and control restrictions, alliances are a suboptimal choice that airlines resort to. (For a detailed discussion, see Chapter 5: Airline Alliances in Northeast Asia.)

---

25   *Ibid.* at 544.
26   Isabelle Lelieur, *Law and Policy of Substantial Ownership and Effective Control of Airlines: Prospects for Change* (Aldershot & Burlington, Vermont: Ashgate, 2003) at 1.
27   ICAO notes that "evidence of principal place of business is predicated upon: the airline is established and incorporated in the territory of the designating Party in accordance with relevant national laws and regulations, has a substantial amount of its operations and capital investment in physical facilities in the territory of the designating Party, pays income tax, registers and bases its aircraft there, and employs a significant number of nationals in managerial, technical and operational positions." ICAO, *Consolidated Conclusions, Model Clauses, Recommendations and Declaration,* ICAO Doc. ATConf/5 (31 March 2003, REVISED 10 July 2003) at 5.
28   ICAO notes that "evidence of effective regulatory control is predicated upon but is not limited to: the airline holds a valid operating licence or permit issued by the licensing authority such as an Air Operator Certificate (AOC), meets the criteria of the designating Party for the operation of international air services, such as proof of financial health, ability to meet public interest requirement, obligations for assurance of service; and the designating Party has and maintains safety and security oversight programmes in compliance with ICAO standards." See *ibid.*

1 Introduction to Northeast Asian Open Skies

In the context of regional liberalization, the concept of "community carrier" has been developed (such as in the E.U. and ASEAN). This concept means that ownership and control of air carriers in the member states of a given community no longer necessarily mean national ownership and control, but instead have been redefined as community ownership and control.[29] (This will be further discussed in Chapter 2: Comparative Analysis of Regional Liberalization Models.)

While many regional liberalization models have substantially relaxed market access or ownership and control restrictions (or both) in various ways,[30] no meaningful progress has been made in Northeast Asia on a regional approach to liberalization, except some liberalization of market access via bilateral air services agreements. This is regrettable, since Northeast Asia has tremendous potential for regional liberalization. For instance, the Centre for Aviation (CAPA) has estimated that opening up regional markets in China, Japan, and Korea would have the potential for incremental growth of 300 million short-haul passengers.[31]

In fact, Northeast Asia is one of the few regions where a stable, developed economy co-exists with enormous potential for further growth. Although the level of political tensions among the three states – China, Japan and Korea – fluctuates, they regard each other as important economic partners and share the goal of promoting peace and common prosperity in the region.[32] Hence, negotiations for regional liberalization will and must continue. There have been two suggestions for how to approach Northeast Asian open skies: the bilateral approach and the trilateral approach.[33] The bilateral approach emphasizes bilateral air services agreements between countries in the region. In other words, this involves establishing three bilateral open skies agreements between China and Korea, Korea and Japan, and Japan and China.[34] Notably, this bilateral approach would only focus on easing market access.

The trilateral approach involves taking gradual steps to create Northeast Asian open skies among the three countries negotiating together. Here, attention should be drawn to several principles that the other regional liberalization models teach about market access relaxation: i) cargo services are more easily liberalized than passenger services; ii) third

---

29 Peter P.C. Haanappel, *The Law and Policy of Air Space and Outer Space: A Comparative Approach* (The Hague: Kluwer Law International, 2003) at 136 [Haanappel, "Law and Policy"].
30 See Chapter 2: Comparative Analysis of Regional Liberalization Models.
31 Centre For Aviation (CAPA), "Japan and South Korea reach historic 'open skies' deal" (3 August 2007), online: <http://centreforaviation.com/analysis/japan-and-south-korea-reach-historic-open-skies-deal-1928>.
32 With this goal, the Trilateral Cooperation Secretariat consisting of China, Japan and Korea was established. See the homepage of the Trilateral Cooperation Secretariat at <www.tcs-asia.org>.
33 See *e.g.* Sang-Do Kim, "Strategy for Liberalized Air Transport Market in NE Asia" (Presentation material presented to the 2009 ICAO Legal Seminar in Asia-Pacific Region, Seoul, 2 April 2009) [unpublished].
34 It is important to note that Korea and Japan have already implemented an open skies agreement. For more detailed explanation, see section 3.3.2 Japan–Korea.

and fourth freedom flights can be liberalized stage by stage, first allowing limited designated points, then capital cities, and finally unlimited designated points; and iii) rights for fifth freedom flights and beyond are typically discussed only after third and fourth freedom flights have been established.

Liberalizing ownership and control restrictions can be discussed as a final step to form Northeast Asian open skies. Alternately, ownership and control reform could precede or otherwise be tied to the earlier stages of market access reform.[35] It is noteworthy that ASEAN adopted the community carrier concept in the 2009 ASEAN Multilateral Agreement on Air Services by relaxing traditional ownership and control restrictions before fully liberalizing market access.

All these steps require a concrete timeline and robust framework. Interestingly, China, Japan and Korea signed and ratified the Agreement on the Establishment of the Trilateral Cooperation Secretariat (TCS) in 2010, and TCS was officially inaugurated in 2011. Ideally, TCS could provide a framework for regional liberalization of air transport in Northeast Asia. (This will be discussed in Chapter 6: Towards Northeast Asian Open Skies.)

Regional liberalization proceeds slowly even when one member state of the region fails to join an agreement. If that member state happens to be an important regional player, the impact is even more substantial.[36] However, this deadlock can be mitigated by airline-led liberalization. Indeed, a potential game changer in Northeast Asian open skies is the airline industry. This is because air carriers themselves can have a considerable impact on liberalization, particularly by means of alliances. (This will be dealt with in Chapter 5: Airline Alliances in Northeast Asia.)

If all the states but one have concluded open skies agreements in the relevant market and if furthermore, business activities among their national carriers have enjoyed antitrust immunity to the level of integrated joint ventures, the remaining party that has yet to join regional liberalization will be comparatively isolated, and their national carriers will be placed at a substantial disadvantage.

The scenario described above may become a reality in Northeast Asia if China continues to protect its air transport market. Korea, Japan, and the US have concluded open skies agreements, and, more importantly, their national air carriers have received antitrust immunity for co-operation among themselves. China, on the contrary, has not concluded any open skies agreement with the three states, thus preventing any Chinese carrier from receiving antitrust immunity. Actively providing airline alliances with antitrust immunity

---

35 In connection with the ASEAN Single Aviation Market, see Bonin, *supra* note 7 at 430-431.
36 A prime example is Indonesia, the largest economy in ASEAN. Indonesia has not fully ratified the implementing protocols of the 2009 Multilateral Agreement for the Full Liberalization of Air Freight Services (MAFLAFS) and the 2010 Multilateral Agreement for the Full Liberalization of Passenger Air Services (MAFLPAS). See section 2.3 The ASEAN Single Aviation Market Model.

could eventually lead to a breakthrough in discussions about Northeast Asian open skies. This will form the basis of analysis in Chapter 5: Airline Alliances in Northeast Asia.

As a background, this research will first review the history of economic regulation of international air transport.

1.2 MULTILATERAL AIR LAW TREATIES

Air law is a legal area known for its rapid development. Given that the first controlled and powered airplane took to the air around the turn of the 20th century, the real history of air law spans less than 120 years. To be sure, scholarly discussion about air law predated this, including the seminal work *De Jure Principis Aereo* in 1687, which argued that the air belongs to everyone but reserves special rights for rulers.[37]

However, until human flight became subject to some degree of control, there was little need for legal regulation.[38] The complex relationship of conflicting interests that air law must deal with only started to become apparent in the twentieth century. As long-haul (and therefore trans-boundary) carriage became feasible and common, the need for *international* air law became evident.

The first multilateral attempt to make laws for international aviation was the Paris Conference of 1910, which laid the foundation for the Convention Relating to the Regulation of Aerial Navigation (the Paris Convention of 1919),[39] the first multilateral *public* air law treaty. A few years later, the First International Conference on Air Law established the Comitè International Technique d'Experts Juridiques Aeriens (CITEJA) in 1925, and the CITEJA's proposal was adopted during the Second Conference on Private Air Law in Warsaw, Poland, in 1929. This was the Convention for the Unification of Certain Rules Relating to International Carriage by Air (the Warsaw Convention), the first multilateral *private* air law treaty and the predecessor of the current Montreal Convention of 1999.[40]

While World War II was still raging on the European and Pacific fronts, the allies were earnestly preparing for their peacetime needs, and regulating postwar air transport was perceived to be an urgent priority.[41] Accordingly, the International Civil Aviation Conference was held in Chicago in 1944, producing the Chicago Convention. The Chicago Convention set forth the fundamental principles of international civil aviation and established the ICAO, a specialized agency of the United Nations. The ICAO began operations

---

37 Milde, *supra* note 14 at 5-6.
38 Ivan A. Vlasic, ed., *Explorations in aerospace law, selected essays by John Cobb Cooper, 1946-1966* (Montreal: McGill University Press, 1968) at 5.
39 Dempsey, "Air Law", *supra* note 19 at 12-13.
40 *Convention for the Unification of Certain Rules for International Carriage by Air done at Montreal on 28 May 1999*
41 Milde, *supra* note 14 at 13.

in 1947, when the Chicago Convention entered into force. Since then, the ICAO has developed extensive rules for international law related to aviation. Major multilateral air law treaties that the ICAO has sponsored can be broadly categorized as shown in the diagram below:

Figure 1.2   Major Multilateral Air Law[42]

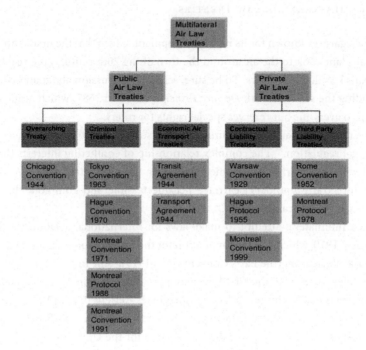

---

42   Full names of the treaties are as follows: *Convention on International Civil Aviation* (Chicago Convention 1944); *Convention on Offences and Certain Other Acts Committed on Board Aircraft* (Tokyo Convention 1963); *Convention for the Suppression of Unlawful Seizure of Aircraft* (Hague Convention 1970); *Convention for the Suppression of Unlawful Acts against the Safety of Civil Aviation* (Montreal Convention 1971); *Protocol for the Suppression of Unlawful Acts of Violence at Airports Serving International Civil Aviation, Supplementary to the Convention for the Suppression of Unlawful Acts against the Safety of Civil Aviation done at Montreal on 23 September 1971* (Montreal Protocol 1988); *Convention on the Marking of Plastic Explosives for the Purpose of Detection* (Montreal Convention 1991); *International Air Services Transit Agreement* (Transit Agreement 1944); *International Air Transport Agreement* (Transport Agreement 1944); *Convention for the Unification of Certain Rules Relating to International Carriage by Air* (Warsaw Convention 1929); *Protocol to Amend the Convention for the Unification of Certain Rules Relating to International Carriage by Air signed at Warsaw on 12 October 1929* (Hague Protocol 1955); *Convention for the Unification of Certain Rules for International Carriage by Air* (Montreal Convention 1999); *Convention on Damage Caused by Foreign Aircraft to Third Parties on the Surface* (Rome Convention 1952); *Protocol to Amend the Convention on Damage Caused by Foreign Aircraft to Third Parties on the Surface signed at Rome on 7 October 1952* (Montreal Protocol 1978).

Generally, states have demonstrated their willingness to comply with the rules of international law, as evidenced by the large number of contracting states to these air law treaties.[43] Indeed, international air law is recognized as a field of international law in which states find it relatively easy to cooperate and coordinate.[44] Considering the international and foreign nature[45] of air transport, coordination is logically necessary. Coordinating through international air law treaties makes air travel more efficient and its regulation more effective.[46]

However, two kinds of multilateral air law treaties have not received strong support from most states: economic air transport treaties and third party liability treaties (see Figure 1.2). In the area of third party liability (treaties dealing with how to provide compensation for damage – physical damage caused by an aircraft or parts thereof on the surface of the earth or to aircraft in flight), the Rome Convention of 1952 and the Montreal Protocol of 1978 are considered lame treaties since only 49 member states and 12 member states have ratified them, respectively (none of which have a strong presence in international air transportation).[47] While two more third party liability treaties[48] were adopted in 2009, they have not received much support from states either. These two instruments have been largely criticized as being unnecessary.[49]

---

43   As of June 1 2015, number of contracting parties are: 191 in Chicago Convention 1944; 186 in Tokyo Convention 1963; 185 in Hague Convention 1970; 188 in Montreal Convention 1971; 173 in Montreal Protocol 1988; 148 Montreal Convention 1991; 130 in Transit Agreement 1944; 11 in Transport Agreement 1944; 152 in Warsaw Convention 1929; 137 in Hague Protocol 1955; 112 in Montreal Convention 1999; 49 in Rome Convention 1952; and 12 in Montreal Protocol.
44   Andrew T. Guzman, *How International Law Works* (Oxford: Oxford University Press, 2008) at 25-27.
45   Paul Dempsey and Michael Milde note that various foreign elements in international carriage by air could involve the nationality of the airline (air carrier); nationality/domicile of the passenger/shipper; points of origin, destination and agreed stopping places; place of conclusion of the contract of carriage; place of accident causing death or injury to passengers or damage to or loss of the baggage or cargo. See Paul Stephen Dempsey & Michael Milde, *International air carrier liability: the Montreal Convention of 1999* (Montreal: McGill University, Centre for Research of Air & Space Law, 2005) at Preface.
46   Guzman, *supra* note 44 at 27.
47   Jae Woon Lee, "The Regime of Compensable Damage in the Modernized Rome Conventions: a Comparison between Article 3 of the General Risks Convention of 2009 and Article 17 of the Montreal Convention of 1999" (2010) 35 Ann. Air & Sp. L. 215-216; Katsutoshi Fujita has summarized the reasons why States have delayed ratifying and/or refused to join the Convention as follows: (1) that limited amounts of damages stipulated in the Convention are too low, (2) that it is considered unnecessary to introduce international rules because domestic laws already provide for sufficient limited amounts of damages in terms of rights of third parties on the surface, (3) that the Convention does not provide for such matters as noise, sonic boom, and nuclear disasters, and (4) that there is an objection against the single jurisdiction. See Katsutoshi Fujita, "Some Considerations for the Modernization of the Rome Convention, in case of Unlawful Interference" (2008) 23 Korean J. Air & Sp. L. 59.
48   *Convention on Compensation for Damage to Third Parties, Resulting from Acts of Unlawful Interference Involving Aircraft* (Unlawful Interference Compensation Convention 2009); *Convention on Compensation for Damage Caused by Aircraft to Third Parties* (General Risks Convention 2009).
49   See *e.g.* George N. Tompkins Jr, "Some Thought to Ponder when Considering Whether to Adopt the New Aviation General Risks and Unlawful Interference Convention Proposed by ICAO"(2008) 33 Air & Space L. 81 at 82-83.

One fundamental reason why states have showed little enthusiasm for third-party liability treaties is the common understanding that the damage in question is governed by the law of the state where the damage occurred (*lex loci damni*), which makes it easy to establish the applicable law or jurisdiction.[50] In other words, most states believe that there is little need, if any, to establish international air law governing third-party liability since their domestic laws can adequately deal with the issue.

The lack of interest in the economic air transport treaties, however, cannot be explained by this rationale. Economic air transport treaties entail granting the airlines of each state party the privilege of carrying passengers, cargo, or a combination of both to, from, over, and beyond their respective territories.[51] In this area, robust international coordination between states is required for *international* air transport. As noted above, although state representatives at the Chicago Conference in 1944 had sought to include the area of economic air transport within the Chicago Convention itself, they could not reach agreement about the scope of the freedoms of the air.

Instead, states at the Chicago Conference adopted two separate and distinct instruments (as mentioned above): the International Air Services Transit Agreement (often called the "Transit Agreement" or "two freedoms agreement") and the International Air Services Transport Agreement (also called the "Transport Agreement" or "five freedoms agreement"). Since the Transit Agreement does not grant any commercial rights (only dealing with the freedoms of overflight (the first freedom) and technical landing (the second freedom)), the number of contracting states is relatively high: 130 states.[52]

On the other hand, the number of contracting states to the Transport Agreement (dealing with the first five freedoms) is just 11,[53] meaning that the Transport Agreement has had little practical significance. The unpopularity of the Transport Agreement has had to do with the economic protectionism that the majority of states have practiced to shield their airlines from competition. More specifically, the inclusion of the fifth freedom was the fundamental reason why a majority of states never accepted the Transport Agreement. The failure of the Transport Agreement proved that states are naturally reluctant to grant the fifth freedom to other states in a multilateral fashion, as doing so would subject their own carriers and protected markets to more competition.

---

50   Milde, *supra* note 14 at 301.
51   Brian F. Havel & Gabriel S. Sanchez, *The Principles and Practice of International Aviation Law* (New York: Cambridge University Press, 2014) at 69 [Havel & Sanchez, "Aviation Law"].
52   Although 130 is a substantial number representing about two thirds of ICAO Member States, the States that are not parties to the Agreement, which include the Russian Federation, China, Canada, Brazil and Indonesia, have very large territories, so in practical terms the universal freedom of the air does not exist. See Jae Woon Lee "Revisiting Freedom of Overflight in International Air Law: Minimum Multilateralism in International Air Transport" (2013) 38 Air & Space L. 351 at 361.
53   Contracting states are Bolivia, Burundi, Costa Rica, El Salvador, Ethiopia, Greece, Honduras, Liberia, Netherlands, Paraguay, and Turkey (reservation on the fifth freedom).

China, Japan, and Korea are not that different from the majority trend. All three are parties to most major multilateral air law treaties except the economic air transport treaties and the third party liability treaties. One noteworthy fact is that Japan and Korea are contracting parties to the Transit Agreement, while China is not. Indeed, the fact that some of the largest states, including China, are not parties to the agreement has been pointed out as one of its major defects.[54]

Together with the Transport Agreement, the ICAO has made several other attempts to initiate global multilateral governance of economic air transport.[55] However, it has yet to create international rules that a majority of countries are willing to adopt related to economic air transport. This prompts the question of why the area of economic air transport is *exceptional* compared to other areas of multilateral air law despite the clear need for international coordination and cooperation. This question—one of the key questions of this research—will be discussed in the following section.

1.3 Exceptionalism in Economic Air Transport

1.3.1 Historical Background

Discussion at the Chicago Conference in 1944 focused, among other things, on how states could reach a multilateral agreement on the safety and economics of international civil aviation.[56] While a multilateral agreement of this sort was achieved in the area of safety, the Chicago Conference failed to reach a consensus on a multilateral means of economic regulation with regard to the commercial aspects of international air transport. Article 6 of the Chicago Convention made it clear that granting traffic rights was contingent on special permission or other authorization by the partner state, inducing states to deal with those aspects primarily through *bilateral* air services agreements.

As noted, the vast divide between the positions of liberalized and protectionist advocates was the primary reason, but not the only reason, for this failure. The short timeframe of the Chicago Conference is believed to be another important reason why the economic aspect was not included in the Chicago Convention. The Chicago Conference took place between November 1, 1944, and December 7, 1944, and the Chicago Convention was successfully adopted during this time. Considering that the Chicago Conference essentially had to create everything from scratch (that is, there were no preliminary meetings, no

---

54 See note 52; See also Milde, *supra* note 14 at 110.
55 See below section 1.3.2 ICAO or WTO: Institutional Problems?
56 Haanappel, "Law and Policy" *supra* note 29 at 19.

draft convention,[57] and no Secretariat to prepare for the conference), it is remarkable that such a comprehensive convention could have been adopted in such a short period.

Indeed, the *Proceedings of the International Civil Aviation Conference* (1944) reveal the frustration felt by delegates as they concluded the protracted discussions about the economic sphere of international civil aviation.[58] Considering the deadlock that would have been impossible to overcome in the available time, adopting the Transit Agreement and the Transport Agreement separately from the Chicago Convention was a skillful "way out" of the impasse.[59] However, as noted above, the Transport Agreement has been a failure, with only 11 contracting states. Even the US, a proponent of the agreement during the Chicago Conference, withdrew from it in 1946.[60] The US concluded at an early stage that poor adoption of the Transport Agreement made it an unreliable medium for the establishment of international air routes.[61]

In 1946, American and British negotiators met in Bermuda in an attempt to reconcile their respective aviation policies and succeeded in reaching a compromise, the so-called Bermuda I agreement.[62] This agreement was important not only because it represented a compromise between the two most important aviation powers of the time, but also because it served as a precedent for the subsequent agreements made by many other countries.[63] Following the failure in Chicago and the success in Bermuda, the bilateral treaty became regarded as the principal diplomatic and political vehicle for the exchange of traffic rights.[64] Reportedly, more than 4,000 bilateral air services agreements are in existence.[65]

---

57   There were, however, United States Proposal of a Convention on Air Navigation, United Kingdom Proposal on International Air Transport, and Canadian Preliminary Draft of an International Air Transport. See U.S. Dept of State, "Proceedings", *supra* note 13; Dempsey also argues that the delegates at Chicago were not drafting from scratch. The delegates examined the provisions of the Paris, Madrid and Havana models (referring to The Convention Relating to the Regulation of Aerial Navigation (Paris Convention of 1919), Ibero-American Convention Relating to Aerial Navigation (signed at Madrid in 1926), and Convention on Commercial Aviation (signed at Havana in 1928)) and the Annexes that had been drafted by CINA(the Commission Internationale de la Navigation Aerienne). See Dempsey, "Air Law", *supra* note 19 at 28.
58   For instance, Minister of Iceland spoke: "It is our understanding that the only remaining question in this: Shall we now, in a hurry, solve differences of opinion regarding the burden of traffic to be allowed to each nation and leave the remaining aspects of this single problem to a later decision, or shall we refer this important question, in its entirety, to the scrutiny and decision of the Interim Council and the Interim Assembly?" see U.S. Dept of State, "Proceedings", *supra* note 13 at 500.
59   Milde, *supra* note 14 at 15.
60   Withdrawal of the United States of America, U.S. Dept. of the State Press Release No.510, reprinted in [Oct. 1998] 3 Av. L. Rep. (CCH) §26,016 at 21.117 (25 July 1946).
61   See Havel, "Open Skies", *supra* note 22 at 106 (citing "Withdrawal of the United States of America", U.S. Dept. of State Press Release No. 510, reprinted in [Oct. 1998] 3 Av. L. Rep. (CCH)).
62   Dempsey, "Foreign Policy", *supra* note 17 at 53.
63   Martin Dresner, "Chapter 23 US Bilateral Air Transport Policy" in Peter Forsyth *et al.* eds., *Liberalization in Aviation: Competition, Cooperation and Public Policy* (Farnham: Ashgate, 2013) 429 at 431.
64   Havel, "Open Skies", *supra* note 22 at 109.
65   See World Trade Organization (WTO), *Air Services Agreements Projectors* (2011), online: <www.wto.org/asap/index.html>.

1.3.2 ICAO or WTO: Institutional Problems?

The ICAO has tried to regain its leadership role in the economic aspects of international air transport. Since the late 1970s, when "deregulation" and "liberalization" became key words in the area of international air transport (a topic that will be discussed in the next section: 1.4 Economic Liberalization), the ICAO has held six Air Transport Conferences: in 1977, 1980, 1985, 1994, 2003 and 2013. While these conferences addressed then-pending issues and proposed necessary guidelines,[66] they were nothing more than forums for discussion and information sharing.

A significant point is that the ICAO does not possess any regulatory authority with respect to economic air transport (unlike its strong mandate in the field of air navigation and technical matters), and therefore it cannot do more than provide a forum for debate and draft guidance materials without any legally binding force.[67]

However, the reason why economic air transport is an exception in multilateral air law governance cannot be explained in institutional terms alone. That is to say, it is not because ICAO lacks regulatory authority. There was a new opportunity in the 1990s with the General Agreement on Trade in Services (GATS) under the World Trade Organization (WTO). However, the WTO has confirmed that WTO law will not revoke or otherwise affect bilateral air services agreements to which a member state is a contracting party.[68]

There are four reasons why coverage of air transport services was avoided when GATS was finalized in 1994. First, the Uruguay Round negotiators understood that international air transport was governed by an intricate system of bilateral agreements that was based on a balanced and reciprocal exchange of rights between states.[69] Second, the principles of non-discrimination under the WTO system (unconditional mandatory most-favored nation (MFN) treatment and national treatment) contrasted with the existing bilateralism in air transport based on bilateral reciprocity, and it was widely held at the time that putting MFN into place could hold back the ongoing process of liberalization of air transport between like-minded states.[70] Third, neither states nor national airlines wished to see a

---

66 See Wasim Zaidi, *Breaking the Shackles: Foreign Ownership and Control in the Airline Industry* (LL.M. Thesis, McGill University Institute of Air and Space Law, 2008) at 81-94 [unpublished].

67 Milde, *supra* note 14 at 124.

68 *ANNEX on Air Transport Services of Annex 1B General Agreement on Trade in Services* "This Annex applies to measures affecting trade in air transport services, whether scheduled or non-scheduled, and ancillary services. It is confirmed that any specific commitment made or obligation assumed under this Agreement shall not reduce or affect a Member's obligations under bilateral or multilateral agreements that are in effect at the entry into force of the Agreement establishing the WTO."

69 International Air Transport Association (IATA), "Liberalization of Air Transport and the GATS", IATA Discussion Paper to WTO (October 1999) at 2, online: <www.wto.org/english/tratop_e/serv_e/iac-posit41.pdf>. [IATA, "GATS"].

70 Henri A. Wassenbergh "The Future of International Air Transport Law: A Philosophy of Law and the Need for Reform of the Economic Regulation of International Air Transport in the 21st Century" (1995) 20 Ann. Air & Sp. L. 405.

dual regulatory regime emerge for air traffic rights, in which some states applied the GATS obligations while others held to existing bilateral arrangements.[71] Fourth, it was the general view that, if new trade concepts were to be applied to air transport, the ICAO was best qualified to pursue this—in other words, that aviation rather than trade interests should continue to play the predominant role at the state level.[72]

In short, the WTO conceded that the ICAO is the organization that should lead the multilateral approach to international air transport. This conclusion unavoidably faces the harsh reality that the ICAO does not possess any regulatory authority over the economic aspects of air transport.

Multilateralism has not failed because of uncertainty about which institution should be responsible for it. States want to keep control of and remain flexible in the political and economic policy-making process so long as such decisions do not violate legal or moral principles (*jus cogens*, for example). In addition, a multilateral approach could lead states to surrender their negotiating positions without the freedom to differentiate their approach according to what individual trading partners have to offer.[73]

1.3.3   Nationalism

It is not uncommon for governments to want to protect their national airlines, and each time they negotiate air services agreements with other states, they calculate what their national airlines stand to gain or lose. In the view of Peter Forsyth, the traditional approach to air services negotiation has been steeped in *mercantilist* notions; negotiations were excessively airline-centric, and little attention was given to the passenger.[74]

Close links between airlines and aviation authorities are nothing new or unusual.[75] Since airlines are large, labor-intensive employers and can generate large profits (and tax revenues), governments are tempted to continue shielding them from competition, particularly when they regard foreign carriers as being more competitive.[76] In recent years, a number of countries seem increasingly willing to remove bilateral restrictions and thereby

---

71   IATA, "GATS", *supra* note 69 at 3.
72   *Ibid.*
73   See Tan, "Horizontal Mandate", *supra* note 9 at 438-439.
74   Peter Forsyth, "Chapter 21 Economic Evaluation of Air Services Liberalization: The New Calculus" in Peter Forsyth *et al.* eds., *Liberalization in Aviation: Competition, Cooperation and Public Policy* (Farnham: Ashgate, 2013) 403 at 403.
75   Sean McGonigle, "Past its Use-By Date: Regulation 868 Concerning Subsidy and State Aid in International Air Services" (2013) 38 Air & Space L. 1 at 13.
76   United Kingdom Civil Aviation Authority, *Ownership and Control Liberalisation: A Discussion Paper* (London: The Stationery Office, 2006), online: <www.caa.co.uk/docs/33/CAP769.pdf>. at 4.15 & 4.16.

expose national airlines to greater competition.[77] Yet protectionism still prevails in the aviation market.

Arguments grounded in national security are still made to justify protectionism although the weight of such arguments has decreased dramatically since the post-war period. A more substantial reason, which cannot be fully justified economically, is nationalism, or the sentimental attachment to national air carriers. In many cases, the biggest and oldest air carrier in each country is named after its home country,[78] and flag carriers have long been symbols of national pride, especially in developing countries.[79]

Michael Paris observed the deeply rooted nationalism in aviation in his book *From the Wright Brothers to Top Gun: Aviation, Nationalism and Popular Cinema*:

> The development of an aviation industry… and the founding of national airlines all played their part in promoting a positive and technologically dynamic image of the state: an important means of enhancing national prestige and status… Aeronautical progress was one means by which the state could demonstrate progress and achievement, a way of fostering and maintaining national pride.[80]

Although the extent of the sentimental attachment to national air carriers has been diminishing in a more globalized society, it has not disappeared entirely. This notion plays an important role in states' preference for bilateral regulation in international air transport since bilateral regulation enables states to control the level of competition that their national carriers will face.

None of the Northeast Asian aviation powers are exceptions to the sentimental attachment to national air carriers. Though the degree of this attachment differs and change has been occurring in recent years (see Chapter 3), China, Japan, and Korea have been accused of using aviation policy to protect their national carriers.[81] In particular, China's special treatment of Air China is no secret. As Peter Harbison, chairman of the Centre for

---

77 *Ibid.*
78 To name a few, Air France, British Airways, Air Canada, American Airlines, Singapore Airlines, Korean Air, Japan Airlines, Air China, Air India, Thai Air, Malaysian Airlines, Qatar Airways, and Air New Zealand.
79 See *e.g.* Edward M. Young, *Aerial Nationalism: A History of Aviation in Thailand* (Washington: Smithsonian Institution Press, 1995).
80 Michael Paris, *From the Wright Brothers to Top Gun: Aviation, Nationalism, and Popular Cinema* (Manchester: Manchester University Press, 1995) at 88.
81 Although it cannot be characterized reasonably as contemporary, see *e.g.* Tae Hoon Oum & Yeong Heok Lee, "The Northeast Asian Air Transport Network: Is There a Possibility of Creating Open Skies in the Region?" (2002) 8 J. Air Trans. Man. 325 at 327 (noting that "[t]he Japanese government's overriding concern is in protecting its flag carriers from competition" and at 328 "(For Koreans) the need to adopt a more liberal approach towards foreign carriers clashes with the current needs to look after the short-term interests of its flag carriers.").

Aviation, once said, "Air China has always been the favorite child" of the Chinese government.[82]

This favoritism was also confirmed by Li Jiaxiang, Vice-Minister and Deputy Secretary of the Leading Party Group of the Ministry of Transport and Director of the General Administration of Civil Aviation, a very influential aviation policymaker in China.[83] Li Jiaxiang candidly explained his dream of transforming Air China into an "international mega carrier" in his 2008 book *Route to Fly*.[84] In the book, he argues that the banner of open skies—"equal competition, equal treatment and equal benefits"—actually disguises a reality of unfairness, inequality and disproportional benefits.[85] In the same vein, Li implies his approval of protectionism for Chinese national carriers.[86]

Regardless of whether it is intended to support liberalization or protectionism, all regulation involves regulatory process, regulatory structure and regulatory content.[87] It is undisputed that regulatory content, or the particular matters that are being regulated, has been considerably changing over the past two decades. Though these changes differ in style and substance, air transport liberalization has spread all over the world. Indeed, the relevant question is shifting from *whether* to liberalize to *how* to liberalize.[88]

1.4   Economic Liberalization in International Air Transport

1.4.1   Scope: Relaxation of "Market Access" and "Ownership and Control" Restrictions

As noted, liberalization is a complex concept that is commonly used in various fields. In the context of international air transport, liberalization can be measured by the level of relaxation of the two main legal hurdles: 1) market access and 2) ownership and control restrictions.

The Chicago Convention 1944 recognizes that each state has complete and exclusive sovereignty over the airspace above its territory and that states can therefore impose limitations on the flight of foreign aircraft through their airspace.[89] Although the freedoms of

---

82   Jamil Anderlini, "China's private airlines facing cross-winds" *Financial Times* (22 March 2010), online: <www.ft.com/intl/cms/s/0/6c9e60bc-35d5-11df-aa43-00144feabdc0.html#axzz2eB2aRTYj>.
83   For Mr. Li's short bio, see <www.chinavitae.com/biography/Li_Jiaxiang%7C4095>.
84   Li Jiaxiang, *Route to Fly* (Beijing: China Machine Press, 2007) [translated by Jolyn Hong] at 188.
85   *Ibid.* at 179.
86   *Ibid.* at Chapter 7: Path for the Future.
87   ICAO, "Regulation", *supra* note 10 at (iii).
88   Taleb Rifai (Secretary General, United Nations World Tourism Organization), Keynote Address to the Sixth ICAO Worldwide Air Transport Conference, 18 March 2013), online: <www.icao.int/Meetings/atconf6/Documents/ATConf-6_Speech_UNWTO_en.pdf>.
89   Diederiks-Verschoor, *supra* note 4 at 53.

the air are frequently referred to in international air transport, none of these freedoms are genuinely free. The following example may better illustrate the characteristics of these freedoms.

Assume that Korean Air (KE) wishes to carry passengers from Seoul to Los Angeles. To take advantage of the most efficient route, KE aircraft will need to operate over Japan. In most cases, KE aircraft will simply fly over Japan without landing (first freedom). Sometimes, KE aircraft may stop in Tokyo for the purpose of refueling or maintenance (second freedom). Since both Korea and Japan are contracting parties to the Transit Agreement (two freedoms agreement), Korea (the state with which Korean Air is registered) does not have to ask Japan for permission for overflights or technical landings. If Korean Air wishes to fly to Paris from Seoul and operates over China, however, Korea has to seek permission from China through a bilateral agreement since China is not a contracting party to the Transit Agreement.

The freedoms of the air that are commercial in nature start with the third freedom. Returning to our example, once the KE aircraft arrives in Los Angeles, Korean Air will want to disembark its passengers (third freedom). The third freedom by itself would be economically impractical if the aircraft were to return home empty.[90] Thus, Korean Air will want to embark passengers destined for Seoul in Los Angeles (fourth freedom). The third and fourth freedoms are governed by a bilateral air services agreement between Korea and the US If Korean Air wishes to carry passengers from Tokyo to Los Angeles and vice versa, it will require additional permission (fifth freedom) from all states concerned: Korea, Japan, and the US through a series of bilateral agreements.

Hence, the freedoms of the air can only become genuinely free through liberal bilateral (or regional) air services agreements, which open up the airspace of the parties concerned to the operation of international air services by the carriers of other states.[91] The level of openness in the international air services agreements determines the level of market access.

Broadly speaking, protective air services agreements allow limited third/fourth freedom flights (direct flights between the home country and a foreign country by national air carriers of the home country) for passengers and cargo while liberalized air services agreements allow unlimited third/fourth freedom flights for passengers and cargo. Some liberalized air services agreements allow unlimited fifth freedom flights (flights between two foreign countries by national air carriers originating in their home country).

A simple comparison of the number of flights and operating airlines in capital cities in Northeast Asia can hint at the different output resulting from the level of openness in international air services agreements. For instance, during the second week of June 2015, seven different airlines operated 374 passenger flights per week on the route between Seoul

---

90 Milde, *supra* note 14 at 113.
91 Diederiks-Verschoor, *supra* note 4 at 53.

(Incheon Airport and Gimpo Airport) and Tokyo (Narita Airport and Haneda Airport) while four different airlines operated only 176 passenger flights per week on the route between Seoul (Incheon Airport and Gimpo Airport) and Beijing (Beijing Capital Airport).[92] This is largely due to the fact that Japan and Korea concluded a liberalized air services agreement while the air services agreement between China and Korea is a protective one which limits the number of third/fourth freedom flights.

The other base on which liberalization rests is relaxing ownership and control restrictions. Essentially, ownership and control restrictions are embedded in the forms of an "internal lock" (domestic law) as well as an "external lock" (air services agreements).[93] To be specific, the internal lock is each country's domestic legislation requiring national ownership and control of its air carriers while the external lock is the nationality clause included in all air services agreements.[94] The most common form of restriction relates to the "substantial ownership and effective control" nationality clause that commonly appears in bilateral air services agreements. This clause mandates that the majority ownership in an airline must reside in the nationals of the state designating that airline (This issue will be discussed in Chapter 4: Ownership and Control Issues in Northeast Asia.)

Such restrictions have their origins in US domestic law. The U.S. Air Commerce Act of 1926 became the first law to require that 51 percent of voting stock at US air carriers be held by US citizens and that 66 percent of the members of the board of directors be US citizens. The Civil Aeronautics Act of 1938 increased from 51 percent to 75 percent the amount of an airline's voting stock that must be in the hands of US nationals for the carrier to qualify as a US operator. The 25 percent cap on foreign voting equity in US airlines is still in effect today.[95]

The US government has explained that there are four main reasons why it has limited ownership and control of its airlines to American citizens: the need to protect the fledgling US airline industry, the desire to regulate international air services through bilateral agreements, safety concerns about foreign aircraft gaining access to US airspace, and military reliance on civilian airlines to supplement airlift capacity.[96]

The issue of ownership and control restrictions was first raised in multilateral discussions during the Chicago Conference.[97] Wanting to block enemy states (principally Germany) from establishing airlines in Latin America to operate into US airspace, US officials sought

---

92   The information is available at <www.airportal.go.kr/knowledge/statistics/index.jsp?pg=01>.
93   See Havel, "Open Skies", *supra* note 22 at 165.
94   *Ibid.* at 135-136.
95   49 U.S.C. § 40102(a).
96   U.S. General Accounting Office, *Airline Competition Impact of Changing Foreign Investment and Control Limits on U.S. Airlines Foreign Investment in U.S. Airlines*, GAO/RCED-93-7 (1992) at 12-13, online: <www.gao.gov/assets/160/152884.pdf>. [US GAO, "Investment and Control"].
97   Alexandrakis G. Constantine, "Foreign Investment in U.S. Airlines: Restrictive Law is Ripe for Change" (1993-1994) 4:1 U. Miami Bus. L.Rev. 71 at 74.

the right to prohibit carriers from operating when their substantial ownership and effective control raised questions of a political nature or threatened national security.[98] Although these restrictions were not included in the Chicago Convention, they were articulated in both the Transit Agreement and the Transport Agreement as follows:

> Each contracting State reserves the right to withhold or revoke a certificate or permit to an air transport enterprise of another State in any case where it is not satisfied that substantial ownership and effective control are vested in nationals of a contracting State, or in case of failure of such air transport enterprise to comply with the laws of the State over which it operates, or to perform its obligations under this Agreement.[99]

More importantly, states started to require the ownership and control restrictions based on the above provision in each of their bilateral air services agreements.[100] Indeed, the first bilateral agreement between the US and the UK in 1946 (Bermuda type 1 agreement) included language about the substantial ownership and effective control of air carriers.[101] A majority of states have viewed the Bermuda type 1 as the standard bilateral air services agreement, and this notion of "flag carrier" has become the norm in worldwide aviation policy.[102]

In recent times, attempts have been made to liberalize ownership and control restrictions. Broadly, the new developments can be divided into four categories: 1) multilateral/plurilateral regulatory reform, 2) regional reform, 3) bilateral preferential concessions, and 4) unilateral (and voluntary) relaxation. (These issues are thoroughly discussed in Chapter 4.)

Ownership and control restrictions are intertwined with market access restrictions. States, however, do not necessarily coordinate their positions on these two legal pivots. For example, although the US has been proactive in liberalizing market access both multilaterally and bilaterally, US domestic law contains stricter ownership rules (75% of voting stock owned by nationals) than most states (51% owned by nationals), and the traditional

---

98 *Ibid.*
99 Article 1 Section 5 of the Transit Agreement and Article 1 Section 5 of the Transport Agreement
100 Lelieur, *supra* note 26 at 2.
101 Article 6 of the Bermuda type 1 Agreement "Each Contracting Party reserves the right to withhold or revoke the exercise of the rights specified in the Annex to this Agreement by a carrier designated by the other Contracting Party in the event that it is not satisfied that substantial ownership and effective control of such carriers are vested in nationals of either Contracting Party."
102 P.P.C. Haanappel, "Airline Ownership and Control and Some Related Matters" (2001) 26 Air & Space L. 90 at 90.

ownership and control requirement has been maintained in the US open skies agreement model.[103]

1.4.2 Economic Impact of Air Transport Liberalization

Liberalization has often entailed deregulation, especially the reduction of state ownership (privatization) and of structural controls.[104] Empirical research has shown that, in many industries, deregulation leads to lower prices for consumers, higher quality of service, and greater access to services, including greater adoption by consumers, in part due to increased competition among providers, lower prices and higher levels of investment.[105] In the same vein, a large body of research has shown that liberalizing air transport has a considerable positive impact on the economy.[106]

In a nutshell, liberalization of air transport has generally fostered greater competition, resulting in lower fares for travelers, more people traveling, more choices in airlines and routes for passengers, and improved services levels (*e.g.* higher frequencies).[107] As to the impact on the wider economy, liberalization leads to increased air service levels and lower fares (which in turn boost the volume of traffic).[108] This can bring about increased economic growth and employment as illustrated below.[109]

---

103 See section 4.1 Ownership and Control Restrictions.
104 Sol Picciotto, "Introduction: What Rules for the World Economy?" in Sol Picciotto & Ruth Mayne, ed., *Regulating International Business: Beyond Liberalization* (New York: St. Martin's Press, 1999) at 2.
105 Ian Kincaid & Michael Tretheway, "Chapter 19 Economic Impact of Aviation Liberalization" in Peter Forsyth *et al.* eds., *Liberalization in Aviation: Competition, Cooperation and Public Policy* (Farnham: Ashgate, 2013) 345 at 349.
106 See *e.g.* Intervistas-ga2, *The Economic Impact of Air Service Liberalization* (2006), online: <www.intervistas.com/downloads/Economic_Impact_of_Air_Service_Liberalization_Final_Report.pdf>.; David Gillen, Richard Harris & Tae Hoon Oum, "Measuring the Economic Effects of Bilateral Liberalization on Air Transport" (2002) 38 *Transportation Research Part E: Logistics and Transportation Review*; Roberta Piermartini & Linda Rousova, *Liberalization of Air Transport Services and Passenger Traffic*, Staff Working Paper ERSD-2008-06, World Trade Organization (2008); OECD, *Liberalisation of International Air Cargo Transport* (May 2002).
107 Ian Kincaid & Michael Tretheway, "Chapter 19 Economic Impact of Aviation Liberalization" in Peter Forsyth *et al.* eds., *Liberalization in Aviation: Competition, Cooperation and Public Policy* (Farnham: Ashgate, 2013) 345 at 349.
108 *Ibid.* at 354.
109 *Ibid*; Kincaid & Tretheway further elaborate the impact on the wider economy in a plain language: "Aviation Sector: additional economic activity in the aviation sector is generated by the servicing, management and maintenance of the additional air services. This includes activities at airlines, airports, air navigation and other businesses that support the aviation sector. The impact can 'spin-off' into the wider economy (called indirect or multiplier impacts) – e.g., food wholesalers that supply food for catering on flights, trucking companies that move goods to and from the airport, refineries processing oil for jet fuel, etc. Tourism sector: air service facilitates the arrival of larger numbers of tourists to a region or country. This includes business as well as leisure tourists. The spending of these tourists can support a wide range of tourism-related businesses: hotels, restaurants, theaters, car rentals, etc. Of course, air service also facilitates outbound tourism, which can be viewed reducing the amount of money spent in an economy. However, even outbound tourism

Figure 1.3   The Economic Impact of Air Service[110]

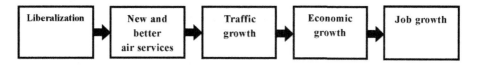

1.4.3   General Trends of Air Transport Liberalization

As seen in the first bilateral agreement between the US and the UK in 1946 and numerous bilateral agreements subsequently concluded, international air transport was once governed by protectively written bilateral air services agreements. The first 30 years (1946-1975) were no doubt the ones with the most stringent international regulation of the economics of air transport.[111]

Since the mid-1970s, however, the air transport industry has undergone a remarkable degree of deregulation. 1978, in particular, was deemed the year of deregulation in aviation history because of the Airline Deregulation Act of 1978 in the US and the first liberalized bilateral air services agreement between the US and the Netherlands. In 1992, the first open skies agreement was concluded between the same two countries.

The U.S. DOT lists eleven components that should be encompassed in the US open skies regime: 1) open entry on all routes, 2) unrestricted capacity and frequency on all routes, 3) unrestricted route and traffic rights (or full fifth freedom access), 4) double-disapproval pricing in third and fourth freedom markets, 5) liberal charter arrangements, 6) liberal cargo regimes, 7) conversion and remittance arrangements, 8) open code-sharing opportunities, 9) self-handling provisions (granting a carrier the right to provide its own

---

involves spending in the home economy, on travel agents, taxis, etc. In any case, it is not necessarily the case that money spent by tourists flying abroad would be spent on tourism at home if there were no air service. Catalytic impacts: also known as wider economic benefits. Air transportation facilitates employment and economic development in the national and regional economy through increased trade, attracting new businesses to the region and encouraging investment. Industries and activities that would otherwise not exist in a region can be attracted by improved air transport connectivity. In particular, catalytic effects can include some or all of the following: Trade effects – air transport liberalization opens new markets to many businesses as a result of new destinations, better flight connections and higher frequencies offered. This leads to a broader demand for existing products. Investment effects – a key factor many companies take into account when taking decisions about location of office, manufacturing or warehouses is proximity of an international airport. Productivity effects – air transportation offers access to new markets which in term enables businesses to achieve greater economies of scale. Air access also enables companies to attract and retain high quality employees."

110   Intervistas-ga2, *supra* note 106.
111   P.P.C. Haanappel, "The Transformation of Sovereignty in the Air" in Chia-Jui Cheng ed., *The Use of Air and Outer Space Cooperation and Competition* (The Hague: Kluwer Law International, 1998) 13 at 15.

support operations), 10) pro-competitive provisions on commercial opportunities, and 11) commitment to nondiscriminatory computer reservation system (CRS) access.[112]

Notably, the US model of an open skies agreement includes unlimited market access rights for the fifth freedom.[113] Typically, however, air services agreements granting largely unrestricted market access rights to the third and fourth freedoms alone are already considered to be open skies agreements. From 1992 to 2012, more than 400 open skies agreements (which of course vary in their details and extent of openness) were concluded by 145 states, representing 76 percent of the ICAO membership.[114]

Among the Northeast Asian aviation powers, Korea has been the most active in reaching open skies agreements. As of December 2013, Korea had concluded 39 open skies agreements (including cargo-only agreements).[115] Korea has reached open skies agreements with major economies like the US, Japan, and Canada as well as medium and smaller economies.

Japan substantially changed its aviation policy in 2007 from protectionism to liberalization, declaring itself the "Asian Gateway." Accordingly, in August 2007, Japan concluded its first open skies agreement with Korea, permitting unlimited third and fourth freedom passenger and cargo flights for all designated points except airports in Tokyo.[116] Since then, Japan has been very proactive in entering open skies agreements. Japan concluded an open skies agreement with the US in 2009 and a quasi-open skies agreement with China in 2012. (The agreement between Japan and China will be discussed in Chapter 3.) According to a publicly available source, Japan had signed open skies agreements with 27 states.[117]

---

112 US DOT Order 92-8-13 (In the Matter of Defining "Open Skies"), Docket 48130.
113 See current U.S. Model Open Skies Agreement Text, online: <www.state.gov/documents/organization/114970.pdf>; see also U.S. State Department press release regarding U.S. Open Skies Agreement with Bangladesh: "Open Skies agreements allow air service by the airlines of both countries between and beyond the other's territory, allowing airline managements to determine how often to fly, the kind of aircraft to use, and the prices to charge. This agreement will strengthen and expand our strong trade, tourism and people-to-people links with Bangladesh, benefitting U.S. and Bangladeshi businesses and travelers by expanding opportunities for air services and encouraging vigorous price competition by airlines, while preserving our commitments to aviation safety and security." online: <www.state.gov/r/pa/prs/ps/2013/08/213192.htm>.
114 ICAO, *Expanding Market Access For International Air Transport*, ICAO Doc ATConf/6-WP/13 (13 December 2012) (Presented by ICAO Secretariat), online: <www.icao.int/Meetings/atconf6/Documents/WorkingPapers/ATConf6-wp013_en.pdf>.
115 Yeong Heok Lee, "Open Sky and Common Aviation Market in Northeast Asia" (Presentation material presented to the 51th International Conference on Law and Policy in Air and Space Field – Enhancing International Cooperation in Air Transport between Korea and China, Seoul, 6 December 2013) [unpublished].
116 The reason for excluding Tokyo was the lack of slots at Narita Airport and Haneda Airport. The restriction on Narita airport was removed in March 2013 when the shortage of slots at the airport was corrected.
117 Japan Ministry of Land, Infrastructure, Transport and Tourism, Press Release, "Aeronautical Consultations between Japan and Austria" (21 February 2014), online: <www.mlit.go.jp/common/001042207.pdf>.

The only significant open skies agreement that China has concluded thus far is the 2010 ASEAN–China Air Transport Agreement.[118] The agreement offers unlimited third/fourth freedom access between the ASEAN States and China. As noted above, China also reached a quasi-open skies agreement with Japan, allowing designated carriers from the two countries to operate an unlimited number of passenger and cargo flights between any Chinese and Japanese cities except Beijing, Shanghai, and Tokyo. Though China has been taking the least liberalized stance among the Northeast Asian states, China is expected to slowly come to adopt a progressive approach to making its market more accessible for international air transport.[119]

The process and structure of international air transport regulation have three distinct venues—national, bilateral, and multilateral.[120] While no one disputes that bilateral air services agreements are still the principal instruments for regulating the economic sphere of international air transportation, the regional approach is becoming increasingly common and will be the central focus of this research.[121]

1.5 REGIONAL LIBERALIZATION

1.5.1 Definition

In a larger context, *regional* liberalization is part of *multilateral* liberalization. Indeed, "multilateral" literally means "in which three or more groups, nations, etc. take part" or "having many sides or parts."[122] Thus, any agreement involving more than two state parties (*e.g.* a regional agreement) is, by definition, a multilateral agreement.[123] More specifically, however, multilateral approaches in international air transport involving liberalization can be divided into the global multilateral approach (full multilateralism), the plurilateral approach (phased multilateralism), and the regional approach.

---

118 For the details of the 2010 ASEAN–China Air Transport Agreement, see Alan Khee-Jin Tan, "The 2010 ASEAN–China Air Transport Agreement: Placing the Cart before the Horse?" (2012) 37 Air & Space L. 35 [Tan, "ASEAN-China"].
119 ICAO, *Expansion of Market Access for International Air Transport in a Proactive, Progressive, Orderly and Safeguarded Manner*, ICAO Doc ATConf/6-WP/97 (6 March 2013) (Presented by China), online: <www.icao.int/Meetings/atconf6/Documents/WorkingPapers/ATConf.6.WP.97.2.1.en.pdf>.
120 ICAO, "Regulation", *supra* note 10.
121 See Chapter 2: Comparative Analysis of Regional Liberalization Models.
122 *Oxford Advanced American Dictionary*, under the word "multilateral".
123 See also ICAO, "Regulation", *supra* note 10 at 3.0 (noting that "[M]ultilateral regulation is regulation undertaken jointly by three or more States, within the framework of an international organization and/or a multilateral treaty or agreement, or as a separate specific activity, and may be broadly construed to include relevant regulatory processes and structures, outcomes or outputs written as treaties or other agreements, resolutions, decisions, directives, or regulations, as well as the observations, conclusions, guidance and discussions of multinational bodies, both intergovernmental and non-governmental.").

The global multilateral approach entails a truly international level playing field[124] and could be achieved in a number of possible fora, including aviation-specific worldwide diplomatic conferences under the ICAO and the WTO.[125] The key principles of global multilateralism are equal rights and obligations, non-discrimination, and the participation as equals of many countries regardless of their size or share of international air transport.[126]

The plurilateral approach (or phased multilateralism) involves a gradual branching out from a core of like-minded states that establish a fully liberalized air transport market among themselves.[127] Generally, a plurilateral agreement is an agreement negotiated between a limited number of states with a particular interest in the subject matter.[128] In the international air transport sector, the Multilateral Agreement on the Liberalization of Air Transportation (MALIAT) is a representative plurilateral agreement. (MALIAT will be reviewed in Chapter 2). Phased multilateralism would allow like-minded member states to come together fairly quickly and avoid forcing reluctant states into a rapid change in policy.[129]

The regional approach is the core of this study and has distinct features as opposed to the first two multilateral approaches. Regional liberalization is different from global multilateral liberalization (full multilateralism) in the sense that its membership is limited to the states in a certain region. Also, while the plurilateral approach is open to any other states, regional liberalization is typically based on closed membership for various reasons: political and economic union, physical proximity, political and economic organization, and so on.

1.5.2 Rationale for the Regional Approach in International Air Transport

In 2013, ICAO acknowledged that more than a dozen agreements for liberalization of intra-regional air transport services are in effect.[130] There are also less formalized groups

---

124 Francesco Fiorilli, "International Air Transport Economic Regulation: Globalization vs Protection of National Interest" (2011) 10:3 Aviation and Space Journal 8 at 12.
125 International Chamber of Commerce (ICC) Committee on Air Transport, "Policy Statement: The Need for Greater Liberalization of International Air Transport" (1 December 2005) at 5.
126 See e.g. Walter Goode, *Dictionary of Trade Policy Terms*, 5th ed. (Cambridge: Cambridge University Press, 2007) under the word "multilateralism". In trade law and policy, "multilateralism" is understood as "an approach to the conduct of international trade based on cooperation, equal rights and obligation, non-discrimination and the participation as equals of many countries regardless of their size or share of international trade."
127 ICC, *supra* note 125 at 5.
128 Anthony Aust, *Modern treaty law and practice,* 2nd ed. (Cambridge: Cambridge University Press, 2007) at 139.
129 ICC, *supra* note 125 at 5.
130 See ICAO Secretariat, "Regulatory and Industry Overview" (20 September 2013), online: <www.icao.int/Meetings/a38/Documents/REGULATORY%20AND%20INDUSTRY%20OVERVIEW.pdf>. [ICAO, "Regulatory Overview"] (noting that the regional agreements for liberalization are: a) the Single

in which discussion about regional liberalization has begun without achieving any substantial results. Indeed, the various regional approaches are at different stages of development and implementation, but they have the common objective of liberalizing the market amongst the member states concerned.¹³¹

It is important to remember that bilateralism is still the principal instrument for liberalizing international air transport. However, the emergence of regional liberalization prompts the questions of why this approach is becoming more common and why some states that are not willing to accept the global multilateral approach take a more flexible position on the regional approach.

Various global multilateral approaches have been initiated, but none of them have been wholly successful. As previously discussed, the failure of global multilateral liberalization is not an institutional problem; rather, it stems from the fact that states want to keep control of and remain flexible in their negotiating positions on international air transport.¹³² Hence, global multilateralism still plays a limited role in the economic sphere of international air transport. The Sixth Worldwide ICAO Air Transport Conference (2013), a highly antici-

---

Aviation Market within the European Union (EU, then European Community); b) the North American Free Trade Area (NAFTA), formed by United States, Canada and Mexico (1994); c) the Decision on Integration of Air Transport of the Andean Community (CAN, then Andean Pact) (1991); d) the Banjul Accord for an Accelerated Implementation of the Yamoussoukro Declaration (1997); e) the Multilateral Air Services Agreement for the Banjul Accord Group (2004); f) the Agreement on the Establishment of Sub-regional Air Transport Cooperation among Cambodia, Lao People's Democratic Republic, Myanmar and Viet Nam (CLMV) (1998; the Multilateral Agreement on Air Services was signed in 2003); g) the Multilateral Air Services Agreement (MASA) of the Caribbean Community (CARICOM) (1998); h) the Agreement on Sub-regional Air Services (Fortaleza Agreement) of the Southern Common Market (MERCOSUR) (1999); i) the Agreement on Air Transport of the Economic and Monetary Community of Central Africa (CEMAC) (1999); j) the Regulations for the implementation of Liberalization of Air Transport Services of the Common Market for Eastern and Southern Africa (COMESA) (1999); k) the Decision relating to the implementation of the Yamoussoukro Declaration concerning the liberalization of access to air transport markets in Africa (Yamoussoukro II Ministerial Decision) of the African Union (AU) (2000); l) the Agreement on the Liberalization of Air Transport of the Arab League States (2007). This agreement formalized the Intra-Arab Freedoms of the Air Programme devised in 2000 by the Arab Civil Aviation Commission (ACAC); m) the Pacific Islands Air Services Agreement (PIASA) of the Pacific Island Forum (2007); and n) the Air Transport Agreement of the Association of Caribbean States (ACS, 2008)).; While ASEAN is not listed, ICAO noted that "The ASEAN Single Aviation Market is expected to fully liberalize air travel between member states in the ASEAN region, allowing ASEAN countries and airlines operating in the region to directly benefit from the growth in air travel around the world, and also freeing up tourism, trade, investment and services flows between member states. Since 1 December 2008, restrictions on Third and Fourth Freedoms between capital cities of member states for air passenger services have been removed while full liberalization of air freight services in the region took effect from 1 January 2009. On 1 January 2011, full liberalization on Fifth Freedom traffic rights between all capital cities took effect." (See section 2.3 ASEAN Single Aviation Market Model.) Also, there is the 2010 Latin American Civil Aviation Commission (LACAC) Open Skies Agreement which will be discussed in Chapter 2.4.3 Regional Liberalization in Latin America. Was the LACAC Agreement listed in the 2013 ICAO document? If so, it should be listed alongside the other agreements above.

131 *Ibid.* at 2.
132 See section 1.3 Exceptionalism in Economic Air Transport.

pated once-a-decade event, again proved that states are not ready – or willing – to harmonize their economic air transport policies through a uniform multilateral approach, at least not for the foreseeable future.[133]

An analogy with the global trading system may partly explain the challenges of the global multilateral approach. While a global multilateral system would ideally maximize benefits by exploiting the competitive advantages of all countries, thereby passing these benefits on to the consumer, the hard reality is that states do not altruistically place the global welfare and common interest over their own immediate self-interest.[134] The Doha Round stalemate is often cited to call into question the WTO's role as a global multilateral forum for negotiating 21st century trade agreements, and an increasing focus is being placed on regional trade deals.[135]

Indeed, the role of global multilateralism is inherently limited on policy issues which are normatively neutral. As Ronald Dworkin noted, policy is different from "principle" in that, whereas principles concern justice, fairness, and other aspects of morality, policy has to do with social, political, and economic goals.[136] Dworkin added that, although goals tend to be improvements, some goals are negative in that they stipulate that some present feature is to be protected from adverse change.[137]

A. LeRoy Bennett succinctly summarized the seven reasons for states to prefer the regional approach over the universal (global multilateral) approach. The first three reasons are worth ruminating on in this discussion about the regional liberalization of international air transport:

1. There is a natural tendency toward regionalism based on the homogeneity of interests, traditions, and values within small groups of neighboring states.
2. Political, economic, and social integration is more easily attained among fewer states within a limited geographic area than on a global basis.
3. Regional economic cooperation provides more efficient economic units than smaller states, and these larger units can compete successfully in world markets.[138]

---

133 See also Havel & Sanchez, "Aviation Law" *supra* note 51 at 109 (noting that "[M]ultilateralism as enjoyed by other globally minded service sectors like telecommunications and finance remains imaginable, although unlikely to materialize in the foreseeable future.").
134 Michael Ewing-Chow, "Multilateral or Regional – WTO "and/or" FTAs? An Academic's View of the Trenches" in C L Lim & Margaret Liang eds., *Economic Diplomacy* (Singapore: World Scientific Publishing, 2011) 257 at 261-262.
135 See *e.g.* Evan Rogerson, "Emerging Issues and Challenges of the WTO" (Speech to National University of Singapore Centre for International Law Distinguished Speaker Series, 19 June 2013) [unpublished] online: <http://cil.nus.edu.sg/programmes-and-activities/past-events/emerging-issues-and-challenges-of-the-wto/>.
136 Ronald Dworkin, *Taking Rights Seriously* (London: Duckworth, 1981) at 22.
137 *Ibid.*
138 A. LeRoy Bennett, *International Organizations: Principles and Issues*, 6th ed. (Englewood Cliffs: Prentice Hall, 1995) at 230-231 (The rest of the reasons, which are not that closely related to regional air transport liberalization, are as follows: 4)Local threats to the peace are more willingly and promptly dealt with by the governments of that area than by disinterested states at greater distance from the scene of conflict; 5) By

In fact, the adoption of regional liberalization has been an alternative to regulatory change and adjustment for many states.[139] Generally, regional agreements can be more detailed and have more chances of being implemented than global multilateral treaties. The mix of fewer states, greater coincidence of interests, and particularly high levels of economic integration and interdependence make for more practicable forms of regional cooperation.[140] It is clear that regional treaties permit more of the flexibility and control that states are so reluctant to lose. In addition, they allow states to pursue their common interest.

Apart from the internal economic benefits resulting from air transport liberalization (i.e. new and better air services, traffic growth, economic growth, job growth, and so on), external relations have been mentioned as an important benefit of regional liberalization for developing countries (or smaller countries) as well as developed countries.[141]

The external relations vis-à-vis third countries and regions is a clear advantage of the regional approach since the member states in the same regional group can "reap the benefits of a stronger negotiating position enabling their airlines to compete on more favorable terms in the international market place".[142] This advantageous position would not be possible if each state in the same regional group *individually* negotiated (for example, market access issues) with a stronger economy outside of the region. In a nutshell, smaller countries in the same region can cooperate to form a stronger aviation community that can compete with other stronger states, blocs of states, or regions. Similarly, regional liberalization is a way for developed countries to improve their negotiating position with other strong regions or states.

---

combining states into regional groupings a global balance of power will be maintained and world peace and security will be promoted. 6) The world is not ready to establish global authority sufficient to maintain peace and promote world welfare. Regionalism is the first step in gaining experience and building areas of consensus toward eventual intergovernmental coordination or integration.; 7) Universalists fail to take into account the heterogeneity of political, economic, social, and geographical factors throughout the world that militate against unity. These differences can be more easily accommodated within a regional framework.); See also Erwin Von Den Steinen, *National Interest and International Aviation* (Alphen aan den Rijn: Kluwer Law International, 2006) at 115 (noting that "[F]irst, we can view the phenomenon with respect to its entirely internal effects; in other words, what shared effect will regional market integration have on services conducted within the region? Second, we can ask what extent the states within the region continue to draw lines between each other; where do the states consider it necessary or advisable to retain sovereign powers in their dealings with each other? Third, we can consider how... the region... now relates to third parties, to states outside the region ; do, for example, the member states find it advantageous to act collectively in some or all areas of their aviation relationships with others?").

139 ICAO Secretariat, "Overview of Trends and Developments in International Air Transport" (24 March 2009), online: <www.icao.int/sustainability/Documents/OverviewTrends.pdf>.
140 Bonin, *supra* note 7 at 44-45.
141 See *e.g.* Tan, "Prospects for SAM", *supra* note 3; Lelieur, *supra* note 26 at 118; Steinen, *supra* note 138 at 114-115.
142 Lelieur, *supra* note 26 at 118.

1.5.3 Progress in Regional Liberalization

The ICAO Secretariat presented global quantitative indicators for evaluating the degree of air transport liberalization in 2010 and 2013.[143] The major findings of the analysis indicate that there has been a steady development of air transport liberalization since the mid-1990s.[144] In 2012, about 35 percent of the country pairs with non-stop scheduled passenger services and about 58 per cent of the frequencies offered were between countries that have embraced liberalization (compared with about 22 and 42 percent, respectively, a decade ago).[145] Much of this liberalization was achieved through bilateral means.

This analysis also confirms that the degree of liberalization varies widely among different regions. Generally speaking, Europe and North America show a more liberal picture while the Asia-Pacific region has been slow to adopt this trend.[146]

Importantly, liberalization achieved at the intra-regional level (i.e. within the same region) has moved ahead of the inter-regional level due to the expansion of regional/plurilateral liberal air services agreements (leading to a big jump in intra-regional passenger movement numbers between 2000–2001 and 2004–2005).[147]

---

143 The original report was released during the 37th ICAO General Assembly in 2010 and an updated version of the report was released just before the 38th ICAO General Assembly in 2013. Online: <www.icao.int/Meetings/atconf6/Documents/Global%20Quantative%20Indicator_en.pdf>.
144 ICAO, "Regulatory Overview", *supra* note 130 at A-3; ICAO, however, noted the incompleteness of the analysis by stating that "[I]t is recognized that the selected liberalized ASAs, especially the regional/plurilateral ones, have heterogeneities in terms of the degree of 'openness' in their provisions, and effective/actual implementation in practice. However, quantifying such differences is difficult and unwarranted due to insufficient details available on some agreements, as well as the need to minimize an element of subjective judgments".
145 *Ibid.*
146 *Ibid.*
147 *Ibid.*; ICAO noted that "[A]greements/arrangements which liberalize Third, Fourth and Fifth Freedoms in respect of scheduled passenger services amongst the parties to the agreement, were selected as "regional/plurilateral liberal ASAs."

1 INTRODUCTION TO NORTHEAST ASIAN OPEN SKIES

Figure 1.4 Liberalized Country Pair Routes with Non-Stop Flights[148]

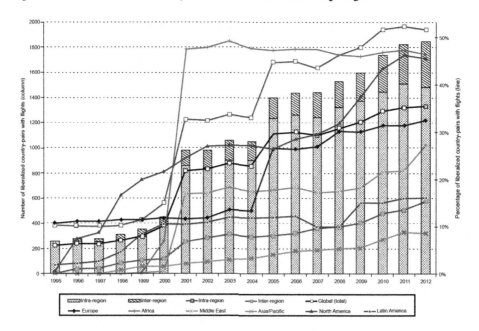

1.5.4 Challenges to Regional Liberalization

Despite ample justifications and encouraging progress, regional liberalization continues to face considerable challenges. The most significant challenge comes from the fact that regional liberalization with multiple member states (*e.g.* 10 states in ASEAN and 22 states in the League of Arab States (the Arab League)) is essentially *multilateral* liberalization on a smaller scale. Hence, regional liberalization cannot avoid the problems of multilateral approaches, *i.e.* states with bigger markets but less competitive air carriers that are not willing to participate in the arrangement. Except the European Union (EU), which is equipped with a mandatory enforcement mechanism, nearly all regional liberalization models have a similar setback: namely, the biggest economy is typically resistant to regional liberalization.

The reluctance of Indonesia, the biggest economy and aviation market in Southeast Asia, to participate fully in the ASEAN Single Aviation Market (SAM) continues;[149] states with larger markets in the Arab League such as Egypt and Saudi Arabia have not ratified

---

148 *Ibid.* at A-4.
149 Indonesia, however, has ratified Protocols 5 and 6 of the Multilateral Agreement on Air Services (MAAS) opening up Jakarta on 5 June 2014 (see more in section 2.3 The ASEAN Single Aviation Market Model).

the Damascus Agreement toward an Arab Single Aviation Market;[150] and China is not willing to create an intra-Northeast Asian single aviation market. All of these issues will be reviewed in the following sections. The reluctance of these states is unquestionably based on "the primacy of aero-politics and geography in the complex calculations of governments and their airlines."[151] As Alan Tan says,

> The reality is that in a grouping of countries with vastly divergent population and geographical sizes and with airlines of varying strengths, the entity with a small population and limited points but with formidable airlines will likely benefit the most from liberalisation agreements, particularly if unlimited fifth freedom opportunities were made available.[152]

Despite the insurmountable obstacle, the number of regional open skies agreements and participating states continues to grow. Generally, the regional approach to air transport counterbalances the shortcomings of the bilateral markets while making it possible to achieve (to some extent) the liberalization of market access and of ownership/control rules.

For air carriers, the regional approach would allow more flexibility, easing their multi-country operations in the region. However, the fact is that the regional approach is still a form of regulation. Even a completely single aviation market—the EU single aviation market, for example—cannot fully satisfy air carriers' business-oriented desires. Although regional liberalization can provide a better business opportunity than sets of bilateral air services agreements, by no means does it provide a satisfactory business environment for airlines. Because of existing legal barriers in international air transport (that is, restrictions on market access and on ownership and control) as well as economic incentives (such as increasing revenue and reducing costs), airlines cooperate under the name of "alliances."

1.6   Airline Alliances

1.6.1   Rationale for Airline Alliances

The limitations of state-led liberalization have led the airlines to turn to private agreements among themselves. In particular, they have formed alliances that represent "a flexible

---

150 See Alan Khee-Jin Tan "The 2004 Damascus Agreement: Liberalizing Market Access and Ownership Rules for Arab Air Carriers" (2010) 35 Ann. Air & Sp. L. 1.
151 Alan Khee-Jin Tan, "Chapter 15 The Future of Multilateral Liberalization of Air Transport in Asia" in David Duval, ed., *Air Transport in the Asia Pacific* (Burlington: Ashgate, 2014) 259 at 264.
152 Ibid.

organizational form offering rapid growth potentials," the kind of potentials enjoyed by firms in other sectors.[153]

Three multinational global alliances—Skyteam, Star Alliance and Oneworld—are well-known to the public. They offer integrated global coverage through the networks of their member airlines. Indeed, the key business motivation for airline alliances starts from the simple fact that "no single airline's network encompasses all possible 'point A to point B' combinations."[154] While airlines differ in many ways—including pricing policies, fleet mix, and production process, which involves ticketing, baggage handling, and passenger catering—they all share this fundamental limitation.[155] As a result, many passengers are required to "interline," or change an airline during their journey.[156]

"Code-sharing" is a more advanced form of cooperation among airlines. In fact, it is the cornerstone of most airline alliances.[157] Code-sharing refers to including the flights of one airline in the schedules of its partner airlines; through a code-sharing arrangement, an airline can expand its network without having to service additional flights.[158] Clearly, this business practice offers airlines three major benefits. First, it is cost-efficient, since airlines are able to provide connections to foreign cities through their partner airlines without using their own aircraft. Second, it represents a means of circumventing the route access restrictions that affect non-open skies agreements.[159] In some cases, however, code-sharing is allowed only if the underlying traffic right is available to the foreign carrier.[160] Third, it allows foreign carriers to make inroads into another nation's domestic market without violating foreign ownership and market access restrictions.[161]

Indeed, airline alliances were at least partially formed to maximize airlines' business opportunities in response to rigid governmental regulation. In particular, the inability of airlines to merge across borders (due to ownership and control restrictions – see more in Chapter 5 on Airline Alliances in Northeast Asia) was an important reason to form alliances.

---

153 Kostas Iatrou & Lida Mantzavinou, "Chapter 13 The Impact of Liberalization on Cross-border Airline Mergers and Alliances" in Peter Forsyth *et al.* eds., *Liberalization in Aviation: Competition, Cooperation and Public Policy* (Farnham: Ashgate, 2013) 233 at 233.
154 Volodymyr Bilotkach & Kai Hüschelrath, "Chapter 14 Economic Effects of Antitrust Immunity for Airline Alliances: Identification and Measurement" in Peter Forsyth *et al.* eds., *Liberalization in Aviation: Competition, Cooperation and Public Policy* (Farnham: Ashgate, 2013) 247 at 248.
155 Ibid.
156 Ibid.
157 Havel, "Open Skies", *supra* note 22 at 208.
158 See The US General Accounting Office, *International Aviation: Airline Alliances Produce Benefits, But Effect on Competition is Uncertain*, GAO/RCED-95-99 (April 1995) at 13.
159 Havel, "Open Skies", *supra* note 22 at 210.
160 See Alan Khee-Jin Tan, "Antitrust Immunity for Trans-Pacific Airline Alliance Agreements: Singapore and China as 'Beyond' Markets" (2013) 38 Air & Space L. 275 at 292 [Tan, "Antitrust Immunity"].
161 Jacob A. Warden ""Open Skies" at a Crossroads: How the United States and European Union Should Use the ECJ Transport Cases to Reconstruct the Transatlantic Aviation Regime" (2003) 24 Northwestern Journal of International Law & Business 227 at 237.

Since the 1990s, airline executives have been pursuing global strategies for cooperation and integration, strategies that seek to loosen the grip of the legal restraints imposed by bilateral diplomacy.[162]

There are three major types of code-share agreements: parallel operation on a trunk route, unilateral operation on a trunk route, and behind and beyond route (see Figure 1.5).[163] Of the three, parallel operation on a trunk route can counterbalance restricted intergovernmental agreements by sharing (and *de facto* increasing) frequency and capacity in the given routes.

An example of this is flights between Beijing and Seoul operated by China Southern and Korean Air, which have each other's codes as well as their own. Due to the restricted market access allowed by the China–Korea air services agreement (under which traffic rights are still distributed to each air carrier by their respective governments), both China Southern and Korean Air have reached their maximum frequency and capacity and could not expand any more on their own. By means of a code-share agreement, however, they can indirectly increase their frequency and capacity on the Beijing-Seoul route. This practice is clearly beneficial to airlines that cannot increase frequency and capacity through their own aircraft due to restrictions in the air services agreement.

---

162 Havel, "Open Skies", *supra* note 22 at 198.
163 Steer Davies Gleave, *Competition Impact of Airline Code-Share Agreements* (London: Steer Davies Gleave, 2007) at 8 ("Parallel operation on a trunk route: two carriers both operate the same sector (flown airport pair), and each gives its code to the other's operated flights; Unilateral operation on a trunk route: a carrier puts its code on a sector operated by another carrier, but not by itself, and not (necessarily) connecting to one of its own operated flights; Behind and beyond route (connecting to a trunk route service): a carrier puts its code on sectors operated by another carrier to provide connections with its own operated services. Such connecting code-shares generally require the marketing carrier to sell an interline journey, *i.e.* one involving travel on its own service and then on the service of the partner carrier (and this kind of code-share is therefore sometimes known as an "interline code-share")).

Figure 1.5 Types of Code-Share Operations[164]

Parallel trunk route code-share operation

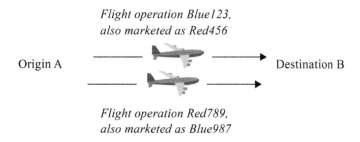

Flight operation Blue123, also marketed as Red456

Origin A → Destination B

Flight operation Red789, also marketed as Blue987

Unilateral trunk route code-share operation

Flight operation Blue234, also marketed as Red567

Origin A ─────→ Destination B

Behind and beyond code-share operation

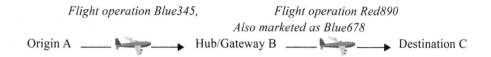

Flight operation Blue345,   *Flight operation Red890*
                                 Also marketed as Blue678

Origin A ─────→ Hub/Gateway B ─────→ Destination C

1.6.2 Antitrust Immunity

While a basic level of cooperation is required by members of an airline alliance (generally involving standard code-share agreements), some alliance members also seek higher levels of cooperation to enhance the benefits of the alliance.[165] Indeed, there is a broad spectrum of cooperation by alliance partners, ranging from basic, arms-length arrangements to highly integrated joint ventures.[166] The level of airline cooperation is broadly described below:

---

164 *Ibid.* at Appendix B-1.
165 The European Commission & the United States Department of Transportation, *Transatlantic Airline Alliances: Competitive Issues and Regulatory Approaches* (16 November 2010) at 4, online: <http://ec.europa.eu/competition/sectors/transport/reports/joint_alliance_report.pdf>.
166 *Ibid.* at 5.

Figure 1.6   Spectrum of Alliance Cooperation[167]

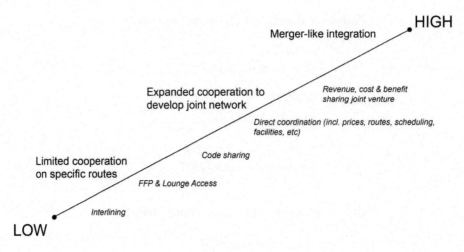

As shown above, alliance members cooperate in many areas; however, they remain competitors until the middle stage of cooperation. For instance, airlines in code-share agreements still compete with each other to maximize their profits. That is to say, each airline tries to sell its own tickets for the sector(s) it operates.

However, highly integrated joint ventures obviate the question of which air carrier's tickets are being sold since the carriers share the revenues and profits in the end. In highly integrated joint ventures, alliance partners are effectively indifferent about which of them provides the actual "metal" (that is, the plane) on particular routes.[168] (Metal neutrality will be examined below in section 1.5.3 on Metal Neutrality and more thoroughly in Chapter 5: Airline Alliances in Northeast Asia.) Such a high degree of alliance cooperation inevitably prompts governmental intervention since it can become anti-competitive.

In fact, highly integrated airline alliances involve two pillars of government regulations (or deregulations). One pillar is liberalization. This has been the major factor behind the formation of airline alliances, and these alliances have developed in response to the opportunities provided by liberalization initiatives.[169] The other pillar of regulation is competition law. Generally, competition law prohibits conduct that interferes with free competition in the marketplace.

---

167   *Ibid*.
168   See Paul Mifsud, "Metal Neutrality and the Nation-Bound Airline Industry" (2011) 36 Air & Space L.117 at 122; see also Tan, "Antitrust Immunity", *supra* note 160 at 279.
169   Iatrou & Mantzavinou, *supra* note 153 at 234 & 244.

Although a number of studies confirm that airline alliances benefit the consumers and carriers concerned,[170] the business activities of airline alliances may result in market allocation, capacity restriction, restriction on schedules, high fares and price fixing, all of which may negatively impact consumers. If the airlines participating in the alliance possess dominant positions in the allocated market, the impact can be much more significant.

In principle, these types of activities must be prevented. However, if the benefits that an airline alliance provides consumers outweigh the alleged anti-competitiveness of the alliance, the competition authorities may grant *antitrust immunity*. Antitrust immunity refers to "immunity from the provisions of antitrust legislation that would otherwise prevent certain forms of co-operation as illegal anti-competitive activities."[171]

National competition authorities in countries with developed legal systems generally have laws in place dealing with antitrust immunity. In order to assess the competitive effects of a given alliance, competition authorities must engage in a fact-finding inquiry to determine the structure, scope, and overlap created by each transaction.[172]

Most national and regional authorities responsible for granting antitrust immunity opine that an open skies agreement is the *precondition* for the approval of antitrust immunity for an airline alliance.[173] Obviously, this is a reasonable requirement. Granting antitrust immunity for airlines in a market where market access is restricted would sharply reduce competition by limiting the actual number of market players (airlines). This would only benefit the airlines that were provided immunity. On the other hand, an "open skies" environment would allow for unlimited entry by a multitude of airlines, thus reducing the anti-competitive concerns arising from the granting of antitrust immunity.

---

170 See *e.g.* Jan K. Brueckner, "International Airfares in the Age of Alliances: the Effects of Codesharing and Antitrust Immunity" (2003) 85 Review of Economic and Statistics 105; W. Tom Whalen, "A Panel Data Analysis of Code Sharing, Antitrust Immunity and Open Skies Treaties in International Aviation Market" (2007) 30 Review of Industrial Organization 39; Volodymyr Bilotkach "Price Effects of Airline Consolidation: Evidence from a Sample of Transatlantic Markets" (2007) 33 Empirical Economics 427; Angela Cheng-Fui Lu, *International Airline Alliances* (The Hague: Kluwer Law International, 2003) at 63-67; See also IATA, *Economics Briefing the Economic Benefits Generated by Alliances and Joint Ventures*, (2011) online: <www.iata.org/whatwedo/Documents/economics/Economics%20of%20JVs_Jan2012L.pdf>. (IATA summarized the benefits of the airline alliances as follows: 1) lower fares for interlining passengers; 2) lower fares resulting from economies of traffic density; 3) passengers can more easily combine fares in an itinerary; 4) airlines can offer passengers a much wider range of schedules; and 5) the passenger enjoys benefits from more seamless service and similar products.)
171 CAPA, *Airlines in Transition report, Part 1: The natural history of airline alliances* (16 April 2013), online: <http://centreforaviation.com/analysis/capa-airlines-in-transition-report-part-1-the-natural-history-of-airline-alliances-105278>.
172 The EU Commission & the US DOT, *supra* note 165 at 5.
173 See generally ICAO, *Antitrust Immunity for Airlines Alliances*, ICAO Doc ATConf/6-WP/85 (4 March 2013) (Presented by the Republic of Korea), online: <www.icao.int/Meetings/atconf6/Documents/WorkingPapers/ATConf6-wp85_en.pdf>.

US Supreme Court Justice Stephen Breyer argued for the importance of potential competition in the airline industry, that is, the awareness that airlines not currently serving a given market are capable of entering it.[174] Justice Breyer continued:

> [T]he nearer the potential competitor and the easier it is to enter a particular city pair, the greater the threat of entry and the closer to the competitive level prices are likely to be. Given the importance of potential competition, every unnecessary removal of a significant carrier as an independent entry-threatening entity gratuitously raises the probability of unwarranted price increases.[175]

By this logic, an open skies agreement that allows unrestricted market access to other airlines should be implemented in the market in question *before* antitrust immunity is granted to a particular airline alliance. More interestingly, antitrust immunity for an airline alliance of which a foreign carrier is a member can be an incentive to conclude an open skies agreement with the home state of that carrier. Historically, the first antitrust immunity granted by the U.S. DOT with regard to airline alliances (Northwest-KLM in January 1993) was part of the US's first open skies agreement negotiated with the Netherlands in 1992.[176] Gillespie and Richard noted how antitrust immunity influenced the open skies agreement:

> [M]any grants of antitrust immunity to international alliances were used in large part to further foreign policy goals, such as Open Skies Agreements. Grants of antitrust immunity presumably provided assurances to a country's policymakers that decisions within an alliance would be made in the joint interests of all participating carriers, including the smaller country carriers in the alliance.[177]

1.6.3   Metal Neutrality

While the benefits of airline alliances have been proven, their effect on competition is less clear.[178] In particular, it is argued that a significant part of the efficiencies generated by airline alliances do not necessarily require immunity as they can already be realized by

---

174   Stephen Breyer, "Regulation and Deregulation in the United States: Airlines, Telecommunications and Antitrust" in Giandomenico Majone, ed., *Deregulation or Re-regulation?* (London: Pinter Publishers, 1990) 7 at 26.
175   *Ibid.*
176   Mifsud, *supra* note 168 at 121.
177   William Gillespie & Oliver M. Richard, "Antitrust Immunity Grants to Joint Venture Agreements: Evidence from International Airline Alliances" (2012) 78 Antitrust Law Journal 443.
178   See the US GAO, *supra* note 158.

interline or code-share agreements.[179] In response to criticisms that antitrust immunity had led to reduced competition, the U.S. DOT, which has limited authority to grant immunity from the US antitrust law to airlines to improve international air service, has recently added a new condition for antitrust immunity: *metal neutrality*. Metal neutrality means "a commercial environment in which joint venture partners have common economic incentives to promote the success of the alliance over their individual corporate interests."[180]

In the trans-Pacific market, and especially in Northeast Asia, the U.S. DOT's 2010 decision to accord antitrust immunity and require metal neutrality led to new regulatory developments. American Airlines and Japan Airlines (JAL) received antitrust immunity from the U.S. DOT on November 10, 2010, for their proposed joint venture (JV), while United Airlines and All Nippon Airways (ANA) received similar antitrust immunity on the same date. However, a significant limitation on the trans-Pacific JVs between these US and Japanese carriers is that US carriers cannot access codeshare services on ANA and JAL to China since China prevents airlines from a third country (i.e. the US) from code-sharing on these routes. (The details will be discussed in Chapter 3: Market Access Issues in Northeast Asia).[181]

Interestingly, the Delta-Korean Air antitrust immunity, which was granted in 2002, did not have the metal neutrality requirement. Although the DOT allowed joint ventures between Delta and Korean Air, a metal neutral joint venture was not a prerequisite for granting antitrust immunity.[182] Due to the new environment, Delta and Korean Air recently started to explore closer cooperation, which could include establishing a JV with metal neutrality.[183]

A far more interesting development is the possibility of Chinese carriers entering into joint venture agreements with their US alliance partners. In fact, media reports confirm a

---

179 Bilotkach & Hüschelrath, *supra* note 154 at 272.
180 U.S. DOT, Joint Application of Air Canada, The Austrian Group, British Midland Airways Ltd, Continental Airlines, Inc., Deutsche Lufthansa AG, Polskie Linie Lotnicze LOT S.A., Scandinavian Airlines System, Swiss international Air Lines Ltd., TAP Air Portugal, and United Air Lines, Inc. to Amend Order 2007-2-16 under 49 U.S.C. ss. 41308 and 41309 so as to Approve and Confer Antitrust Immunity, Dkt No DOTOST-2008-0234-0253, Order 2009-7-10, Final Order (10 July 2009).
181 CAPA, "US-Japan airline alliances become lopsided as JAL, ANA expand while US to shift to other markets" (4 February 2013), online: CAPA <http://centreforaviation.com/analysis/us-japan-airline-alliances-become-lopsided-as-jal-ana-expand-while-us-to-shift-to-other-markets-95799>. [CAPA, "US-Japan airline alliance"].
182 U.S. DOT, Joint Application of Delta Air Lines, INC. Korean Air Lines CO., LTD., Societe Air France, Alitalia-Linee Aeree Italiane-S.p.A. Czech Airlines under 49 U.S.C. §§ 41308 and 41309 for approval of and antitrust immunity for alliances agreements, Dkt OST-2002-11842 ORDER GRANTING APPROVAL AND ANTITRUST IMMUNITY FOR ALLIANCE AGREEMENTS Final Order (27 June 2002) (noting that "[S]ince the antitrust laws allow competitors to engage in joint ventures that are pro-competitive, we think it unlikely that the integration of the Joint Applicants' services would be found to violate the antitrust laws, subject to the conditions being imposed here by us.").
183 See CAPA, "Delta Air Lines puts trans-Atlantic worries to rest as it posts strong 2Q2014 results" (24 July 2014), online: <http://centreforaviation.com/analysis/delta-air-lines-puts-trans-atlantic-worries-to-rest-as-it-posts-strong-2q2014-results-179297>.

"Mexican stand-off" in which China Southern's offer to Delta to form a JV would clash with the U.S. DOT's policy of only approving JV antitrust immunities where open skies agreements already exist (in this case, between the US and China).[184] Paul Mifsud predicts that Delta's experience with metal neutral joint ventures could be put to use if its Chinese partner could successfully press its government to adopt an open skies agreement with the US[185] Nothing can be certain at this stage, but it is highly interesting to see how airline alliances can impact the dynamics of air services agreements to which China, Japan and Korea are parties.

1.7 Object and Structure of the Research

The primary object of my research is to analyze possible regional and bilateral approaches to liberalizing market access and ownership and control restrictions in Northeast Asia and to propose the steps that need to be taken to achieve Northeast Asian open skies, including a possible "trilateral" solution among the three states.[186] A secondary object is to take a step back from the orthodox position that intergovernmental agreements (*e.g.* air services agreements) solely determine the level of air transport liberalization and to argue instead that air carriers themselves can enter into private agreements such as alliances that can have a substantial impact on liberalization.

After the general introduction to Northeast Asian open skies presented in this chapter, Chapter 2: Comparative Analysis of Regional Liberalization Models analyzes different regional approaches for air transport liberalization. It first examines the rationales for regional liberalization. The chapter will discuss examples of regional liberalization, ranging from regions whose member states are still pursuing the common vision of liberalizing their markets to those that have fully achieved integrated single aviation markets. In the process, the chapter will assess in detail the developments in the EU (including its agreements with the US) and in ASEAN (including its agreement with China), critically analyzing them from two angles: benefits and challenges. In this context, both the justifications for and barriers to Northeast Asian open skies are discussed, along with an outline of progress in the discussion about Northeast Asian open skies.

Chapter 3: Market Access Issues in Northeast Asia begins with a detailed outline of the market access issue in international air transport. After describing national policies on market access in Northeast Asia, this chapter identifies specific market access issues in Northeast Asia on the national, bilateral, and regional levels. Specifically, the questions of

---

184 CAPA, "US-Japan airline alliance", *supra* note 181.
185 Mifsud, *supra* note 168 at 129.
186 Multilateral, trilateral, regional – the three terms have essentially the same meaning in the special context of Northeast Asia. For more, see section 2.5 Regional Liberalization in Northeast Asia.

what is preventing the liberalization of access in the Northeast Asian market, including aero-political impediments (and particularly the position of China), and what can initiate market access liberalization in Northeast Asia are discussed. In particular, the role of low-cost carriers (LCCs) in moving forward the liberalization agenda for market access is analyzed.

Chapter 4: Ownership and Control Issues in Northeast Asia parallels the previous chapter because ownership and control restrictions are the other significant legal hurdle to air transport liberalization. The origin of the legal framework for ownership and control is examined first. After exploring national law and policy on ownership and control restrictions in Northeast Asia, various mechanisms for liberalizing ownership and control in Northeast Asia on the multilateral, regional, bilateral, and national levels are examined. Following that, airlines' response to ownership and control restrictions are discussed.

Chapter 5: Airline Alliances in Northeast Asia begins by investigating the rationales for airline alliances. While introducing various industry practices, Chapter 5 explains that airline alliances play an important role in overcoming, albeit not completely, the restrictions on market access and ownership and control in the air transport market. It then identifies in what ways and to what extent airline alliances in Northeast Asia have developed. After pointing out that the business activities of airline alliances can be anti-competitive, Chapter 5 explains the need to ensure that airline alliances comply with competition/antitrust law in order to safeguard fair and free competition in the air transport market. Chapter 5 further addresses under what circumstances antitrust immunity is given to airline alliances. After discussing the origin and rationale of antitrust immunity, this chapter elaborates on how national and regional competition authorities discuss and decide whether to grant antitrust immunity to an airline alliance. Chapter 5 then deals with how antitrust immunity for airline alliances can reshape the dynamics of Northeast Asian open skies.

Chapter 6: Towards Northeast Asian Open Skies: Liberalization by the Airline Industry and States provides a prescriptive analysis of what is needed to bring about Northeast Asian open skies. After summarizing the key findings of the research, this chapter proposes short-term (through 2020), mid-term (through 2025) and long-term (through 2030) steps for Northeast Asian open skies.

2 Comparative Analysis of Regional Liberalization Models

2.1 Overview

The various regional liberalization models that exist are at different stages of development and implementation. Among these, the single aviation market (SAM) is the most advanced model of regional liberalization. As the term illustrates, multiple aviation markets that are usually segmented by states are becoming one market under the concept of SAM. The EU created a SAM for the first time through adopting a series of legislative acts (discussed in the following section).

However, the EU has not provided an official definition for SAM even though the term is commonly used by many bodies including the European Commission and EU member states.[1] The Association of Southeast Asian Nations (ASEAN) SAM (discussed in the section 2.3) provides the following features of a SAM:

- Some restrictions are removed for designated ASEAN carriers on the operation of passenger and freight transport and associated commercial activities within the states in the ASEAN region;
- a common policy is adopted for user charges, tariffs, competitive behavior and other forms of regulation; and
- majority ownership and effective control of designated carriers is vested in ASEAN states and or nationals in the aggregate.[2] (otherwise known as the "community carrier" concept).

The EU Single Aviation Market is the most structured and consolidated model of any regional liberalization model seen thus far. Although the EU model is highly exceptional, it is worth studying how the EU adopted a single aviation market and what it has achieved

---

[1] See *e.g.* The European Commission homepage, online: <http://ec.europa.eu/transport/modes/air/internal_market/index_en.htm>; Daniel Calleja (Director of Air Transport, European Commission), "Aviation in the European Union – an Overview" (Presentation to EU-Latin America Civil Aviation Summit, Rio de Janeiro, 24-26 May 2010), online: <http://clacsec.lima.icao.int/Reuniones/2010/Cumbre/Presentaciones/Sesion1/Calleja.pdf>; *The European Union's Commitment to Cooperation with the World Aviation Community*, (Presented by Portugal, on behalf of the European Community and its Member States), online: <http://ec.europa.eu/transport/modes/air/international_aviation/european_community_icao/doc/info_paper_icao_en.pdf>.

[2] Ian Thomas, David Stone, Alan Khee-Jin Tan, Andrew Drysdale, & Phil McDermott, *Developing ASEAN's Single Aviation Market and Regional Air Services Arrangements with Dialogue Partners* (CAPA Final Report, June 2008, REPSF II Project No. 07/003) at 13 [CAPA, "Final Report"].

through the EU SAM.[3] In Asia, the ASEAN SAM is a fairly good and realistic example of what regional liberalization can achieve.[4]

In the following sections, the EU SAM and ASEAN SAM models (section 2.2 and section 2.3, respectively) will be fully analyzed in terms of three key liberalizing features: namely, market access, ownership and control, and external relations. Next, other regional liberalization models in the Australia-New Zealand SAM, Asia-Pacific Economic Cooperation (APEC)'s Initiative, Arab League, Latin America, Pacific Islands, and Africa will be discussed mainly in terms of two key features: market access and ownership and control restrictions (section 2.4). Recognizing that regional liberalization of Northeast Asia is at a preliminary discussion stage, the brief history, justifications, and barriers will be examined in the last section (section 2.5).

2.2 THE EU SINGLE AVIATION MARKET MODEL

2.2.1 Overview

As the most integrated of any regional organization in the world, the EU is the gold standard for other regions seeking to move in a similar direction.[5] Among the four stages of economic integration – free trade area (zero tariffs between member countries and reduced non-tariff barriers),[6] customs union (free trade area and common external tariffs),[7]

---

3   Related but different concepts are the Common Aviation Area (CAA) and the Single European Sky (SES). CAA refers to the open market between the EU and its neighboring countries, which entails regulatory convergence through the implementation of EU aviation rules. SES is involved in air transport management (ATM). The implementation of SES aims to put ATM under EU control while reducing the fragmentation of European airspace. See European Commission, ' Aviation Policy, online: <http://ec.europa.eu/transport/modes/air/international_aviation/external_aviation_policy/neighbourhood_en.htm>; European Commission, *Report from the Commission to the European Parliament and the Council on the Implementation of the Single Sky legislation: time to deliver* (Brussels: EC, 2011), online: <http://ec.europa.eu/transport/modes/air/single_european_sky/doc/reports/2011_11_14_com_2011_0731_f_rapport_en.pdf>.
4   But see the criticism on its slow implementation, *e.g.* Alan Khee-Jin Tan, "Clear take-off on Asean Open Skies" *The Straits Times* (5 April 2013), online: <www.straitstimes.com/the-big-story/asia-report/opinion/story/clear-take-asean-open-skies-20130405>.
5   Fraser Cameron, "The European Integration Model: What Relevance for Asia?" in G. John Ikenberry, ed., *Regional Integration and Institutionalization Comparing Asia and Europe* (Kyoto: Shoukadoh Publishers, 2012) 33 at 33.
6   For more, see Nicholas Moussis, *Access to European Union: law, economics, policies*, 16th ed. (Rixensart: European Study Service, 2007) at 69-70 (noting that "[A] free trade area is based on intergovernmental cooperation. In such an area, member countries abolish import duties and other customs barriers to the free movement of goods manufactured in the territory of their partners. However, each country retains its own external tariff and its customs policy vis-à-vis third countries. It also retains entirely its national sovereignty.").
7   See *ibid.* at 70 (noting that "[I]n a customs union, which is the first stage of the evolutionary multinational integration process, free movement concerns not only products manufactured in the territory of the partners,

common market (customs union, free movement of capital and labor, and some policy harmonization),[8] and economic union (common market and common economic policies and institutions) – the EU is at the stage of economic union.

Economic unions not only require coordinated monetary and fiscal policies but also key economic policies relating to, *inter alia*, the labor market and transportation.[9] Since all countries in the economic union essentially share "the same economic space," operating conflicting policies in those areas is considered to be counter-productive.[10]

The aviation sector in Europe has been directed by the EU's common economic policies, and therefore the EU Single Aviation Market is remarkably structured and consolidated compared to other regional liberalization models in the world. Although the EU has been referred to as the best model for regional liberalization in the air transport sector, it is important to note that the EU model is highly exceptional.

Indeed, no other regional liberalization model can match the EU's level of systemic integration. Two key ideas that help explain the EU's successful regional liberalization are the *institutions* that have consolidated the process and the common European *identity* that has allowed the integration to take place without repulsion.

The EU has solid institutions (executive, legislative and judicial bodies) that are involved in the decision-making process and have the authority to enforce those decisions. Known as "the principal actors of European integration,"[11] these institutions comprise four main organs: the European Commission, the European Parliament, the Council of the European Union (formerly the Council of the Ministers, also informally known as the EU Council),[12] and the Court of Justice of the European Union (CJEU), formerly the European Court of Justice.[13] Essentially, the ultimate enforcement of EU law has been entrusted to the CJEU,

---

but all products, irrespective of origin, situated in the territory of the member countries. Furthermore, the latter lose their customs autonomy and apply a common external customs tariff to third countries.").

8   See *ibid.* (noting that "[i]f the members would like to turn a customs union into a real internal market, they would need to ensure not only the free movement of goods and services, but also the free movement of production factors, namely labour and capital. In order to obtain these fundamental freedoms of a common market, the member states had to develop a great number of common policies in pre-established and in new fields, such as social, environment and consumer protection, calling for further sharing of national sovereignties.").

9   Michel Holden, *Stages of Economic Integration: From Autarky to Economic Union* (13 February 2003), online: <http://dsp-psd.pwgsc.gc.ca/Collection-R/LoPBdP/inbrief/prb0249-e.htm#freetxt>.

10 *Ibid.*

11 Moussis, *supra* note 6 at 42.

12 The Council of the European Union should not be confused with the European Council which is essentially the summit where EU leaders meet to decide on broad policy priorities and major initiatives. The European Council has no power to pass law.

13 See European Union, *EU institutions and other bodies*, online: <http://europa.eu/about-eu/institutions-bodies/index_en.htm>.

and the CJEU has had an extraordinary impact on the emergence of the EU SAM policy.[14] (For more discussion, see below section 2.2.2.3 External Relations.)

To be sure, it is not the object of this research to analyze European identity. However, it is important to note the rich literature that discusses the concept of European identity and to recognize the link between European identity and the growth of the EU, which is to say the success of European economic integration.[15] While arguing that European identity does not necessarily decrease one's national identity or other kinds of identities, Claire Wallace and Kristin Stromsnes drew an interesting analogy between the European identity and the Euro coins – national on one side and standardized European on the other.[16] In other words, the EU has successfully established (more accurately, consolidated) the concept of European identity without detracting from national identity.

The first steps toward a common air transport policy did not surface until 1970 when the European Commission adopted a draft proposal for a Council Decision on common action in Community air transport.[17] After that, the Commission took several actions preparing for the development of community air transport services. The Commission recommended to the Council joint actions for improving the air service network of the Community in 1972. More significantly, the Commission released the memorandum *Contribution of the European Communities to the Development of the Air Transport Services* in 1979.[18]

The possibility of creating a single aviation market started receiving more attention in the mid-1980s.[19] The ECJ decision in the Nouvelles Frontiéres case (1986)[20] created conditions that were favorable for taking an important step forward in liberalizing the air transport industry.[21] Although the 1957 Treaty of Rome granted the EC the authority to create the framework of a common transport policy (Article 74),[22] sea and air transport were originally categorized as exceptions that required unanimous approval from member

---

14   Brian Havel, *Beyond Open Skies: A New Regime for International Aviation* (Alphen aan den Rijn: Kluwer Law International, 2009) at 394. [Havel, "Open Skies"].
15   See *e.g.* Jeffrey T. Checkel & Peter J. Katzenstein, ed., *European Identity* (Cambridge: Cambridge University Press, 2009); Kaija E Schilde, "Who are the Europeans? European Identity Outside of European Integration" (2014) 52 Journal of Common Market Studies 650.
16   Claire Wallace & Kristin Stromsnes, "Introduction: European Identities" (2008) 9 Perspectives on European Politics and Society 378 at 379.
17   Jeffrey Goh, *European Air Transport Law and Competition* (Chichester: John Wiley & Sons, 1997) at 21. [Goh, "European Air Transport"].
18   EC, Commission, *Contribution of the European Communities to the development of air transport services* (Luxembourg: EC, 1979) EC Bulletin, Supplement 5, para 12. The Commission produced three memoranda which set out its vision on the direction of air transport within the Community and beyond. This was the first memorandum. See *ibid.* at 22.
19   The second and the third memoranda were released in 1984 and 1986.
20   *Ministere Public v. Asjes*, C-209-213/84 [1986] E.C.R. I-1425.
21   Martin Staniland, *A Europe of the air?: The Airline Industry and European Integration* (Lanham: Rowman & Littlefield, 2008) at 78.
22   *Treaty Establishing the European Economic Community*, done at Rome, 25 March 1957, Article 74.

states to implement a common transport policy (Article 84).[23] However, in the Nouvelles Frontiéres case, the ECJ held that "Article 84 of the Treaty cannot be interpreted as excluding air transport from the general rules of the Treaty, including competition rules."[24]

Another major impetus for the EU SAM was the Single European Act (signed in February 1986 and became effective in July 1987). Indeed, the creation of the EU SAM was part of the move toward a single internal market across a wide range of economic activity, as embodied in the Single European Act.[25] The Single European Act amended the Treaty of Rome and reinforced the EC's ability to direct common policies (including air transport policy) for the EC at large.[26]

The EU officially liberalized its air transport sector through three "packages": the first in December 1987,[27] the second in November 1990,[28] and the third in January 1993.[29] The first package started to relax the established rules. It was particularly significant that this package allowed any EU carrier to operate on major hub routes within the EU without restriction on the number of designated air carriers. It also provided EU air carriers with the right to operate 5th freedom services within EU member states at up to 30 percent of total capacity.

The second package expanded the scope of liberalization. It gave all EU carriers the right to carry unlimited 3rd and 4th freedom flights between their home country and another EU member state and relaxed restrictions on 5th freedom services to up to 50

---

23 *Ibid.* Article 84.
24 *Ministere Public v. Asjes*, C-209-213/84 [1986] E.C.R. I-1425.
25 EU Member States, *European Experience of Air Transport Liberalization* (2003 February), online: <www.icao.int/sustainability/CaseStudies/StatesReplies/EuropeLiberalization_En.pdf>.
26 Jacob A. Warden, ""Open Skies" at a Crossroads: How the United States and European Union Should Use the ECJ Transport Cases to Reconstruct the Transatlantic Aviation Regime" (2003) 24 Northwestern Journal of International Law & Business 227 at 233.
27 EC, *Council Regulation 3975/87 laying down the procedure for the application of the rules on competition to undertakings in the air transport sector* [1987]; EC, *Council Regulation 3976/87 on the application of Article 85(3) of the EC Treaty to certain categories of agreements and concerted practices in the air transport sector* [1987]; EC, *Council Directive 87/601 on fares for scheduled air services between Member States* [1987]; and EC, *Council 87/602 on the sharing of passenger capacity between air carriers on scheduled air services between Member States and on access for air carriers to scheduled air service routes between Member States,* [1987].
28 EC, *Council Regulation 2342/90 on fares for scheduled air services* [1990]; EC, *Council Regulation 2343/90 on access for air carriers to scheduled intra-Community air service routes and on the sharing of passenger capacity between air carriers on scheduled air services between Member States* [1990]; and EC, *Council Regulation 2344/90 amending Regulation 3976/87 on the application of Article 85(3) of the Treaty to certain categories of agreements and concerted practices in the air transport sector* [1990].
29 EC, *Council Regulation 2407/92 on licensing of air carriers* [1992]; EC, *Council Regulation 2408/92 on access for Community air carriers to intra-Community air routes* [1992]; EC, *Council Regulation 2409/92 on fares and rates for air services* [1992]; EC, *Council Regulation 2410/92 amending Council Regulation 3875/87 laying down the procedure for the application of the rules on competition to undertakings in the air transport sector* [1992]; and EC, *Council Regulation 2411/92 amending Council Regulation 3976/87 on the application of Article 85(3) of the Treaty to certain categories of agreements and concerted practices in the air transport sector* [1992].

percent of total capacity. The first two packages were deliberately modest and incremental since the Commission and the EU member states were determined to ensure a gradual transition rather than a radical change.[30]

The most important change came with the third package, which virtually created the EU Single Aviation Market. While the first two packages had relaxed the existing regime, "the third package abandoned virtually all restrictions in favor of a fully-fledged open market regime".[31] The Commission envisioned that the third package would complete the liberalization of traffic rights from bilateral control, severing the link between each state's airspace sovereignty and the award of access rights to its air transport market.[32]

In brief, while the EU air transportation market prior to 1987 was still heavily regulated and rigorously protected by individual member states, for the next decade through 1997, the market was significantly liberalized with the goal of establishing a single aviation market in the EU.

Table 2.1   Summary of Market Access and Ownership and Control Liberalization of the EU Packages[33]

First Package (From 1 January 1988)	Second Package (From 1 November 1990)	Third Package (From 1 January 1993)
– 3rd/4th freedom to hub routes in the EU – 5th freedom traffic allowed up to 30% of capacity	– 3rd/4th freedom between all airports in the EU – 5th freedom traffic allowed up to 50% of capacity	– Full access to all international and domestic routes within the EU (e.g. 3rd, 4th, 5th, and 7th freedoms) – 8th freedom is allowed for 50% of capacity – Cabotage is unrestricted (including 9th freedom) from April 1997 – EU Concept of Community ownership and control replaces national ownership and control

2.2.2   Main Features

2.2.2.1   Market Access

It is worth reiterating that removing (or lowering) the two main legal hurdles (market access and ownership and control restrictions) are the most fundamental features of any liberalization effort for international air transport services.

Market access was fully liberalized by EU Regulation 2408/92, a key measure of the third package. Once an air carrier is recognized as a "community carrier" (see discussion

---

30   Staniland, *supra* note 21 at 87-88.
31   *Ibid.* at 96.
32   Havel, *supra* note 14 at 405.
33   CAPA, "Final Report", *supra* note 2 at 71.

in the following section) and maintains the requirements thereof, it can fly any route within the EU with no restrictions on flights (*e.g.* 3rd, 4th, 5th, and 7th freedoms as well as domestic cabotage routes) or capacity with only a few exceptions. These exceptions include public service obligations, such as subsidized routes to remote, sparsely populated regions, and limitations on areas with serious congestion or environmental problems.

The third package also initially allowed a community carrier to operate consecutive cabotage services as extensions to service to or from their own state (the 8th freedom), unless the cabotage sector amounts to more than 50 percent of capacity. Since April 1997, however, EU member states' domestic markets have been completely open to any EU community carriers (the 9th freedom). This marked the completion of the third package. Full 7th, 8th, and 9th freedom rights yielded "a comprehensive, uniform, and open route network across the entire airspace of the EU."[34] An EU carrier can thus today connect any number of points within the EU without any economic restrictions as to frequency or capacity.

2.2.2.2 Ownership and Control

The third package introduced the concept of the "community carrier" for the first time. As dictated by EU Regulation 2407/92 on the licensing of air carriers, EU member states grant an air carrier an operating license if the air carrier meets safety and finance requirements and is majority-owned and effectively controlled by EU member states and/or their nationals. Thus, ownership and control of air carriers in EU member states no longer necessarily means national ownership and control but has instead been redefined as EU ownership and control.[35]

EU Regulation 2407/92 still requires the licensee to have its "principal place of business" (this concept will be discussed in Chapter 4: Ownership and Control Issues in Northeast Asia) located in the licensing member states and then "multilateralizes" the nationality rule by requiring that EU member states and/or their nationals own more than 50 percent of the undertaking and effectively control it.[36]

From a business point of view, one of the practical results of EU Regulation 2407/92 was that an EU carrier from one EU member state could establish itself or a subsidiary air

---

34 Havel, *supra* note 14 at 405.
35 Peter P.C. Haanappel, *The Law and Policy of Air Space and Outer Space: A Comparative Approach* (Alphen aan den Rijn: Kluwer Law International, 2009) at 136. [Haanappel, "Law and Policy"].
36 Havel, "Open Skies", *supra* note 14 at 408-409; Article 2(g) of Council Regulation No 2407/92 defines 'effective control' as follows: "Effective control means a relationship constituted by rights, contracts or any other means which, either separately or jointly and having regard to the considerations of fact or law involved, confer the possibility of directly or indirectly exercising a decisive influence on an undertaking, in particular by: "(a) the right to use all or part of the assets of an undertaking; (b) rights or contracts which confer a decisive influence on the composition, voting or decisions of the bodies of an undertaking or otherwise confer a decisive influence on the running of the business of the undertaking."

carrier or franchised air carrier in other EU member states. This is advantageous because outside the EU, joint venture airlines can only be formed between non-nationals and the local (national) interest in order to fulfill the ownership and control restrictions. In the EU, the nationals of any member state can cross national borders and freely establish airlines, even fully-owned ones, in any other member state. .

2.2.2.3 External Relations

Through the three packages, the EU became a common aviation market (the EU Single Aviation Market). However, common economic policies, an important feature of economic unions, were still developing even after the conclusion of the third package in 1997. In particular, a coordinated external aviation policy was not formulated until almost a decade later (see discussion below on the Open Skies cases). In fact, neither the adoption of a common air transport policy nor the emergence of a single aviation market persuaded EU member states to concede the EU's exclusive competence concerning external aviation policy.[37]

Since the creation of the EU SAM in 1992, the European Commission had consistently argued that member states should work through EU institutions to manage international air services because a coherent approach would benefit the EU as a whole.[38] Moreover, the proliferation of open skies agreements between the US and individual EU states made the European Commission concerned that the EU was losing out when member states negotiated with the US on an individual level rather than as a bloc.[39] EU member states, however, consistently resisted and successfully thwarted the Commission's efforts.[40]

In 1998, the EU Commission started an infringement procedure against eight EU member states (seven EU member states that had signed open skies agreements with the US[41] and the UK, which had been renegotiating the Bermuda 2 agreement with the US[42]). Soon after the member states reconfirmed in 2001 that they would not comply with the opinion of the Commission, the Commission finally brought a lawsuit against them before the European Court of Justice.[43]

---

37 See Havel, *ibid.* at 425.
38 EC, Commission, *Communication from the Commission on the consequences of the Court judgements of 5 November 2002 for European air transport policy*, [2002].
39 Alan Khee-Jin Tan, "Liberalizing Aviation in the Asia-Pacific Region: The Impact of the EU Horizontal Mandate" (2006) 31 Air & Space L. 432 at 443. [Tan, "Horizontal Mandate"].
40 Allan I. Mendelsohn, "The USA and the EU- Aviation Relations: An Impasse or an Opportunity?" (2004) 29 Air & Space L. 263 at 264.
41 They are Denmark, Sweden, Finland, Belgium, Luxemburg, Austria, and Germany. The Netherlands/U.S. bilateral was allowed to stand since it predated the Third Package. (See Paul Dempsey, *Public International Air Law* (Montreal: Institute of Air and Space Law, 2008) at 570.) [Dempsey, "Air Law"].
42 H.S. Rutger Jan toe Laer, "The ECJ Decisions: 'Blessing in Disguise'?" (2006) 31 Air & Space L. 19 at 19.
43 *Ibid.*

In essence, there were both legal and aero-political reasons for the legal action. From a legal perspective, the EU's community carrier concept created potential conflicts with preexisting bilateral air services agreements between EU member states and non-EU member states. Bilateral air services agreements contain the "ownership and control" provision (or nationality provision), giving a state (State B) the right to revoke the permit of an air carrier from the other state (State A) if that air carrier is not majority owned and effectively controlled by nationals of the state (State A).

Thus, there was the danger that if an air carrier acquired a majority stake in a foreign air carrier, the foreign carrier's traffic rights could be lost on the basis of the nationality provisions in the bilateral agreements.[44] In this scenario, an EU community carrier (owned, for instance, by four EU states with equal 25% shares) and designated by those four states could lose traffic rights arising from bilateral agreements between these states and non-EU states. Thus, explicit consent from the third party partner states was needed. (See below for a discussion of horizontal agreements.)

While the above legal conflict was concerned with ownership and control, another important legal conflict involved market access. In the view of the European Commission, the nature of bilateral air services agreements and the individual manner in which these were negotiated (that is, only the two states in the bilateral agreement enjoy exclusive traffic rights) created conflicts with the unified regulations developed inside the Community.[45] Jeffery Shane, former US Undersecretary of Transportation for Policy, US Department of Transportation, succinctly explained the logic as follows:

> Since EU law, dating as far back as the Treaty of Rome, includes the right of establishment and national treatment for all Member States, any provision in which an EU Member State agrees to allow the United States to veto services by an airline owned or controlled by citizens of a second EU Member State represents discrimination by the first Member State against the second. In other words, Germany is not allowed to discriminate against the airlines of France by agreeing that the U.S. may reject services offered between Germany and the U.S. by any carrier that isn't substantially owned and effectively controlled by German citizens – which Air France certainly is not.[46]

---

44 Isabella H.Ph. Diederiks-Verschoor, *An Introduction to Air Law*, 9th ed. revised by Pablo Mendes de Leon (Alphen aan den Rijn: Kluwer Law International, 2012) at 93-94.
45 See EC, Commission, *Communication from the Commission on the consequences of the Court judgements of 5 November 2002 for European air transport policy*, [2002].
46 Jeffery Shane, "Open Skies Agreements and the European Court of Justice" (Speech presented to the American Bar Association's forum on Air and Space Law, November 2002) online: <http://2001-2009.state.gov/e/eeb/rls/rm/2002/19501.htm>.

In the above example provided by Shane, the end result would be that under the Germany-US bilateral air services agreement, Air France could not be designated by Germany to operate services between Germany and the United States. This aero-political issue was likely the most important reason why the European Commission took legal action against the member states. The Commission believed that negotiating an open skies agreement with the US at the community level (in other words, negotiating between the US and the EU as a whole) was ideal since a bloc approach could advance the full benefits of the EU Single Aviation Market.[47] In this regard, the Commission interpreted the member states' individual approaches as a threat to the ideal of the European common market.[48]

The ECJ judgment was rendered on 5 November 2002, and this so-called "open skies judgment" marked the start of EC external aviation policy.[49] In the underlying cases,[50] the Commission accused the member states of 1) infringing the external competence of the European Union by entering into air services agreements with third countries and 2) infringing the EC treaty on the right of establishment through the nationality clause in their air services agreements with the US.

With regard to the first argument, the ECJ held the EU Regulation in question "[did] not govern the granting of traffic rights on intra-Community routes to non-Community carriers,"[51] allowing EU member states to grant "fifth freedom" rights to third countries. However, the ECJ importantly concluded that "the Community has acquired *exclusive competence* (by the Regulation No. 2409/92) to enter into commitments with non-member countries relating to the [fifth] freedom of non-Community carriers to set fares and rates."[52]

With regard to the second argument, the European Court of Justice concluded that the nationality restrictions infringed Article 43 of the EC Treaty regarding the right of establishment[53] (see Mr. Shane's explanation above) and that the relevant open skies

---

47 toe Laer, *supra* note 42 at 23. See also EC, Commission, *Communication from the Commission on the consequences of the Court judgements of 5 November 2002 for European air transport policy,* [2002] at 11.
48 toe Laer, *ibid.* at 23.
49 EC, Commission, *Communication from the Commission, Developing the agenda for the Community's External Aviation Policy* [2005].
50 Collectively *Commission of the European Communities v. United Kingdom of Great Britain and Northern Ireland,* C-466/98 [2002] E.C.R. I-09427; *Commission of the European Communities v. Kingdom of Denmark,* C-467/98 [2002] E.C.R. I-09519; *Commission of the European Communities v. Kingdom of Sweden,* C-468/98, [2002] E.C.R. I-09575;*Commission of the European Communities v. République de Finlande,* C-469/98 [2002] E.C.R. I-09627; *Commission of the European Communities v. Kingdom of Belgium,* C-471/98, [2002] E.C.R. I-09681; *Commission of the European Communities v. Grand Duchy of Luxemburg,* C-472/98, [2002] E.C.R. I-09741; *Commission of the European Communities v. Republic of Austria,* C-475/98 [2002] E.C.R. I-09797; *Commission of the European Communities v. Federal Republic of Germany,* C-476/98, [2002] E.C.R. I-09865.
51 *Commission of the European Communities v. Federal Republic of Germany,* C-476/98, [2002] E.C.R. I-09865 [*Commission v. Germany*] at para. 117.
52 *Ibid.* at para. 124.
53 See Article 43 of *The E.C. Treaty*: "Within the framework of the provisions set out below, restrictions on the freedom of establishment of nationals of a Member State in the territory of another Member State shall

agreements with the US and the UK-US air services agreement covered issues within the exclusive competence of the Commission.[54] The second finding has had a dramatic impact since it essentially means that all air services agreements to which member states are parties contain an illegal nationality clause.[55]

It is noteworthy to mention that the right of establishment under EU law entails permanent installation by the nationals of a member state in any other EU member state so as to pursue an economic activity in that state.[56] The EU's understanding of the right of establishment is less strict than a 'principal place of business' criterion,[57] which will be discussed in Chapter 4. In essence, while an EU airline can have only one principal place of business, multiple establishments are allowed for an EU airline.[58]

On 20 November 2002, soon after the open skies decision was rendered, the European Commission requested EU member states to terminate their bilateral air services agreements with the US and asked the Council of European Union to authorize the Commission to open community negotiations with the US.[59] On 5 June 2003, the Council of European Union finally authorized the Commission to resume negotiations with the US on a new transatlantic air transport agreement.[60]

After much political wrangling, the European Commission also received authorization from the Council of European Union to enter into so-called "horizontal agreements" with non-EU states on 29 March 2005.[61] The horizontal agreement led non-EU states to recognize

---

be prohibited. Such prohibition shall also apply to restrictions on the setting-up of agencies, branches or subsidiaries by nationals of any Member State established in the territory of any Member State."

54 U.K., Authority of the House of Lords London, *"Open Skies" or Open Markets? The Effect of the European Court of Justice (ECJ) Judgments on Aviation Relations Between the European Union (EU) and the United States of America (USA)* (London: The Stationary Office, 2003), online: <www.publications.parliament.uk/pa/ld200203/ldselect/ldeucom/92/92.pdf>.

55 toe Laer, *supra* note 42 at 26.

56 See Moussis, *supra* note 6 at 101. See also *Commission v. Germany supra* note 51 at para. 147 (noting that "freedom of establishment includes the right to take up and pursue activities as self-employed persons and to set up and manage undertakings, in particular companies or firms within the meaning of the second paragraph of Article 58 of the EC Treaty (now the second paragraph of Article 48 EC) under the conditions laid down for its own nationals by the legislation of the Member State in which establishment is effected".).

57 Tan, "Horizontal Mandate", *supra* note 39 at 443.

58 *Ibid.*

59 See EC, Commission, *Communication from the Commission on relations between the Community and third countries in the field of air transport*, COM (2003) 94, online: <http://eur-lex.europa.eu/legal-content/EN/TXT/HTML/?uri=CELEX:52003DC0094&from=EN>.

60 See EC, Commission, *New Era for Air Transport: Loyola de Palacio welcomes the mandate given to the European Commission for negotiating an Open Aviation Area with the US*, IP/03/806 (5 June 2003), online: <http://europa.eu/rapid/press-release_IP-03-806_en.htm>.

61 See EC, Commission, *Commission Decision on approving the standard clauses for inclusion in bilateral air service agreements between Member States and third countries jointly laid down by the Commission and the Member States*, COM(2005)943, online: <http://ec.europa.eu/transport/modes/air/international_aviation/doc/standard_clauses_en.pdf>; See also Brian F. Havel & Gabriel S. Sanchez, *The Principles and Practices of International Aviation Law* (New York: Cambridge University Press, 2014) at 97-98 [Havel & Sanchez, "Aviation Law"].

the EU "community carrier" designation clause instead of the traditional nationality clause in all the bilateral air services agreements between EU member states and those non-EU states.[62] However, unlike the agreement adopted with the US, the horizontal agreements did not affect the hard rights; that is, no additional traffic rights were created.[63]

In fact, only with separate authorization to negotiate a comprehensive open skies agreement, the so-called "vertical mandate," can the European Commission negotiate an overall air services agreement with a non-EU state.[64] Among the comprehensive agreements that the EU Commission has completed with so-called global partners, the EU-US Air Transport Agreement (2007) is extremely significant given the two parties' clout and size in international aviation.

Indeed, the EU-US Air Transport Agreement (2007) is historic largely because it is a deal between two regions encompassing a geographic area with an estimated 60 percent of the world's air traffic.[65] Martin Dresner summarizes the key elements of the EU-US Air Transport Agreement (2007):

- The concept of "EU Community airline" is recognized;
- All US and EU airlines have the right to compete on all routes between the US and the EU, as well as on all fifth freedom routes;
- The right for cargo airlines to operate 7th Freedom routes, including routes between EU countries for US cargo carriers is allowed;
- No capacity or frequency restrictions are imposed;
- Fares are established at the discretion of each airline, and are not subject to government approval.[66]

After the agreement took effect in March 2008, the US–EUsecond stage negotiations began.[67] Although the EU and US agreed on a second-stage open skies agreement in March

---

62 Alan Khee-Jin Tan, "Singapore' New Air Services Agreements with the E.U. and The U.K.: Implications for Liberalization in Asia" (2008) 73 J. Air L. & Com. 351 at 354 [Tan, "Singapore's Agreements"].
63 Peter Van Fenema, "EU Horizontal Agreements: Community Designation and the 'Free Rider' Clause" (2006) 31 Air & Space L. 172 at 177-178.
64 Havel & Sanchez, "Aviation Law", *supra* note 61 at 98; See also EC, Commission, *External Aviation Policy*, online: <http://ec.europa.eu/transport/modes/air/international_aviation/external_aviation_policy/index_en.htm>.
65 James L. Devall, "The U.S.-EU Agreement – A Path to a Global Aviation Agreement" (2008) Issues in Aviation Law and Policy. 13295 at 13295.
66 Martin Dresner, "Chapter 23 US Bilateral Air Transport Policy" in Peter Forsyth *et al.* ed., *Liberalization in Aviation: Competition, Cooperation and Public Policy* (Farnham: Ashgate, 2013) 429 at 436.
67 The Article 21 of the U.S.-EU Agreement 2007 specifies that "[T]he Parties shall begin negotiations not later than 60 days after the date of provisional application of this Agreement, with the goal of developing the next stage expeditiously."

2010, the scope of the changes is not significant.[68] In essence, the 2010 agreement allows additional liberalization of airline ownership and control but involves no important developments for market access issues. Furthermore, it is unlikely the second-stage open skies agreement will be implemented in the near future since it requires legislative changes about ownership restriction in the US. The legal reform on the ownership restriction is generally a daunting task (this will be discussed in the Chapter 4) and US labor groups, which have traditionally exerted a powerful influence on certain members of Congress, fiercely oppose ownership changes.[69]

That said, what the EU has achieved with the US in the Air Transport Agreement (2007) is remarkable. To sum up, because the EU forms an economic union with central institutions governing *inter alia* the aviation market, it was able to achieve liberalized market access, relax ownership and control regulations, and make unified external policies.

2.2.3 Benefits of the EU Single Aviation Market

Competition is the primary justification for liberalization, and competition is what allows the EU SAM to provide new and better services. For instance, the EU saw a 170 percent increase in intra-EU routes – and a 310 percent increase in routes with more than two carriers – between 1992 and 2009 following the introduction of its Three Packages.[70] More cities and remote regions are being served by air transport, with passengers enjoying greater choice of destinations and more direct flights.[71]

The most significant development in the post-liberalization period is the emergence and growth of low-cost carriers (LCCs). While the capacity share of LCCs in the EU aviation market was just 1.6 percent in 1996, their share grew to 20.2 percent in 2003.[72] Even more important is the pace of this growth. While the capacity controlled by legacy carriers has only grown an average of 1 percent each year from 2004 to 2013, LCCs' capacity in Europe has grown an average of 14 percent each year.[73] The OAG FACTS (Frequency and Capacity Trend Statistics) report, which was released in May 2013, shows that LCCs now control over 50 percent of both international and domestic markets in some EU states.

---

68 The airline industry expressed its disappointment at the second agreement. See *e.g.* James Kanter & Nicola Clark, "U.S. and E.U. Agree to Expand Open Skies Accord", *The New York Times* (25 March 2010), online: <www.nytimes.com/2010/03/26/business/global/26skies.html>.
69 See Dresner, *supra* note 66 at 437.
70 ICAO Secretariat, "Regulatory and Industry Overview" (20 September 2013), online: <www.icao.int/Meetings/a38/Documents/REGULATORY%20AND%20INDUSTRY%20OVERVIEW.pdf>. [ICAO, "Regulatory Overview"].
71 CAPA, "Final Report" *supra* note 2 at 51.
72 Intervistas-ga2, *The Economic Impact of Air Service Liberalization* (2006) at 33, online: <www.intervistas.com/downloads/Economic_Impact_of_Air_Service_Liberalization_Final_Report.pdf>.
73 OAG, May FACTS (2013) at 3, online: <www.oag.com/sites/default/files/May%20FACTS.pdf>.

Figure 2.1   LCC's Market Shares in Europe[74]

International Seats Market Share

Latvia	
Slovakia	
Lithuania	
Poland	
Hungary	
Spain	
Romania	
Italy	
Portugal	
Ireland	
UK	
Belgium	
Sweden	
Cyprus	
Greece	
Estonia	
Denmark	
Czech...	
Netherlands	
Bulgaria	
France	
Germany	
Austria	
Finland	
Slovenia	
Luxembourg	

0%   50%   100%

■ LCC ■ Legacy

Domestic Seats Market Share

Spain	
Netherlands	
Italy	
Denmark	
UK	
Sweden	
France	
Finland	
Germany	
Portugal	
Romania	
Greece	

0%   50%   100%

■ LCC ■ Legacy

The creation of the EU Single Aviation Market also facilitated the development of alliances among European airlines and later of outright mergers (*e.g.* Air France/KLM).[75] (This will be further discussed in Chapter 4) There were various benefits on a macro-economy level, including 44 million additional passengers attributable to the new market regime (an increase of 33 percent), 1.4 million full-time equivalent jobs resulting from liberalization, and a USD 85 billion increase in European GDP.[76]

2.2.4   *Challenges to the EU Single Aviation Market*

Arguably, it can be said that the EU Single Aviation Market is *complete*. That is, all EU member states (currently 28 states) enjoy all nine freedoms within the Union without

---

74   *Ibid.* at 4.
75   Intervistas-ga2, *supra* note 72 at 36.
76   *Ibid.* at 37.

restrictions, and all EU community carriers (at least legally) can enjoy traffic rights resulting from bilateral air services agreements between any EU states and non-EU states without discrimination (for those non-EU states that have concluded vertical or horizontal agreements with the EU). By virtue of the EU-US Air Transport Agreement (2007), for instance, EU carriers can fly between any EU city and any US city with unlimited capacity, and a merger between EU carriers would not carry the risk of losing traffic rights since the US recognizes the EU community carrier clause.

The fact that some non-EU states are not willing to sign EU "horizontal" agreements[77] is a remaining task for the EU. A more significant issue is that the EU Commission's power to act as a "super-negotiator" on air services agreements with non-EU states on behalf of all EU member states is restricted since the Commission is still required to attain the so-called "vertical mandate" from the Council of the EU.[78] Therefore, EU member states continue to retain "the piecemeal system of bilateral air services agreements in their aero-political relations with third countries" in most air services negotiations.[79]

Nonetheless, it is safe to say that the EU has achieved nearly all attainable goals. Hence, it is hard to pinpoint the work that still needs to be done to further consolidate regional liberalization within the EU. Nevertheless, some legal and policy-based challenges arising from the fully consolidated regional liberalization have been noticed. The most commonly cited legal challenge has to do with conflict between EU community law (the three packages) and Article 7 of the Chicago Convention, which is labeled as "cabotage."

Cabotage refers to domestic carriage (i.e. between two or more points within the same state) by foreign aircraft. The Chicago Convention's Article 7[80] stipulates in the second paragraph that "[E]ach contracting State undertakes not to enter into any arrangements which specifically grant any such privilege on an exclusive basis to any other State or an

---

77 To check the status of bilateral air services agreements, See EC, "Bilateral Air Services Agreements brought into legal conformity since the Court of Justice of the EU judgments of 5 November 2002", online: <http://ec.europa.eu/transport/modes/air/international_aviation/external_aviation_policy/doc/table_-_asa_brought_into_legal_conformity_since_ecj_judgments-_january_2013.pdf>.; Some countries have not signed "horizontal" agreements with the EC, but instead have inserted "community carrier" designation clauses when revising their existing bilateral agreements with certain EU member states. See Tan, "Singapore's Agreements", *supra* note 62 at 355; See also Dempsey, "Air Law", *supra* note 41 at 575 (noting that "[s]ome nations might be unwilling to allow the designation of an unlimited number of EU carriers over routes between their countries and Europe".).
78 Havel & Sanchez, "Aviation Law", *supra* note 61 at 98.
79 *Ibid.* at 99.
80 Chicago Convention, Article 7 – Cabotage: "Each contracting State shall have the right to refuse permission to the aircraft of other contracting States to take on in its territory passengers, mail and cargo carried for remuneration or hire and destined for another point within its territory. Each contracting State undertakes not to enter into any arrangements which specifically grant any such privilege on an exclusive basis to any other State or an airline of any other State, and not to obtain any such exclusive privilege from any other State."

airline of any other State, and not to obtain any such exclusive privilege from any other State."

Obviously, EU community law grants exclusive cabotage rights to EU carriers. Thus, EU law (especially, the Third Package permitting unrestricted cabotage from April 1997) arguably violates the second sentence of Article 7 of the Chicago Convention since Article 7 prohibits discriminatory granting of cabotage rights.[81] Although there have been attempts at the ICAO to amend Article 7[82] and some respected scholars have argued that Article 7 requires clarification,[83] the ICAO did not see the urgent need to do so.[84]

A more substantial challenge relates to arguments about policy. Since the development of regional trade blocs is criticized as a fragmentation of the WTO regime in trade law,[85] the EU SAM, a fully consolidated regional liberalization model, could be interpreted as a deviation from the ideal of global multilateralism. However, since full multilateral liberalization with the "most favored nation" principle does not apply in international aviation,[86] it is hard to criticize the outcome of the EU SAM.

If a new global approach is adopted in the future, the EU's regional approach should harmonize with the global approach. Peter Haanappel warned that the failure of harmonization between worldwide and regional developments could lead to regional blocs adopting defensive, protectionist attitudes towards other blocs.[87] Despite this concern, it is noteworthy that the EU has been actively promoting the global approach.[88]

As of 1 November 2008, the third package was replaced by EU Regulation 1008/2008 on common rules for the operation of air services in the European Community,[89] and the EU internal market is now governed by this regulation.[90] While Regulation 1008/2008 continues to provide the economic framework for air transport in the European Commu-

---

81 See Dempsey, "Air Law", *supra* note 41 at 565.
82 See Michael Milde, *International Air Law and ICAO*, 2nd ed. (Utrecht: Eleven International Publishing, 2012) at 43.
83 See *e.g.* Diederiks-Verschoor, *supra* note 44 at 55.
84 See Pablo Mendes de Leon, *Cabotage in Air Transport Regulation* (London: Martinus Nijhoff, 1992) at 63-66.
85 See *e.g.* Mailhard Hilf & Tim Rene Salomn, "Running in Circles: Regionalism in World Trade and How It will lead back to Multilateralism" in Ulrich Fastenrath, ed., *From Bilateralism to Community Interest: Essays in Honour of Bruno Simma* (Oxford: Oxford University Press, 2011) at 257.
86 See section 1.3.2 ICAO or WTO: institutional problems? for reasons why coverage of air transport services was avoided.
87 Peter P.C. Haanappel, "Multilateralism and Economic Bloc Forming in International Air Transport" (1994) 19 Ann. Air & Sp. L. 279 at 304-305.
88 See *e.g.* EU, *The European Union's Commitment to Cooperation with the World Aviation Community*, online: <http://ec.europa.eu/transport/modes/air/international_aviation/european_community_icao/doc/info_paper_icao_en.pdf>.
89 See European Commission, *Internal Market*, online: <http://ec.europa.eu/transport/modes/air/internal_market/integration_en.htm>.
90 Diederiks-Verschoor, *supra* note 44 at 86.

nity, the EU has also made a great deal of effort toward further integration by forging the Single European Sky (SES).

The SES is an initiative to reform the architecture of European air traffic management (ATM) in order to meet future capacity and safety needs at a European rather than a local level, thereby increasing the overall efficiency of the European air transport system.[91] Daniel Calleja Crespo, former Director for Air Transport in the European Commission, and Timothy Fenoulhet, Head of the EU Liaison Office at Eurocontrol (see below for the role of Eurocontrol), stated that the initiative to create the SES can be considered the "last frontier" in EU aviation.[92]

The vision of SES was developed in 1999 when the EU Commission called for structural reform that would permit "the creation of a single European sky by way of integrated management of airspace and the development of new concepts and procedures of air traffic management."[93] The SES was formally adopted in 2004, with the SES framework comprising four regulations.[94] In 2009, the second package of the SES (Regulation 1070/2009) updated the four basic regulations (2004), commonly called the Single European Sky II.

Eurocontrol is deeply involved in the SES. Established in 1960, Eurocontrol was the first organization tasked with air transport management on a regional level.[95] Eurocontrol now contributes to both the regulatory and the technological aspects of the SES.[96] Another goal that the EU is pursuing is technical harmonization in air transport, and the European Aviation Safety Agency (EASA) is playing an important role in achieving this. The EASA has extended this role to include the key safety fields of aerodromes, air transport management, and air navigation services.[97]

---

91 See EUROCONTROL, *Frequently Asked Questions (FAQ) on EUROCONTROL*, online: <https://www.eurocontrol.int/faq/corporate>.

92 Daniel Calleja Crespo & Timothy Fenoulhet, "Chapter 1 The Single European Sky (SES): 'Building Europe in the Sky'" in Pablo Mendes de Leon & Daniel Calleja Crespo, ed., *Achieving the Single European Sky: Goals and Challenges* (Alphen aan den Rijn: Kluwer Law International, 2011) 3 at 6.

93 EC, *Communication from the Commission to the council and the european parliament – The creation of the single European sky*, online: <http://eur-lex.europa.eu/legal-content/EN/ALL/?uri=CELEX:51999DC0614>. at 19.

94 Namely, Regulation (EC) No 549/2004 of the European Parliament and of the Council of 10 March 2004 laying down the framework for the creation of the single European sky (the framework Regulation); Air Navigation Services Regulation (EC) No. 550/2004 on the provision of air navigation services for the Single European Sky; Airspace Regulation (EC) No. 551/2004 on the organisation and use of the airspace in the Single European Sky; and Interoperability Regulation (EC) No. 552/2004 on the interoperability of the European Air Traffic Management network.

95 Diederiks-Verschoor, *supra* note 44 at 40.

96 See EUROCONTROL, *Single European Sky*, online: <https://www.eurocontrol.int/dossiers/single-european-sky>.

97 See EC, *European Parliament legislative resolution of 12 March 2014 on the proposal for a regulation of the European Parliament and of the Council amending Regulation (EC) No 216/2008 in the field of aerodromes,*

Having succeeded with economic integration, the EU is now forging a more advanced single market in order to take the EU SAM beyond economic integration. Overall, even though the EU single aviation market is complete internally (that is, market access is completely free and ownership and control restrictions are entirely removed), the EU continues to seek, among other things, more coordinated external aviation policy, more consolidated air transport control, and more uniform safety standards.

2.3 THE ASEAN SINGLE AVIATION MARKET MODEL

2.3.1 Overview

ASEAN has designated air travel (or air transport) as one of the 12 priority sectors for economic integration.[98] Similarly, members of ASEAN share the view that air transport is an integral component in the proposed establishment of an ASEAN Economic Community (AEC), which is scheduled to come into effect in 2015.[99] Therefore, negotiations on liberalizing air services have taken place in the context of ASEAN's larger economic integration.

The push towards ASEAN regional liberalization has been incorporated in several declarations adopted by the organization.[100] In 1995, ASEAN initiated discussion on "open skies" at a leaders' summit held in Bangkok, Thailand. Since then, the idea of ASEAN open skies has been reinforced by meetings of the ASEAN transport ministers and various policy documents. In 2002, the ASEAN Memorandum of Understanding (MOU) on Air Freight Services, a first step towards the full liberalization of ASEAN air freight services, was signed.[101]

In 2004, the 10th meeting of the ASEAN transport ministers adopted the Action Plan for ASEAN Air Transport Integration and Liberalization 2005–2015 and the Roadmap for

---

air traffic management and air navigation services, online: <www.europarl.europa.eu/sides/getDoc.do?type=TA&reference=P7-TA-2014-0221&language=EN&ring=A7-2014-0098>.

98   See *ASEAN Framework Agreement for the Integration of Priority Sectors* done at Vientiane, Lao PDR, 29 November 2004. Originally there were 11 priority sectors; namely, agro-based products, air travel, automotives, e-ASEAN, electronics, fisheries, healthcare, rubber-based products, textiles and apparels, tourism and wood-based products; Logistics was added as a twelfth priority sector in 2006. See Thitipha Wattanapruttipaisan, "Priority integration sectors: performance and challenges" *Bangkok Post* (29 August 2006), online: <http://www.asean.org/resources/publications/published-articles/item/asiaviews-regional-insights-global-outreach-columns-commentaries-priority-integration-sectors-performance-and-challenges-asiaviews-edition-33iiiaug2006-2>.

99   See ASEAN, *ASEAN Economic Community Blueprint Blueprint* (Jakarta: ASEAN Secretariat, 2008), online: <www.asean.org/archive/5187-10.pdf>.

100 Peter Forsyth, John King, & Cherry Lyn Rodolfo, "Open skies in ASEAN" (2006) 12 Journal of Air Transport Management 143 at 144.

101 *Ibid.*

Integration of the Air Travel Sector (RIATS).[102] The Action Plan set the long-term goal of ASEAN regional liberalization as the "conclusion of an ASEAN Multilateral Agreement on Air Services by 2015 by significantly removing restrictions on market access so as to achieve a single air transport market."[103] Concurrently, the Roadmap for Integration of the Air Travel Sector (RIATS) identified the following specific goals and target dates:

Table 2.2 The ASEAN Roadmap for Integration of the Air Travel Sector

Deadline	Passenger	Cargo
2005	- Unlimited 3rd and 4th freedom flights for all designated points within ASEAN sub-regions	
2006	- At least two designated points in each country in the ASEAN sub-regions	Unlimited 3rd and 4th freedom flights
	- Unlimited 5th freedom traffic between designated points in the ASEAN sub-regions	
2008	- At least two designated points in each country in the ASEAN sub-regions	Unlimited 3rd, 4th, and 5th freedom flights
	- Unlimited 3rd and 4th freedom flights between the capital cities	
2010	- Unlimited 5th freedom flights between the capital cities by 2010	

The roadmap has been successfully incorporated into three formal legal agreements for the acceptance of ASEAN member states.[104] The three agreements are the 2009 Multilateral Agreement on Air Services (MAAS),[105] the 2009 Multilateral Agreement for Full Liberal-

---

102 *Action Plan for ASEAN Air Transport Integration and Liberalization* done at Phnom Penh, Cambodia, 23 November 2004. See The ASEAN Secretariat, *ASEAN Documents Series 2004* (Jakarta: ASEAN Secretariat, 2005) at 221-226.
103 *Ibid.* at 223.
104 Alan Khee-Jin Tan, "Toward a Single Aviation Market in ASEAN: Regulatory Reform and Industry Challenges" 2013 Economic Research Institute for ASEAN and East Asia (ERIA) Discussion Paper 2013-22 at 3 [Tan, "SAM in ASEAN"], online: <www.eria.org/publications/discussion_papers/toward-a-single-aviation-market-in-asean-regulatory-reform-and-industry-challenges.html>.
105 *ASEAN Multilateral Agreement on Air Services*, done at Manila, Philippines, 20 May 2009, online: <www.asean.org/communities/asean-economic-community/item/asean-multilateral-agreement-on-air-services-manila-20-may-2009-2>.

ization of Air Freight Services (MAFLAFS),[106] and the 2010 Multilateral Agreement for Full Liberalization of Passenger Air Services (MAFLPAS).[107]

Although the Action Plan has not been fully implemented according to the suggested timetable (with several states missing the stipulated deadlines, as will be examined below), substantial liberalization has been realized in the region. The fact that ASEAN used a concrete action plan to push ahead with regional liberalization was instrumental in achieving meaningful results.

2.3.2   Main Features

2.3.2.1   Market Access

Pursuant to the goals set out in the Action Plan for ASEAN Air Transport Integration and Liberalization 2005–2015 and RIATS, the 2009 Multilateral Agreement on Air Services (MAAS) provided a step-by-step approach by laying out several implementing protocols that aim to ease market access liberalization in the region.

Table 2.3   The 2009 Multilateral Agreement on Air Services (MAAS)[108]

Protocol	Scope	State Parties
Protocols 1 to 4*	Limited impact, covering mainly secondary cities in growth areas (sub-regions) straddling borders of neighboring states**	All 10 member states
Protocol 5	Unlimited 3rd and 4th freedom between capital cities (A's carriers between A's capital and another capital) *E.g. Thai Airways' (TG) Bangkok-Hanoi and vice versa*	All 10 member states
Protocol 6	Unlimited 5th freedom between capital cities (A's carriers from A's capital to C's capital via B's capital) *E.g. TG's Bangkok-Kuala Lumpur-Singapore and vice versa*	All 10 member states

* Protocol 1 – Unlimited Third and Fourth Freedom Traffic Rights Within ASEAN Sub-Region; Protocol 2 – Unlimited Fifth Freedom Traffic Rights Within ASEAN Sub-Region; Protocol 3 – Unlimited Third and Fourth Freedom Traffic Rights Between ASEAN Sub-Regions; and Protocol 4 – Unlimited Fifth Freedom Traffic Rights Between ASEAN Sub-Regions.

** Tan, "SAM in ASEAN", *supra* note 104 at 4 (noting that "[F]our such sub-regions have so far been identified (new sub-regions may be declared or existing ones expanded): the Brunei, Indonesia, Malaysia and Philippines East ASEAN Growth Area (BIMP-EAGA); the Sub-regional Cooperation in Air Transport among Cambodia,

---

106 *ASEAN Multilateral Agreement on the Full Liberalisation of Air Freight Services*, done at Manila, Philippines, 20 May 2009, online: <http://cil.nus.edu.sg/2009/2009-asean-multilateral-agreement-on-the-full-liberalisation-of-air-freight-services-signed-on-20-may-2009-in-manila-the-philippines-by-the-transport-ministers/>.
107 *ASEAN Multilateral Agreement on Full Liberalisation of Passenger Air Services*, done at Bandar Seri Begawan, Brunei Darussalam, 12 November 2010, online: <http://cil.nus.edu.sg/2010/2010-asean-multilateral-agreement-on-full-liberalisation-of-passenger-air-services/>.
108 Centre for International Law (CIL), "AVIATION, Lifting-The-Barriers Roundtables" (Preliminary paper presented to the 2013 Network ASEAN Forum, August 2013) at 4, online: <www.cariasean.org/pdf/Aviation-Prelim-Paper.pdf>.

Lao PDR, Myanmar and Vietnam (CLMV); the Indonesia, Malaysia, Singapore Growth Triangle (IMS-GT); and the Indonesia, Malaysia, Thailand Growth Triangle (IMT-GT)").

Alan Tan describes the above gradual approach as "ASEAN's incrementalist philosophy of starting with modest goals first and pursuing more ambitious relaxations at a later stage."[109] Indeed, given that ASEAN has no central government or supranational institutions (unlike the EU) and that there are 10 states (more member states than is ideal for close negotiations), starting with liberalization in the border-area sub-regions (Protocols 1 to 4) was a sensible approach.

However, since the designated points in the sub-regions covered by Protocols 1 to 4 are mostly secondary cities, the impact on air traffic volume has been negligible. The substantial air transport liberalization in ASEAN began with Protocol 5 since this step addresses unlimited 3rd and 4th freedom traffic rights between ASEAN capital cities. Further, Protocol 6 provides unlimited 5th freedom traffic rights between ASEAN capital cities. Indonesia ratified both Protocols 5 and 6 in May 2014, a long-awaited development, and the Philippines only became party to the Protocols in February 2016. (See more discussion in section 2.3.4 Challenge) However, Protocol 6 would not have much commercial impact since the ASEAN capital cities are not very far apart and few airlines would seek to operate a 5th freedom capital city stop within ASEAN.[110]

The 2010 Multilateral Agreement for the Full Liberalization of Passenger Air Services (MAFLPAS) was designed to supplement MAAS and to include the rest of the ASEAN cities.[111]

---

109 Tan, "SAM in ASEAN", *supra* note 104 at 6.
110 Alan Khee-Jin Tan, "The ASEAN Multilateral Agreement on Air Services: En Route to Open Skies?" (2010) 16 Journal of Air Transport Management 289 at 290 [Tan, "ASEAN Multilateral Agreement"]; however, some air carriers are attempting to use 5th freedom rights as if they were 7th freedom rights, which is not allowed under the ASEAN agreements. For instance, Malaysia-based AirAsia's application to operate 5th freedom flights departing from Kuala Lumpur to Yangon via Singapore is a *de facto* 7th freedom because is the Singapore-Yangon sector entails "backtracking" traffic such that few passengers would actually use this flight to get from Kuala Lumpur to Yangon. The reality would be that the aircraft will unload all its passengers taken on in Kuala Lumpur when it arrives in Singapore and take on a fresh new load of passengers in Singapore bound for Yangon – an effective 7th freedom. See Alan Tan's presentation to the 2013 Network ASEAN Forum, 22 August 2013, online: <www.cariasean.org/pdf/RT/Aviation%20RT%20Presentation.pdf>. at 16. The question of whether to recognize such proposed operations as 5th or 7th freedom is currently being discussed by the ASEAN member states.
111 Tan, "SAM in ASEAN", *supra* note 104 at 8.

Table 2.4 The 2010 Multilateral Agreement for the Full Liberalization of Passenger Air Services (MAFLPAS)[112]

Protocol	Scope	State Parties
Protocol 1	Unlimited 3rd and 4th freedoms between all cities (A's carriers from A's capital to B's non-capital, A's non-capital to B's capital, and A's noncapital to B's non-capital) *E.g. TG Bangkok-Cebu, Phuket-Manila, Phuket-Cebu*	All except Indonesia and Laos
Protocol 2	Unlimited 5th freedom between all cities (except capital-capital-capital) *E.g. TG Phuket-Ho Chi Minh-Cebu, Phuket-Ho Chi Minh-Manila, Phuket-Hanoi-Cebu, Phuket-Hanoi-Manila, Bangkok-Hanoi-Cebu, Bangkok- Ho Chi Minh-Manila, Bangkok-Ho Chi Minh-Cebu*	All except Indonesia and Laos

Laos and, more substantially, Indonesia are not parties to MAFLPAS. The fact that Indonesia, the largest economy in ASEAN and the country with 40 percent of the entire ASEAN population, has not accepted the 2010 MAFLPAS and the 2009 Multilateral Agreement for the Full Liberalization of Air Freight Services (MAFLAFS, see below) is currently the biggest setback to the ASEAN Single Aviation Market. (This issue will be discussed in section 2.3.4 Challenges to the ASEAN SAM.)

Table 2.5 The 2009 Multilateral Agreement for the Full Liberalization of Air Freight Services (MAFLAFS)[113]

Protocol	Scope	State Parties
Protocols 1	Unlimited 3rd, 4th, and 5th freedom between designated points *E.g. Thai Airways Cargo's Bangkok-Clark, Bangkok-Vientiane-Hanoi routes*	All 10 member states except Indonesia
Protocol 2	Unlimited 3rd, 4th, and 5th freedom between all points with international airports *E.g. Thai Airways Cargo's Bangkok-Singapore, Bangkok-Singapore-Manila routes*	All except Indonesia

Notably, 7th freedom and domestic cabotage (8th and 9th freedoms) are missing from the ASEAN regional agreements. Thus, from the perspective of market access, ASEAN is not a true single aviation market. The fact that the ASEAN SAM has not permitted the 7th freedom has crucial implications both internally and externally. The question of allowing the 7th freedom is presumably slated for post-2015 negotiations (further discussed in sections 2.3.2.3 External Relations and 2.3.4 Challenge).

---

112 CIL, *supra* note 108 at 5.
113 *Ibid.*

2.3.2.2 Ownership and Control

In the bilateral air services agreements between the individual ASEAN states, it is a common condition that designated carriers must be "substantially owned and effectively controlled" by the designating state and/or its nationals.[114] Interestingly, the 2009 Multilateral Agreement on Air Services (MAAS) and the 2010 Multilateral Agreement for the Full Liberalization of Passenger Air Services (MAFLPAS) provide for a so-called ASEAN community carrier, which is similar to the EU community carrier or the Australia-New Zealand SAM carrier concepts. (This will be discussed in section 2.4.1 Australia-New Zealand Single Aviation Market.)

MAAS and MALFAS provide that all contracting states have the right to designate multiple airlines to enjoy the relevant traffic rights so long as the airlines fulfill the following criteria on ownership and control:

a. substantial ownership and effective control of that airline are vested in the Contracting Party designating the airline, nationals of that Contracting Party, or both (Article 3(2)(a)(i); or
b. subject to acceptance by a Contracting Party receiving such application, the designated airline which is incorporated and has its principal place of business in the territory of the Contracting Party that designates the airline, is and remains substantially owned and effectively controlled by one or more ASEAN Member States and/or its nationals, and the Contracting Party designating the airline has and maintains effective regulatory control (Article 3(2)(a)(ii); or
c. subject to acceptance by a Contracting Party receiving such application, the designated airline is incorporated in and has its principal place of business in the territory of the Contracting Party that designates the airline in which the Contracting Party designating the airline, has and maintains effective regulatory control of that airline, provided that such arrangements will not be equivalent to allowing airline(s) or its subsidiaries access to traffic rights not otherwise available to that airline(s) (Article 3(2)(a)(iii).

Since Article 3(2)(a)(ii) provides that ownership and control requirement can be met by "one or more ASEAN Member States and/or its nationals," this lays the groundwork for what can be termed an "ASEAN community carrier."[115] Hence, an airline that is substantially owned and effectively controlled by ASEAN interests in the aggregate would fulfill the

---

114 Tan "SAM in ASEAN", *supra* note 104 at 17.
115 Tan, "ASEAN Multilateral Agreement", *supra* note 110 at 291.

ownership and control requirement.[116] For instance, a Cambodian-registered carrier need not be majority-owned by Cambodians; instead, it can be owned by 20 percent Cambodian, 20 percent Malaysian, and 11 percent Vietnamese interests.[117] Thus, the majority ownership can be spread out among ASEAN interests as long as effective regulatory control remains with the Cambodian authorities.[118]

Strictly speaking, Article 3(2)(a)(iii) says that there need not even be *any* Cambodian interests as long as the airline has its place of incorporation and principal place of business in Cambodia and the Cambodian government maintains effective regulatory control over it. (For a discussion of the difference between "effective economic control" and "effective regulatory control" which entails safety, security, and other important regulatory matters, see Chapter 4: Ownership and Control Issues in Northeast Asia.)

The legal problem with the ASEAN community carriers is that there is a risk that the contracting state will reject the application of an ASEAN community carrier, even if the airline is substantially owned and effectively controlled by ASEAN interests.[119] This is because Article 3(2)(a)(ii) starts with a prior condition: "subject to acceptance by a Contracting Party receiving such application." This means that there is no guarantee that an ASEAN community carrier will be able to access all countries in ASEAN, and this uncertainty is a manifest disadvantage for any such airline or for any investor planning to establish one.[120] This legal challenge is another important feature of the ASEAN SAM that requires further liberalization in the post-2015 negotiations.

2.3.2.3 External Relations

The ASEAN SAM has also attempted to establish a common external relations strategy for the grouping. This is significant given the fact that ASEAN does not have strong institutions with enforcement functions like the EU. Indeed, since the early stage of the ASEAN SAM, the member states have been aware of the need to establish some form of external common strategy vis-à-vis third countries and regions.[121]

In 2007, ASEAN agreed with China to work toward an ASEAN-China Regional Air Services Agreement at the 6th ASEAN-China Transport Ministers Meeting.[122] Accordingly,

---

116 Ibid.
117 CIL, *supra* note 110 at 7.
118 Ibid.
119 Article 3(2)(a)(ii) of MAAS and Article 3(2)(a)(ii) of MAFLPAS begins with "subject to the acceptance of the contracting party receiving the application of a designated airline".
120 Alan Khee-Jin Tan, "Toward a Single Aviation Market in ASEAN: Regulatory Reform and Industry Challenges" 2013 Economic Research Institute for ASEAN and East Asia (ERIA) Discussion Paper 2013-22 at 20.
121 Alan Khee-Jin Tan, "Aviation Policy in the Philippines and the Impact of the Proposed Southeast Asian Single Aviation Market" (2009) 34 Air and Space L. 285 at 303 [Tan, "The Philippines"].
122 Gong Yu, "U.S. – E.U. Open Skies Deal and Its Implication for the Liberalization of International Air Transport Services: A Chinese Perspective" (2009) 2 Journal of East Asia and International Law. 129 at 153.

the 2007 ASEAN-China Aviation Cooperation Framework was adopted with provisions for the gradual liberalization of cargo and passenger services.[123]

It is worth noting that the ASEAN-China Free Trade Agreement was the explicit justification for the ASEAN-China Regional Air Services Agreement that was subsequently adopted in 2010. The 2007 ASEAN-China Aviation Cooperation Framework states that the ASEAN-China Regional Air Services Agreement should be concluded by 2010 "to support the realisation of the ASEAN-China Free Trade Agreement in 2010" and "to implement the agreement thereafter in line with the establishment of the ASEAN-China FTA."[124]

The ASEAN-China free trade area came into effect on 1 January 2010[125] and, not surprisingly, the Air Transport Agreement between ASEAN and China was adopted in November 2010.[126] The ASEAN–China Air Transport Agreement and its Protocol 1 provide for unlimited 3rd and 4th freedom access for airlines on both sides and effectively supersede the capacity restrictions in the bilateral agreements that exist between the individual ASEAN states and China (the bilateral agreements are still in place – only the capacity is changed).[127] The ASEAN–China Air Transport Agreement is already in force among China, Singapore, Malaysia, Thailand, Myanmar and Vietnam.[128]

The interesting thing about this Agreement is the fact that the ASEAN states concluded it with China even without having forged a complete SAM within ASEAN first. Although the incomplete ASEAN Single Aviation Market leaves ASEAN carriers at a relative disadvantage to Chinese carriers (this will be discussed in section 2.3.4. Challenge), it is clear that ASEAN *regional* liberalization has accomplished far more than 10 separate bilateral air services agreements between the 10 ASEAN member states and China would have otherwise achieved. In other words, ASEAN has proved that regional liberalization confers the advantage of a stronger negotiating position.

---

123 See *2007 ASEAN-China Aviation Cooperation Framework,* issued in Singapore on 2 November 2007, para 6. "6. The substantive elements of this ASEAN-China Regional Air Services Arrangement would include, but not limited to, provisions for gradual liberalisation of cargo services as well as passenger services: 1) removal of restrictions to the number of points in the route schedule; 2) no limitations on third and fourth freedom traffic rights between ASEAN and China; 3) no limitations on fifth freedom traffic rights between ASEAN and China; 4) no limitations on frequency and capacity, as well as the type of aircraft; 5) charter operation as an element; and 6) multiple airline designation.", online: <http://cil.nus.edu.sg/rp/pdf/2007%20ASEAN-China%20Aviation%20Cooperation%20Framework-pdf.pdf>.
124 *Ibid.*
125 For the discussion of ASEAN-China FTA, See *e.g.* Sarah Y. Tong & Catherine Chong, "CHINA-ASEAN Free Trade Area in 2010: A Regional Perspective", 2010 East Asia Institute, National University of Singapore, Background Brief No. 519, online: <www.eai.nus.edu.sg/BB519.pdf>.
126 For the details, see Alan Khee-Jin Tan, "The 2010 ASEAN–China Air Transport Agreement: Placing the Cart before the Horse?" (2012) 37 Air & Space L. 35. [Tan, "ASEAN-China"].
127 See *the ASEAN–China Air Transport Agreement* Article 23(3). online: <www.asean.org/archive/transport/Air%20Transport%20Agreement%20between%20ASEAN+China.pdf>.; see also Tan "SAM in ASEAN", *supra* note 104 at 22.
128 Tan, *ibid.* at 23.

2.3.3 Benefits of the ASEAN Single Aviation Market

Since the ASEAN SAM is still being implemented, it is too early to fully assess ASEAN developments in the post-liberalization period. The goal of providing the 3rd, 4th, and 5th freedoms by 2015 has not been completed yet, and the 7th freedom has not even been discussed. Similarly, the 8th and 9th freedoms (cabotage operations) are not even on the negotiating table as a future agenda item.

Nonetheless, fairly relaxed regional liberalization has already led to distinctively positive results. Once again, the growth of low-cost carriers (LCCs) is noticeable. The LCC penetration rate in the Southeast Asian market is above 50 percent, having steadily increased from less than 5 percent in 2003.[129]

Figure 2.2 LCCs' Share of Capacity within Southeast Asia[130]

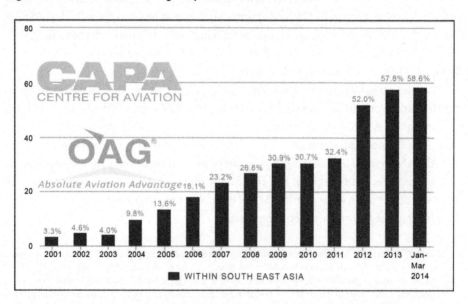

In terms of market access, except the non-capital cities in Indonesia and Laos, ASEAN carriers are free to fly from points in their home states to any other points in ASEAN and vice versa. This business environment is beneficial for LCCs that mainly focus on 3rd and

---

129 CAPA, "Competition in Southeast Asia's low-cost airline sector heats up as capacity surges" (5 September 2013), online: <http://centreforaviation.com/analysis/competition-in-southeast-asias-low-cost-airline-sector-heats-up-as-capacity-surges-126798>.

130 CAPA, "Southeast Asia low-cost airline fleet to expand by almost 20% in 2014. Are more deferrals needed?" (11 March 2014), online: <http://centreforaviation.com/analysis/southeast-asia-low-cost-airline-fleet-to-expand-by-almost-20-in-2014-are-more-deferrals-needed-156726>. (noting that the surge in penetration rate from 2011 to 2012 is driven by re-classification of Lion Air from FSC to LCC).

4th freedom traffic. Although the problem of slot shortages at congested airports such as Jakarta and Manila may hamper LCCs' operations (that is, landing and take-off slots are not available even on the open market), that is a separate issue from the openness of traffic rights (slot problems in Jakarta and Manila will be discussed in the following section.)

LCCs are particularly well placed to target the surging middle class in Southeast Asia, since such carriers are focused primarily on short-haul markets and their lower fares make flying more affordable.[131] Although there is no official distinction between short-haul and long-haul flights, a generally accepted industry convention is that short-haul flights are less than 3,000 km and can be operated by standard narrow-body aircraft (*e.g.* Boeing 737 and Airbus 320).[132] LCCs derive their competitive advantage from the operational efficiencies in short-haul flights,[133] and most intra-ASEAN routes are shorter than 3,000 km. Thus, ASEAN has an ideal environment for LCCs, and six intra-ASEAN routes are ranked in the top 10 international LCC routes:

Table 2.6 Top 10 International LCC Routes (2014)[134]

Rank	Origin	Destination
1	Singapore Changi Airport	Jakarta Soekarno-Hatta International Airport
2	Singapore Changi Airport	Kuala Lumpur International Airport
3	Dubai International Airport	Kuwait International Airport
4	Kuala Lumpur International Airport	Bangkok Don Mueang International Airport
5	Kuala Lumpur International Airport	Jakarta Soekarno-Hatta International Airport
6	Barcelona El Prat Airport	London Gatwick Airport
7	Dubai International Airport	Doha Hamad International Airport
8	Manila Ninoy Aquino International Airport	Singapore Changi Airport
9	Singapore Changi Airport	Bangkok Suvarnabhumi International Airport
10	Dublin Airport	London Stansted Airport

---

131 CAPA, "Competition in Southeast Asia's low-cost airline sector heats up as capacity surges" (5 September 2013), online: <http://centreforaviation.com/analysis/competition-in-southeast-asias-low-cost-airline-sector-heats-up-as-capacity-surges-126798>.
132 Jost Daft & Sascha Albers, "A profitability analysis of low-cost long-haul flight operations" (2012) 19 Journal of Air Transport Management 49 at 54.
133 John G. Wensveen & Ryan Leick, "The long-haul low-cost carrier: A unique business model" (2009) 15 Journal of Air Transport Management 127 at 128.
134 CAPA, "Lion's Malindo Air to compete vs AirAsia, Jetstar & Tigerair on world's top international LCC route" (12 October 2014), online: <http://centreforaviation.com/analysis/lions-malindo-air-to-compete-vs-airasia-jetstar--tigerair-on-worlds-top-international-lcc-route-191075>.

As much as ASEAN regional liberalization has served as the catalyst leading to the growth of LCCs, the role of LCCs in ASEAN regional liberalization cannot be underestimated. The development of national LCCs helped change governments' mindset toward ASEAN regional liberalization. For instance, Malaysia, which used to be much less enthusiastic about regional liberalization, has joined all the ASEAN regional liberalization agreements. The success of Malaysia-based AirAsia has definitely affected the country's policy changes.

In addition to the intra-ASEAN liberalization, the new ASEAN–China Air Transport Agreement provides an enormous opportunity for both LCCs and full-service carriers. Now ASEAN carriers have unlimited penetration into all of China (with the exception of Hong Kong, Macao and Taiwan, points excluded in the ASEAN-China Agreement), which would have not been possible if the 10 states had negotiated with China separately, providing them with an important growth engine.

Although there has been encouraging progress on the liberalization of market access, ownership and control restrictions are still in place in ASEAN. The concept of the ASEAN "community carrier" was formulated under the ASEAN agreements, but there is a substantial restriction (that is, a state can exercise its veto) (Article 3(2)(a)(ii) of MAAS and MALFAS).

Indeed, an ASEAN community carrier with multiple ASEAN interests in the aggregate has never been established. In other words, the community carrier concept sounds good in theory, but it has not been put into practice. All the LCC joint ventures in recent years still use the old 51/49 model (that is, majority ownership by the local interest and minority ownership by the foreign parent airline). Table 2.7 summarizes the ownership and control structure of LCC joint ventures in ASEAN. A more thorough discussion of joint ventures can be found in Chapter 4: Ownership and Control Issues in Northeast Asia.

Table 2.7 The Ownership and Control Structure of ASEAN LCC Joint Ventures

Country/Territory	Joint Venture Airline	Local Shareholder/s	Foreign Shareholder/s
Indonesia	Indonesia AirAsia	Pin Harris – 20% and Sendjaja Windjaja – 31%	AAIL (wholly-owned subsidiary of AirAsia Berhad) – 49%
Indonesia	Indonesia AirAsia X	PT Kirana Anugerah Perkasa (PTKAP) – 51%	AirAsia X Berhad – 49%
Malaysia	Malindo Air	National Aerospace and Defence Industries – 51%	Lion Air – 49%
Philippines	Philippine AirAsia	F&S Holdings – 16%; TNR Holdings – 16%; Alfredo Yao – 13% and Michael Romero – 16%	AAIL (wholly-owned subsidiary of AirAsia Berhad) – 40%;
Philippines	AirAsia Zest	AirAsia Inc. (Philippine AirAsia) – 49% and Alfredo Yao – 51%	-

Country/Territory	Joint Venture Airline	Local Shareholder/s	Foreign Shareholder/s
Thailand	Thai Lion Air	2 Thai businessmen (names undisclosed) – 51%	Lion Air Group – 49%;
Thailand	Thai AirAsia X	Tassapon Bijleveld – 41% and Julpas Kruesopon – 10%	AirAsia Berhad – 49%;
Thailand	NokScoot	Nok Mangkang Co. Ltd. (wholly-owned subsidiary of Nok Airlines) – 49% and Pueannammitr Co. Ltd. – 2%	Scoot Pte. Ltd. – 49%
Thailand	Thai AirAsia	Asia Aviation – 55%	AAIL (wholly-owned subsidiary of AirAsia Berhad) – 45%
Thailand	Thai Vietjet Air	Kan Air (Somphong Sooksanguan) – 51%	Vietjet – 49%
Singapore	Jetstar Asia	Westbrook Investments Pte. Ltd. – 51%	Qantas Airways – 49%
Vietnam	Jetstar Pacific	Vietnam Airlines – 69% and Saigontourist Travel Services – 1%	Qantas Airways – 30%;

Along with the tangible benefits, the intangible effect of regional liberalization must be considered. On a global level, various commercial approaches by airlines have been initiated to circumvent ownership and control restrictions. Examples of such approaches are establishing joint ventures with local interests. This joint venture model is an *incorporated* joint venture that forms a separate company (mostly initiated by LCCs). This model is different from the *unincorporated* joint venture model (normally conducted between full-service carriers such as the JAL/AA and ANA/UA joint ventures), which does not form a separate legally incorporated company. (This will be fully discussed in Chapter 4: Ownership and Control Issues in Northeast Asia.)

AirAsia pioneered the incorporated joint venture model in the region. In the case of AirAsia's subsidiaries in other ASEAN states (namely, Indonesia AirAsia, Thai AirAsia, and Philippines AirAsia), the local owners hold a majority share, while the parent airline group only has a minority stake.[135] This adheres to the traditional 51/49 practice.[136] However, the requirement of "effective control" is less clear since the managing expertise and strategic decisions may come from the parent foreign airline (the minority owner).[137] Typically, the local majority shareholders have no experience with aviation.

A unique feature of LCC JVs in the region is that ASEAN governments have disregarded (or at least mitigated) the effective control test. In other words, "effective control" inquiries

---

135 Tan, "SAM in ASEAN", *supra* note 104 at 17.
136 However, see Philippines AirAsia. Under the laws of the Philippines, at least 60% of its capital must be held by Filipino citizens.
137 Tan, "SAM in ASEAN", *supra* note 104 at 18.

have not been conducted strictly. (This will be further discussed in the Chapter 4) These joint ventures were only possible because ASEAN cooperation, liberalization, and integration were in progress. It is doubtful that the same joint ventures would have been possible if a totally foreign carrier (*e.g.* a US carrier) had proposed the subsidiaries to the local governments.

On the macro-economy level, CAPA estimated that ASEAN SAM has brought the 10 states a total of USD 1,074 million in GDP gains.[138]

2.3.4 Challenges to the ASEAN Single Aviation Market

The biggest challenge faced by the ASEAN Single Aviation Market is rooted in the immense diversity of economic development and competitiveness of the national air carriers.[139] The basic indicators in Table 2.8 briefly show the diversity of ASEAN states.

Table 2.8 Basic ASEAN Indicators (2014)

Countries	Total land area (Km2)	Total population (Thousand)	Population density (persons per km2)	Gross domestic product (USD million)	Gross domestic product per capita
Brunei Darussalam	5,769	406.2	70	16,117.5	39,678.7
Cambodia	181,035	14,962.6	83	15,659.0	1,046.5
Indonesia	1,860,360	248,818.1	134	862,567.9	3,466.7
Lao PDR	236,800	6,644.0	28	10,002.0	1,505.4
Malaysia	330,290	29,948.0	91	312,071.6	10,420.5
Myanmar	676,577	61,573.8	91	56,408.0	916.1
Philippines	300,000	99,384.5	331	269,024.6	2,706.9
Singapore	715	5,399.2	7,550	297,945.8	55,183.3
Thailand	513,120	68,251.0	133	387,534.1	5,678.1
Viet Nam	330,951	89,708.9	271	171,219.3	1,908.6
ASEAN	4,435,617	625,096.3	139	2,398,549.6	3,837.1

---

138 CAPA, "Final Report" *supra* note 2 at 137 (noting GDP gains by states: Brunei Darussalam USD 12 million; Cambodia 7 million; Indonesia 364 million; Lao PDR 4 million; Malaysia 157 million; Myanmar 12 million; The Philippines 118 million; Singapore 132 million; Thailand 207 million; and Viet Nam 61 million).
139 See Forsyth *et al*, *supra* note 100 at 143 (noting that "[T]he ASEAN countries are very diverse. Some are populous, others are not; some have high per capita incomes, while others are amongst the poorest in the world some have well-developed aviation sectors, while others have embryonic aviation industries, at best; and some have efficient, financially strong airlines, while others do not.").

Airlines in the ASEAN have varying strengths and sizes. The fact that Laos and, more importantly, Indonesia have yet to implement full intra-ASEAN liberalization for even the 3rd, 4th and 5th freedoms has to do with the competitiveness of their national carriers.

As the largest market in ASEAN, Indonesia's participation will virtually determine the effectiveness of the proposed ASEAN Single Aviation Market.[140] In this regard, Indonesia's recent ratification of Protocols 5 and 6 of the 2009 Multilateral Agreement on Air Services, which opened Jakarta to 3rd, 4th, and 5th freedom traffic to and from other capital cities, is welcome news. However, a separate but related problem is the scarcity of slots. Indeed, Jakarta's Soekarno-Hatta airport is heavily congested, with existing terminals operating well above capacity (the airport has a capacity of 22 million passengers, but it served about 60 million passengers in 2014[141]), and the airport's two runways are fully utilized during peak hours.[142] Airlines seeking to add flights at the Soekarno-Hatta airport have to operate in very unpopular periods such as prior to 6:00 a.m.[143] Thus, Indonesia's ratification of Protocols 5 and 6 of the 2009 MAAS does not effectively change anything since few new flights can be launched from Jakarta.

Similarly, the late ratification of the Philippines regarding Protocols 5 and 6 of the 2009 Multilateral Agreement on Air Services has to do with the country's aviation policy of restricting access to Manila's congested Ninoy Aquino International Airport while fully opening Clark Airport, which is located about 80 km from downtown Manila.[144] Alan Tan is critical of this practice, arguing that "linking slots to access rights is a negative precedent in that it encourages governments to use congestion and lack of slots as excuses to delay their adherence to regional commitments."[145]

Another important weakness of the ASEAN SAM is that the 7th freedom and cabotage rights (8th and 9th freedoms) have not been discussed. This setback is aggravated by the new ASEAN–China Air Transport Agreement. Now that ASEAN and China have agreed to unlimited 3rd and 4th freedom between the two regions, "[The ASEAN–China Air Transport Agreement] may create network imbalance as ASEAN airlines can fly to China

---

140 See Batari Saraswati & Shinya Hanaoka, "Aviation Policy in Indonesia and Its Relation to ASEAN Single Aviation Market" (2013) 9 Proceedings of the Eastern Asia Society for Transportation Studies 2.
141 Emirsyah Satar (CEO of Garuda Indonesia), "The next biggest growth opportunities for Indonesia's airline market" (Address to the 7th Annual Aviation Outlook Asia Conference, 29 October 2014) [unpublished].
142 Saraswati & Hanaoka, *supra* note 140 at 5.
143 CAPA "Jakarta Halim Airport re-opening frees Soekarno-Hatta slots for Citilink, Garuda, AirAsia, Lion Air" (12 January 2014), online: <http://centreforaviation.com/analysis/jakarta-halim-airport-re-opening-frees-soekarno-hatta-slots-for-citilink-garuda-airasia-lion-air-147479>; For instance, Mandala Airlines started flights at 4:30 a.m. in Jakarta because the carrier cannot get any airport slots later in the day. See Kyunghee Park & Jasmine Wang "Jakarta 4:30 A.M. Flights Show Budget Carriers Outgrow Airports" *Bloomberg* (4 February 2013), online: <www.bloomberg.com/news/2013-02-03/jakarta-4-30-a-m-flights-show-budget-carriers-outgrow-airports.html>.
144 See Tan, "The Philippines", *supra* note 121.
145 Tan, "SAM in ASEAN", *supra* note 104 at 4.

only originally from points in their own territory, while China can connect any point in their domestic hinterland with any point in ASEAN."[146]

The lesson that ASEAN can learn from the EU is that the unlimited 7th freedom is permitted by the EU's Third Package and the ECJ's "open skies" decision so that EU airlines can operate from any EU point to any US point if they wish to. In other words, "all flights between the US and the EU are now straightforward 3rd/4th freedom operations for all airlines from both sides."[147] Logically, ASEAN needs to discuss the 7th freedom in order to redress the imbalance with China.

At the same time, the inherent reluctance to 7th freedom operations for passengers should not be overlooked. 7th freedom for passengers is typically viewed as a serious threat to local air carriers.[148] Most ASEAN states would not move toward relaxing the 7th freedom without a tangible benefit for their national carriers or people. Given the circumstances, a modest introduction of 7th freedom operations (such as allowing 7th freedom only when there were previously no direct flights) could be a way to initiate discussion.[149]

Overall, the ASEAN Single Aviation Market model should be praised for its relatively speedy acceptance by member states and regarded as a fairly good and realistic example of what regional liberalization can achieve.

2.4 Other Regional Liberalization Models

In this section, other regional liberalization models are discussed with a focus on the key features of market access and ownership and control restrictions, along with a brief discussion of the impediments to each regional liberalization model.

2.4.1 Australia-New Zealand Single Aviation Market

Clearly, the formation of the Australia-New Zealand Single Aviation Market corresponded to the *bilateral* approach given that there are only these two countries involved. However, it is worth pausing to examine how the Australia-New Zealand SAM has developed since it is a truly advanced model. Australia and New Zealand have been actively cooperating in many areas including air transportation because of their geographical proximity, shared colonial history and consequential regional interdependence.[150]

---

146 Saraswati & Hanaoka, *supra* note 140 at 13.
147 Tan "SAM in ASEAN", *supra* note 104 at 24-25.
148 Alan Khee-Jin Tan, "Prospects for a Single Aviation Market in Southeast Asia" (2009) 34 Ann. Air & Sp. L. 253 at 271. [Tan, "Prospects for SAM"].
149 *Ibid.* at 272.
150 Jeffrey Goh, *The Single Aviation Market of Australia and New Zealand* (London: Cavendish Publishing Limited, 2001) at 43. [Goh, "Australia and New Zealand"].

The two countries signed the Closer Economic Relations Trade Agreement (CER) covering goods and services that came into effect in 1983 and expanded this even further with the CER Trade in Services Protocol in 1988. However, the CER never included civil aviation and, consequently, the liberalization of air transportation between Australia and New Zealand was dealt with through bilateral air services agreements.[151]

The integration of air transportation between the two countries has been significantly affected by the deregulation of the domestic aviation market and the privatization of national airlines.[152] In Australia, the domestic aviation market was deregulated in 1990, and state-owned Qantas was fully privatized in 1995. In New Zealand, meanwhile, deregulation of the domestic market took place in 1983, and state-owned Air New Zealand (ANZ) became a private company in 1989.[153]

In July 1992, Australia and New Zealand signed a Memorandum of Understanding aiming to create a single aviation market in three stages from 1992 to 1994.[154] Although the two countries had trouble adhering to the schedule outlined in the 1992 MOU,[155] they did make some progress on domestic access issues later through the 1996 Single Aviation Market Arrangements. Finally, Australia and New Zealand signed a new Air Services Agreement in 2002 that replaced all previous arrangements.[156]

Through the removal of all restrictions on air services between, within, and beyond the two countries for Australian and New Zealand airlines (thus, 1st, 2nd, 3rd, 4th, 5th, 6th, 8th, and 9th freedoms for passenger and cargo flights and 7th freedom only for cargo flights), the 2002 Air Services Agreement created a single aviation market.

However, the MoU signed by the two states in November 2000 provides that, in the event that Australia grants the airline(s) of a third party 7th freedom operations for passengers, both Australia and New Zealand would grant 7th freedom operations for passengers to the airline(s) of each party that have been designated under the agreement.[157] For instance, if Singapore Airlines is allowed to operate 7th freedom flights from Australia (such as Sydney to Jakarta), Air New Zealand can do the same, and Qantas can start to operate 7th freedom flights from New Zealand (such as Auckland to Los Angeles).

It is important to note that the 5th freedom is not unlimited due to the involvement of third countries. For instance, since the air services agreement between Australia and

---

151 CAPA, "Final Report" *supra* note 2 at 52.
152 ICAO Secretariat, "Trans Tasman Single Aviation Market" (July 2007), online: <www.icao.int/sustainability/CaseStudies/StatesReplies/Trans-Tasman_En.pdf>.
153 *Ibid.*
154 Similar to the EU's gradual approach, the original plan was to increase market access annually, culminating in the removal of all route and capacity restrictions between the two countries and full access to each other's domestic markets by 1994.
155 See CAPA, "Final Report" *supra* note 2 at 52.
156 They are: the 1961 Air Services Agreement; the 1992 Memorandum of Understanding on Air Services Arrangements; and the 1996 Single Aviation Market Arrangements.
157 CAPA, "Final Report" *supra* note 2 at 53.

Korea is not an open skies agreement (that is, there is a capacity limit even on 3rd and 4th freedom operations), Air New Zealand cannot exercise unlimited 5th freedom (Auckland–Sydney–Seoul routes). By the same token, the 7th freedom was excluded from the 2002 agreement. Thus, the relevant privileges are strictly limited to activities within the two countries.

This is different from what EU carriers are entitled to (unlimited 1st to 9th freedoms), a difference arising simply because of the number of member states. Whilst EU community carriers can enjoy the 5th and 7th freedoms as long as the origins and destinations are within the EU single aviation market, the air services agreement between Australia and New Zealand only involves two countries and thus cannot deal with the traffic rights of third countries.

The 2002 Air Services Agreement defines two types of airlines: namely, designated airlines[158] and SAM airlines. While designated airlines can operate 1st freedom to 6th freedom, 7th freedom (only for cargo) and 8th freedom, SAM airlines can operate 1st freedom to 4th freedom and have full cabotage rights (8th freedom and 9th freedom) in the other party's market. The SAM airline is conceptually similar to the EU community carrier. An airline is entitled to be a SAM airline if 1) it is majority owned and effectively controlled by nationals of either or both states (Australia and New Zealand), 2) the chairperson of the airline and at least two-thirds of its board members are nationals of either state, and 3) the head office is based in the territory of one of the states.

The unique character of the Australia-New Zealand SAM might be related to non-intervention with respect to external relations. The privileges of the SAM airlines are strictly limited to activities within the two countries, and the Australia-New Zealand Air Services Agreement does not include provisions for horizontal agreement the way the EU arrangement does. In other words, despite the completion of an *internal* single aviation market, Australia and New Zealand still maintain sovereignty over their bilateral rights with third countries.[159]

2.4.2   Asia-Pacific Economic Cooperation (APEC)'s Initiative

The 2001 APEC Multilateral Agreement on the Liberalization of International Air Transport (MALIAT) is a plurilateral agreement (that is, an agreement amongst several like-minded states that is open for others to join)[160] aiming for a multilateral open skies arrangement.

---

158 See *ibid.* at 53 (noting that designated airlines must be 1) incorporated and have its principal place of business in the territory of the Party concerned and 2) effectively controlled by that Party, its nationals or both).
159 *Ibid.* at 60.
160 ICAO Secretariat, "Overview of Trends and Developments in International Air Transport" (24 March 2009), online: <www.icao.int/sustainability/Documents/OverviewTrends.pdf>.

MALIAT was the first modern multilateral open skies agreement that deals with both the main pillars of liberalization: relaxation of market access and of ownership and control.

The key features of MALIAT regarding market access are multiple airline designation, unrestricted route schedules, unrestricted traffic rights including fifth freedom passenger services and seventh freedom cargo services, and unrestricted capacity and frequency.[161] (MALIAT's innovative approach to liberalizing the traditional ownership requirement restrictions will be discussed in Chapter 4: Ownership and Control Issues in Northeast Asia.)

But contrary to early optimism, MALIAT has not been widely accepted. There are only nine contracting states to the agreement (most of which are not major economies except the US).[162] Simply put, two of the main reasons for low acceptance were inherent in the very nature of MALIAT—it was multilateral, and it was liberal.[163] More specifically, as Alan Tan points out, there are three multi-faceted reasons why most APEC economies have not ratified MALIAT: 1) countries like China are not prepared to enter into an "open skies" relationship with the US; 2) most APEC countries are not willing to abandon the "substantial ownership" restriction (discussed in Chapter 4); and 3) the possibility of unlimited fifth freedom for the carriers of other contracting states has huge implications for individual states and their carriers.[164]

Indeed, resistance to MALIAT has a great deal to do with its liberalization of fifth freedom routes and the presence of Singapore and the US as contracting states.[165] This means that any MALIAT party would have to grant, say, (since this is an example) Singapore Airlines full fifth-freedom services between its cities and the US, *e.g.* Singapore–Shanghai–LA or Singapore–Seoul–New York (all routes without capacity or frequency restrictions for Singapore Airlines). In return, Singapore, as a small market and because of its location in Southeast Asia, would not be able to offer the Northeast Asian airlines a viable fifth freedom operation to the US Thus, states in the Asia-Pacific region with larger markets (that is, a bigger population and a greater number of airports and airlines) are not willing to join MALIAT.[166]

China, Japan, and Korea are member economies of APEC, but none of them is a contracting state to MALIAT, and for the above reasons, there is no sign that they are interested

---

161 Dempsey, "Air Law", *supra* note 41 at 558.
162 Brunei, Chile, Cook Islands, New Zealand, Samoa, Singapore, Tonga, United States, and Mongolia (cargo only). See online: <www.maliat.govt.nz/country/>.
163 Sean McGonigle, "Assessing the APEC Multilateral Agreement After 5 Years of Inactivity" (2013) 38 Ann. Air & Sp. L. 429 at 430.
164 See Alan Khee-Jin Tan, "Chapter 15 The Future of Multilateral Liberalization of Air Transport in Asia" in David Duval, ed., *Air Transport in the Asia Pacific* (Burlington: Ashgate, 2014). [Tan, "Future of Multilateral"].
165 See Tan, "Horizontal Mandate", *supra* note 39 at 438-439.
166 *Ibid.*

in the agreement.[167] For such larger economies in APEC, the unlimited fifth freedom provision in MALIAT is something from which they have much to lose but little to gain. In fact, "MALIAT's remarkable boldness in removing fifth freedom restriction ended up being its own undoing."[168]

Two parties to MALIAT, New Zealand and the US, made an effort to keep the agreement relevant at the ICAO Sixth Worldwide Air Transport Conference in 2013.[169] Indeed, the Transport Conference realistically represented the best opportunity in recent times for MALIAT to reach wider acceptance.[170] But despite this effort, no substantial progress was made to further liberalize market access through MALIAT.[171] Interestingly, however, attention was drawn to the fact that states may join MALIAT on a cargo-only basis.[172] It is worth mentioning that Mongolia accepted MALIAT on a cargo-only basis.[173]

2.4.3 Regional Liberalization in the League of Arab States

The League of Arab States, which consists of 22 Arab countries located in the Middle East and Africa, has discussed liberalizing intra-regional air transport services. The Arab Civil Aviation Commission (ACAC) was established in June 1996 as a regional organization for coordination and cooperation in the area of aviation among Arab countries. The ACAC devised the Intra-Arab Freedoms of the Air Program in 2000 and prepared a timetable for gradual liberalization in four stages as follows:

---

167 But see McGonigle, *supra* note 163 at 438 (noting that Japan was initially interested in the MALIAT.)
168 Tan, "Future of Multilateral", *supra* note 166 at 264; Even in 1960's, states' reluctance to grant the fifth freedom to other states was recognized. D.H.N. Johnson touched on the heart of the fifth freedom controversy in his book *Rights in Air Space* (1965). "Basically, [the fifth freedom] controversy arises from the fact that some countries feel that the sovereignty which they possess over their land territory, and their air space, must be in aviation matters be exploited for all that it is worth as an economic asset... If we may take as an example countries A, B, and C, A will be suspicious of C's fifth freedom operations lest they impair A's own share of the traffic between A and B." in D.H.N. Johnson, *Rights in Air Space* (Manchester: Manchester University Press, 19765) at 66.
169 See ICAO, *The Multilateral Agreement on the Liberalization of International Air Transportation: A Basis for the Future Economic Regulation of Air Services*, ICAO Doc ATConf/6-WP/34 (12 February 2013) (Presented by New Zealand), online: <www.icao.int/Meetings/atconf6/Documents/WorkingPapers/ATConf6-wp034_en.pdf>; ICAO, *Liberalization of Market Access*, ICAO ATConf/6-WP/60 (14 February 2013) (Presented by United States of America), online: <www.icao.int/Meetings/atconf6/Documents/Working-Papers/ATConf6-wp060_en.pdf>.
170 McGonigle, *supra* note 163 at 442.
171 See ICAO, *the Report on Agenda Item 2.1*(summary report of the Air Transport Conference), ICAO ATConf/6-WP/104 (22 March 2013) at para 2.1.3.1, "e) in the short term, States should continue to pursue market access liberalization according to situations and requirements, using existing avenues such as the Multilateral Agreement on the Liberalization of International Air Transportation (MALIAT), while ICAO should continue to provide guidance and assistance to States in facilitating the process.", online: <www.icao.int/Meetings/atconf6/Documents/FinalReport/ATConf6_wp104-2-1_en.pdf>.
172 *Ibid.* at para 2.1.6.2.
173 See MALIAT, *Country Matrix*, online: <www.maliat.govt.nz/country/matrix.php>.

Table 2.9 Guidelines for Arab Regional Liberalization[174]

Phase / Starting Point	Passenger	Cargo
Phase 1 / November 2000	Deregulating non-scheduled passenger operations	Deregulation of cargo
Phase 2 / March 2003	Deregulating 3rd and 4th freedom rights for passenger traffic by allocating capacity of 60% and 40% between the parties	
Phase 3 / March 2005	Unrestricted deregulation of 3rd and 4th freedom rights for passenger traffic	
Phase 4 / March 2007	Deregulating 5th freedom rights	

In 2004, the League of Arab States adopted the Agreement for the Liberalization of Air Transport between the Arab States in Damascus, Syria. The Agreement required at least five countries' acceptance to come into effect, and this requirement was fulfilled in December 2007 when the UAE, ratified it.[175]

With regard to market access, the 2004 Damascus Agreement allows designated air carriers to enjoy unlimited 3rd, 4th, and 5th freedom flights among parties to the agreement.[176] Whereas the ASEAN SAM took a gradual or incremental approach (from sub-region to whole region and from secondary cities to capital cities and eventually to all cities), the Damascus Agreement opted for swift change (including full 5th freedom from the beginning).

In terms of ownership and control, the Damascus Agreement also allows for the creation of Arab "community carriers"[177] in addition to traditional air carriers with substantial ownership and effective control reposed in the designating state or its nationals. Thus, there is the potential for forming new regional carriers that are owned by a group of states or their nationals and serving points among these states.[178]

Even though a fairly liberal regional agreement has been adopted, actual acceptance by states has been slow. According to publicly available sources, only eight countries (out of 22 countries in the Arab League) have ratified the Damascus Convention so far.[179] One

---

174 United Nations, "Economic and Social Commission for Western Asia(ESCWA) Study on Air Transport in the Arab World" (2007) at 32 online: <www.escwa.un.org/information/publications/edit/upload/grid-07-3-e.pdf>.
175 Alan Khee-Jin Tan "The 2004 Damascus Agreement: Liberalizing Market Access and Ownership Rules for Arab Air Carriers" (2010) 35 Ann. Air & Sp. L. 1 at 3. [Tan, "Damascus"].
176 Similar to the ASEAN SAM, there is no provision for 7th freedom and cabotage rights in the Agreement.
177 Air carriers can be a designated carrier if they are i) substantially owned and effectively controlled by several Arab League states or their nationals and ii) the main headquarters is located in one of the states. See Tan, "Damascus" *supra* note 175 at 8.
178 *Ibid.* at 9.
179 Arab Air Carriers Organization (AACO), "Agenda Item 9: Air Transport, Air Transport Relations between the Arab World & the European Union" at the First Meeting of Directors General of Civil Aviation – Middle East Region, DGCA-MID/1-WP/31 22/02/2011, online: <www.icao.int/MID/Documents/2011/

of the main reasons for the lack of state interest in the agreement is the unequal strengths of the various state-owned carriers in the region.[180] Moreover, the competitive gap has been increasing between premier air carriers (Dubai-based Emirates, Abu Dhabi-based Etihad, and Doha-based Qatar Airways) and the other traditional flag carriers in the region. While those premier air carriers are making rapid progress with their competitive hub airports, new aircraft, and aggressive marketing campaigns, the other mostly state-owned traditional flag carriers such as Saudi Arabian Airlines, Egypt Air, Royal Jordanian Airlines and Royal Air Maroc are losing market share.

Emirates, Etihad, and Qatar Airways are typical "6th freedom" carriers. Put simply, 6th freedom carriers effectively regard geographically strategic "hub" airports as a transit stop and make use of liberalized 3rd and 4th freedom rights to operate numerous "spokes."[181] As a result, many states with larger markets are reluctant to grant unlimited 3rd and 4th freedom rights to smaller states with good location and strong airlines. Together with resistance to the "6th freedom" carriers, the unlimited 5th freedom permitted by the Damascus Agreement is a great concern for bigger states like Saudi Arabia and Egypt. If Saudi Arabia and Egypt ratify the Damascus Agreement, it means that Emirates and Etihad, two formidable airlines in the UAE, could operate trunk routes such as Dubai-Riyadh-Cairo or Abu Dhabi-Jeddah-Cairo, which would be undesirable for the relatively uncompetitive airlines Saudi Arabian Airlines and Egypt Air.

Despite steady efforts to push the implementation of the Damascus Agreement,[182] the imbalance of aviation competitiveness in the region will not be redressed in the foreseeable future, which will remain an obstacle on the road to a single aviation market for Arab countries.

---

dgca_mid1/docs/wp31_en.pdf>; Lebanon, Jordan, Syria, Palestine, Oman, Yemen, the United Arab Emirates and Morocco have both signed and ratified the agreement. Bahrain, Tunisia, Sudan, Iraq, Egypt and Somalia have only signed the agreement without ratifying it.

180 Tan, "Damascus" *supra* note 175 at 3.
181 Tan "SAM in ASEAN", *supra* note 104 at 12.
182 See *e.g.* Declaration AACO / IATA Aeropolitical Forum, Abu Dhabi, (16 January 2012) online: <www.aaco.org/Library/Files/AACO%20IATA%20Aeropolitical%20Forum%20Declaration.pdf>, IATA (Speech at Arab Air Carriers Organization (AACO) Assembly, Cairo, 20 October 2010) (noting that "[t]he Damascus Convention of 2004 provides a framework to remedy this with regional liberalization. But the number of countries ratifying it is disappointing."), online <www.iata.org/pressroom/speeches/pages/2010-10-20-01.aspx>.; Arab Air Carriers Organization (AACO), "Agenda Item 9: Air Transport, Air Transport Relations between the Arab World & the European Union" at the First Meeting of Directors General of Civil Aviation – Middle East Region, DGCA-MID/1-WP/31 (22 February 2011), online: <www.icao. int/MID/Documents/2011/dgca_mid1/docs/wp31_en.pdf>; and Annual Report Arab Air Carriers Organization 45th Annual General Meeting – Algeria (5-7 November 2012), online: <www.aaco.org/Library/Files/Publications/Annual%20Reports/2012/Annual%20Report%20english%202012.pdf>.

2.4.4 Regional Liberalization in Latin America

Latin America is a vast continent (Latin America and the Caribbean are approximately five times larger than the EU).[183] Understandably, regional liberalization in Latin America has mainly developed on a sub-regional basis. Broadly, three sub-regional groups have formed air transport agreements for intra-regional liberalization; namely, the Decision on Integration of Air Transport of the Andean Community (CAN, then Andean Pact) (1991); the Agreement on Sub-regional Air Services (Fortaleza Agreement) of the Southern Common Market (MERCOSUR) (1996); and the Air Transport Agreement of the Association of Caribbean States (2004). Apart from the sub-regional agreements, the Latin American Civil Aviation Commission (LACAC) has spearheaded the adoption of an ambitious open skies agreement covering the whole of Latin America.

The Andean Community of Nations is currently composed of Bolivia, Colombia, Ecuador, and Peru).[184]

Table 2.10 Basic Indicators for Andean Community (2014)

Countries	Total land area (Km2)	Total population (Thousand)	Gross domestic product (USD million)	Gross domestic product per capita (USD)
Bolivia	1,098,580	10,556	30,600	2,867
Columbia	1,138,910	48,320	378,100	7,825
Ecuador	283,560	15,740	90,020	5,720
Peru	1,285,220	30,380	202,300	6,659
Andean Community	3,806,270	104,996	701,020	5,757

Since the adoption in 1991 of Decision 297, which provides the framework for regional air transport market liberalization, there has been gradual progress.[185] In 2004, the Commission of the Andean Community of Nations issued Decision 582, which allows free

---

183 Latin America and Caribbean (20.44 million sq km) and the European Union (4.32 million sq km). See online: <www.nationmaster.com/country-info/compare/European-Union/Latin-America-and-Caribbean>.
184 The original Andean Pact was established in 1969 by Bolivia, Chile, Colombia, Ecuador, and Peru. In 1973, its sixth member, Venezuela joined the pact, but Chile withdrew in 1976. In 2006, Venezuela announced its withdrawal.
185 See ICAO, "Evolution of the Liberalization of the Services of Air Transport in the Services of Air Transport in the State Members of the Latin American Civil Aviation Commission – LACAC", ICAO Doc A36-WP/282 (21 September 2007) (Presented by the Latin American Civil Aviation Commission) at 3, online: <www.icao.int/Meetings/AMC/MA/Assembly%2036th%20Session/wp282_en.pdf>.

market access for intra-sub-regional air transport for airlines of member states.[186] Advanced regional liberalization is taking place in the Andean Community including cabotage rights.[187] While the initiatives have been ambitious, the limited number of countries involved limits its reach. Interestingly, there has been discussion about the possibility of negotiating as a group with MERCOSUR (see below) in order to broaden the scope to the entire South American region.[188]

MERCOSUR (Mercado Común del Sur, or Southern Common Market) is a sub-regional bloc comprising Argentina, Brazil, Paraguay, Uruguay and Venezuela. The Fortaleza Agreement (1996), the first agreement on air services negotiated by MERCOSUR countries, allows freedoms of the air for intra-regional traffic on routes which are not served by existing bilateral agreements.[189] In addition to all the official MERCOSUR member states except Venezuela, three associated member states, Bolivia, Chile and Peru, are contracting states to the Fortaleza Agreement.

Table 2.11 Basic Indicators for the Parties of the Fortaleza Agreement

Countries	Total land area (Km2)	Total population (Thousand)	Gross domestic product (USD million)	Gross domestic product per capita (USD)
Argentina	2,780,400	43,669	536,155	12,778
Bolivia	1,098,580	10,556	30,600	2,867
Brazil	8,515,767	202,656	2,244,000	11,067
Chile	756,096	17,819	264,095	14,911
Paraguay	406,752	6,800	45,901	6,758
Peru	1,285,220	30,380	202,300	6,659

---

186 ICAO, "Status of the International Air Transport Services Regulation in the Latin American and Caribbean States" (4 September 2004) (Presented by the Latin American Civil Aviation Commission), online: <www.icao.int/Meetings/AMC/MA/Assembly%2035th%20Session/wp196_en.pdf>.
187 Bruno Macedo, *A Potential Open Sky Agreement Between the EU and MERCOSUR Based on the EU-US Agreement* (Master Thesis, Universidade do Porto, 2008) [unpublished] at 24, online: <http://repositorio-aberto.up.pt/bitstream/10216/60024/2/Texto%20integral.pdf>; See ASEAN, "ASEAN AND THE ANDEAN COMMUNITY" (8 May 2000), online: <www.asean.org/asean/external-relations/international-regional-organisations/item/asean-and-the-andean-community-cooperating-in-the-new-millennium-presentation-of-h-e-rodolfo-c-severino-secretary-general-of-the-association-of-southeast-asian-nations-at-the-1st-symposium-on-asean-andean-cooperation-in-the-new-millennium>.
188 ICAO, "Status of the International Air Transport Services Regulation in the Latin American and Caribbean States" (4 September 2004) (Presented by the Latin American Civil Aviation Commission), online: <www.icao.int/Meetings/AMC/MA/Assembly%2035th%20Session/wp196_en.pdf>.
189 UNCTAD (United Nations Conference on Trade and Development) Secretariat, *Air Transport Services: The Positive Agenda for Developing Countries* (16 April 1999) at 8-9, online: <http://unctad.org/EN/docs/c1em9d2.EN.pdf>.

Countries	Total land area (Km2)	Total population (Thousand)	Gross domestic product (USD million)	Gross domestic product per capita (USD)
Uruguay	176,215	3,324	58,238	17,121
Fortaleza Member States	15,019,030	315,204	3,381,289	10,308

The Fortaleza Agreement (1996) would seem to be a pivotal regional liberalization model in Latin America mainly because of its membership, which includes larger regional economies, Argentina and Brazil in particular, along with Chile, which is home to LAN, the biggest and most successful airline in the region. Nevertheless, it is fairly restrictive compared to the Andean Decisions. First, the Fortaleza Agreement only deals with the 1st to 4th freedoms. Second, all bilateral agreements between member states are still in place and have not been replaced by a regional framework.[190]

Given the many scattered islands of which it is composed, the Caribbean is an area that is particularly dependent on air transport.[191] The Caribbean States Association (consisting of 28 states[192]) adopted the Air Transport Agreement among its members and associated states in 2004.[193] The Caribbean Air Transport Agreement (2004) is the basic instrument for liberalizing air services among its member states.[194] Although traffic rights are fairly liberalized (granting the five freedoms of the air)[195] and the concept of the Caribbean community carrier has been adopted,[196] the Caribbean Air Transport Agreement

---

190 Diederiks-Verschoor, *supra* note 44 at 70.
191 Association of Caribbean States, *20 Years Promoting Cooperation in the Greater Caribbean* (April 2014) at 110, online: <http://6aec.sre.gob.mx/ebooks/ebookacseng.pdf>.
192 Antigua and Barbuda, Bahamas, Barbados, Belize, Colombia, Costa Rica, Cuba, Dominica, Dominican Republic, El Salvador, Grenada, Guatemala, Guyana, Haiti, Honduras, Jamaica, Mexico, Nicaragua, Panama, St Kitts and Nevis, St Lucia, St Vincent and the Grenadines, Suriname, Trinidad and Tobago, Venezuela.
193 Full name is "the Air Transport Agreement Among the Member States and Associate Member of the Association of Caribbean States".
194 ICAO, "Evolution of the Liberalization of the Services of Air Transport in the Services of Air Transport in the State Members of the Latin American Civil Aviation Commission – LACAC", ICAO Doc A36-WP/282 (21 September 2007) (Presented by the Latin American Civil Aviation Commission), online: <www.icao.int/Meetings/AMC/MA/Assembly%2036th%20Session/wp282_en.pdf>.
195 ICAO, "Status of the International Air Transport Services Regulation in the Latin American and Caribbean States" (4 September 2004) (Presented by the Latin American Civil Aviation Commission), online: <www.icao.int/Meetings/AMC/MA/Assembly%2035th%20Session/wp196_en.pdf>.
196 *The Caribbean Air Transport Agreement (2004)*: "Article 3 – A. Designation and Authorization. 2. Upon receipt of such designation and application from the designated airline, in the form and manner prescribed for operating authorizations, the Aeronautical Authorities of the other Party shall grant appropriate authorization with minimum procedural delay, provided that: a. Substantial ownership and effective control of that airline are vested in one or more Parties, its or their nationals or both; and b. The headquarters of the designated airline are located in the territory of the Party designating the airline; and c. The designated airline is qualified to meet the conditions prescribed under the laws and regulations normally applied to the operation of international air transport by the Party considering the application or applications; and d. The Party that designates the airline is maintaining and administering."

does not replace bilateral agreements between member states, just as with the Fortaleza Agreement.[197]

More importantly, actual acceptance of the Agreement (that is, ratification) has been slow. According to publicly available sources, only eight states and two territories are contracting parties to the Caribbean Air Transport Agreement (2004).[198] The fact that Cuba (the most populous island state in the Caribbean with approximately 11 million people) and Jamaica (2.7 million) are parties to the Agreement is hopeful. However, other populous and relatively rich states such as the Dominican Republic (9.7 million) and Trinidad and Tobago (1.3 million with more than US$20,000 GDP per capita) are missing from the agreement. Not surprisingly, Panama—home to Copa Airlines, the most competitive airline in the region—has ratified the Caribbean Air Transport Agreement (2004). Indeed, Panama's presence in the agreement, which would permit Copa Airlines to engage in unlimited five freedom operations in the region, seems to be the root cause of other states' hesitation to join the Caribbean Air Transport Agreement.[199]

On the broad regional level (but not including the most Caribbean island states), the Ad Hoc Group of the Latin American Civil Aviation Commission (LACAC) (consisting of 22 member states[200]) was established in 2010 to draft and propose an open skies agreement for Latin America.[201] The goal was a greater regional liberalization which can be achieved among Latin American countries as a whole rather than fragmented approach.[202] LACAC member states embraced the draft agreement and enacted the Multilateral Open

---

197 *The Caribbean Air Transport Agreement (2004)*: "Article 17 – Existing Agreements Bearing in mind the provisions in Article 2, this Agreement shall not affect any memorandum of understanding, bilateral or multilateral agreement showing similar authorizations that are already in force among the Parties or among the Parties and a non- Party nor the renewal thereof."
198 See ICAO, "Regional/Plurilateral Agreements and Arrangements for Liberalization" (updated 22 July 2009), online: <www.icao.int/sustainability/Documents/RegionalAgreements.pdf>. (noting that "Antigua and Barbuda*, Bahamas*, Barbados, Belize, Colombia*, Costa Rica**, Cuba, Dominica*, Dominican Republic**, El Salvador*, Grenada*, Guatemala, Guyana*, Haiti**, Honduras*, Jamaica, Nicaragua**, Panama, Saint Kitts and Nevis*, Saint Lucia*, Saint Vincent/Grenadines*, Suriname, Trinidad and Tobago**, Mexico*, Venezuela, Guadeloupe/French Guiana/Martinique (France)*, Aruba (Netherlands), Netherlands Antilles (Netherlands) and Turks and Caicos Islands (United Kingdom, became an associate member of ACS in 2006)*; [States with * mark did not sign the Caribbean Air Transport Agreement; States with ** mark did not ratify the Caribbean Air Transport Agreement].").
199 Copa Airlines has been developing a significant route network in the Caribbean while no other airlines in the Caribbean are genuinely profitable. See David Jessop, "Who Will Save Caribbean Aviation?" *The Gleaner* (28 April 2013), online: <http://jamaica-gleaner.com/gleaner/20130428/business/business5.html>.
200 Argentina, Aruba, Belize, Bolivia, Brazil, Chile, Colombia, Costa Rica, Cuba, Dominican Republic, Ecuador, El Salvador, Guatemala, Honduras, Jamaica, Mexico, Nicaragua, Panama, Paraguay, Peru, Uruguay and Venezuela.
201 ICAO, "Developments in the Liberalization of International Air Transport Services in the Latin American Region" (5 March 2013) (Presented by LACAC), online: <www.icao.int/Meetings/atconf6/Documents/WorkingPapers/ATConf6-ip006_en.pdf>.
202 Lucas Braun, "Liberalization or Bust: A Double Step Approach to Relaxing the Foreign Ownership and Control Restrictions in the Brazilian Aviation Industry" (2014) 39 Air & Space L. 343 at 351.

Skies Agreement for Member States of the Latin American Civil Aviation Commission (LACAC Agreement) at the 14th LACAC Ordinary Assembly in Punta Cana, Dominican Republic, in 2010.[203]

The LACAC initiative embodies the most liberal position in the region.[204] The LACAC Agreement explicitly allows unlimited traffic rights up to the 6th freedom.[205] Also, member states can specify their level of openness by way of reserving separate paragraphs that grant the 7th freedom for cargo services alone, the 7th freedom for combined passenger and cargo services, and the right to cabotage.[206]

The LACAC Agreement is open for ratification by all LACAC member states. However, acceptance has been slow, and many states have merely signed the agreement without ratifying it. The Latin American Civil Aviation Commission confirmed that nine states (namely, Brazil, Chile, Columbia, Guatemala, Honduras, Panama, Paraguay, the Dominican Republic, and Uruguay) have signed the LACAC Agreement.[207] According to publicly available sources, however, none of them have ratified the agreement yet.[208] Moreover, seven states (out of the nine signatories) have chosen to reserve Article 2 (Granting of Rights)[209] of the agreement. Thus, although the LACAC agreement (2010) is ambitious, it has a long way to go before it can have a real impact on the region.

---

203 ICAO, "Developments in the Liberalization of International Air Transport Services in the Latin American Region" (5 March 2013) (Presented by LACAC), online: <www.icao.int/Meetings/atconf6/Documents/WorkingPapers/ATConf6-ip006_en.pdf>.
204 Jose Ignacio Garcia-Arboleda, "Transnational Airlines in Latin America Facing the Fear of Nationality" (2012) 37 Air & Space L. 93 at 109.
205 See Article 2 (Granting of Right) of the LACAC Agreement, online: <www.icao.int/Meetings/atconf6/Documents/WorkingPapers/ATConf6-ip006_en.pdf>.
206 See Article 2 (Grating of Rights) and Article 37 (Reservations) of the LACAC Agreement, online: <www.icao.int/Meetings/atconf6/Documents/WorkingPapers/ATConf6-ip006_en.pdf>.
207 ICAO, "Developments in the Liberalization of International Air Transport Services in the Latin American Region" (5 March 2013) (Presented by LACAC), online: <www.icao.int/Meetings/atconf6/Documents/WorkingPapers/ATConf6-ip006_en.pdf>.
208 It is certain that Brazil has not ratified the LACAC Agreement. See Braun, *supra* note 202 at 351 (noting that "[a]pproval by the Brazilian Congress is still pending and only time will tell if Brazil is willing to adopt such an overreaching commitment.").
209 They are Brazil, Columbia, Guatemala, Honduras, Panama, Paraguay, and Dominican Republic. For the explanation about reservation provision in the LACAC agreement, see *RESOLUTION A20-27 GUIDELINES FOR ADDRESSING RESERVATIONS (formulation, acceptance and objection) IN THE MULTILATERAL OPEN SKIES AGREEMENT FOR MEMBER STATES OF THE LATIN AMERICAN CIVIL AVIATION COMMISSION* (noting that "[W]hereas, according to Article 2, each Party to the Agreement grants all traffic rights to the other Parties, making the multilateral agreement an Open Skies Agreement; and freedoms of the air are grouped in such a way as to facilitate their acceptance as well as possible reservations. Those traffic rights that might cause problems to other countries are granted in separate subparagraphs, listed in order of increasing difficulty, that is, the seventh freedom for cargo; the seventh freedom for combined flights and for cabotage."), online: <<www.icao.int/Meetings/atconf6/Documents/WorkingPapers/ATConf6-ip006_en.pdf>.

In 2008, the Latin American states established the Union of South American Nations[210] as part of the continuing process of South American integration. If Latin American states share the vision of forging an economic union and the role of the Union of South American Nations becomes more substantial, it is conceivable that more states will agree to accept the LACAC Agreement as part of economic integration.

Meanwhile, more substantial liberalization has been carried out by airlines with respect to ownership and control restrictions. By way of establishing joint ventures with local interests (LAN Airlines' subsidiaries in Argentina, Columbia, Ecuador, and Peru) and creating holding companies for multiple airlines (LATAM Airlines Group S.A. for LAN Airlines and TAM Airlines and Avianca Holdings S.A. for Avianca and TACA Airlines), we are witnessing substantial relaxation of ownership and control rules.

As AirAsia takes advantage of the intangible benefits of regional cooperation, liberalization, and integration in ASEAN (that is, the more relaxed "effective control" inquiries, see section 2.3.3 Benefits of the ASEAN Single Aviation Market), some Latin American airlines (particularly LAN Airlines) have also adroitly utilized these intangible benefits. (This will be further discussed in section 4.4 Airlines' Response to Ownership and Control Restrictions.)

2.4.5   Regional Liberalization in the Pacific Islands

At the request of the ministers of the Pacific Islands Forum in 1998, the Pacific Islands Air Services Agreement (PIASA) was developed and finally endorsed for signature at the 2003 Pacific Forum Leaders meeting.[211] PIASA is designed to gradually replace the existing system of bilateral air services agreements between the 14 island members[212] of the Pacific Islands Forum with one cooperative agreement to liberalize air services.[213] By setting three stages of increasing liberalization, the PIASA places the importance on actual implementation.

---

210 See online: <www.unasursg.org>.
211 Christopher Findlay, Peter Forsyth & John King, "Developments in Pacific Islands' Air Transport" in Satish Chand ed., *Pacific Islands Regional Integration and Governance* (Canberra: Asia Pacific Press, 2005) at 173-174.
212 Cook Islands, Federated States of Micronesia, Fiji, Kiribati, Nauru, Niue, Palau, Papua New Guinea, Republic of Marshall Islands, Samoa, Solomon Islands, Tonga, Tuvalu and Vanuatu. Australia and New Zealand are members of Pacific islands forum but they are not the members of the Agreement.
213 The Pacific Islands Forum Secretariat, "The Pacific Islands Air Services Agreement (PIASA): Phased Development of a Single Aviation Market in the Pacific" (February 2003), online: <www.icao.int/sustainability/CaseStudies/StatesReplies/PacificMarket_En.pdf>.

Table 2.12 The Snapshot of the Pacific Islands Air Services Agreement[214]

Timeframe	Market Access	Ownership and Control
Six months after the agreement comes into force	3rd, 4th and 6th freedoms are liberalized.	Community carrier is allowed. Permits a state with no existing flag carrier to designate another country's airline, so long as its place of residence and principal place of business is in the territory of the designating state.
Twelve months after the agreement comes into force	5th freedom rights amongst the parties are liberalized.	No change
Thirty months after the agreement comes into force	5th freedoms on routes to non-members of the agreement are open to all member airlines (subject to the bilateral agreements with the non-member states). Australia and New Zealand may accede to the agreement only at the beginning of the third phase.	Extending the earlier use of place of residence and business to all member states

The step-by-step scheme allows governments and airlines to adapt gradually as the system is introduced incrementally.[215] Since the Pacific region is characterized by low density and remoteness, which make the routes costly to serve, regional liberalization and particularly 5th freedom traffic make good sense.[216]

PIASA took effect in October 2007. However, the non-adherence to the agreement by Fiji, the central node of the regional network[217] and a relatively large economy in the region, is a crucial challenge for PIASA.[218] Indeed, Fiji is the largest of the Pacific island states, the home of around 880,000 of the total 3.4 million people living in the region.[219]

Fiji's reluctance to accept PIASA is largely due to the effect that the unlimited 5th freedom granted by the agreement would have on the country's national carrier, Fiji Airways. Fiji has expressed its concern that Fiji Airways (formerly Air Pacific), a Fiji state-owned company with a minority share held by Qantas, would suffer from the unrestricted access to 5th freedom traffic that PIASA would provide to other airlines in the region.[220]

---

214 *Ibid.*
215 *Ibid.*
216 See Findlay *et al., supra* note 211 at 168-169.
217 *Ibid.* at 174.
218 CAPA, "Air Pacific's trouble in paradise" (19 June 2009), online: <http://centreforaviation.com/analysis/air-pacifics-trouble-in-paradise-7964>.
219 The World Bank, Pacific Islands Overview (updated 1 October 2014), online: <www.worldbank.org/en/country/pacificislands/overview>.
220 ICAO, *FIJI'S Position on Multilateral Air Service Agreements: Pacific Islands Air Services Agreement (PIASA)*, ICAO Doc. ATConf/5-WP/45 (23 January 2003) (Presented by Fiji), online: <www.icao.int/Meetings/ATConf5/Documents/ATConf5_wp045_en.pdf>.

Even in a small market such as this one, the aero-political aspect of impediments continues to prevail.

2.4.6 Regional Liberalization in Africa

Although air transport plays an important role in the economic development of Africa by fostering trade and foreign investments, air services in the continent have long been restrictive and inefficient.[221] In order to promote air transport liberalization in Africa, African ministers in charge of civil aviation met in Yamoussoukro, Ivory Coast, in 1999, and adopted the Yamoussoukro Decision.[222] Essentially, the Yamoussoukro Decision is "the continental agreement with the aim of gradual liberalization of scheduled and non-scheduled intra-African air transport services."[223]

With regard to market access, the Yamoussoukro Decision allows the multilateral exchange of up to 5th freedom air traffic rights between any member states on a simple notification.[224] On airline ownership and control, Article 6 replaced the traditional "substantial ownership and effective control" with the concept of "principal place of business and effective regulatory control". (This concept will be discussed in detail in Chapter 4.) Members of the African Civil Aviation Commission (AFCAC) stated that "the importance of this provision (Article 6) lies in the opportunities it creates for increased access to international foreign equity participation in African airlines and the possibility of encouraging the restructuring of African airlines through cross-border capital injection and consolidations."[225]

As a huge continent with numerous countries (54[226]), it was recognized early on that implementation of the Yamoussoukro Decision depended mainly on sub-regional initiatives

---

221 Charles E. Schlumberger, "Africa's Long Path to Liberalizing Air Services – Status Quo of the Implementation of the Yamoussoukro Decision" (2008) 33 Ann. Air & Sp. L. 194 at 197. [Schlumberger, "Yamoussoukro Decision"].

222 Official name is "Decision Relating to the Implementation of the Yamoussoukro Declaration concerning the Liberalization of Access to Air Transport Markets in Africa".

223 ICAO, "Relaxing the Rules for Airline Designation", ICAO Doc. ATConf/6-WP/46 (13 March 2013) (Presented by Members of the African Civil Aviation Commission (AFCAC)), online: <www.icao.int/meetings/atconf6/documents/workingpapers/atconf6-wp046_en.pdf>.

224 Schlumberger, "Yamoussoukro Decision", *supra* note 221 at 196.

225 ICAO, *Relaxing the Rules for Airline Designation*, ICAO Doc. ATConf/6-WP/46 (13 March 2013) (Presented by Members of the African Civil Aviation Commission (AFCAC)), online: <www.icao.int/meetings/atconf6/documents/workingpapers/atconf6-wp046_en.pdf>.

226 Algeria, Angola, Benin, Botswana, Burkina Faso, Burundi, Cameroon, Cap Verde, Central African Republic, Chad, Comoros, Congo, Cote d'Ivoire, Democratic Republic of the Congo, Djibouti, Egypt, Equatorial Guinea, Eritrea, Ethiopia, Gabon, Gambia, Ghana, Guinea, Guinea-Bissau, Kenya, Lesotho, Liberia, Libyan Arab Jamahiriya, Madagascar, Malawi, Mali, Mauritania, Mauritius, Morocco, Mozambique, Namibia, Niger, Nigeria, Rwanda, Sao Tome and Principe, Senegal, Seychelles, Sierra Leone, Somalia, South Africa,

in regional economic groupings.[227] The East African Community (EAC), the common market for East South Africa (COMESA), and the South African Development Community (SADC) are examples of such regional economic groupings.[228]

The vast majority of African states (including bigger economies like Cameroon, Egypt, Ethiopia, Ghana, Kenya, and Nigeria) have already ratified the Yamoussoukro Decision,[229] but the Decision is not being put into practice. Some countries are failing to implement certain elements of the Decision, whilst others are simply ignoring it by continuing to honor traditional restrictive bilateral air services agreements with other countries, which is a bigger problem.[230] For instance, it has been reported that only 19 of Ethiopia's 46 bilateral air services agreements with other African states are in accordance with the Yamoussoukro Decision.[231]

The aero-political reasons for ignoring the Yamoussoukro Decision can be inferred from Charles Schlumberger's summary of the impacts of the Decision on the African air transport sector:

- the relative strengthening of a limited number of stronger African carriers, such as Ethiopian Airlines and Kenya Airways, that reaped the benefits of their comparative advantages in terms of geographical location; financial, commercial and managerial strength; and access to intercontinental markets;
- the marginalization of many already weak carriers, some of which ultimately disappeared, for instance, Air Tanzania, Nigerian Airways, and Cameroon Airlines;
- the consolidation of networks through the phasing out of a number of low-density routes and growth of routes to and from the main hubs, most significant in East Africa;
- the development of fifth freedom traffic, especially in regions and country pairs that lacked strong local carriers, often offered by dominant carriers at marginal cost, effectively resulting in pressure on regional fares, which is forcing locally-based third and fourth freedom carriers to accept lower fares; and

---

Southern Sudan, Sudan, Swaziland, Togo, Tunisia, Uganda, United Republic of Tanzania, Zambia, and Zimbabwe.

227 Charles E. Schlumberger, *Open Skies for Africa Implementing the Yamoussoukro Decision* (Washington, D.C.: The World Bank, 2010) at 61. [Schlumberger, "Open Skies for Africa"].

228 See *ibid.* at Chapter 4; See also Pablo Mendes De Leon, "Competition in International Markets: A Comparative Analysis" Paper to Organisation for Economic Co-operation and Development(OECD) (13 June 2014), online: <www.oecd.org/officialdocuments/publicdisplaydocumentpdf/?cote=DAF/COMP/WD(2014) 77&docLanguage=En>.

229 See ICAO, "Regional/Plurilateral Agreements and Arrangements for Liberalization" (updated 22 July 2009), online: <www.icao.int/sustainability/Documents/RegionalAgreements.pdf>.

230 Schlumberger, "Open Skies for Africa", *supra* note 227 at 6.

231 *Ibid.* at 39; see also *ibid.* at 58 (noting that "Kenya temporarily refused Ethiopian Airlines the right to conduct fifth freedom operations between Nairobi and Kigali, Rwanda, in breach of the Yamoussoukro Decision.").

- the significant development of sixth freedom traffic, fostered by the liberalization of third and fourth freedom capacities within Africa, and in some cases with intercontinental counterpart countries.[232]

Simply put, the Yamoussoukro Decision has created "winners" and "losers" just as other regional liberalization models have. While Kenya and Ethiopia, for example, have benefited from regional liberalization, it has led to the disappearance of already weak national carriers in Nigeria, Cameroon, and Tanzania.

The challenge of African regional liberalization is unique since the problem is not "acceptance" but "implementation." Although there is a call for implementing the Yamoussoukro Decision,[233] it seems unlikely that the status quo, whereby African states rely on bilateral air services agreements rather than the Yamoussoukro Decision, will be altered in the near future.

2.5   REGIONAL LIBERALIZATION IN NORTHEAST ASIA

It is difficult to make any direct comparisons between the regional aviation markets discussed above and Northeast Asian regional liberalization. Those regional aviation markets are either well-established single aviation markets or proposed single aviation markets with specific goals and a phased timeline. While there is wide variation in terms of actual acceptance, most regions have adopted some forms of agreement for intra-regional liberalization, often with the prodding of a regional organization like ASEAN or the Arab League. In contrast, regional liberalization in Northeast Asia is still at a preliminary discussion stage with no dedicated organization tasked with promoting the cause.

2.5.1   History

The possibility of regional liberalization in Northeast Asia was raised in the early 2000s.[234] In June 2006, the prospect of Northeast Asian open skies was openly discussed by China, Japan and Korea for the first time when the 1st International Symposium on Liberalizing

---

232 *Ibid.* at 146-147.
233 See *e.g.* ICAO, *Africa's Strategy for Market Access and Catalyst for Air Transport Growth*, ICAO Doc. ATConf/6-WP/35 (18 February 2013) (Presented by Members of the African Civil Aviation Commission (AFCAC)); ICAO, *Relaxing the Rules for Airline Designation*, ICAO Doc. ATConf/6-WP/46 (18 February 2013) (Presented by AFCAC).
234 See e.g. Tae Hoon Oum & Yeong Heok Lee, "The Northeast Asian air transport network: is there a possibility of creating Open Skies in the region?" (2002) 8 Journal of Air Transport Management. 325; Anming Zhang & Hongmin Chen, "Evolution of China's Air Transport Development and Policy towards International Liberalization" (2003) 42 Transportation Journal. 31.

Air Transport in Northeast Asia was held in Korea. The symposium brought together government policy makers, industry experts, and academics from the three countries.

Participants at the symposium noted the recent substantial increase in commerce and tourism among the countries and agreed that creating Northeast Asian open skies would be ultimately advantageous for all three countries by increasing the movement of people and goods and reducing logistics costs. The Symposium was held for five consecutive years including the inaugural event: 2007 (Tokyo, Japan), 2008 (Guizhou, China), 2009 (Busan, Korea), and 2010 (Osaka, Japan). However, the negotiations have not moved forward, and the regular annual symposium was halted in 2011.

On a bilateral level, there has been some progress since then such as the Korea-Japan open skies agreement in 2007 (which was partially triggered by the discussions for regional liberalization in Northeast Asia). In August 2012, China and Japan concluded a much more liberalized air services agreement allowing designated carriers to operate an unlimited number of passenger and cargo flights between any Chinese and Japanese cities except Beijing, Shanghai, and Tokyo. While this *quasi* open skies agreement did not include significantly expanded services to the major cities on each side (owing to slot restrictions), it opened the door for an explosion in services to and from secondary cities.[235] With regard to China–Korea relations, the air services consultation in June 2006, which was held a week after the 1st International Symposium on Liberalizing Air Transport in Northeast Asia, led to some partial liberalization, such as opening up China's Shandong province. (See sections 3.2 National Policy on Market Access in International Air Transport and 3.3 Bilateral Positions on Market Access.)

Nevertheless, the reality is that the speed and scope of Northeast Asian open skies have not kept up with expectations. At the moment, it is not possible to assert that substantial change is occurring. As discussed below, however, there are solid reasons to focus on Northeast Asian open skies.

2.5.2   Justifications

Broadly, there are five main factors that provide a justification for Northeast Asian open skies. First is the fact that China, Korea, and Japan rely heavily on each other's markets and influence each other in significant ways. Take, for example, the export markets for China, Japan and Korea. For China, Japan and Korea ranked as the third and fourth largest

---

235   CAPA, "China–Japan traffic bottoms out but faces massive challenge; Spring Airlines to launch new routes" (17 January 2013), online: <http://centreforaviation.com/analysis/China–Japan-traffic-bottoms-out-but-faces-massive-challenge-spring-airlines-to-launch-new-routes-94109>.

export markets (after the US and Hong Kong) in 2012. For Japan, China and Korea ranked first and third. For Korea, China and Japan ranked first and third.[236]

A similar picture can be seen in the number of foreign visitors. For China, Koreans and Japanese ranked first and second in terms of the number of visitors in 2013.[237] For Japan, Korean and Chinese visitors ranked first and third (Taiwan being second).[238] For Korea, Chinese and Japanese visitors ranked first and second.[239] Importantly, while Chinese visitors in 2012 represented 23 percent of all visitor arrivals to Korea, they accounted for 40 percent of all inbound tourists to Korea in 2014.[240] Given that there is no means of land transportation between the three countries and that the few sea routes (including Weihei, China, to Incheon, Korea, and Fukuoka, Japan, to Busan, Korea) have limited capacity and involve relatively significant travel time, air transport is the key means of inter-state travel in the region.

Second, as explained above, aviation blocs are emerging or have already emerged in most regions of the world. Due to the advantages of regional liberalization[241] and the unpopularity of global multilateral agreements, it seems very likely that the regional approach will be adopted more commonly and that the scope of regional liberalization will increase. One possible outcome of such collaboration is the creation of an aviation bloc that can increase the bargaining power of the bloc's members when negotiating with other parties (whether states or aviation blocs). If China, Japan, and Korea succeed in forming an aviation bloc, they too will be better able to respond with one voice to unilateral

---

236   Trilateral Cooperation Secretariat (TCS), *2013 Trilateral Statistics – Trade* (March 2014), online: <www.tcs-asia.org/skin/default/design/file_manager/files/tcs/TCS%20-%202013%20Trilateral%20Statistics-5.pdf>.
237   China National Tourism Administration, *To China (FOREIGN VISITOR ARRIVALS BY MODE OF TRANSPORT,JAN-DEC 2013)*, online: <http://en.cnta.gov.cn/html/2014-1/2014-1-16-15-55-74745.html>.
238   Japan National Tourism Organization, *2013 Foreign Visitors & Japanese Departures,* online: <https://www.jnto.go.jp/eng/ttp/sta/PDF/E2013.pdf>.
239   Lee Hyun-jeong, "Foreign visitors to Seoul exceed 10 million in 2013" *The Korea Herald* (23 January 2014), online: <www.koreaherald.com/view.php?ud=20140123000963>.
240   CAPA, "Outbound Chinese tourists to surpass 100 million in 2014. Northeast Asian airlines first to benefit" (16 July 2014), online: <http://centreforaviation.com/analysis/outbound-chinese-tourists-to-surpass-100-million-in-2014-northeast-asian-airlines-first-to-benefit-177128>.
241   See section 2.1 Overview; See also Jason Bonin "Regionalism in International Civil Aviation: A Re-evaluation of the Economic Regulation of International Air Transport in the Context of Economic Integration" (2008) 12 Singapore Year Book of International Law 113 at 122 (noting that regional approaches "represent a manifestation of cooperative political will, and as such a means to progressively liberalize the economic regulation of the air transport industry while protecting the legitimate interests of states in, as well as the suppliers and consumers of, air transportation."); See also Erwin Von Den Steinen, *National Interest and International Aviation* (Alphen aan den Rijn: Kluwer Law International, 2006) at 55. Although Steinen did not differentiate 'plurilateral' from 'regional' in the section: "The Emerging Plurilateral Alternative", most of the examples he enumerated are regional arrangements (*e.g.* Yamoussoukro, ASEAN, and the Caribbean Common Aviation Area). He notes that "[t]hese types of agreements are likely to be more comprehensive in scope than either bilaterals or multilaterals considered separately; plurilateral agreements will cover a wider range of issues, possibly even in greater depth, and can in fact evolve into a fairly systematic set of rules that create a unified regional aviation market.").

actions from other aviation blocs or larger countries and effectively protect their common interests.

Third, it is important to note that there are only three parties in these negotiations. This is an ideal number for efficient negotiations, and furthermore the three countries already have in place more than 50 trilateral consultative mechanisms on various matters including 18 ministerial meetings and over 100 cooperative projects in addition to the annual Trilateral Summit.[242] In particular, the China–Japan–Korea Free Trade Agreement (FTA) has been under negotiation since 2012 for the countries' mutual economic benefit,[243] and the China–Japan–Korea Ministerial Conference on Transport and Logistics has been held every two years since 2006.[244]

Fourth, Northeast Asia is one of the few regions where a stable, developed economy coexists with enormous potential for economic growth. According to the World Bank, China's GDP in 2013 ranked number two in the world, Japan number three, and Korea number fourteen,[245] while the annual growth rate in 2013 was 7.7 percent in China, 1.5 percent in Japan and 3.0 percent in Korea.[246] The economic strengths of the three countries are fairly evenly matched. This is a comparatively advantageous environment since the experience of other aviation blocs shows that an imbalance in the economic competitiveness of the states involved creates too many obstacles to overcome. But Northeast Asian open skies, on the other hand, would enjoy considerable synergy.

Last but not least, national carriers are by and large becoming more competitive, and LCCs are growing quickly in Northeast Asia. Seven legacy carriers in the region – namely, Air China, China Eastern, China Southern, Korean Air, Asiana Airlines, Japan Airlines, and All Nippon Airways (or ANA) – have positioned themselves as leading air carriers not only in Asia but also in the world. All of them are members of the branded global alliances (Skyteam, Star Alliance, and Oneworld) and generally have a high rank in fleet number, capacity and connectivity. (See the snapshot of the seven carriers.)

---

242 Trilateral Cooperation Secretariat, "Overview of TCS", online: <www.tcs-asia.org>.
243 Shannon Tiezzi, "China–Japan-South Korea Hold FTA Talks Despite Political Tension" *The Diplomat*, (5 March 2014), online: <http://thediplomat.com/2014/03/China–Japan-south-korea-hold-fta-talks-despite-political-tension> (noting that "South Korea's chief negotiator, Assistant Trade Minister Woo Tae-hee told, 'The three countries are well aware of the fact that the Korea–China–Japan FTA will stimulate the countries' economic growth while also contributing to regional integration.'").
244 The 5th Trilateral Ministerial Conference on Transport and Logistics was held in Yokohama, see Trilateral Cooperation News, online: <http://en.tcs-asia.org/dnb/board/view.php?board_name=2_1_news&view_id=245>.
245 China's GDP in 2013 was USD 9,240,270 million, Japan was USD 4,901,530 million and, Korea was USD 1,304,554 million. See The World Bank, "GDP 2013", online: <http://databank.worldbank.org/data/download/GDP.pdf>.
246 The World Bank, "GDP Growth", online: <http://data.worldbank.org/indicator/NY.GDP.MKTP.KD.ZG>.

Table 2.13 Northeast Asian Legacy Carrier Profile[247]

Country	Airlines (Code)	Fleet Size	Service Starting Date	Key share-holder and/or parent company	Main Hub
China	Air China (CA)	331	1988	China National Aviation Corporation (100%)	Beijing Capital International Airport
	China Eastern Airlines (MU)	385	1988	Chinese government (about 60%)	Shanghai's Pudong and Hongqiao Airports
	China Southern Airlines (CZ)	490	1988	Chinese government (more than 51%)	Guangzhou Baiyun Airport
Japan	Japan Airlines (JL)	163	1951	No key share-holder (no government share)	Tokyo Narita Airport / Tokyo Haneda Airport
	All Nippon Airways (NH)	214	1952	No key share-holder (no government share)	Tokyo Narita Airport / Tokyo Haneda Airport
Korea	Korean Air (KE)	155	1969	Hanjin Group (no government share)	Seoul Incheon International Airport
	Asiana Airlines (OZ)	85	1988	Kumho Asiana Group (no government share)	Seoul Incheon International Airport

In addition, all three countries are witnessing the emergence and significant growth of low cost carriers. (The role of LCCs will be discussed in Chapter 3.)

2.5.3 Barriers

However, Northeast Asian open skies face complicated impediments, which include not only purely aviation-related issues but also political and historical issues. Indeed, some Chinese scholars have suggested that political relations among the three countries are the *actual* barriers to Northeast Asian open skies.[248]

Conflicts rooted in political and historical disagreements are nothing new in the region. Tension still remains among the three states, and the antagonism continues. These are not negligible risk factors for sustainable developments in the Northeast Asian aviation market, and they are in, particular, major barriers for Northeast Asian open skies. For instance,

---

247 CAPA, "Profiles", online: <http://centreforaviation.com/profiles/>; airline homepage.
248 Zheng Xingwu, "China's Approaches to Aviation Market Liberalization in Northeast Asia: An Academic Viewpoint" in Yeon Myung Kim *et al.* eds., *Negotiating Strategies for Creating a Liberalized Air Transport Bloc in Northeast Asia* (Ilsan: Korea Transport Institute, 2009) 295 at 321.

when a territorial dispute flared up between China and Japan over uninhabited islands (Diaoyu in Chinese and Senkaku in Japanese) in September 2012, 18,800 tickets for travel between the two countries with All Nippon Airways (which accounts for about 24% of the capacity in the China–Japan aviation market) were immediately cancelled.[249] Subsequently, most air carriers operating between China and Japan cut their capacity.[250]

With respect to more aviation-related issues, the asymmetry between the three states is a fundamental obstacle to Northeast Asian open skies. Broadly speaking, there are three aspects to this asymmetry: different geographical locations, the varying competitiveness of their national carriers, and diverse market sizes.[251]

The imbalance arising from geographical location becomes significant in the context of the lucrative China–US market. Both Japan and Korea are strategically located for the China–US market. Moreover, there is no open skies agreement between China and the US. Although the US has initiated negotiations with China about open skies, China shows no signs of moving toward an open skies agreement with the US in the near term.[252]

Two stories are told to explain why China and the US have not reached an open skies agreement. China argues that since there are many unused frequencies for Chinese carriers, largely due to the visa restrictions on Chinese wanting to travel to the US, it does not feel the need to open up the China–US aviation market.[253] Li Jiaxiang, an influential aviation policymaker in China, stated in his 2008 book *Route to Fly* that the US government's strict visa policies and complicated immigration procedures put Chinese airlines at a serious disadvantage. Li also put an emphasis on the 1:4 ratio of Chinese nationals going to the US to US nationals going to China in the US–China aviation market at the time.[254]

However, China's "one-route-one-airline policy" is also blamed for the low market share of Chinese carriers.[255] This policy means that only one Chinese carrier is designated for each international route (though some changes have been noticed recently—see section 3.2.2.1 Protecting the Big Three Airlines). The policy is based on the national champion theory, which presumes that "with suppressed competition in domestic markets, firms

---

249 CAPA, "China's territorial disputes with Japan and the Philippines see traffic dips" (21 September 2012) online: <https://centreforaviation.com/analysis/chinas-territorial-disputes-with-japan-and-the-philippines-see-traffic-dips-83336>.
250 *Ibid.*
251 Yeon Myung Kim & Sean Seungho Lee "Chapter 9 Air Transport in Korea and Northeast Asia" in *The Impacts and Benefits of Structural Reforms in the Transport, Energy and Telecommunications Sector* (Singapore: Asia-Pacific Economic Cooperation, 2011) 219 at 226.
252 See, *e.g.*, Jay Boehmer, "Slots, Visas Stymie U.S.-China Open Skies", *Business Travel News* (11 April 2011), online: <www.businesstravelnews.com/article.aspx?id=20338&ida=Airlines&a=btn>.
253 *Ibid.*
254 Li Jiaxiang, *Route to Fly* (Beijing: China Machine Press, 2007) at 177 [translated by Jolyn Hong].
255 See *e.g.* CAPA, "Chinese carriers in for the long haul but face stumbling blocks along the way" (26 December 2012), online: <http://centreforaviation.com/analysis/chinese-carriers-in-for-the-long-haul-but-face-stumbling-blocks-along-the-way-91991>.

can achieve large scales which enable them to obtain large market shares and profits in export markets."[256]

In contrast with the Chinese plan, however, the one-route-one-airline policy has created more inefficiency and allowed foreign carriers to seize a greater market share on China–US routes.[257] Taking the Shanghai-Los Angeles route as one example, Delta will be the third US carrier to operate the route on a daily basis from July 2015, following United Airlines and American Airlines with one daily service each.[258] However, China Eastern is the sole Chinese carrier operating one daily flight on the route according to the one-route-one-airline policy. As a consequence, Chinese carriers on the route are hampered from reversing their under-representation in international markets.[259]

Indeed, there are some sectors—including the airline industry—in which the national champion theory rarely plays out, and competition is the very thing that brings innovation and improvements in the long run.[260] Although there are signs that China is adjusting its aviation policy (see section 3.2.2 China), the country is unlikely to reassess its attitude toward open skies with the US in the near future.[261]

In the absence of a China–US open skies agreement, Northeast Asian open skies entailing the exchange or generous or unlimited third and fourth freedom rights could enable Japanese and Korean carriers to use Tokyo and Incheon as gateway hubs from China to North America and vice versa.[262] This is a major hurdle to Northeast Asian open skies as illustrated below:

> The Northeast Asia Air Transportation Bloc may divert more China–US traffic via China–Japan or China–Korea to US, which will reduce the amount of both air traffic and revenues of airlines from China. Thus the airlines from China may look at the bloc as an 'I lose-you win' game, which must lead to strong opposition from those airlines. Furthermore the diversion will strengthen the East Asia hub positions of NRT (Tokyo) and ICN (Seoul), which could block the efforts of PEK (Beijing) and PVG (Shanghai) to become main hubs in East Asia. These airports may join in the opposition camp. Although there are prosperous bilateral aviation markets in this region, the unbalanced distribution

---

256 Xiaowen Fu & Tae Hoon Oum, "Dominant Carrier Performance and International Liberalization", Presented to OECD International Transport Forum (June 2014) at 5.
257 Alan Khee-Jin Tan, "Antitrust Immunity for Trans-Pacific Airline Alliance Agreements: Singapore and China as 'Beyond' Markets" 38 Air & Space L. 275 at 293. [Tan, "Antitrust Immunity"].
258 CAPA, "China Eastern, Delta and Hainan Airlines' new routes accelerate US-China aviation development" (23 February 2015), online: <http://centreforaviation.com/analysis/china-eastern-delta-and-hainan-airlines-new-routes-accelerate-us-china-aviation-development-210537>.
259 Tan, "Antitrust Immunity", *supra* note 257 at 293.
260 Fu & Oum, *supra* note 256 at 16.
261 Tan, "Antitrust Immunity", *supra* note 257 at 295.
262 Fu & Oum, *supra* note 256 at 19.

of benefits would prevent China's government from the determination in favor of the Bloc.²⁶³

The varying competitiveness of national carriers in Northeast Asia is another impediment. Although the gap of the competitiveness has been narrowed, China claims that Chinese air carriers' insufficient competitiveness is a major barrier to reaching open skies agreements.²⁶⁴ It is important to note that Li Jiaxiang, Director of the General Administration of Civil Aviation, explained his dream of transforming Air China into an "international super-carrier" in his book *Route to Fly*.²⁶⁵ Given that Korean and Japanese carriers, especially Korean Air, actively supply the China–US market by 6th freedom operations (*e.g.* Beijing-Seoul-Los Angeles),²⁶⁶ Northeast Asian open skies might be seen as a threat to Air China's ambitions of becoming an international super carrier.

Lastly is the issue of varying market sizes, which should come as no surprise. China has many more airports than Japan and Korea, and this number continues to increase.²⁶⁷ This may prompt Chinese carriers to be concerned that the network benefits of Northeast Asian open skies will primarily be enjoyed by Japanese and Korean airlines, as they will be able to connect more spoke markets to their hubs than Chinese airlines.²⁶⁸

2.5.4 Paths to Northeast Asian Open Skies

Admittedly, we have yet to see any compromises made or substantial results achieved involving Northeast Asian open skies. While sufficient justification can be provided for Northeast Asian open skies, it is not yet adequate to overcome the serious impediments to liberalization in the region. It is no secret that China, the biggest market and the least liberalized state, holds the key to Northeast Asian open skies. China still takes an extremely cautious stance in multilateral and regional approaches to air transport liberalization and is reluctant to engage in discussions about it.

As explored in this chapter, it is no surprise that bigger players are resistant to the trend of regional liberalization. Some examples are Indonesia in ASEAN, Egypt and Saudi Arabia

---

263 Zheng Xingwu, "China's Approaches to Aviation Market Liberalization in Northeast Asia: An Academic Viewpoint" in Yeon Myung Kim *et al.* eds., *Negotiating Strategies for Creating a Liberalized Air Transport Bloc in Northeast Asia* (Ilsan: Korea Transport Institute, 2009) 295 at 340.
264 Bin Li, "Open China's Skies or Not? – From the Perspective of a Chinese Scholar" (2010) 9 Issues of Aviation Law and Policy 209 at 212.
265 *Financial Times*, "China's private airlines facing cross-winds" (March 22, 2010), online at <www.ft.com/intl/cms/s/0/6c9e60bc-35d5-11df-aa43-00144feabdc0.html#axzz2eB2aRTYj>; See also online: <www.chinavitae.com/biography/Li_Jiaxiang%7C4095>.
266 See Tan, "Antitrust Immunity", *supra* note 257 at 287-295.
267 See *e.g.* Yang Xiuyun & Yu Hong, *China's airports: recent development and future challenges* (Singapore: East Asian Institute, National University of Singapore, 2010).
268 Fu & Oum, *supra* note 256 at 20.

among the Arab states, Brazil in Latin America, Fiji among the Pacific islands, and Nigeria in Africa. In contrast, smaller countries with competitive airlines are the drivers of regional liberalization. Some examples of this are Singapore in ASEAN, UAE in the Arab region, Chile in Latin America, and Ethiopia in Africa. Clearly, they have more to gain than to lose in their respective regional liberalization groups. It will not be easy to mitigate the deeply embedded aero-political implications of regional liberalization.

In the context of Northeast Asian open skies, the fact is that China has more to lose than Japan and Korea combined. We can easily imagine a three-way dynamic. On one side is Korea, which is motivated to promote open skies; on the other is China, which is ambivalent to the idea; and somewhere in the middle is Japan, which has a bigger market than Korea but a smaller one than China. China's assessment about whether (and to what extent) it would benefit from regional liberalization in Northeast Asia is the most important factor determining the future of a single aviation market in Northeast Asia.

Meanwhile, China, Japan, and Korea have started to cooperate closely on bilateral liberalization in recent years. In fact, one of the three bilateral agreements in the region, the Korea-Japan air service agreement, has already established open skies, removing all restrictions on Tokyo's Narita airport in 2013. Another bilateral air services agreement between China and Japan is a *quasi*-open skies agreement allowing unlimited 3rd and 4th freedom flights except to Beijing, Shanghai, and Tokyo. Thus, the China–Korea air services agreement is the only restrictive one among the three bilateral agreements in Northeast Asia. While Korea is keenly interested in reaching an open skies agreement with China, China is concerned that the formidable Korean Air and Asiana will dominate the market.[269]

Interestingly, Beijing is beginning to appreciate the "Air India Syndrome," by which the Indian flag carrier was protected almost to death, letting other carriers become more efficient.[270] Li Jiaxiang confirmed that the regulator plans to study new policies to promote low-cost carriers and also urged established airlines to learn from successful low-cost airlines to improve management standards and operating efficiency.[271] (China's national aviation policy will be discussed in Chapter 3.)

The future role of LCCs in Northeast Asia cannot be overstated. In 2013, LCCs accounted for only 9 percent of intra-Northeast Asia seats compared to over 50 percent in Southeast Asia.[272] This stark difference indirectly shows the potential for LCCs in

---

269 CAPA, "Korean Air seeks new markets after betting the house on N America, seemingly without SkyTeam support" (30 September 2013), online: <http://centreforaviation.com/analysis/korean-air-seeks-new-markets-after-betting-the-house-on-n-america-seemingly-without-skyteam-support-130189>.
270 CAPA, "North Asian LCC, Round 1: Inertia prevails over innovation in 2013" *Airline Leader* 18 (Aug-Sep 2013) 36 at 38.
271 Joanne Chiu, "China's Air Regulator Will Consider Ways to Boost Budget-Carrier Market" The *Wall Street Journal* (29 July 2013), online: <http://stream.wsj.com/story/latest-headlines/SS-2-63399/SS-2-288619/>.
272 CAPA, "North Asian LCC, Round 1: Inertia prevails over innovation in 2013" *Airline Leader* 18 (Aug-Sep 2013) 36 at 39.

Northeast Asia. Most Northeast Asian LCCs are well established now, and more LCCs are in the process of entering the market. (Chapter 3 will further examine LCCs in Northeast Asia.)

In particular, China-based Spring Airlines is the largest LCC and is recognized as one of the most efficient LCCs in Northeast Asia.[273] It has even started a Japanese subsidiary, Spring Airlines Japan (it will be discussed in Chapter 4.) Since the new Chinese LCC policy will likely include open skies on short-haul routes,[274] this policy will have tremendous impact on the discussion of regional liberalization in Northeast Asia.

Obviously, the seven major legacy carriers in Northeast Asia will continue to play an important role in Northeast Asian open skies. Fu and Oum assert that protecting China's big three airlines (the largest carriers in Asia and the largest carriers in the world within a decade) is like "treating giants as babies."[275] Once China works harder to reform its aviation policy, change is likely to come without delay. Meanwhile, the airline alliances in which Northeast Asian legacy carriers participate will play an important role in developing the idea of Northeast Asian open skies. (Chapter 5 will discuss this topic.)

2.6 Conclusion

This chapter compared the different regional liberalization models from the legal and aero-political perspectives. As demonstrated in this chapter, discussions about regional open skies agreements are underway in most parts of the world, and regional liberalization is becoming increasingly common. This contrasts with the fact that not a single global multilateral approach to the economic aspects of international air transport has ever been successfully implemented.

However, it is clear that regional liberalization is not free from the "winners and losers" paradigm. Regional liberalization tends to be less appealing to bigger countries and more appealing to smaller countries with competitive airlines. Thus, in the process of promoting Northeast Asian open skies, we must bear in mind the aero-political challenges that liberalization commonly faces.

From the next chapter, the focus will shift to Northeast Asia. Chapter 3: Market Access Issues in Northeast Asia will provide an in-depth analysis of market access issues in air transport with a focus on Northeast Asia.

---

273 *Ibid.* at 37-38.
274 *Ibid.* at 38.
275 Fu & Oum, *supra* note 256 at 29.

3 Market Access Issues in Northeast Asia

3.1 Market Access Restrictions in International Air Transport

3.1.1 Overview

In the context of international trade, market access generally describes "the extent to which an imported good or service can compete in another market with goods or services made there."[1] As previously discussed, however, international air transport has developed separately from general governance of international trade mainly because of its exceptional nature.

Theoretically, one could ask whether the air transport sector is really that peculiar, given that air transport could be regarded as trade in services that include, among others, banking, telecommunications, and tourism. In fact, there is no convincing explanation (at least economically) as to why international air transport is so different and why it should be regarded as exceptional. But though the justifications for this status are groundless (or weak at best), the reality is that the airline industry is likely to retain its exceptional status. (See section 1.3 Exceptionalism in Economic Air Transport.)

Nonetheless, understanding the definition of market access under international trade law, and especially the WTO's General Agreement on Trade in Services (GATS), is worthwhile for comparing the similarities and differences in the elements of market access in air transport. In particular, GATS is recognized as having gone the furthest among the various WTO agreements in seeking to overcome market access impediments caused by globalization and the rapid growth of trade in services.[2]

Although GATS does not explicitly define market access, Article 16 (Market Access) of GATS lists six types of measures that are prohibited in sectors where market access commitments are undertaken.[3] Interestingly, the first three have significant implications

---

[1] Walter Goode, *Dictionary of Trade Policy Terms*, 5th ed. (Cambridge: Cambridge University Press, 2007) under the word "Market access".
[2] Ibid.
[3] *General Agreement on Trade in Services*, 15 April 1994, 1869 U.N.T.S.183, art.16, 33 ILM 1167 (entered into force 1 January 1995) [GATS]. "Art XVI Market Access – 2. In sectors where market-access commitments are undertaken, the measures which a Member shall not maintain or adopt either on the basis of a regional subdivision or on the basis of its entire territory, unless otherwise specified in its Schedule, are defined as: (a) limitations on the number of service suppliers whether in the form of numerical quotas, monopolies, exclusive service suppliers or the requirements of an economic needs test; (b) limitations on the total value of service transactions or assets in the form of numerical quotas or the requirement of an economic needs test; (c) limitations on the total number of service operations or on the total quantity of service output expressed in terms of designated numerical units in the form of quotas or the requirement of an economic

for the market access elements of international air transport. These three measures—the number of service suppliers, the total value of service transactions, and the total number of service operations—conceptually match the international air transport elements of carrier designation, capacity, and frequency.

Despite the notable similarities with general trade in services, it is an undeniable fact that air transport does have some unique aspects. This difference largely derives from the scope of "market." In air transport, the market is traditionally defined as each individual route that connects a point of origin to a point of destination (O&D city pair). Indeed, the concept of the "freedom of the air," the underlying framework for air transport market access that was discussed in Chapter 1, is based on the O&D city pair market classification.

In the following sections, the elements of market access liberalization in international air transport will be elaborated. Prior to this explanation, however, it is important to grasp the relationship between market access and ownership and control requirements in the context of an air services agreement. (Ownership and control requirements have related but different implications for domestic laws that will be reviewed in Chapter 4.)

In a nutshell, ownership and control requirements can be regarded as the precondition for market access. The crucial prerequisite for market access is whether an air carrier is *entitled* to operate in the market. Since ownership and control requirements are essentially the test used to assess entitlement, they are directly intertwined with market access. In other words, an airline from State A can be designated by State A to enjoy the market access privileges granted by State B pursuant to an air services agreement between State A and State B. To do so, an airline from State A must satisfy the ownership and control conditions under the said air services agreement as well as the national law of State A. (Ownership and control issues will be separately discussed in Chapter 4.)

3.1.2   Direct Market Access Issues

3.1.2.1   Carrier Designation

A designated airline means an airline that has been designated and authorized in accordance with the bilateral air services agreement in question. An airline that satisfies the ownership and control requirements in domestic law and the air services agreement is entitled to be a designated airline. There are three types of designation systems: single designation (one

---

needs test; (d) limitations on the total number of natural persons that may be employed in a particular service sector or that a service supplier may employ and who are necessary for, and directly related to, the supply of a specific service in the form of numerical quotas or the requirement of an economic needs test; (e) measures which restrict or require specific types of legal entity or joint venture through which a service supplier may supply a service; and (f) limitations on the participation of foreign capital in terms of maximum percentage limit on foreign shareholding or the total value of individual or aggregate foreign investment."

carrier on each side),[4] dual designation (two carriers on each side),[5] and multiple designation.[6]

Historically, the Bermuda type 1 agreement, the prototype for many bilateral air services agreements, adopted the multiple designation system.[7] However, many post-Bermuda I agreements applied the single designation system largely because many states had only one international carrier.[8] States with a single international airline were reluctant to accept dual designation or multiple designation due to the fear of open competition with countries with several international air carriers such as the US.[9]

The US traditionally insisted on a system of multiple designation by using the language "carrier or carriers" in the carrier designation provision.[10] Even though the language did not limit the number of designated carriers *per se*, many states interpreted the words to mean a maximum of two, and the US government continued to designate only as many US carriers as there were foreign carriers operating in the relevant bilateral market.[11] The US deregulatory initiative in 1978 clarified the carrier designation provision by changing the relevant language to "as many airlines as it wishes," which more clearly indicates unlimited multiple designation.[12]

As many states started to have more than two international carriers over this time period, it was necessary to switch from single designation to dual or multiple designation.

---

4   See ICAO, *ICAO Template Air Services Agreement* (28 September 2009) at 9. "Article 3 Designation and authorization [Traditional] Each Party shall have the right to designate in writing to the other Party an airline to operate the agreed services [in accordance with this Agreement] and to withdraw or alter such designation." This traditional approach refers to one airline or a single designation, online: <www.icao.int/Meetings/AMC/MA/ICAN2009/templateairservicesagreements.pdf>. [ICAO, "Template Agreement"].

5   *Ibid.* at 10. "Article 3 Designation and authorization [Transitional] Each Party shall have the right to designate in writing to the other Party one or more airlines to operate the agreed services [in accordance with this Agreement] and to withdraw or alter such designation." The transitional approach refers to one or more airlines or multiple designation."

6   *Ibid.* at 12. "Article 3 Designation and authorization [Full liberalization] Each Party shall have the right to designate in writing to the other Party as many airlines as it wishes to operate the agreed services [in accordance with this Agreement] and to withdraw or alter such designation." The full liberalization approach refers to many airlines or puts no quantitative limit on the number of airlines that can be designated."

7   See *Air Service Agreement Between the Government of the United States of America and the Government of the United Kingdom of Great Britain and Northern Ireland*, signed at Bermuda, 11 February 1946, Article 2 using the language of "air carrier or carriers."

8   Paul Dempsey, *Public International Air Law* (Montreal: Institute of Air and Space Law, 2008) at 585. [Dempsey, "Air Law"].

9   Brian F. Havel & Gabriel S. Sanchez, *The Principles and Practices of International Aviation Law* (New York: Cambridge University Press, 2014) at 101. [Havel & Sanchez, "Aviation Law"].

10 Dempsey, "Air Law", *supra* note 8 at 584-585.

11 See Peter P.C. Haanappel, *The Law and Policy of Air Space and Outer Space: A Comparative Approach* (Alphen aan den Rijn: Kluwer Law International, 2009) at 117-118. [Haanappel, "Law and Policy"]; See also *ibid.* 586.

12 See Dempsey, *ibid.* at 586.

Since unlimited multiple designation removes a fundamental market entry barrier for new entrants, it is one of the most important characteristics of market access liberalization.

3.1.2.2 Route Designation

Most bilateral agreements only have one article in the main text of the agreement dealing with the exchange of rights about routes and leave all the crucial details to an annex labelled "Route Schedule."[13] While the article in the main text typically grants the first freedom (overflight) and second freedom (technical landing), the remaining freedoms are typically enumerated in the annex and an accompanying Memorandum of Understanding, which is periodically modified.[14]

The traditional approach limits air transport services to cities named on specified route(s).[15] Departing from the restricted approach, there are various approaches to liberalizing the designation of routes, thereby increasing the level of market access. Route designation can provide for open entry for the third and fourth freedom traffic;[16] open entry for the fifth freedom traffic; explicitly include unlimited sixth freedom;[17] open seventh freedom for all-cargo services;[18] open seventh freedom for passenger services and limited cabotage;[19] and open eighth and ninth freedom rights to parties in both international and domestic markets.[20]

Although air services agreements seldom explicitly use the aviation jargon "freedoms of the air,"[21] these freedoms are conceptually embedded in route designation. Since route designation specifies routes (or opens entry to all routes) on which the designated carriers are allowed to operate, it essentially provides the architecture for exercising the nine freedoms of the air.[22]

---

13 Haanappel, "Law and Policy", *supra* note 11 at 115.
14 *Ibid.* at 115 & 117.
15 See ICAO, "Template Agreement", *supra* note 4 at 88. "Annex I Route schedules [Traditional] A. Routes to be operated by the designated airline (or airlines) of Party A: From (named cities) in Party A via (intermediate points) to (named cities) in Party B and beyond (beyond points)."
16 *Ibid.* "Annex I Route schedules [Transitional Option 1] A. Routes to be operated by the designated airline (or airlines) of Party A: From any point or points in Party A via (intermediate points) to any point or points in Party B and beyond (beyond points)."
17 *Ibid.* at 89. "Annex I Route schedules [Transitional Option 2] A. Routes to be operated by the designated airline (or airlines) of Party A: 1. From points behind Party A via Party A and intermediate points to any point or points in Party B and beyond."
18 *Ibid.* "Annex I Route schedules [Transitional Option 2] A. Routes to be operated by the designated airline (or airlines) of Party A: 2. For all-cargo service(s), between Party B and any point or points."
19 *Ibid.* "Annex I Route schedules [Transitional Option 3] A. Routes to be operated by the designated airline (or airlines) of Party A: From points to and from the territory of Party B with limited cabotage."
20 *Ibid.* at 90. "Annex I Route schedules [Full liberalization] A. Routes to be operated by the designated airline (or airlines) of Party A: Points to, from and within the territory of Party B."
21 Havel & Sanchez, "Aviation Law", *supra* note 9 at 96.
22 See Figure 1.1 The Nine Freedoms of the Air in Chapter 1.

3.1.2.3 Capacity and Frequency

Capacity in air transport is the supply of passenger seats and cargo space by airlines, and it can be expressed in the total number of seats or volume of cargo space.[23] Broadly speaking, capacity embodies frequency, the number of flights flown over a given time period. Frequency specifically refers to the number of flights per day (usually on heavily traveled short-haul routes) or per week (usually for less traveled long-haul routes).[24] There are three types of capacity provisions in air services agreements: predetermination, Bermuda 1, and free-determination.[25]

Predetermination is the least liberalized but most widely used type of capacity regulation.[26] It is often called "Bermuda II type," referring to the air services agreement that the US and the UK adopted in 1977, once again, in Bermuda. After the UK denounced the Bermuda I Agreement of 1946 due to its dissatisfaction over capacity provisions under the agreement, the US and the UK reached a new agreement (Bermuda II) that, among other changes,[27] specifically limits capacity. Peter Haanappel noted the significance of Article 11, Paragraph 5, of the Bermuda II agreement,[28] which requires states to avoid overcapacity.[29] Article 11 of the Bermuda II agreement was essentially designed to prevent Pan Am and TWA (American carriers that are now both defunct) from exercising their traffic rights to a much greater extent than British Airways in the North Atlantic market.[30]

Under a predetermination capacity article, designated airlines may offer capacity based on predetermination in which both states jointly agree in advance on the total capacity to

---

23 Haanappel, "Law and Policy", *supra* note 11 at 120.
24 Ibid.
25 For details, see ICAO, *Policy and Guidance Material on the Economic Regulation of International Air Transport*, 2008, ICAO Doc 9587.
26 See ICAO, "Template Agreement", supra note 4 at 32. Article 16 Capacity [Traditional – Predetermination].
27 See Brian Havel, *Beyond Open Skies: A New Regime for International Aviation* (Alphen aan den Rijn, Kluwer Law International: 2009) at 116 -119. [Havel, "Open Skies"].
28 Article 11 paragraph 5 of *Bermuda II agreement* "(5) The Contracting Parties recognize that airline actions leading to excess capacity or to the under provision of capacity can both run counter to the interests of the travelling public. Accordingly, in the particular case of combination air services on the North Atlantic routes specified in paragraph (1) of Annex 2, they have agreed to establish the procedures set forth in Annex 2. With respect to other routes and services, if one Contracting Party believes that the operations of a designated airline or airlines of the other Contracting Party have been inconsistent with the principles set forth in this Article, it may request consultations pursuant to Article 16 (Consultations) for the purpose of reviewing the operations in question to determine whether they are in conformity with these principles. If such consultations there shall be taken into consideration the operations of all airlines serving the market in question and designated by the Contracting Party whose airline or airlines are under review. In the Contracting Parties conclude that the operations under review are not in conformity with the principles set forth in the Article, they may decide upon appropriate corrective or remedial measures, except that, where frequency or capacity limitations are already provided for a route specified in Annex 1, the Contracting Parties may not vary those limitations or impose additional limitations except by amendment of this Agreement."
29 Peter Haanappel, "Bilateral Air Transport Agreements – 1913-1980" (1980) 5 International Trade Law Journal 241 at 260.
30 Ibid.

be offered on each route.[31] Predetermination typically aims to equal competition *exactly* by splitting capacity fifty-fifty.[32]

Bermuda 1, as the name suggests, originally comes from the Bermuda 1 agreement between the US and UK in 1946. Under Bermuda 1, designated airlines determine their capacity individually based on the capacity principle that both states have adopted subject to *ex post facto* review by both states.[33] The capacity principle under the Bermuda 1 agreement states that an airline's capacity should be primarily determined by traffic demand between the two states (third and fourth freedom traffic) and that fifth freedom traffic should be only a secondary consideration.[34]

Compared to many later agreements of the fifty-fifty predetermined type, Bermuda 1 could qualify as liberal.[35] That is, Bermuda 1 initially allows each airline the freedom to determine its own capacity based on its analysis of market requirements, even if that capacity can later be challenged by *ex post facto* review.[36]

Free determination is widely found in open skies agreements. Under a free-determination capacity provision, designated airlines can choose what capacity to offer without government approval or intervention. Free determination is a market-oriented approach, and genuine market access liberalization is only possible with this type of capacity provision.

Indeed, carrier designation, route designation, and capacity (and frequency) are three issues that directly determine market access liberalization, and full market access is impossible when any of these three elements is restricted.

3.1.3 Indirect Market Access Issues

For air carriers, the issues of constraints on airport capacity, restrictions on airspace use and visa policies are as important for their operation as issues related to direct market access. Even in a legally liberalized market in which direct market access issues have been more or less solved, air carriers seeking new commercial opportunities may encounter serious difficulties due to indirect market access issues.

---

31 See ICAO, "Template Agreement", *supra* note 4 at 33. Article 16 Capacity [Traditional – Predetermination]
32 Havel, "Open Skies" *supra* note 27 at 118; See also Havel & Sanchez, "Aviation Law", *supra* note 9 at 103 (explaining that "[T]he notion that an airline has the primacy claim on the custom of its own national is part of a "managed trade" mindset in the supply of international air transport services…Managed trade is the use of protectionist artifices such as preset restrictions on imports by or from a foreign supplier to favor proportionally the weaker domestic supplier.").
33 See ICAO, "Template Agreement", *supra* note 4 at 33. Article 16 Capacity [Transitional – Bermuda I].
34 See Dempsey, "Air Law", *supra* note 8 at 524; see also Barry Diamond, "The Bermuda Agreement Revisited: A Look at the Past, Present and Future of Bilateral Air Transport Agreements" (1975) 41 J. Air L. & Com 419 at 444-447.
35 Havel, "Open Skies" *supra* note 27 at 112.
36 See ICAO, "Template Agreement", *supra* note 4 at 33. Article 16 Capacity [Transitional – Bermuda I].

3.1.3.1 Airport Capacity

The basic problem with constraints on airport capacity is the fact that demand exceeds supply for airport use. As growth in air traffic surpasses the available runways, parking, and passenger processing capacity in terminals, airport slot shortage is becoming an issue in many airports around the world.[37] Airport slots are defined as "specific time periods allotted for an aircraft to land or take off at an airport."[38]

More specifically, airport capacity can be divided into "airside" capacity and "landside" capacity. Airside capacity generally refers to the number of aircraft operations (takeoffs and landings) that the airport and the supporting air traffic control (ATC) system can accommodate in a unit of time, while landside capacity refers to the number of passengers that an airport terminal can accommodate.[39]

Clearly, the fundamental solution to capacity shortage is to increase capacity. However, expanding airport infrastructure is by no means an easy project, and it requires a long-term approach. Furthermore, since many of the world's highest-demand airports are in dense urban areas, expanding these airports significantly is even more problematic.[40] Therefore, in the short term, a more realistic question is how slots can be allocated effectively and fairly.

In brief, slots are negotiated with airport authorities, and the incumbent airlines at the airport normally act as slot coordinators. Thus, airport authorities and government regulators are faced with the dilemma of striking a balance between the interests of incumbents that have spent years investing to establish their presence and the interests of new airlines.[41]

---

37 ICAO, *Slot Allocation*, ICAO Doc. ATConf/6-WP/11 (10 December 2012) at 1-2 (noting that "[A]ccording to the International Air Transport Association (IATA), the total number of capacity constrained airports that have been labelled as a fully-coordinated or Level 3 Airport(airports where the demand for runway and gate access exceeds the capacity of the airport, resulting in the need for slots to be allocated to airlines through the IATA Schedule Coordination System) subject to slot allocation under the IATA Schedule Coordination System continues to increase: 136 in 2000, 155 in 2010, and by 2012, the number is expected to reach 159 (104 in Europe, of which 92 are in the 27 EU Member States, 43 in Asia Pacific, and the remaining 11 scattered in the Middle East, North America, and South Africa). In addition, 121 airports across the world are experiencing some level of congestion. If traffic volumes continue to increase at a pace faster than investment in capacity expansion, it is expected that many of these 121 airports experiencing congestion will become fully-coordinated or Level 3 airports."), online: <www.icao.int/Meetings/atconf6/Documents/WorkingPapers/ATConf6-wp011_en.pdf>. [ICAO, "Slot Allocation"].
38 *Ibid.* at 1.
39 U.S., Congress, Office of Technology Assessment, *Airport and Air Traffic Control System* (1982) (Washington, D.C.: U.S. Government Printing Office, 1982) at 101.
40 Havel & Sanchez, "Aviation Law", *supra* note 9 at 116.
41 Isabella H.Ph. Diederiks-Verschoor, *An Introduction to Air Law*, 9th ed. revised by Pablo Mendes de Leon (Alphen aan den Rijn: Kluwer Law International, 2012) at 89.

Many problems caused by slot shortage have been identified[42] (the slot shortage issue and its implications for Northeast Asia will be separately discussed in section 3.2 below), and various approaches to reducing these problems have been suggested.[43] Since the issue of slot allocation is also related to restricting night flights (also known as the airport curfew),[44] it must be balanced with the issue of aircraft noise at the airport as well. In fact, slot allocation is a vast legal and economic topic, and a detailed analysis is outside the scope of this research.

Nonetheless, it is important to note that the insufficiency of slots affects the ability of air carriers to exercise market access rights granted to states under air services agreements.[45] Even though slot issues are typically not dealt with in bilateral air services agreements, which determine market access rights, slot shortage has also been adduced as a barrier to opening market access in some states.[46]

3.1.3.2 Airspace Use

One of the most important principles in international air law is Article 1 of the Chicago Convention (1944), which states that "[T]he contracting States recognize that every State has complete and exclusive sovereignty over the air space above its territory." Thus, state sovereignty over airspace means that air transport is subject to permission or consent from the governments of the states from which a flight takes off or lands or that it overflies.[47]

In protecting the sovereignty of their national airspace, most countries seek to strike a balance between the freedom enjoyed by various types of civil aviation and military activities by the national air force, ranging from training flights to real emergencies.[48] However, some states have disproportionately demarcated their airspace for military activity, creating serious operational limitations for airlines that are scheduled to depart, land, or overfly. For instance, the military controls some 80 percent of China's total national

---

42   See generally, ICAO, *Slot Allocation*, ICAO Doc. ATConf/6-WP/11 (10 December 2012) at 7, Appendix B Present and Future Airport Capacity Constraints, online: <www.icao.int/Meetings/atconf6/Documents/WorkingPapers/ATConf6-wp011_en.pdf>.
43   See generally, ICAO, *Regulatory Implications of the Allocation of Flight Departure and Arrival Slots at International Airports*, ICAO Circular 283 (2001); Achim Czerny et al eds., *Airport Slots: International Experiences and Options for Reform* (Burlington: Ashgate, 2008).
44   See ICAO, *Night Flight Restriction*, ICAO Doc. ATConf/6-WP/8 (10 December 2012) at 2 (noting that "[A]s of mid-2012, approximately 250 domestic and international airports worldwide imposed some form of night time operational restrictions", online: <www.icao.int/Meetings/atconf6/Documents/WorkingPapers/ATConf6-wp008-rev_en.pdf>.
45   ICAO, "Slot Allocation", *supra* note 37 at 2.
46   See *e.g.* the Philippines's position at section 2.3 and China's position at section 3.2.
47   Henri Wassenbergh, *Principles and Practices in Air Transport Regulation* (Paris: Institut du Transport Aérien, 1993) at 82.
48   Alan Williams, *Contemporary Issues Shaping China's Civil Aviation Policy: Balancing International with Domestic Priorities* (Burlington, VT: Ashgate, 2009) at 194.

airspace,[49] which is an enormous obstacle to market access for all airlines flying from, to, or over China, including the Chinese airlines themselves. (The problems related to China's congested airspace will be further discussed in section 3.2.2.3 Managing Airspace Better.)

Another market access issue relating to airspace use has to do with charging royalties for overflight. The Russian Federation has been openly accused of illicitly collecting money from foreign airlines in exchange for granting them the right to overfly Russian territory along the trans-Siberian route.[50] Even though charging money for overflight is a breach of Article 15 of the Chicago Convention,[51] this improper practice has continued.

A fundamental reason for charging a fee for the trans-Siberian route is presumably to protect Russian carriers, especially Aeroflot. However, it is not even clear whether this money is being used to shore up Aeroflot's bottom line. Indeed, it was reported in 1999 that about USD 600 million of overflight fees charged by Aeroflot had been laundered and transferred to the Swiss bank accounts of former Aeroflot executives.[52]

Russia has argued that since Russian carriers should have the same rights for flights between Europe and Northeast Asia (even though those flights do not touch down on Russian soil and have no direct link to the Russian market), Russian carriers must be compensated for not using these rights.[53] If Russian carriers use their traffic rights to a lesser extent than European and Northeast Asian airlines, those carriers can pay to "borrow" unused rights from Russian carriers.[54]

This bizarre position has indirectly affected the level of market access that is legally allowed by air services agreements between the states of the EU and of Northeast Asia, whose airlines must overfly Russian airspace to exercise traffic rights under these agreements. According to the assessment of the Association of European Airlines (AEA), European carriers paid approximately USD 430 million on overflight royalties to Russian airlines in 2008.[55] Thus, European and Northeast Asian carriers must take into account the additional operating cost—a substantial amount of money—when they plan to operate routes between Europe and Northeast Asia.

In addition, alternatives to Siberian routes can push up airlines' fuel costs. For instance, one European airline said that avoiding Siberian airspace—for example, by flying further south over Kazakhstan—would add 30 minutes to eastbound flights and 45 minutes to

---

49 *Ibid.* at 196.
50 See *e.g.* Michael Milde, "Some question marks about the price of 'Russian air'" (2000) 49 Zeitschrift für Luft- und Weltraumrecht (ZLW) 147, [Milde, "Russian Air"]; Johannes Baur, "EU-Russia Aviation Relations and the Issue of Siberian Overflights" (2010) 35 Air & Space L. 225.
51 Chicago Convention Article 15 "…No fees, dues or other charges shall be imposed by any contracting State in respect solely of the right of transit over or entry into or exit from its territory of any aircraft of a contracting State or persons or property thereon."
52 Milde, "Russian Air", *supra* note 50 at 148.
53 Baur, *supra* note 50 at 226.
54 *Ibid.* at 227.
55 *Ibid.* at 230.

westbound ones.[56] Obviously, this is a huge burden for carriers that wish to exercise their market access rights.

3.1.3.3 Visa Openness

The relationship between air transport and tourism is an "intrinsic symbiosis."[57] Since visa policies are among the most important formalities influencing tourism, visa openness constitutes an indirect market access issue in international air transport. For instance, the visa restrictions on Chinese wanting to travel to the US have been identified as the main reason why China is not interested in an open skies agreement with the US.[58] Li Jiaxiang also said that the US government's strict visa policies put Chinese airlines at a serious disadvantage.[59]

On a global level, gradual progress has been made in the area of visa relaxation. Overseas travel used to be heavily impacted by customs regulations and visa formalities. According to the study by the United Nations World Tourism Organization (UNWTO) in 2014, 19 percent of the world's population is not required to obtain a visa at all when traveling for tourism purposes while another 19 percent of the population can apply for either an electronic visa (eVisa) or a visa on arrival.[60] Nonetheless, 62 percent of the global population still needs to obtain a visa before traveling overseas.[61]

UNWTO categorizes the functions of visas as follows: "to ensure security; to control immigration and limit the entry, duration of stay, or activities of travelers; to generate revenue and apply measures of reciprocity; and to ensure a destination's carrying capacity is not exceeded and control tourism demand."[62] Compelling or legitimate as these rationales may be, travelers generally see visas as an inconvenient formality. Due to visa-related inconveniences, some potential travelers decide not to make a particular journey or end up choosing an alternative destination.

In contrast, visa facilitation leads to the growth of the tourism market and, as a natural consequence, the aviation market as well. For instance, after the US expanded its visa waiver program in November 2008 to include the Czech Republic, Estonia, Hungary, Latvia, Lithuania, Slovakia, and Korea, arrivals from these countries collectively grew 46

---

56 Andrew Parker, "Moscow kickback set to squeeze western airlines" *Financial Times* (6 August 2014).
57 Taleb Rifai (Secretary General, United Nations World Tourism Organization), Keynote Address to the Sixth ICAO Worldwide Air Transport Conference, 18 March 2013), online: <www.icao.int/Meetings/atconf6/Documents/ATConf-6_Speech_UNWTO_en.pdf>.
58 Jay Boehmer, "Slots, Visas Stymie U.S.-China Open Skies", *Business Travel News* (11 April 2011), online: <www.businesstravelnews.com/article.aspx?id=20338&ida=Airlines&a=btn>.
59 Li Jiaxiang, *Route to Fly* (Beijing: China Machine Press, 2007) at 177 [translated by Jolyn Hong].
60 UNWTO (World Tourism Organization), *Visa Openness Report 2014* (November 2014) at 6, online: <http://dtxtq4w60xqpw.cloudfront.net/sites/all/files/docpdf/2014visaopennessreport2ndprinting.pdf>.
61 *Ibid.* at 6.
62 *Ibid.* at 3.

percent over the following three-year period.⁶³ To meet the surge of Korean passengers wanting to go to the US, and in particular tourist destinations such as Hawaii, Korean Air and Asiana Airlines increased their frequencies and Hawaiian Airlines started to operate in Korea.

According to research jointly conducted by UNWTO and the World Travel & Tourism Council (WTTC), easing visa requirements causes tourist arrivals from the affected market to increase from 5 percent to 25 percent per year.⁶⁴ Thus, visa policies restrain the actual demand of consumers, and relaxing visa processes and policies indirectly but significantly affects the aviation market.

Northeast Asian states are in the process of relaxing their visa policies toward their neighbors' nationals. Table 3.1 below shows the status of visa requirements among the three countries and their nationals.

Table 3.1   Visa Status between Three Countries and Their Nationals

Nationality	Destination		
	China	**Japan**	**Korea**
Chinese	--	Visa Required	Visa Required (except Jeju Island)
Japanese	No Visa Required	--	No Visa Required
Korean	Visa Required	No Visa Required	--

Among the six scenarios above, three options are already open (that is, no visa is required) and the remaining three options are when 1) Chinese enter Japan; 2) Chinese enter Korea; and 3) Koreans enter China. It should be noted that it is not too inconvenient for Koreans to obtain a Chinese visa.

Interestingly, both Korea and Japan are in the process of relaxing visa requirements for Chinese visitors. In addition to adding China to Korea's visa waiver program for Jeju Island in 2006, Korea started to provide multiple-entry visas to select demographics of Chinese citizens and double-entry visas allowing Chinese citizens to enter the country

---

63   UNWTO & World Travel & Tourism Council (WTTC), *The Impact of Visa Facilitation in ASEAN Member States* (January 2014) at 15, online: <www.wttc.org/-/media/files/reports/policy%20research/impact_asean.pdf>.

64   *Ibid.* at 8.; In the study of ASEAN market, the potential gain in international tourism arrivals by visa facilitation policies is between 6 million and 10 million, representing an increase between 3.0% and 5.1%, see *ibid.* at 10; In another similar study, it was projected that by improving visa facilitation, the APEC region stands to gain 38 to 57 million international tourist arrivals, between 9% and 13% above the baseline forecast under current visa policies, see World Tourism Organization (UNWTO) & World Travel & Tourism Council (WTTC), *The Impact of Visa Facilitation in APEC Economies* (Madrid: Centro Español de Derechos Reprográfico, 2013) at 21, online: <www.wttc.org/-/media/files/reports/policy%20research/the_impact_of_visa_facilitation_in_apec_economies_high_res_2oct13.pdf>, at 5-6.

twice within a set period of time for tourism purposes.[65] In a similar fashion, Japan announced a series of reforms for Chinese visitors in October 2014.[66]

3.2 NATIONAL POLICIES ON MARKET ACCESS IN NORTHEAST ASIA

3.2.1 Overview

As explained in previous chapters, this research principally deals with the architecture of international treaties with respect to economic air transport. Undeniably, however, there are considerable national policy aspects that also affect international treaties. Indeed, it has been argued that much of the substance of air services agreements is a matter of policy based on economic considerations.

At this juncture, it is worth mentioning that economic analysis of international law, or the "law and economics" methodology,[67] has received special attention in the area of international law.[68] In particular, adherents to rational choice theory in the law and economics school insist that "states are assumed to be rational, self-interested, and able to identify and pursue their interests"[69] and "states only enter into agreements when doing so makes them *better off*."[70] Since international air transport entails economic and other

---

65 APEC, *Ibid.* at 21.
66 See CAPA, "Japan relaxes Chinese visas to stimulate visitor & airline growth, following Southeast Asia success" (13 January 2015), online: <http://centreforaviation.com/analysis/japan-relaxes-chinese-visas-to-stimulate-visitor--airline-growth-following-southeast-asia-success-204156>. "(1) Requirements for multiple-entry visa for applicants with a short-term business purpose, and for cultural or intellectual figures will be partially relaxed. (2) The financial requirement will be relaxed for individual tourists applying for multiple-entry visas for Okinawa and three prefectures in Tohoku, who have travel record to Japan in the last three years. (3) For individual tourists, a new multiple-entry visa without the requirement of visiting either Okinawa or one of three prefectures in Tohoku will be introduced, for those applicants with substantially high incomes."
67 See *Black's Law Dictionary*, 9th ed., under the word "law and economics." "Law and Economics is a discipline advocating the economic analysis of the law, whereby legal rules are subjected to a cost-benefit analysis to determine whether a change from one legal rule to another will increase or decrease allocative efficiency and social wealth. [Although it is] originally developed as an approach to antitrust policy, law and economics is today used by its proponents to explain and interpret a variety of legal subjects."
68 See generally, Eric Posner & Alan Sykes, *Economic Foundations of International Law* (Cambridge: Harvard University Press, 2013); For summary of the methods of international law, see generally Steven Ratner & Anne-Marie Slaughter, "Appraising the Methods of International Law: a Prospectus for Readers" (1999) 93 Am. J. Int'l L. 291 at 294 (noting that "Law and Economics is a discipline advocating the economic analysis of the law, whereby legal rules are subjected to a cost-benefit analysis to determine whether a change from one legal rule to another will increase or decrease allocative efficiency and social wealth. [Although it is] originally developed as an approach to antitrust policy, law and economics is today used by its proponents to explain and interpret a variety of legal subjects.").
69 Andrew T. Guzman, *How International Law Works* (Oxford: Oxford University Press, 2008) at 17.
70 *Ibid.* at 121.

national interest implications, rational choice theory is helpful in understanding the relevant international legal framework.[71]

Defining the national interest is within the ambit of national policy. States (or their policy makers) determine their national interest on their own, and the power of international law is limited when national interest is at stake.[72] Obviously, however, once policies turn into international treaties, contracting states to these treaties are bound by the rules set out in them.

The process by which a policy becomes international law and the outcome of such a process require in-depth legal analysis. In the same vein, the relationship between policy and international law demands wide-ranging discussion. Although these theoretical questions are not within the scope of this research, a relevant assumption is that policies are generally perceived as paths of a political nature because they are produced outside the legal world and because political evaluations and decisions are inserted into the legal system through policies.[73]

In other words, national policies are rooted in different political backgrounds with the natural consequence that policy on international air transport varies from state to state. Understanding the national air transport policies of China, Japan, and Korea and their policy priorities is essential for further analyzing the impediments to and opportunities for Northeast Asian open skies. Since national policy is not always static and can change even during a short period, it should be noted that the views here reflect the three countries' national policies as of 2015.

3.2.2 China

3.2.2.1 Protecting the "Big Three" Airlines

The central pillar of China's aviation policy on international air transport is to protect its "big three" state-owned airlines: Air China, China Southern, and China Eastern. This policy has remained in place since 2002, when the Chinese government restructured nine air carriers and consolidated them into these three groups.[74] This market consolidation essentially led to geographical market allocation of China's three primary hubs: Beijing to

---

71 Havel & Sanchez, "Aviation Law", *supra* note 9 at 10.
72 Guzman, *supra* note 69 at 125.
73 Mauro Zamboni, *The Policy of Law – A Legal Theoretical Framework* (Oxford: Hart Publishing, 2007) at 115-117.
74 See Alan Williams, *Contemporary Issues Shaping China's Civil Aviation Policy: Balancing International with Domestic Priorities* (Burlington, VT: Ashgate, 2009) at 87. "Air China Group, formerly Air China (based in Beijing), China Southwest (based in Chengdu), and CNAC (based in Hong Kong); China Southern Group, formerly, China Southern (based in Guangzhou), China Northern (based in Shenyang), and China Xinjiang (based in Urumqi); China Eastern Group, formerly China Eastern (based in Shanghai), China Yunnan (based in Kunming), and China Northwest (based X'ian)."

Air China, Shanghai to China Eastern, and Guangzhou to China Southern. This market allocation was solidified when the Chinese government stopped accepting applications for new airlines in 2007.[75] In 2013, however, China lifted the ban on establishing new airlines (see the next section 3.2.2.2).

The government-driven market consolidation had two motivations. First, a number of small airlines were facing various difficulties including the possibility of imminent collapse due to a combination of several factors such as the aftermath of the Asian financial crisis, unsatisfactory safety issues, and lack of management skill.[76] Second, China hoped to have super-carriers in order to compete with large international rivals.[77]

China has been protecting its aviation industry by maintaining strict control of market access. The Civil Aviation Authority of China (CAAC), the regulator of civil aviation in China as well as the government body responsible for negotiating air services agreements with foreign countries, has followed three principles in protecting the national airlines.

First, it applies the "one route, one carrier" rule.[78] Usually, only one Chinese carrier and one foreign carrier have been designated to minimize competition on a particular international route. This dovetails with the geographical allocation of the three major hubs to the Big Three, as explained above. The "one route, one carrier" principle has been watered down for short-haul routes. Yet, the general practice is that only one Chinese carrier can fly a long-haul international route.

Nonetheless, Air China has been observed to receive special treatment, such as Air China' flights from Shanghai to Frankfurt, Milan, Paris and Sydney.[79] In other words, Beijing-based Air China can fly long-haul routes from Shanghai but China Eastern (Shanghai-based) cannot fly long-haul routes from Beijing.[80] It is important to recall that Air China is the country's only official flag carrier although all three are state-owned.[81] As the "favorite child" of the Chinese government,[82] special treatment for Air China is an established practice.

---

75   Joanne Chiu, "China's Air Regulator Will Consider Ways to Boost Budget-Carrier Market" *The Wall Street Journal* (29 July 2013), online: <http://online.wsj.com/news/articles/SB10001424127887323854904578634920047272886>.
76   See Williams, *supra* note 74 at 86; See also Anming Zhang & Hongmin Chen, "Evolutions of China's Air Transport Development and Policy towards International Liberalization" (2003) 42:3 Transportation Journal 31 at 37-38.
77   See Williams, *ibid.* at 213.
78   See Zhang & Chen, *supra* note 76 at 37.
79   CAPA, "Chinese carriers in for the long haul but face stumbling blocks along the way" (26 December 2012), online: <http://centreforaviation.com/analysis/chinese-carriers-in-for-the-long-haul-but-face-stumbling-blocks-along-the-way-91991>.
80   See CAPA, "Chinese airlines pioneer new international strategies: JVs to overcome internal limitations" (12 March 2014), online: <http://centreforaviation.com/analysis/chinese-airlines-pioneer-new-international-strategies-jvs-to-overcome-internal-limitations-156522>.
81   *Ibid.*
82   Jamil Anderlini, "China's private airlines facing cross-winds" *Financial Times* (22 March 2010).

Second, fifth freedom rights are not generally granted to foreign carriers.[83] China has traditionally emphasized the strict reciprocity principle based on the actual market share of national carriers[84] and equal participation of national carriers in the air transport market.[85] By their very nature, fifth freedom operations by foreign carriers are generally viewed by most states as a threat to their own airlines[86] (see section 2.4.2 Asia-Pacific Economic Cooperation (APEC)'s Initiative (that is, MALIAT) for the aero-political aspect of the fifth freedom), and consequently China only sees fifth freedom rights as an obstacle to the participation of the big three airlines.

Exceptions are made for sizeable markets. China made its only significant agreement for fifth freedom exchange of passenger traffic with India. In early 2008, following a trip by then Indian Prime Minister Manmohan Singh to China, the two countries announced they would relax their air services agreement to allow fifth freedom exchanges.[87] Subsequently, India's Jet Airways launched a daily Mumbai-Shanghai-San Francisco service (although it was later terminated for commercial reasons).[88]

A somewhat less significant fifth freedom exchange was made in the ASEAN–China Air Transport Agreement Protocol 2 in 2013.[89] Since the ASEAN–China Air Transport Agreement Protocol 2 only opens up 10 Chinese cities (excluding Beijing, Shanghai and Guangzhou) as ASEAN carriers' fifth freedom intermediate points,[90] it is unclear whether fifth freedom operations here would actually be possible (or profitable).

Third, third-party code sharing (a commercial agreement in which an airline code is shared between an airline of the bilateral partners and an airline other than the bilateral partners) is prohibited. For instance, American Airlines cannot codeshare with Japan Airlines on the route between Tokyo's Narita Airport and Beijing Capital Airport, on which Japan Airlines operates, because this would be a third-party code share. In other words, foreign carriers operating to and from China can code-share with Chinese carriers, but no other third-party carriers.[91]

83　Zhang & Chen, *supra* note 76 at 37.
84　*Ibid.* at 36.
85　Wu Zhouhong (Department of International Affairs and Cooperation, General Administration of Civil Aviation of China), Comment to "Implementation the Process of the European Common Air Transport Market and the Common Air Transport Policy" by Kenneth Button (2003) 90 at 91 [unpublished, archived at The Korea Transport Institute].
86　Alan Khee-Jin Tan, "The 2010 ASEAN–China Air Transport Agreement: Much Ado over Fifth Freedom Rights?" (2014) 14 Issues in Aviation and Policy 19 at 22. [Tan, "Fifth Freedom Rights"].
87　Alan Khee-Jin Tan, "India's Evolving Policy on International Civil Aviation" (2013) 38 Air and Space L. 439 at 452. [Tan, "India"].
88　*Ibid.*
89　See Tan, "Fifth Freedom Rights", *supra* note 86 at 22.
90　*Ibid.* at 24.
91　Alan Khee-Jin Tan, "Antitrust Immunity for Trans-Pacific Airline Alliance Agreements: Singapore and China as 'Beyond' Markets" 38 Air & Space L. 275 at 292. [Tan, "Antitrust Immunity"].

3.2.2.2 Promoting LCCs

Even though LCCs would normally be considered a threat that could upset China's carefully calibrated policy of protecting the big three airlines, there are signs of a paradigm shift in China's aviation policy, suggesting that China is considering (or has already started) promoting LCCs. Above all, it is noteworthy that China lifted a six-year ban on setting up new independent airlines in May 2013.[92] Table 3.2 shows the list of established Chinese airlines (most of which are planning or likely to have 100 aircraft by 2020).[93]

Table 3.2 Summary of Major Incumbent Chinese Airlines[94]

Airline	Fleet Size
China Southern	457
China Eastern	350
Air China	316
Shenzhen Airlines	139
Hainan Airlines	120
Xiamen Airlines	103
Tianjin Airlines	84
Sichuan Airlines	83
Shanghai Airlines	74
Shandong Airlines	72
Spring Airlines	40
Juneyao Airlines	34
Okay Airways	24
West Air	13
Joy Air	8

In addition to those incumbent airlines, about 20 new Chinese airlines (most of them LCCs) have launched or are planning to launch between 2013 and 2015.[95] Table 3.3 shows some of these airlines.

---

92 Chiu, *supra* note 75.
93 CAPA, "13 Chinese airlines could each have a fleet of over 100 aircraft by 2020" (26 May 2014), online: <http://centreforaviation.com/analysis/13-chinese-airlines-could-each-have-a-fleet-of-over-100-aircraft-by-2020-169778>.
94 Updated from CAPA, "13 Chinese airlines could each have a fleet of over 100 aircraft by 2020" (26 May 2014), online: <http://centreforaviation.com/analysis/13-chinese-airlines-could-each-have-a-fleet-of-over-100-aircraft-by-2020-169778>.
95 CAPA, "For Northeast Asia's airlines, previously slow to adapt, 2015 spells opportunity" *Airline Leader* 26 (February 2015), online: <www.airlineleader.com/categories/regions/for-northeast-asias-airlines-previously-slow-to-adapt-2015-spells-opportunity-209070>.

Table 3.3 Summary of Proposed New Chinese Airlines[96]

Airline	Status
Donghai Airlines	Launched in March 2014
Guilin Airlines	Waiting
Hefei Airlines	Waiting
Jiangxi Airlines	Waiting
Jiu Yuan Airlines	Waiting
Loong Airlines	Launched in December 2013
Qingdao Airlines	Launched in April 2014
Ruili Airlines	Launched in May 2014
Sutong Airlines	Waiting
Urumqi Airlines	Launched in August 2014

Since Spring Airline (China's largest and earliest LCC) achieved great success in China,[97] other Chinese private airlines have been seeking to establish LCCs.[98] In July 2014, China Eastern converted its Shanghai-based subsidiary China United Airlines into an LCC partly because of China's new policy of supporting LCCs, and this venture may encourage Air China and China Southern to follow suit with their respective subsidiaries.[99]

China is also gradually allowing foreign LCCs into both major and medium-sized airports.[100] Foreign LCCs' market access into China is expected to grow, especially in non-hub Chinese airports that are not congested and of secondary importance to the three major hubs of Beijing, Shanghai and Guangzhou.

However, China's priority will continue to be the Big Three airlines. A commonly accepted industry view is that "an influx of new LCCs competing aggressively with the big three is unlikely to be the government's vision."[101] Although protecting the big three airlines

---

96 Modified from CAPA, "China's aviation reforms and a rush of airline start-ups boost growth prospects; and fleets recycle" (3 January 2015), online: <http://centreforaviation.com/analysis/chinas-aviation-reforms-and-a-rush-of-airline-start-ups-boost-growth-prospects-and-fleets-recycle-203328>.
97 See CAPA, "Japan's expanding LCCs drive growth but need cultivating; Spring Airlines and AirAsia re-entry loom" (5 April 2014), online: <http://centreforaviation.com/analysis/japans-expanding-lccs-drive-growth-but-need-cultivating-spring-airlines-and-airasia-re-entry-loom-160039>.
98 Chiu, *supra* note 75.
99 Kyunghee Park & Clement Tan, "China Eastern Sets Up Budget Carrier, Rivals May Follow" *Bloomberg* (2 July 2014), online: <www.bloomberg.com/news/2014-07-02/china-eastern-sets-up-budget-carrier-rivals-may-follow.html>.
100 Xiaowen Fu & Tae Hoon Oum, *Dominant Carrier Performance and International Liberalisation: The Case of North East Asia*, Discussion Paper No 2015-03, International Transport Forum (Paris: OECD, 2015) at 25.
101 Davin Wu (an analyst at Credit Suisse) in Joanne Chiu, "China's Air Regulator Will Consider Ways to Boost Budget-Carrier Market" *The Wall Street Journal* (29 July 2013), online: <http://online.wsj.com/news/articles/SB10001424127887323854904578634920047272886>.

continues to be the central pillar of China's policy on international air transport, China now upholds LCCs as an efficient growth mechanism.[102]

It was largely of symbolic importance when CAAC deputy director Xia Xinghua publicly said that "China will roll out a series of policies to encourage the development of LCCs" on 5 November 2013 during the ICAO/CAAC Symposium on LCCs held in Beijing.[103] The government's policy does encourage the development of LCCs and the increasing number of Chinese LCCs means more market penetration is in progress. (See figure 3.1.)

Figure 3.1   LCCs' Penetration in China[104]

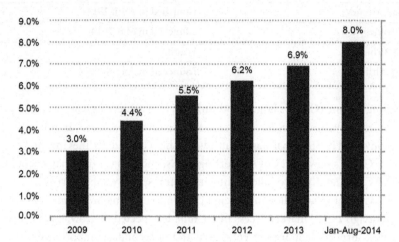

3.2.2.3   Managing Airspace Better

The most notable challenge to China's market access in international air transport is the lack of airspace resources, which has resulted in a bottle neck impeding the growth of civil aviation.[105] Not only do the four major airports (Beijing Capital Airport, Shanghai Hongqiao Airport, Shanghai Pudong Airport, and Guangzhou Baiyun Airport) suffer severe shortages

---

102   CAPA, "North Asia's aviation gradually breaks with tradition but a legacy mindset persists" *Airline Leader* 25 (November 2014), online: <www.airlineleader.com/categories/regions/north-asias-aviation-gradually-breaks-with-tradition-but-a-legacy-mindset-persists-194800>.

103   Izzie Lin, "China Rolls Out Policies to Boost Budget Airlines" *World Civil Aviation Resource Net* (6 November 2013), online: <www.wcarn.com/news/30/30194.html>.

104   CAPA, "North Asia's aviation gradually breaks with tradition but a legacy mindset persists" *Airline Leader* 25 (November 2014), online: <www.airlineleader.com/categories/regions/north-asias-aviation-gradually-breaks-with-tradition-but-a-legacy-mindset-persists-194800>.

105   ICAO, *Expansion of Market Access for International Air Transport in a Proactive, Progressive, Orderly and Safeguarded Manner*, ICAO Doc ATConf/6-WP/97 (6 March 2013) (Presented by China) at 3, online: <www.icao.int/Meetings/atconf6/Documents/WorkingPapers/ATConf.6.WP.97.2.1.en.pdf>.

of airspace, but it is also reported that 17 other airports face similar problems as they approach the saturation point for usable airspace resources.[106]

The main challenge for Chinese airports lies in airside capacity issues rather than landside capacity issues (see section 3.1.3.1 Airport Capacity for the difference between these two terms). Since the airspace that commercial airlines can use is highly limited, busy airports in megacities cannot sufficiently support airlines' on-time performance (that is, on-time departures and arrivals). As a consequence, Chinese airports were ranked as the world's worst in terms of on-time departures and arrivals.

The Civil Aviation Act 1995 provides the civil aviation and military authorities with a framework for joint control of Chinese airspace, and the Chinese military has indeed turned over increasing numbers of air corridors to civilian management.[107] However, just 20 percent of Chinese airspace is open to commercial carriers compared to 80 percent in the US.[108] Although China acknowledged that a new approach to airspace management is necessary for sustainable growth, cooperation between the CAAC and the Chinese military has been slow.[109]

China's airspace shortage creates serious operational delays for many airlines, but it affects Chinese airlines the most since they nearly always use Chinese airspace (except fifth freedom operations). In fact, China's major airlines fared poorly compared with their regional and global counterparts in regard to on-time operation.[110]

---

106 *Ibid.*
107 CAPA, "China's looming airspace squeeze" (21 April 2011), online: <http://centreforaviation.com/analysis/chinas-looming-airspace-squeeze-50355>; See also Williams, *supra* note 74 at 194.
108 CAPA, *Ibid.*
109 *Ibid.*
110 Chuck Thompson, "China airports world's worst for on-time performance" *CNN* (12 July 2013), online: <http://edition.cnn.com/2013/07/12/travel/china-airport-performance/>.

Figure 3.2   On-Time Departures at Major International Airports[111]

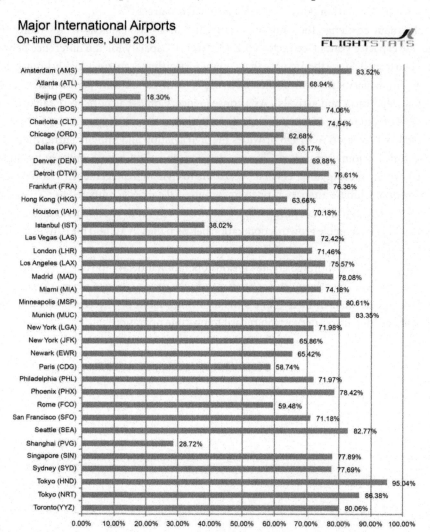

---

111 FlightStats, *On-time Performance Report – June 2013* (15 August 2013), online: <www.flightstats.com/go/story.do?id=1061>.

Figure 3.3 On-time Performance of Asian Airlines[112]

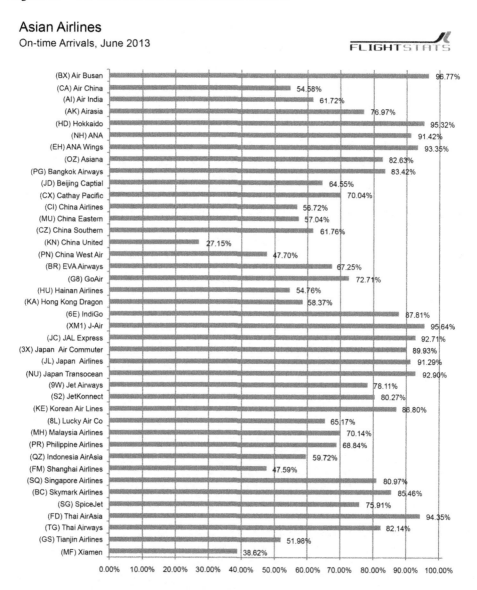

Far-reaching changes are taking place in China. The fact that China's major airports, and especially the Beijing Capital Airport, have reached their capacity is currently a major

---

112 FlightStats, *On-time Performance Report – June 2013* (15 August 2013), online: <www.flight-stats.com/go/story.do?id=1061>.

challenge to developing air transport in China.[113] Li Jiaxiang, head of China's Civil Aviation Administration, once said that "it is now impossible to add even one more flight to the tight daily schedule of the capital airport."[114]

Although the airside capacity shortage is an extremely serious problem due to the lack of airspace for civil aviation, the landside shortage issue remains a major problem, too. Although Beijing Capital Airport's yearly capacity was raised to 82 million passengers in 2008 with the opening of Terminal 3, it has already exceeded its capacity, handling 83.7 million passengers in 2013.[115] Furthermore, annual traffic at Beijing Capital is expected to reach 90 million passengers by 2015.[116]

In order to overcome this obstacle, the idea of a new airport in Beijing was proposed in 2008 and finally approved in 2012.[117] The new Beijing Airport, located south of the city in Daxing and scheduled to open in late 2018, will have eight runways and an initial capacity of 40 million, which is supposed to increase to 70 million by 2025.[118]

---

113 See ICAO, *Expansion of Market Access for International Air Transport in a Proactive, Progressive, Orderly and Safeguarded Manner*, ICAO Doc ATConf/6-WP/97 (6 March 2013) (Presented by China) at 3, online: <www.icao.int/Meetings/atconf6/Documents/WorkingPapers/ATConf.6.WP.97.2.1.en.pdf>.
114 John Walton, "New airport for Beijing: "impossible to add even one more flight" to current airport" *Australian Business Traveller* (13 January 2011), online: <www.ausbt.com.au/new-airport-for-beijing-impossible-to-add-even-one-more-flight-to-current-airport>.
115 Guillaume Dupont, "Beijing New Airports" *New Airport Insider* (24 September 2014), online: <http://dcdesigntech.com/new-airport-insider/beijing-new-airports/>.
116 *Ibid.*
117 *Ibid.*
118 CAPA, "Asia leads the field in airport construction but privatisation opportunities are few" *Airline Leader* 25 (November 2014), online: <www.airlineleader.com/categories/feature/asia-leads-the-field-in-airport-construction-but-privatisation-opportunities-are-few-193963>.

Figure 3.4 Location of Beijing Daxing Airport[119]

Interestingly, China is considering a low-cost terminal in Beijing's new airport.[120] If all goes according to plan, the LCC terminal at China's capital will be another meaningful step in promoting LCCs. It would provide great opportunities to Northeast Asian LCCs that are eager to fly to Beijing.

However, better management of airspace is a prerequisite. Increasing landside capacity would be nearly futile if there is no corresponding increase in airside capacity. The fact that only 20 percent of Chinese airspace is open to commercial carriers is a severe constraint.

Indeed, political pressure for cooperation between civil and military authorities with regard to Chinese airspace has been increasing on an international level. In June 2013, the ICAO Asia and Pacific Regional Sub-Office (APAC RSO) was inaugurated in Beijing. The strategic goals for the sub-office include "enhanc[ing] airspace capacity and efficiency to

---

119 John Walton, "New airport for Beijing: "impossible to add even one more flight" to current airport" *Australian Business Traveller* (13 January 2011), online: <www.ausbt.com.au/new-airport-for-beijing-impossible-to-add-even-one-more-flight-to-current-airport>.
120 Vanessa Zhang, "CAAC Mulls Low-Cost Carrier Terminal at New Beijing Airport" *World Civil Aviation Resource Net* (6 November 2013), online: <www.wcarn.com/news/30/30198.html>.

accommodate Asian aviation growth" and "optimiz[ing] Air Transport Management (ATM) operations via collaborative management of traffic flow."[121]

One of the first major events that the sub-office organized was the APAC Civil-Military Cooperation Lecture-Seminar, which aimed to raise awareness of the high priority and benefits of civil-military cooperation.[122] Although cooperation between the CAAC and the Chinese military has been slow,[123] the interests of Chinese airlines and external pressure from ICAO and neighboring states will hopefully improve the airspace shortage problem.

3.2.3   Japan

3.2.3.1   Policy Transformation through the "Asian Gateway Initiative"

Japan's aviation policy has long been criticized for its protection of national carriers.[124] However, a complete transformation was made when a new comprehensive policy package, the "Asian Gateway Initiative," was endorsed by Japanese Prime Minister Abe Shinzo in May 2007. The Council for the Asian Gateway Initiative,[125] consisting of politicians, academics, and industry experts, prepared the initiative, which covers various policy priorities including aviation.[126]

Conceptually, the Asian Gateway Initiative is rooted in Japan's re-evaluation of Asia. The initiative replaced the old perception of "Japan and Asia"—which had emphasized the difference between the two[127]—with a *de facto* declaration that Japan is a part of Asia.[128] Throughout the "lost decades", Japan has witnessed a drop in global market share in many

---

121   See ICAO Asia & Pacific Regional Sub-Office, "Strategic Framework for the APAC Regional Sub-Office (RSO)", online: <www.icao.int/APAC/RSO-Beijing/Pages/Strategic.aspx>.
122   See ICAO Asia & Pacific Regional Sub-Office, "APAC Civil /Military Cooperation Lecture/Seminar 2014 OVERVIEW", online: <www.icao.int/APAC/RSO-Beijing/Pages/APAC-Overview.aspx>.
123   CAPA, "China's looming airspace squeeze" (21 April 2011), online: <http://centreforaviation.com/analysis/chinas-looming-airspace-squeeze-50355>.
124   See *e.g.* Tae Hoon Oum & Yeong Heok Lee, "The Northeast Asian Air Transport Network: Is There a Possibility of Creating Open Skies in the Region?" (2002) 8 Journal of Air Transport Management. 325.
125   For the explanation for Council for Asian Gateway Initiative, see online: <http://japan.kantei.go.jp/gateway/index_e.html>.
126   The ten major policy priorities are: 1) Change in aviation policy to achieve "Asian Open Skies"; 2) Implement a program for streamlining trade measures; 3) Restructure policy for foreign students in order for Japan to serve as a hub for a human resource network in Asia; 4) Further open up universities to the world; 5) Create a financial and capital market attractive to Asian Customers; 6) Transform agriculture into a successful growth industry during the time of globalization; 7) Create an "Asian Gateway Special Zone"; 8) Implement concrete policies in line with a comprehensive strategy for "creative industries"; 9) Promote Japan's attractiveness overseas; 10) Strengthen Japan's central role in promoting regional study and cooperation for solving common problems.
127   The Council for the Asian Gateway Initiative, "Asian Gateway Initiative" (16 May 2007) at 7, online: <http://japan.kantei.go.jp/gateway/kettei/070516doc.pdf>.
128   The Japanese government unconventionally released the plan in English, Chinese, and Korean. See online: <http://japan.kantei.go.jp/gateway/index_e.html>.

industries, and its position as an Asian hub has also been weakened with the rise of more competitive Asian hubs. Against this background, a newly elected Prime Minister, Abe Shinzo wanted a radical change to improve Japan's position in Asia.[129]

Considering Japan's geography, the Asian Gateway Initiative seemed a reasonable policy direction. Located at the northeastern extremity of Asia, Japan has the great geographical advantage of being the gateway between Asia and the Americas.

The Council for the Asian Gateway Initiative viewed aviation as the most crucial sector for achieving the objectives of the initiative because enhancing the aviation network is a prerequisite to Japan's becoming an Asian gateway.[130] In fact, "form[ing] a strategic international aviation network through aviation liberalization ("Asian Open Skies")" was designated as one of the policy's priorities.[131] Under this priority, several sub-tasks were introduced, some of which are listed below:

> Change the traditional aviation policy in order to strategically promote the rapid liberalization of aviation ("Asian Open Skies");
> Promote aviation liberalization in order to remove restriction on carriers, entry points, and the number of both passenger and cargo flights; and
> Start liberalization negotiations with China and other Asian countries (give high priority to Asia).

Within three months of the proclamation of the Asian Gateway Initiative, Japan signed an open skies agreement with Korea (the first open skies agreement in history by the Japanese government[132]), followed by several other Asian states as promised, including Hong Kong, Macau, Vietnam, Thailand, Malaysia, and Singapore. However, the Tokyo Metropolitan Airports (Narita Airport and Haneda Airport) were excluded from the open skies agreements until slot shortage problems were improved.

3.2.3.2   Increasing Airport Capacity in the Tokyo Area

Established and new airlines operating to and from Tokyo had long been anticipating an expansion of the international networks in the Tokyo metropolitan area for better market access. Both Haneda Airport, located 15 km south of Tokyo Station, and Narita Airport, located 60 km east of Tokyo Station, have long suffered from capacity shortage.

---

129   Personal communication between the author and Dr. Akira Mistumasu.
130   The Council for the Asian Gateway Initiative, "Asian Gateway Initiative" (16 May 2007) at 6, online: <http://japan.kantei.go.jp/gateway/kettei/070516doc.pdf>.
131   *Ibid.* at 8.
132   Yi-Shih Chung & Cheng-Lung Wu, "Chapter 12 Air Market Opening between Taiwan and China: Impact on Airport and Airline Network Developments in Neighboring Asia Pacific Countries" in David Timothy Duval, ed., *Air Transport in the Asia Pacific* (Burlington: Ashgate, 2014) 199 at 211.

Figure 3.5 Distance of Tokyo Area Airports from Downtown Tokyo[133]

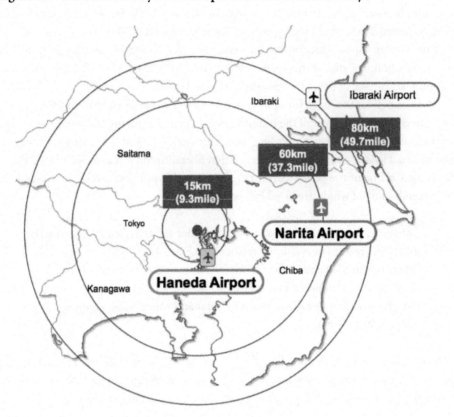

Haneda Airport was Tokyo's main airport until Narita Airport opened in 1978. After the completion of Narita Airport, Haneda became a predominantly domestic airport as international traffic was diverted east to Narita.[134] Reflecting Japan's rapid growth and extraordinary economic success in the 1980s, demand increased significantly, and interim or partial efforts to increase capacity at Haneda and Narita Airports could not keep pace with demand.[135]

---

133 CAPA, "Japan awards international Tokyo Haneda Airport slots, but Narita Airport remains the main hub", (9 October 2013), online: <http://centreforaviation.com/analysis/japan-awards-international-tokyo-haneda-airport-slots-but-narita-airport-remains-the-main-hub-132103>.
134 Patrick M. Cronin, *Taking Off Civil Aviation, Forward Progress and Japan's Third Arrow Reforms* (Washington, D.C.: Center for a New American Security, 2013) at 12.
135 *Ibid.* at 12-13.

Figure 3.6 Aircraft Movements at Haneda and Narita Airports: 1970-2010[136]

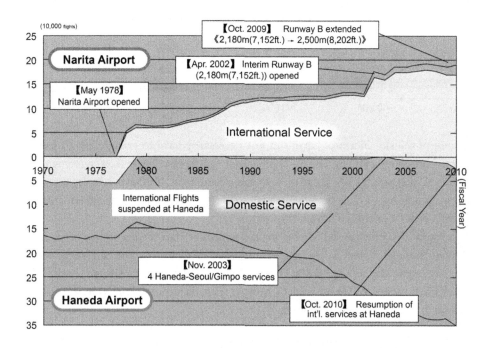

More substantial changes have been made since 2010. By significantly expanding runways and building new terminals, the Japanese authorities have increased the number of slots at the two airports (Narita and Haneda).

Table 3.4 Annual Slot Changes at Tokyo Haneda and Tokyo Narita Airports[137]

Year	Narita	Haneda		Narita + Haneda
	International	International	Domestic	International
2009	200,000	303,000		200,000
2010	220,000	60,000	311,000	280,000

---

136 CAPA, "Japan awards international Tokyo Haneda Airport slots, but Narita Airport remains the main hub", (9 October 2013), online: <http://centreforaviation.com/analysis/japan-awards-international-tokyo-haneda-airport-slots-but-narita-airport-remains-the-main-hub-132103>.

137 Based on the following sources: CAPA, "Japan awards international Tokyo Haneda Airport slots, but Narita Airport remains the main hub" (9 October 2013), online: <http://centreforaviation.com/analysis/japan-awards-international-tokyo-haneda-airport-slots-but-narita-airport-remains-the-main-hub-132103>; Yoshiro Taguchi (Deputy Director, Japan Civil Aviation Bureau), "Updates on Japan's International Aviation Policy" (Presentation to IATA Schedule Committee,13 November 2011), online: <www.schedule-coordination.jp/archives/arc_jcab/pdf/2010/jcab_at_sc127.pdf>.; CAPA, "New runways for Tokyo Haneda and Narita airports would allow Japan to catch up to other Asian hubs" (19 June 2014), online: <http://centre-

Year	Narita	Haneda		Narita + Haneda
	International	International	Domestic	International
2011	235,000	60,000	330,000	295,000
2012	250,000	60,000	330,000	310,000
2013	270,000	60,000	330,000	330,000
2014	270,000	90,000	357,000	360,000
2015	300,000	90,000	357,000	390,000

Because of the slot increase, Japan did not necessarily have to exclude Tokyo when it adopted an open skies agreement. Japan's first full-fledged open skies agreement that included Tokyo was the US–Japan open skies agreement in 2010. Japan has also continued to re-negotiate air services agreements with states that already had such agreements with Japan in order to include Tokyo.[138]

A recent dynamic caused by creating more slots at Haneda airport is a competition between Narita and Haneda airports for international flights. As slots at Haneda airport increased, some airlines (*e.g.*, Delta, United Airlines, and American Airlines) have shifted some of their operations from Narita airport to Haneda airport, which is more attractive because of its proximity to downtown.[139]

3.2.3.3 Promoting LCCs

New market access rights triggered by the Asian Gateway Initiative and successful relaxation of indirect market access (capacity expansion at the Tokyo metropolitan airports) have provided a suitable platform for the development of LCCs. It was rightly anticipated that the post-2010 period would be a "big bang" for Japanese aviation, as the significant capacity expansion at Tokyo's airports would enable LCCs to snap up new slots at Tokyo airports, providing a fresh surge in competition.[140]

In 2012 alone, three new low-cost airlines were established in Japan as subsidiaries of JAL and ANA: JAL's Jetstar Japan, a joint venture with Australia's Jetstar; ANA's Peach, minority held with Hong Kong interests involved; and AirAsia Japan, a joint venture between ANA and AirAsia. AirAsia Japan ceased operations in October 2013 due to a

---

foraviation.com/analysis/new-runways-for-tokyo-haneda-and-narita-airports-would-allow-japan-to-catch-up-to-other-asian-hubs-171788>.
138 Taguchi, *Ibid*.
139 CAPA, "Tokyo Narita Outlook Part 1: once a mega hub, international and transit passengers decline" (23 March 2015), online: <http://centreforaviation.com/analysis/tokyo-narita-outlook-part-1-once-a-mega-hub-international-and-transit-passengers-decline-215202>.
140 CAPA, "Calm before the Big Bang – Japan Airlines on track to report first profit in three years" (11 February 2008), online: <http://centreforaviation.com/analysis/calm-before-the-big-bang---japan-airlines-on-track-to-report-first-profit-in-three-years-2355>.

managerial conflict between ANA and AirAsia. Soon after, ANA established its own LCC, Vanilla Air. The new AirAsia Japan, a JV between Malaysia's AirAsia and Japanese investors (majority owners with no airline experience), is planning to launch its joint venture in 2015. (See section 4.2.3 Japan)

In addition to the three LCCs in which Japanese airlines own a share and partially (or wholly) control, Spring Airlines Japan, a JV between China's Spring Airlines and Japanese investors (majority owners), began its Japanese operations in 2014. (This will be discussed in Chapter 4: Ownership and Control Issues in Northeast Asia.)

3.2.4 Korea

3.2.4.1 Prioritizing Northeast Asia

Promoting open skies agreements with Northeast Asian countries is a key item on the agenda of Korean aviation policy.[141] As a strategically located country with a competitive aviation infrastructure, Korea has a strong incentive to bring about Northeast Asian regional liberalization. Korea's domestic aviation market is only the 22nd-largest in the world (behind the UK but above Vietnam),[142] compared with China (2nd-largest) and Japan (3rd-largest).[143] In addition, it has a formidable rival: namely, the KTX high-speed rail line.

For instance, the Seoul-Busan route (Busan being the second largest city in Korea), the most popular inland route in Korea, was materially affected by the introduction of KTX. While a flight between the two cities takes fifty minutes, KTX only takes two and a half hours. In addition, train stations are conveniently located downtown, while airports are located on the outskirts of Seoul and Busan. Effectively, the three routes in Table 3.5 are the commercially viable domestic routes.

Table 3.5   Major Domestic Routes in Korea[144]

		2011	2012	2013
Seoul (Gimpo)-Jeju	Number of Flights	66,402	69,622	75,116
	Number of Passengers	10,307,531	11,039,071	12,058,614
	Average Load Factor	79.9	83.7	84.6

---

141 See Korean Ministry of Land, Infrastructure and Transport, "Aviation Policy," online: <http://english.molit.go.kr/USR/sectoral/>.
142 CAPA, "Foreign LCCs line up for JVs in South Korea as aviation market changes" (21 January 2013), online: <http://centreforaviation.com/analysis/foreign-lccs-line-up-for-jvs-in-south-korea-as-aviation-market-changes-94372>.
143 CAPA, "LCCs help Japanese domestic market grow for first time in six years, but market situation still dire" (8 August 2013), online: <http://centreforaviation.com/analysis/lccs-help-japanese-domestic-market-grow-for-first-time-in-six-years-but-market-situation-still-dire-121716>.
144 Based on data from <www.airportal.go.kr>.

		2011	2012	2013
Seoul (Gimpo)-Busan (Gimhae)	Number of Flights	19,746	18,734	18,666
	Number of Passenger	2,319,215	2,167,253	1,990,366
	Average Load Factor	66.9	70.0	70.4
Jeju-Busan (Gimhae)	Number of Flights	16,638	17,802	18,461
	Number of Passenger	2,589,974	2,664,567	2,801,853
	Average Load Factor	80.1	80.2	82.4

Thus, Korea would want to promote open skies regimes internationally, especially with China and Japan.[145] Korea also has a strong international origin/destination (3rd/4th freedom) market on its own as well as a population approaching 50 million.

According to the Korean government's Basic Plan for Aviation Policy released in August 2012, building a single aviation market in Northeast Asia consisting of China, Japan, and Korea as core members plus Taiwan and Mongolia is a long-term goal for Korea.[146] The plan proposes a Korea-China open skies agreement as the short-term goal, a Korea-China–Japan single market as the mid-term goal, and expansion of the market to include other states (including Taiwan and Mongolia) as the long-term goal.

3.2.4.2 Focusing on 6th Freedom Traffic

Focusing on the 6th freedom (connecting traffic) is a common interest for the Korean government, Incheon airport (Korea's hub airport), and Korean legacy carriers (Korean Air and Asiana Airlines). Incheon Airport's connecting ratio (the ratio of transfer passengers to the total number of arriving passengers) of 16 percent is much lower than its competitors (Hong Kong 28%, Narita 21%, and Changi 31% in 2011), a problem which the Korean Ministry of Land, Infrastructure, and Transport (MLIT) and Incheon Airport Authority are currently grappling with.[147]

Geographically, Korea is well-positioned as many types of commercial aircraft can operate non-stop flights to the US market (something that cannot be done from Southeast Asia). The shorter distance from Korea to the US allows smaller aircraft to be efficiently used for thinner points, or routes where current demand would be insufficient to fill a

---

145 See Xiaowen Fu, Tae Hoon Oum & Anming Zhang "Air Transport Liberalization and Its Impacts on Airline Competition and Air Passenger Traffic" (2010) 49:4 Transportation Journal. 24 at 33.
146 Korean Ministry of Land, Infrastructure and Transport, "The Aviation Policy Basic Plan" (10 August 2012), online: <www.molit.go.kr/USR/policyData/m_34681/dtl.jsp?search=&srch_dept_nm=&srch_dept_id=&srch_usr_nm=&srch_usr_titl=Y&srch_usr_ctnt=&search_regdate_s=&search_regdate__e=&psize=10&scategory=p_sec_7&p_category=701&lcmspage=1&id=256>. (only Korean language available).
147 Korean Ministry of Land, Infrastructure and Transport, "Plan for Advancing Incheon International Airport Authority" (24 August 2012), online: <www.mltm.go.kr/USR/policyTarget/m_24066/dtl. jsp?idx=153>. (only Korean language available).

larger aircraft.[148] With the dual advantages of geography and market access (the US–Korea open skies agreement had been adopted since 1998), Korean Air was able to establish itself as the largest Asian airline with operations to the US both in terms of destinations and seat capacity.[149]

3.2.4.3   Promoting LCCs

Korean aviation policy towards LCCs can be described as controlled liberalization. In economic theory, the simultaneous occurrence of the birth of new airlines and the disappearance of weaker airlines through bankruptcies or mergers is regarded as an acceptable outcome of liberalization.[150] However, there has been a tendency in Korea to view the bankruptcy of a national airline as a social loss for which the government is in part responsible. Thus, policy makers are cautious about the level of competition posed to the established carriers by LCCs.[151]

In recent years, there has been a marked change in policy toward LCCs. Indeed, the Korean government has been cautiously shifting the focus of its aviation policy priorities from legacy carriers to LCCs by adopting the explicit policy goal of "supporting the growth of LCCs."[152] Mr. Ken Choi, CEO of Jeju Air, Korea's third largest airline and its strongest LCC, acknowledged the Korean government's recent efforts when he said that "2014 is the first year where the Korean Government has really supported LCC development."[153]

The emergence of Korean LCCs has a lot to do with the open skies agreement with Japan. Soon after this agreement took effect in 2007, a number of Korean companies showed an interest in establishing international air carriers targeting short-haul international routes, mainly in the Japanese market. Indeed, four out of five Korean low-cost carriers were established after the 2007 Japan–Korea open skies agreement: Jeju Air (June 2006), Jin Air (July 2008), Air Busan (October 2008), Eastar Jet (January 2009), and T'way (August 2010). All these LCCs started their international operations to Japanese points.

However, the Korean government's focus is on promoting *Korean* LCCs. It, together with the Korean carriers, have opposed the efforts of foreign LCCs (namely Tiger Air and

---

148 CAPA, "Korean Air seeks new markets after betting the house on N America, seemingly without SkyTeam support" (30 September 2013), online: <http://centreforaviation.com/analysis/korean-air-seeks-new-markets-after-betting-the-house-on-n-america-seemingly-without-skyteam-support-130189>.
149 *Ibid*.
150 See Fu *et al, supra* note 145 at 34.
151 Jeong-Ho Choi (Deputy Minister for the Office of Civil Aviation, The Korean Ministry of Land, Infrastructure and Transport), "Keynote address to the 52th Conference of the Korea Society of Air & Space Law and Policy" (23 May 2014) (He mentioned that the Korean government researched the question of whether the number of LCCs in Korea should be controlled and how many Korean LCCs should be allowed to operate.)
152 *Ibid*.
153 CAPA, "Jeju Air: 2014 is first year where Korean Govt has really supported LCC development" (13 October 2014), online: <http://centreforaviation.com/news/jeju-air-2014-is-first-year-where-korean-govt-has-really-supported-lcc-development-382578>.

AirAsia) to establish joint ventures in Korea. (Since this issue is more related to ownership and control restrictions, it will be discussed in Chapter 4: Ownership and Control Issues in Northeast Asia.)

3.3 Bilateral Positions on Market Access

3.3.1 China–Japan

China and Japan concluded their first air services agreement in 1974. Since then, there has been a gradual increase in destinations, flights, passengers carried, and volume of cargo. Chinese air carriers have expanded their operations between the two countries more aggressively than Japanese air carriers, whose expansion of their Chinese operations has been somewhat slow.[154]

In addition to the expansion of regular routes, an agreement on shuttle services between airports with good access to the downtown centers of the major cities of Shanghai (Hongqiao Airport) and Tokyo (Haneda Airport) was adopted at the air services consultation meeting held in June 2007. The two countries had first agreed on this shuttle service when Wen Jiabao, Prime Minister of China at the time, visited Japan in April 2007. His visit to Korea around the same time also helped to establish shuttle services between Gimpo in Seoul and Hongqiao in Shanghai.

In August 2012, China and Japan reached a considerably liberalized air services agreement allowing their designated carriers to operate unlimited numbers of passenger and cargo flights between any Chinese and Japanese cities except for the metropolitan centers of Beijing, Shanghai, and Tokyo. While liberalization of market access between secondary cities was significant on the surface (although major cities like Osaka were also included), more commercial importance came from the substantial increase in "shuttle

---

154 In 2006, for example, 12 designated Chinese air carriers operated from 18 Chinese cities to 17 Japanese cities, with 336 passenger flights per week and 41 cargo flights per week. In contrast, 3 designated Japanese air carriers provided services from 4 Japanese cities to 10 Chinese cities with 270 passenger flights per week and 33 cargo flights per week. Civil Aviation Administration of China, "中日.民航会谈在武汉举行" (13 March 2007), online: <www.caac.gov.cn/L1/L3/L3_16/L3_16_3/200703/t20070313_1673.html>. (Available only in Chinese, translated by the author); In 2012, this trend continued. For Chinese side, 12 designated Chinese air carriers operated from 21 Chinese cities to 17 Japanese cities, with 437 passenger flights per week and 38 cargo flights per week. For Japanese side, 3 designated Japanese air carriers provided services from 4 Japanese cities to 10 Chinese cities with 231 passenger flights per week and 44 cargo flights per week. The Japanese Ministry of Land, Infrastructure, and Transport, "日本.・ 中国 航空関係" (30 July 2012), online: <www.mlit.go.jp/common/000220340.pdf>. (Available only in Chinese, translated by the author).

services".[155] Because of the increased number of slots at Tokyo Haneda airport, the number of services from Haneda to Shanghai and Beijing increased by four services per day.[156] (See section 3.4.1 Shuttle Services among Major Cities in Northeast Asia.)

However, soon after this agreement, the China–Japan market was profoundly affected by a political dispute in September 2012 concerning a series of islands in the East China Sea called Diaoyu in Chinese and Senkaku in Japanese.[157] Due to the political tensions, the aviation market between the two countries lost nine years of growth, with the situation lasting much longer than the airlines had initially expected.[158]

Market access liberalization between secondary cities on both sides is starting to materialize through LCC operations, albeit slowly. For instance, in addition to the launch of Spring Airlines Japan (which will be discussed in Chapter 4), China's Spring Airlines is fostering a strategic partnership with Japan's Ibaraki Airport, 80 km from downtown Tokyo, to launch direct services as a way of taking advantage of the market access liberalization.[159]

3.3.2 Japan–Korea

In the four decades since the 1st Air Services Consultation took place in Tokyo in May 1967, the frequency and capacity of flights between Japan and Korea have steadily increased. A major step forward was taken in February 2006 when the two states decided to exempt visas for Korean nationals who wish to enter Japan and Japanese nationals who wish to enter Korea for a period of 90 days or less.[160] This visa facilitation was a significant stepping stone to an open skies agreement between the two states in 2007.

In August 2007, the two countries signed an open skies agreement permitting unlimited third and fourth freedom passenger and cargo flights for all designated points except airports in Tokyo. The reason for excluding Tokyo was the lack of slots at Narita Airport and

---

155 See Nicholas Olczak, "Japan and China expand bilateral air service" *Business Traveller* (9 August 2012), online: <www.businesstraveller.com/asia-pacific/news/japan-and-china-expand-bilateral-air-service>.
156 CAPA, "Japan and China expand bilateral air services agreement" (9 August 2012), online: <http://centreforaviation.com/news/japan-and-china-expand-bilateral-air-services-agreement-168722>.
157 CAPA, "China–Japan traffic bottoms out but faces massive challenge; Spring Airlines to launch new routes" (17 January 2013), online: <http://centreforaviation.com/analysis/China–Japan-traffic-bottoms-out-but-faces-massive-challenge-spring-airlines-to-launch-new-routes-94109>.
158 *Ibid.*
159 Jonathan Hutt (Strategy and Branding Director at Spring Airlines), "Spring Airlines International Expansion from China into North Asia" (Presentation material to the CAPA LCCs & New Age Airlines, Seoul, 4 September 2013).
160 See Embassy of Japan in Singapore, "Visa Exemption For Nationals Of The Republic Of Korea", online: <www.sg.emb-japan.go.jp/visa_korea.htm>; Jung Kwon-hyun, "Korea-Japan Visa Waiver" *Chosun-ilbo* (7 February 2006), online: <www.chosun.com/national/news/200602/200602060370.html>.

Haneda Airport.[161] Nevertheless, there was an increase in frequency between Gimpo Airport in Seoul and Haneda Airport in Tokyo pursuant to the shuttle service arrangement involving capital airports. In addition, the two countries agreed to expand fifth freedom operations.

The open skies agreement was directly related to Japan's new aviation policy. As already noted, Japan maintained a protectionist stance until 2007. Indeed, when trilateral open skies were openly discussed for the first time in June 2006,[162] Japan's position was even more protectionist than China's.[163] But in April 2007, the Japanese government unveiled the Asia Gateway Initiative, which was designed to remove restrictions on foreign air carriers' access to its airports[164] and to put the emphasis on improving links with neighboring countries.

While market access was significantly liberalized by the 2007 agreement, the limited slots at Haneda and Narita airports delayed the genuine effect of open skies. Japan has since solved this problem by significantly expanding runways and building new terminals at both airports. Once the shortage of slots at these airports had been resolved, Japan and Korea agreed at the air services consultation held in Seoul in December 2010 to add 14 flights on the Korea–Narita routes starting in March 2011 and to remove restrictions on frequency on the same routes starting in March 2013. Eventually, Narita airport was opened up entirely in March 2013, and Haneda airport was made more accessible by significant slot increases.

The real game changer in this market has been LCCs. The fact that LCCs could not fly to and from Tokyo was a huge drawback restricting LCCs' market penetration. Now that LCCs can fly between Tokyo's Narita airport and Seoul's Incheon airport without market access restrictions (although there are still capacity restrictions at Haneda airport and Gimpo airport, which provide better access to downtown Tokyo and Seoul, respectively), Japan and Korea are witnessing robust growth in LCC operations that focus on the Japan–Korea market. Obviously, the Japan–Korea market is an attractive market for LCCs because of the strong demand, short flight time, low operational costs and relatively high airfares set by the incumbent full-service airlines.

---

161 Narita Airport is a gateway airport to Japan, while Haneda Airport is considered a secondary airport. However, Haneda Airport is more accessible to people living in Tokyo: Narita is located 60 km east of Tokyo Station, while Haneda is located 15 km south of Tokyo Station. See Figure 3.5 Distance of Tokyo Area Airports from Downtown Tokyo.
162 The 1st International Symposium on Liberalizing Air Transport in Northeast Asia (see section 2.5.1 History).
163 Personal communication between the author and the Symposium committee member (Prof. Lee Yeong Heok).
164 Tae Hoon Oum, "Liberalization and Future Developments in Asia-Pacific Air Transport, Networks and Policy" (Presentation material to the 3rd Conference on International Air Transport Cooperation, Seoul, May 2010).

3.3.3   Korea–China

The first air services consultation between China and Korea took place in Beijing in July 1994 when China began adopting an open market policy across the board. Since then, air services consultations have taken place quite often—approximately once every two years—leading to increased flight frequency and capacity between the two countries.[165] The results of the air services consultation in June 2006 were particularly remarkable.

First, the two countries agreed to open the Korea–Shandong Province and the Korea–Hainan Province markets immediately with respect to unlimited third and fourth freedom passenger and cargo flights. In fact, China had already opened Hainan up through a policy of unilateral liberalization. In 2003, the CAAC and Hainan provincial government decided to unilaterally open up Hainan to unlimited 3rd, 4th and 5th traffic rights so as to promote the development of local tourism and the overall economy.[166]

Opening up Shandong was a meaningful step forward. It was in fact proposed by the Chinese government (despite strong opposition from Chinese carriers) because Shandong province is geographically close to Korea and many joint ventures between China and Korea were located in the province.[167] As a result of this partial liberalization, the market between Seoul, Korea, and Shandong Province (the location of the cities of Qingdao, Jinan, Weihai, and Yantai) has grown by about 72 percent in the number of flights, 38 percent in passengers and 15 percent in tonnage of cargo transported in the first year since liberalization.[168]

Second, the two governments agreed to expand passenger and cargo operations, which included increasing frequency on existing routes and adopting new routes.

---

165 Between 1994, when China and South Korea concluded their first air services agreement, and 2006, when they agreed to fully liberalize the market by 2010, annual growth had been about 20% in the passenger market and 25% in the cargo market. See J.H. Park, *A Study on the Effects of Air Transport Liberalization on Air Transport Markets*, (PhD Thesis, Department of Logistics Management, University of Incheon, 2011) (in Korean) [unpublished].

166 China, "Chinese Paper on Transportation Industry on Implementation of the Recommendations on More Competitive Air Service" (Paper presented to the 22nd APEC Transportation Working Group Meeting, 1-5 September 2003).

167 Yeong Heok Lee, "The Effects of Open Sky and its Prospects in NE Asia" (Presentation to the International Conference on Air Transport, Air Law and Regulation, Singapore, 24-26 May 2010).

168 *Ibid.*

Table 3.6 China–Korea Air Transport Statistics[169]

Year	Flights			Traffic		No. of airlines			Routes		
	Total	Pax flight	Cargo flight	Pax (no)	Tones (1000 ton)	Total	Pax	Cargo	Total	Pax	Cargo only
2004	38,658	37,260	1,398	5,288,252	280	22	14	8	36	34	2
2005	47,869	44,731	3,138	6,573,175	354	16	12	4	37	37	0
2006	61,804	56,912	4,892	7,321,391	413	20	12	8	37	37	0
2007	86,622	77,177	8,115	9,442,477	535	31	19	12	41	41	0
2008	81,294	72,285	9,009	7,963,624	528	24	14	10	43	43	0

However, there were rather restrictive rules involving the designation of carriers. In terms of passengers, China and Korea agreed to limit the number of designated airlines as follows: one airline each for routes with no more than 11 flights per week, two airlines each for routes with between 11 and 14 flights per week, and three or more airlines each for routes with 15 or more flights per week.[170]

Third, the two sides agreed to increase fifth freedom flights, albeit on a limited basis. Interestingly, China and Korea agreed to preferential relaxation of market access involving the 5th freedom. This stipulates that designated Chinese airlines are entitled to operate up to 21 weekly frequencies with 5th freedom traffic rights through Korean points for passenger and cargo services. However, designated Korean airlines are entitled to operate up to 13 weekly frequencies with 5th freedom traffic rights through Chinese points, among which seven weekly frequencies could only be exercised *three years* after the use of 5th freedom traffic rights by designated Chinese airlines. The remaining six weekly frequencies could be used *six years* after the Chinese airlines use these rights.[171]

In fact, preferential relaxation of market access was used in the Canada-US open skies agreement of 1995. After the agreement was reached, Canadian carriers could immediately access any point in the US from any point in Canada. However, there was a three-year transition period before US carriers could access Toronto/Pearson and a two-year transition period before they could access Montreal/Dorval and Vancouver International.[172] This

---

169 Jae Woon Lee, "Chapter 13 Regional Liberalization in Northeast Asia (China, South Korea, and Japan)" in David Timothy Duval, ed., *Air Transport in the Asia Pacific* (Burlington: Ashgate, 2014) 217 at 225.
170 J.H. Park, *A Study on the Effects of Air Transport Liberalization on Air Transport Markets*, (PhD Thesis, Department of Logistics Management, University of Incheon, 2011) at 99 [unpublished] (noting that "on the cargo side, the 'one route, one carrier' rule was abolished in 2006."). [translated by the author].
171 Memorandum of Understanding to the Air Services Agreement between China and Korea in 2006 [mimeo. restricted].
172 See Sangita Dubey & François Gendron, "The U.S.-Canada Open Skies Agreement: Three Years Later" (1999) 18:3 Travel-Log, online: <http://publications.gc.ca/Collection-R/Statcan/87-003-XIE/0039987-003-XIB.pdf>.

preferential relaxation of market access was an attempt to help Canadian carriers, which were less competitive than American carriers, by imposing a transition period.

In a similar fashion, preferential relaxation of market access gave Chinese carriers (which were less competitive than Korean airlines in 2006) lead time to gain a market advantage. This method has major implications for Northeast Asian open skies as an incentive for China, the key state in Northeast Asian open skies. (See Chapter 6: Towards Northeast Asian Open Skies: Liberalization by the Airline Industry and States.)

Fourth (and most significantly), China and Korea signed a memorandum of understanding permitting unlimited third and fourth freedom passenger and cargo flights for all designated points between the two countries starting in 2010. In the air services consultations between the two countries in 2008, however, China switched its position on open skies with Korea from full liberalization to moderate liberalization. Since then, negotiations have hovered around the status quo and not changed much except for limited increases in some flights. In response to the change in China's stance on open skies, Korea has been pursuing unlimited third and fourth freedom passenger and cargo flights vis-à-vis the five Chinese provinces of Hunan, Shaanxi, Jilin, Zhejiang, and Liaoning.[173]

The drive to reach full liberalization by 2010, which China and South Korea had agreed to in 2006, did not go according to plan. Although China has not returned to rigid protectionism, it seems unlikely that full liberalization of the aviation market between the two countries will be achieved in the near future.

As discussed in section 2.5.3 Barriers, China's aero-political position significantly affects the future of its air transport relationship with Korea. For three key reasons—namely, different geographical locations, the varying competitiveness of their national carriers, and diverse market sizes—the Chinese interpretation of full liberalization of the aviation market between China and Korea is still an "I lose-you win" game.

Nevertheless, since tourism, investment and trade between the two countries are gradually increasing, there will be a need for greater supply and progressive liberalization in the aviation market as well.

3.4 The Prospect of Liberalizing Trilateral Market Access

Except for regularly held negotiations and conferences for Northeast Asian open skies, China, Japan, and Korea have not made much progress through trilateral cooperation. The only thing achieved by the trilateral approach thus far is the shuttle service arrangement among the down airports of the three major cities – Shanghai, Tokyo and Seoul. However, the emergence and development of LCCs in Northeast Asia have been remarkable, and

---

[173] Korean Ministry of Land, Transport and Maritime Affairs (MLTM), "The First Roadmap for Aviation Policy" (December 2009) (available only in Korean).

LCCs have the potential to move the liberalization agenda forward. The role of LCCs in the context of market access liberalization cannot be underestimated. The other significant development in Northeast Asia is lively discussion of bilateral and trilateral free-trade agreements (FTAs). Even though FTAs have traditionally not covered aviation, which has always been reserved for separate negotiations, these FTAs could potentially accelerate liberalization of market access in air transport, especially in the cargo sector.

3.4.1 Shuttle Services among Major Cities in Northeast

Shuttle services between airports with good access to the respective downtown areas in the three major cities of Shanghai, Seoul and Tokyo (Hongqiao, Gimpo, and Haneda Airports, respectively) started in 2007. Given that the three airports have hitherto been considered "domestic" airports in their respective countries, triangular shuttle services among them was recognized as a positive sign for the future of regional liberalization in Northeast Asia.[174] Some commentators also noted that the shuttle program between Seoul's Gimpo Airport and Tokyo's Haneda Airport was a "preparatory step" towards overall liberalization between Korea and Japan.[175]

It can be said that the shuttle service had its conceptual origin in the BESETO (Beijing-Seoul-Tokyo) cooperative scheme that was initially proposed in 1991 as a model for cooperation among the three Northeast Asian mega-cities.[176] In the post-Cold War era, capital cities in Northeast Asia inevitably began to assume a regional role due to increasing interdependency among the three states.[177]

In early 2007, the BESETO Corridor Vision was specifically proposed by a joint study carried out by three government research institutes in China, Korea, and Japan.[178] While identifying air transport as an essential sector for building the BESETO corridor, this joint

---

174 Anming Zhang, "Northeast Asia's Unified, Concerted Approaches to the Inter-continental and Sub-continental Air Services Linkages" in Yeon Myung Kim & Sungwon Lee, eds., *Negotiating Strategies for Creating a Liberalized Air Transport Bloc in Northeast Asia* (Honolulu, HI; The Korea Transport Institute & East-West Center, 2009) 461 at 502-503.

175 Yeon Myung Kim & Sean Seungho Lee, "Korea's Approaches to Aviation Market Liberalization in Northeast Asia" in Yeon Myung Kim & Sungwon Lee, eds., *Negotiating Strategies for Creating a Liberalized Air Transport Bloc in Northeast Asia* (Honolulu, HI; The Korea Transport Institute & East-West Center, 2009) 393 at 416.

176 For the concept of "BESETO", see Hieyeon Keum, "Globalization and Inter-City Cooperation in Northeast Asia" (2000) 18 East Asia. 97.

177 Hieyeon Keum, "Globalization and Inter-City Cooperation in Northeast Asia" (2000) 18 East Asia. 97 at 97.

178 Institute of Spatial Planning & Regional Economy (ISPRE) of the National Development and Reform Commission, P.R. of China, Korea Research Institute for Human Settlements (KRIHS), Korea, and National Institute for Research Advancement (NIRA), Japan; see NIRA, "Proposal for Promotion of the Realization of the BESETO Corridor Vision – Toward sustained development in the Northeast Asia Region" (March 2007), online: <www.nira.or.jp/past/newse/paper/beseto/proposal.pdf>.

study strongly recommended setting up air shuttle service among mega-cities in Northeast Asia.[179]

In China, Shanghai was chosen to be the shuttle destination instead of Beijing. Since Shanghai is the business capital of China (while Beijing is its political and administrative capital), there is naturally more business traffic to and from Shanghai than Beijing, and it is such traffic that would benefit more from having an airport closer to downtown. Another reason is that Shanghai could offer the other Northeast Asian partners Hongqiao Airport, which has better access to downtown Shanghai than Pudong Airport, the main international airport in Shanghai.

Beijing Nanyuan Airport (the secondary airport in Beijing) is closer to downtown Beijing than Capital Airport. However, Nanyuan Airport has not been offered for shuttle services mainly because it is a major military air base. Although Japan and China reached a basic agreement on opening charter services between Haneda Airport and Beijing Nanyuan Airport in 2007, these plans were later scrapped.[180] To paint a more complete picture of shuttle services among the major cities in Northeast Asia, the following tables have been provided.

Table 3.7 Comparison of Travel Times among the Major Cities in Northeast Asia (Downtown Airports vs. Main International Airports)

	Route	Downtown To Airport	Flight Time	Airport To Downtown	Total Time
China – Japan	Hongqio – Haneda	20 m	3 h 20 m	30 m	4 h 10 m
	Pudong – Narita	1 h	3 h 30 m	1 h 20 m	5 h 50 m
Japan – Korea	Haneda – Gimpo	30 m	2 h	40 m	3 h 10 m
	Narita – Incheon	1 h 20 m	2 h 15 m	1 h 10 m	4 h 45 m
Korea – China	Gimpo – Hongqiao	40 m	1 h 50 m	20 m	2 h 50 m
	Incheon – Pudong	1 h 10 m	1 h 50 m	1 h	4 h

Table 3.8 Summary of Airlines Operating Shuttle Services

	Route	Chinese Carriers	Japanese Carriers	Korean Carriers
China – Japan	Hongqiao – Haneda	2 (China Eastern and Shanghai Airlines)	2 (Japan Airlines and ANA)	
	Pudong – Narita	2 (Air China and China Eastern)	2 (Japan Airlines and ANA)	

---

179 See NIRA, ibid.
180 See "Japan gives up on launching flights to Nanyuan Airport before Olympics." *Kyodo News International* (8 May 2008), online: <www.thefreelibrary.com/Japan+gives+up+on+launching+flights+to+Nanyuan+Airport+before...-a0179075052>.

Route		Chinese Carriers	Japanese Carriers	Korean Carriers
Japan - Korea	Haneda – Gimpo		2 (Japan Airlines and ANA)	2 (Korean Air and Asiana Airlines)
	Narita – Incheon		2 (Japan Airline and Vanilla Air)*	4 (Korean Air, Asiana Airline, Jeju Air, and Eastar Jet)
Korea – China	Gimpo – Hongqiao	2 (China Eastern and Shanghai Airlines)		2 (Korean Air and Asian Airlines)
	Incheon – Pudong	4 (China Eastern, China Southern, Shanghai Airlines and Spring)		2 (Korean Air and Asian Airlines)

* United Airway operates (joint venture with ANA).

3.4.2 The Role of LCCs

It is patently obvious that the liberalization of market access has facilitated the development of LCCs. Indeed, this trend has been observed globally. Led by Southwest Airlines, US LCCs have grown with domestic air transport deregulation while European LCCs including Ryanair and EasyJet have flourished under the three liberalization packages promulgated by the European Commission.

In ASEAN, the deregulation of the domestic markets initially paved the way for the birth of LCCs, and several liberalized bilateral air services agreements between ASEAN states further enabled the emergence of LCCs in international routes.[181] In Northeast Asia, the 2007 open skies agreement between Korea and Japan triggered the establishment of most Korean LCCs. The addition of Narita airport to the Korea-Japan open skies agreement in early 2013 was another golden opportunity for Korean and Japanese LCCs that had been launched in 2012.

At the same time, it is crucial to understand the bi-directional relationship between LCCs and liberalization. Although liberalization of market access has evidently facilitated the growth of LCCs, LCCs themselves also promote policy reform and liberalization.[182] Peter Forsyth, John King and Cherry Lyn Rodolfo rightly observed the pressure from LCCs in 2006 when the idea of ASEAN regional liberalization was ripening:

> The rapid development of LCCs in Singapore, Indonesia, Malaysia, and Thailand is now resulting in pressure on regulators for access to more international routes… ASEAN internal routes, with short to medium hauls and low to

---

[181] See Peter Forsyth, John King & Cherry Lyn Rodolfo, "Open skies in ASEAN" (2006) 12 Journal of Air Transport Management 143 at 146.
[182] See Fu *et al*, *supra* note 145 at 35.

moderate density are very suited to the LCCs… These pressures will tend to drive ASEAN to accelerate its liberalisation process.[183]

Indeed, ASEAN member states adopted the Multilateral Agreement on Air Services (MAAS) in 2009, with emerging LCCs serving as one of the main drivers for this development.[184] The significant air traffic growth by LCCs and the success of LCCs (particularly AirAsia) prompted the ASEAN states to push for greater regional liberalization.[185]

Northeast Asia still lags well behind Southeast Asia in terms of LCC penetration, but the door is opening to LCCs in the region. As noted, all of the Northeast Asian states are now witnessing the development of LCCs.

Figure 3.7 LCCs' Capacity Share within Northeast Asia[186]

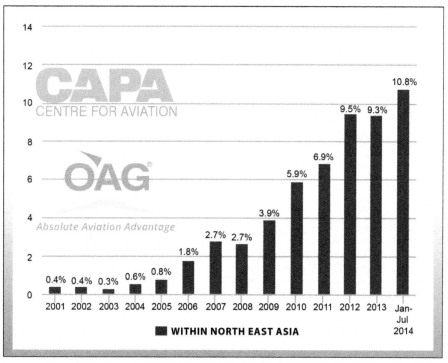

---

183 Forsyth *et al*, *supra* note 181 at 150.
184 See Fu *et al*, *supra* note 145 at 35.
185 *Ibid*.
186 Brendan Sobie, "LCC Subsidiaries of Legacy Carriers" (Presented to the ICAO/CAAC Symposium on Low Cost Carriers, October 2014), online: <www.icao.int/Meetings/LCC-China-2014/Documents/2-03-CAPA_Sobie-EN.pdf>.

Similar to the ASEAN experience—in which pressure from rapidly growing LCCs helped break down restrictions to market access[187]—Northeast Asian LCCs will likely press the aviation authorities in China, Japan, and Korea to move forward with regional liberalization.

3.4.3 Developing a China–Japan–Korea Free Trade Agreement

A free trade agreement is an agreement between two or more countries pursuant to which they give each other preferential conditions for market access rather than the non-discriminatory most-favored-nation treatment.[188] After a long period of preparation including a trilateral summit, a joint study by state-run research institutes, ministerial meetings, and working-level consultations, China, Japan, and Korea launched the trilateral Free Trade Agreement (CJK FTA) talks in March 2013.[189] Most recently, the 7th round of CJK FTA negotiations was held in Seoul in May 2015.[190]

As an FTA aims to cut trade (or transaction) costs, efficient air transport networks and cost-effective air transport are directly correlated to the goals of an FTA. Thus, it follows that air transport liberalization should go hand in hand with discussion of an FTA. For instance, when the ASEAN-China FTA talks were set up in 2002, they were immediately followed by an air transport cooperation initiative and the formation of a ministerial-level coordinating mechanism for transport.[191]

In the process of discussing Northeast Asian open skies, several commentators have suggested a link between FTAs and air services agreements for cargo air transport.[192]

---

187 Forsyth et al, supra note 181 at 151.
188 Walter Goode, *Dictionary of Trade Policy Terms*, 5th ed. (Cambridge: Cambridge University Press, 2007) under the word "Free trade agreement".
189 See online: China FTA Network <http://fta.mofcom.gov.cn/topic/chinarh.shtml>.
190 "The Conference of Chief Negotiators of the 7th Round of China-Japan–Korea Free Trade Area Negotiations held in Korea" *China FTA Network* (14 May 2015), online: <http://fta.mofcom.gov.cn/enarticle/chinarihen/chinarihennews/201505/21555_1.html>.
191 Wu Zhouhong (Department of International Affairs and Cooperation, General Administration of Civil Aviation of China), Comment to "Implementation the Process of the European Common Air Transport Market and the Common Air Transport Policy" by Kenneth Button (2003) 90 at 92 [unpublished, archived at The Korea Transport Institute].
192 Zheng Xingwu, "China's Approaches to Aviation Market Liberalization in Northeast Asia: An Academic Viewpoint" in Yeon Myung Kim and Sungwon Lee, eds., *Negotiating Strategies for Creating a Liberalized Air Transport Bloc in Northeast Asia* (Honolulu, HI; The Korea Transport Institute & East-West Center, 2009) 295 at 343 (noting that "[I]n future, a liberalized bilateral ASA may be signed after the conclusion of the bilateral FTA."); Yeon Myung Kim & Sean Seungho Lee, "Korea's Approaches to Aviation Market Liberalization in Northeast Asia" in Yeon Myung Kim and Sungwon Lee, eds., *Negotiating Strategies for Creating a Liberalized Air Transport Bloc in Northeast Asia* (Honolulu, HI; The Korea Transport Institute & East-West Center, 2009) 393 at 408 (noting that "[D]uring the process of a bilateral FTA meeting, issues such as the integration and liberalization of the air transport market must be handled with the utmost priority."); Fang Liu, "Comments in Part III: Negotiating Strategies for Coping with the Key Barriers to Liberalization of Northeast Asian Aviation Markets" in Yeon Myung Kim and Sungwon Lee, eds., *Negotiating Strategies for Creating a Liberalized Air Transport Bloc in Northeast Asia* (Honolulu, HI; The Korea Transport

3   MARKET ACCESS ISSUES IN NORTHEAST ASIA

Although there is a structural difference in their positions (that is, some supported incorporating market access conditions for cargo into the FTA discussions[193] while others argued that air transport discussions should be kept separate from FTA negotiations),[194] it was repeatedly acknowledged that liberalization of market access in the air cargo business was important for the success of the FTA.

As seen in Chapter 2, it has been easier to liberalize cargo service than passenger service.[195] Indeed, states have traditionally shown far more willingness to provide market access for foreign carriers carrying cargo than passengers. For instance, the ASEAN Single Aviation Market approach has shown that the cargo market is more flexible than the passenger market. The reason why cargo liberalization tends to be less controversial for states and their carriers was well documented in the CAPA consulting report:[196]

> After all, the participation of foreign carriers in freight transport can help lift exports from a particular State. Freight carriers often develop so-called "milk

---

Institute & East-West Center, 2009) 423 at 425 (noting that "[t]here is a possibility and need for the integration of air transportation after the economic integration comes to a high degree of the free trade area. The establishment of the free trade zone in Northeast Asia would certainly provide great opportunity to create the Northeast Asia air transport bloc, and speeding up of productive factor and people movement by air transport would also greatly promote free trade and economy development in this region. Therefore, in my view, the aviation authorities of the Northeast Asian countries should make common contributions in support of the free trade zone in this region so as to help create a liberalized air transport bloc in Northeast Asia at early stage."); Anming Zhang, "Northeast Asia's Unified, Concerted Approaches to the Inter-continental and Sub-continental Air Services Linkages" in Yeon Myung Kim and Sungwon Lee, eds., *Negotiating Strategies for Creating a Liberalized Air Transport Bloc in Northeast Asia* (Honolulu, HI; The Korea Transport Institute & East-West Center, 2009) 461 at 509 ("Appendix 2. Air Cargo Liberalization and Integration Strategies in Northeast Asia. 1) Tie airfreight liberalization with negotiations of free trade area (FTA): Make the option open of incorporating bilateral airfreight traffic rights negotiations into negotiations for the trade liberalization in broader goods and services. That is, aviation sector may be part of the large negotiations for establishing "Northeast Asian Economic Cooperation" or a Northeast Asian FTA. In this way, there will be a bigger room for a give-take bargaining over traffic rights. In addition, several issues of key importance to air carriers can be addressed relatively easily. For example, customs clearance procedures for transshipments can be dealt with under the trade facilitation program of an FTA, whereas restrictions on inter-modal and airport handling rights fall under the market access program.").

193 See *e.g.* Zhang, *ibid*.
194 See *e.g.* Kim & Lee, *supra* note 192 at 402 (noting that "[T]he best recourse would be viewing NEA's air transport policy separately from that of any FTA. An FTA's air transport agenda will entail another time-consuming policy-making process for the formulation of an integrated market frame; immediate liberalization of the air cargo sector is the best solution for the three NEA countries.").
195 ICAO, *Liberalization of Air Cargo Services*, ICAO ATConf/6-WP/14 (13 December 2012) (Presented by ICAO Secretariat) at 1 para 1.2, online: <www.icao.int/Meetings/atconf6/Documents/WorkingPapers/ATConf6-wp014_en.pdf>. (noting that "[A]s at the end of October 2012, of the 400 plus open skies agreements concluded by States, more than 100 granted Seventh freedom for air cargo or all cargo services, thus providing greater opportunity for the growth of such services.").
196 Ian Thomas, David Stone, Alan Khee-Jin Tan, Andrew Drysdale, & Phil McDermott, *Developing ASEAN's Single Aviation Market and Regional Air Services Arrangements with Dialogue Partners* (Final Report, June 2008, REPSF II Project No. 07/003) at 72.

runs" between destinations which strengthen their overall viability by accessing a series of markets. The presence of 7th freedom cargo carriers may even be welcome if the State's own carriers lack cargo capacity.

Now that not only bilateral FTAs but also a trilateral FTA are being widely discussed, it is likely that liberalization of the cargo sector in Northeast Asia will bear fruit in the near future. More specific suggestions will be discussed in Chapter 6: Towards Northeast Asian Open Skies: Liberalization by the Airline Industry and States. For now, however, it is unlikely that the momentum for FTAs will affect passenger air services, largely because passenger air services cannot easily be disentangled from traditional aero-political calculations.

3.5 Conclusion

The object of this chapter has been to provide a detailed description and analysis of market access issues in international air transport for the three Northeast Asian states. After identifying direct market access issues (carrier designation, route designation, and capacity and frequency) and indirect market access issues (airport capacity, airspace use, and visa openness), I have discussed national policies on market access in Northeast Asia.

Although there are various legal and political barriers to market access liberalization, positive steps toward Northeast Asian open skies have been observed on national, bilateral, and trilateral levels. The next chapter (Chapter 4: Ownership and Control Issues in Northeast Asia) will provide an in-depth analysis of the ownership and control issues in air transport with a focus on Northeast Asia.

4 OWNERSHIP AND CONTROL ISSUES IN NORTHEAST ASIA

4.1 OWNERSHIP AND CONTROL RESTRICTIONS IN INTERNATIONAL AIR TRANSPORT

4.1.1 Overview

Recognizing that the liberalization of air transport depends very much on the level of market access, Chapter 3 delved into market access issues from various angles with a particular emphasis on Northeast Asia. The other pivot on which liberalization rests is the relaxation of ownership and control restrictions, the key theme of this chapter.

Although ownership and control restrictions are closely related to market access restrictions, states do not necessarily coordinate their positions on these two legal pivots. For instance, although the United States has been proactive in liberalizing market access (as discussed in Chapter 3), US domestic law lays down stricter ownership rules than in most states (see the section below). In addition, the traditional ownership and control requirements are entrenched in the US open skies agreement model.

From the outset, it is necessary to note that ownership and control restrictions are more difficult to interpret than market access issues. Generally speaking, the level of market access is stipulated in air services agreement in clear language. Pertinent questions include 1) how many air carriers from each state are allowed to fly, 2) which routes will be allowed, and 3) how many flights will be operated per day or week. Since those questions are not ambiguous to interpret, market access issues are implemented in a relatively straightforward manner.

In contrast, interpreting ownership and control restrictions is not a simple process. Essentially, ownership and control restrictions are embedded in an internal lock (domestic law) as well as an external lock (the air services agreements).[1] The complexity of the ownership and control restrictions not only entails a multilayered regulatory structure but also implies that they are expressed in an opaque manner. Consequently, this requires a more detailed analysis, which may be accomplished by subdividing ownership and control restrictions into the following matrix:

---

1   Brian Havel, *Beyond Open Skies: A New Regime for International Aviation* (Alphen aan den Rijn: Kluwer Law International, 2009) at 135 and 165. [Havel, "Open Skies"].

Table 4.1 Subdivision of Ownership and Control Restrictions

	Substantial Ownership	Effective Control
Internal Restriction (Domestic Law)	A	B
External Restriction (Air Services Agreements)	C	D

Substantial ownership restriction by way of domestic law (Subdivision A) is a quantitative restriction that sets a limit on foreign shares in national air carriers. While domestic laws in many jurisdictions generally provide that the majority share of national carriers must be held by nationals, meaning that foreign shares must not exceed 50 percent, some states have more rigid restrictions on the maximum foreign ownership (*e.g.* Brazil, 20 percent;[2] the US, 25 percent;[3] and the Philippines, 40 percent[4]).

Effective control restriction by way of domestic law (Subdivision B) is a qualitative restriction that focuses on "who controls" national air carriers. Evaluating effective control is trickier than assessing substantial ownership since it is not a mathematical question. Although some national laws provide rules including, *inter alia*, restrictions on the

---

2   See Lucas Braun, "Liberalization or Bust: A Double Step Approach to Relaxing the Foreign Ownership and Control Restrictions in the Brazilian Aviation Industry" (2014) 39 Air & Space L. 343 at 348. (noting that "Article 181 of the Brazilian Aeronautic Code (Law No. 7565/86) provides that, in order for an aviation company to be authorized to engage in air transportation services within Brazil, the following conditions must be met: (i) it must have its principal place of business in Brazil, (ii) 80 percent of its voting stock must be held by Brazilians, and (iii) its overall management (direção) must be entrusted exclusively to Brazilians.").

3   49 U.S.C. § 40102(a) (15) "citizen of the United States" means—(A) an individual who is a citizen of the United States; (B) a partnership each of whose partners is an individual who is a citizen of the United States; or (C) a corporation or association organized under the laws of the United States or a State, the District of Columbia, or a territory or possession of the United States, of which the president and at least two-thirds of the board of directors and other managing officers are citizens of the United States, which is under the actual control of citizens of the United States, and in which at least 75 percent of the voting interest is owned or controlled by persons that are citizens of the United States."

4   *The 1987 Constitution of the Republic of the Philippines Article XII Section 11.* "No franchise, certificate, or any other form of authorization for the operation of a public utility shall be granted except to citizens of the Philippines or to corporations or associations organized under the laws of the Philippines, at least sixty per centum of whose capital is owned by such citizens; nor shall such franchise, certificate, or authorization be exclusive in character or for a longer period than fifty years. Neither shall any such franchise or right be granted except under the condition that it shall be subject to amendment, alteration, or repeal by the Congress when the common good so requires. The State shall encourage equity participation in public utilities by the general public. The participation of foreign investors in the governing body of any public utility enterprise shall be limited to their proportionate share in its capital, and all the executive and managing officers of such corporation or association must be citizens of the Philippines." See also *Metropolitan Cebu Water District (MCWD) v. Margarita A. Adala*, [2007] (the Philippines Supreme Court Decision) stating that "[A] "public utility" is a business or service engaged in regularly supplying the public with some commodity or service of public consequence such as electricity, gas, water, transportation, telephone or telegraph service.", online: <www.lawphil.net/judjuris/juri2007/jul2007/gr_168914_2007.html>.

nationality of the chairperson and the members of the board,[5] it is inevitable that the relevant government body must exercise wide discretion in interpreting effective control. In brief, the practical importance of such restrictions is defined by government policy.

Substantial ownership restriction by way of air services agreements (Subdivision C) is a reciprocal restriction. On routes governed by an air services agreement between two states, a substantial ownership restriction in the agreement requires that a state party designate only carriers that are substantially owned by its own nationals. This effectively restrains national air carriers of one state from attracting sizeable foreign investment.

The concern of the airline seeking foreign investment is that its traffic rights can be revoked or suspended by the other state if it ceases to be substantially owned by its own nationals. The difficulty rests in the definition of what constitutes "substantial ownership." Although states generally interpret "substantial" as "majority" in practice, there is no accepted definition of what is considered to be "substantial ownership" in most air services agreements. Thus, evaluating Subdivision C is more complicated than Subdivision A, as the latter sets a specific limit on ownership restriction in domestic law.

Havel and Sanchez indicate the ambiguity of the "substantial ownership" restriction by positing a hypothetical situation: if Lufthansa were merely to acquire a 25 percent stake in Air Canada, the US could assert that Lufthansa had acquired enough leverage to allow the US to revoke Air Canada's right to fly to the US based on the air services agreement between the US and Canada.[6] This scenario is not unrealistic because the US could conceivably reference its own domestic requirement that limits foreign ownership of US airlines to 25 percent of voting stock.

Finally, effective control restriction by way of air services agreements (Subdivision D) is also a reciprocal restriction. Just as Subdivision B was more complicated than Subdivision A, Subdivision D is also more difficult to interpret than Subdivision C, since interpreting "effective control" varies by state. As there is room for each government's discretionary power to come into play in negotiations, state parties to an air services agreement do not necessarily have a fixed definition of "effective control".

Using the same Air Canada example above, if there were various indicators of Lufthansa's corporate intervention in Air Canada's management and operations that

---

5   The EU, for example, provides a somewhat explicit definition of "effective control." Article 2(g) of Council Regulation No. 2407/92 defines "effective control" as follows: "Effective control means a relationship constituted by rights, contracts or any other means which, either separately or jointly and having regard to the considerations of fact or law involved, confer the possibility of directly or indirectly exercising a decisive influence on an undertaking, in particular by: (a) the right to use all or part of the assets of an undertaking; (b) rights or contracts which confer a decisive influence on the composition, voting or decisions of the bodies of an undertaking or otherwise confer a decisive influence on the running of the business of the undertaking."

6   Brian Havel & Gabriel Sanchez, "The Emerging *Lex Aviatica*" (2011) 42 Geo. Int'l L.J. 639 at 650-651. [Havel & Sanchez, "Lex Aviatica"].

implied that Lufthansa has acquired leverage to exercise "effective control" of Air Canada, the US could revoke Air Canada's right to fly to the US.[7]

4.1.2   Internal (Domestic Law) Restrictions

Substantial ownership and effective control restrictions have origins in US domestic law. The US Air Commerce Act of 1926 was the first law that required US air carriers to maintain 51 percent of voting stock under US citizenship and to ensure that 66 percent of members of the board of directors were US citizens.[8]

In 1925, the US Congress initiated the citizenship requirement to assure the availability of aircraft for national defense purposes.[9] At the time, the US Congress and the head of the US military believed that it was necessary to have "government intervention in commercial air carrier development for the dual purpose of training a reserve corps of pilots and maintaining an auxiliary air force."[10] Given the historical backdrop (the First World War only ended in 1918), it is understandable that the country's political and military leaders did not disassociate the commercial and military roles of aviation. Essentially, commercial pilots were potential military pilots, and commercial aircraft constituted a reserve air fleet in the event of war.

In the 1930s, economic protectionism provided another justification for the ownership and control restrictions in US domestic law.[11] During the Great Depression, the US often chose protectionism as the principal means of strengthening the US economy.[12] Accordingly, The Civil Aeronautics Act of 1938 increased from 51 percent to 75 percent the amount of an airline's voting stock that must be in US hands for the carrier to qualify as a US operator.

---

7   *Ibid.* at 651.
8   See Constantine Alexandrakis, "Foreign Investment in U.S. Airlines: Restrictive Law is Ripe for Change" (1993-1994) 4 U. Miami Bus. L. Rev. 71 at 73-74.
9   See *ibid.* at 73.
10   James E. Gjerset, "Crippling United States Airlines: Archaic Interpretations of the Federal Aviation Act's Restriction on Foreign Capital Investments" (1991) 7 American University Journal of International Law and Policy173 at 180-181.
11   Although some commentators argue that economic protectionism *replaced* the national defense justification (*e.g.* Alexandrakis *supra* note 8 stating that "[M]ilitary protectionism was replaced by economic protectionism during the New Deal era in the 1930s."), it is safe to say that the national defense justification remained valid at least until the 1950s. See Gjerset, *ibid.* at 182 (noting that "[W]ith the advent of the Great Depression and New Deal Legislation, however, the justification for the citizenship requirement changed from strict national security goals to protecting developing industries from foreign competition.).
12   See Bimal Patel, "A Flight Plan Towards Financial Stability – The History and Future of Foreign Ownership Restrictions in the United States Aviation Industry" (2008) 73 J. Air L. & Com. 487 at 490; See also Isabelle Lelieur, *Law and Policy of Substantial Ownership and Effective Control of Airlines: Prospects for Change* (Burlington, Vermont: Ashgate, 2003) at 32.

The Federal Aviation Act of 1958 further narrowed the ownership and control restrictions by specifically defining what "citizen of the United States" meant. This act was first amended as the Airline Deregulation Act of 1978, and these amendments were later codified in separate sections of US Code (USC): Title 49 – Transportation. Specifically, paragraph 15 of 40102(a) in the 49 USC provides that:

> "[C]itizen of the United States" means—
> (A) an individual who is a citizen of the United States;
> (B) a partnership each of whose partners is an individual who is a citizen of the United States; or
> (C) a corporation or association organized under the laws of the United States or a State, the District of Columbia, or a territory or possession of the United States, of which the president and at least two-thirds of the board of directors and other managing officers are citizens of the United States, which is under the actual control of citizens of the United States, and in which at least 75 percent of the voting interest is owned or controlled by persons that are citizens of the United States.

The 25 percent cap on foreign voting equity in US airlines is still in effect as a substantial ownership restriction. On the issue of what constitutes effective (or actual) control, the US Department of Transportation (US DOT) principally focuses on the question of whether a foreign interest will be able to substantially influence the carrier's activities.[13] The US DOT also stated that controlling factors broadly include substantial ownership ties, financial arrangements, or managerial affiliations while emphasizing that each citizenship case presents its own set of facts.[14] Despite these explanations, it is evident that the control test is flexible enough to give the US DOT the discretion to determine whether effective control is in the hands of US nationals.

Indeed, the US DOT's decisions show that the application of the control test remains unsettled.[15] While the DOT's DHL/ASTAR decision (2004)[16] favored DHL's US domestic supplier (ASTAR) without creating many difficulties for the applicant, Virgin America had to pass much stricter foreign control criteria.[17] Brian Havel succinctly noted that the

---

13   U.S., Department of Transportation, *Acquisition of Northwest Airlines by Wings Holdings, Inc.* (Order 89-9-51) (29 September 1989) at 5.
14   U.S., Department of Transportation, *DHL AIRWAYS, INC. n/k/a ASTAR AIR CARGO, INC.* (Docket OST-2002-13089) (10 May 2004) at 8, online: <www.transportation.gov/sites/dot.dev/files/docs/2004-5-10.pdf>.
15   Havel, "Open Skies", *supra* note 1 at 141.
16   U.S., Department of Transportation, *DHL AIRWAYS, INC. n/k/a ASTAR AIR CARGO, INC.* (Docket OST-2002-13089) (10 May 2004).
17   See Havel, *supra* note 1 at 143-155. Havel noted that the DOT's strict "actual control" analysis yielded positive results for Virgin America. For instance, Virgin America removed Frederick Reid as CEO of Virgin

US DOT's citizenship review process is clouded by "the unpredictability of the ad hoc, impressionistic – and unabashedly aeropolitical – analysis which DOT regulators have continued to apply."[18]

Although ownership and control restrictions under domestic law originated in the US, US domestic law is not unique in this regard. In fact, many states have laws with the ownership restriction. (See Table 4.2 for the foreign ownership restriction in selected countries.)

Table 4.2 Foreign Ownership Limits in Selected Countries[19]

Country	Maximum percent of foreign ownership in selected countries
Australia	- 49 percent for international airlines
	- 100 percent for domestic airlines
Brazil	- 20 percent of voting equity
Canada	- 25 percent of voting equity
	- The maximum holding in Air Canada by any single investor is limited to 15 percent
Chile	- The only requirement for designation as a Chilean carrier (domestic or international) is principal place of business
China	- 49 percent
Colombia	- 40 percent
India	- 26 percent for Air India
	- 49 percent for privately-owned domestic carriers
Indonesia	- Airlines designated under bilateral agreements must be substantially owned and effectively controlled by the other party
Israel	- 34 percent
Japan	- 49 percent
Kenya	- 49 percent
Korea	- 49 percent
Malaysia	- 45 percent for Malaysia Airlines, but the maximum holding by any single foreign entity is 20 percent
	- 49 percent for other airlines
Mauritius	- 40 percent

America (although Mr. Reid was the preferred choice of Virgin Group CEO Richard Branson) and cut the Virgin Group's board representation from three to two. See *ibid*. at 153.

18 *Ibid*. at 146-147.
19 Based on Chia-Jui Hsu & Yu-Chun Chang, "The Influences of Airline Ownership Rules on Aviation Policies and Carriers' Strategies" (2005) 5 Proceedings of the Eastern Asia Society for Transportation Studies 557 at 558, online: <www.easts.info/on-line/proceedings_05/557.pdf>. However, I have made updates and corrections for China, Japan, and Korea.

Country	Maximum percent of foreign ownership in selected countries
New Zealand	- 49 percent for international airlines
	- 100 percent for domestic airlines
Peru	- 49 percent
Philippines	- 40 percent
Singapore	- The only requirement for designation as a Singapore carrier is principal place of business
Taiwan	- One third
Thailand	- 49 percent
US	- 25 percent of voting equity

Australia and New Zealand are unique in that they have liberalized foreign ownership in domestic airlines. New Zealand removed the foreign ownership restriction in 1988,[20] and Australia relaxed the ownership rules in 1999. This means that "any foreign person including a foreign airline can acquire up to 100 percent of the equity of an Australian domestic airline, unless it is deemed to be contrary to the national interest."[21]

The lifting of the foreign ownership cap was particularly significant in the creation of low-cost carriers.[22] Virgin Blue (now Virgin Australia), a subsidiary of the Virgin Group, was established in 2000 with 100 percent UK capital, and Tiger Airways Australia had been a wholly owned subsidiary of Singapore's Tiger Airways Holdings Limited since its creation in 2007.[23]

It is very rare for ownership and control to be fully liberalized in a country's domestic law like this. In the vast majority of states, a foreign carrier cannot establish its own airline, either a new airline or a subsidiary or buying over an existing airline, in a domestic market due to these internal restrictions.

---

20 See *ibid*. at 565 (noting that "[I]n June 1986, the New Zealand Government amended the Air Services Licensing Act (1983) removing specific restrictions on overseas investments in domestic airlines. In policy guidelines issued to the Overseas Investment Commission (OIC), it was stipulated that up to 50 percent investment by foreign airlines was acceptable. In February 1988, the Government approved a temporary increase in Ansett Australia's shareholding in Ansett New Zealand to 100 percent, provided a return to 50 percent occurred within two years if a suitable New Zealand shareholder could be found. Seven months later, the Government decided to remove the previous 50 percent limit on investment by foreign airlines. The OIC was thereby able to approve 100 percent investment by any foreign carrier in a domestic airline and as such New Zealand became the first country in the world to remove foreign ownership restrictions on domestic carriers.").

21 Jeffrey Goh, *The Single Aviation Market of Australia and New Zealand* (London: Cavendish Publishing Limited, 2001) at 72.

22 Hsu & Chang, *supra* note 19 at 566.

23 In 2014, Tiger Airways Australia became a fully owned subsidiary of Virgin Australia. See CAPA, "Virgin Australia CEO John Borghetti interview: dual-brand strategies, Asia & being a modern airline" (4 December 2014), online: <http://centreforaviation.com/analysis/virgin-australia-ceo-john-borghetti-interview-dual-brand-strategies-asia--being-a-modern-airline-199511>.

4.1.3 External (Air Services Agreement) Restrictions

The Chicago Conference was the first time that the issues of ownership and control restrictions were raised in international discussions.[24] Since US officials wanted to assure the safety of US airspace, the US sought the right to prohibit carriers from operating there if substantial ownership and effective control raised questions of a political nature or a threat to national security.[25] For the US, the then-war enemies Germany and Italy were the main targets of these sentiments, particularly because they had extensive ties to Latin American airlines operating within the US sphere of influence.[26]

Although these restrictions were not included in the Chicago Convention (1944), both the Transit Agreement (1944) and the Transport Agreement (1944) provided for such restrictions.[27] The identical wording was inserted in the "Standard Form of Agreement for Provisional Air Routes" as a model for future bilateral agreements.[28] More importantly, the first bilateral agreement between the US and the UK in 1946 (Bermuda type 1 Agreement) modeled the language for substantial ownership and effective control of air carriers.[29]

The majority of states have followed the Bermuda type 1 as a standard bilateral air services agreement, and the notion of "flag carrier" defined here has long been the norm in worldwide aviation policy.[30] The current practice is not very far from the agreements made in the 1940s. In 2006, it was reported that substantial ownership and effective control

---

24 Alexandrakis *supra* note 8 at 74.
25 See *ibid*. See also *Proceedings of the International Conference on Civil Aviation, Chicago, 1 November – 7 December 1944* (Washington, D.C.: United States Government Printing Office, 1948) vol. II at 1283. During the Chicago Conference 1944, the US Delegate once spoke that "we would not care to have a group of Germans go abroad and use their ill gotten gains to purchase aircraft and utilize rights we might have accorded a friendly state to fly into the Unites States."
26 Alexandrakis *supra* note 8 at 74.
27 Article 1 Section 5 of the Transit Agreement and Article 1 Section 6 of the Transport Agreement: "Each contracting State reserves the right to withhold or revoke a certificate or permit to an air transport enterprise of another State in any case where it is not satisfied that substantial ownership and effective control are vested in nationals of a contracting State, or in case of failure of such air transport enterprise to comply with the laws of the State over which it operates, or to perform its obligations under this Agreement."
28 Michael Milde, *International Air Law and ICAO*, 2nd ed. (Utrecht: Eleven International Publishing, 2012) at 91.
29 Article 6 of the Bermuda 1 Agreement: "Each Contracting Party reserves the right to withhold or revoke the exercise of the rights specified in the Annex to this Agreement by a carrier designated by the other Contracting Party in the event that it is not satisfied that substantial ownership and effective control of such carriers are vested in nationals of either Contracting Party, or in case of failure by that carrier to comply with the laws and regulations referred to in Article 5 hereof, or otherwise to fulfil the conditions under which the rights are granted in accordance with this Agreement and its Annex."
30 Peter P.C. Haanappel, "Airline Ownership and Control and Some Related Matters" (2001) 26 Air & Space L. 90 at 90.

clauses were found in 90 percent of bilateral air services agreements.[31] One example is Article 3, paragraphs 2 and 3, of the China–Korea air services agreement:

> Article 3 (Airline Designation and Authorization)
> (2) The substantial ownership and effective control of the airlines designated by each Contracting Party shall remain vested in such Contracting Party or its nationals.
> (3) The aeronautical authorities of the other Contracting Party may require the airlines designated by the first Contracting Party to satisfy to them that they are qualified to fulfil the conditions prescribed under the laws and regulations normally and reasonably applied by the said authorities to the operation of international air services.

Article 4, paragraph 1, sub-paragraph (a), of the Agreement also pertains to this issue:

> Article 4 (Revocation, Suspension and Imposition of Conditions)
> (1) Each Contracting Party shall have the right to revoke or suspend the operating authorization granted to the designated airline(s) of the other Contracting Party or to impose such conditions as it may deem necessary on the exercise by the said designated airline(s) of the rights specified in Article 2 of this Agreement, in any of the following cases:
> (a) where it is not satisfied that substantial ownership and effective control of that airline is vested in the other Contracting Party or its nationals.

A very important feature of this external restriction is the fact that the language of the nationality provision in air services agreements is rather flexible. Indeed, the nationality provision is framed as a *right* to revoke, implying that there is an implicit right not to revoke.[32] In other words, states are not obliged to invoke the nationality clause even if they believe that the nationality conditions are not met.[33] For instance, the US did not suspend the traffic rights of Aerolineas Argentinas even though the airline was 85 percent owned by a Spanish holding company backed by Iberia (Spanish carrier).[34] Instead, the US required

---

31 WTO, Council for Trade in Services, *Quantitative Air Services Agreements Review (QUASAR): Part B: PRELIMINARY RESULTS*, S/C/W/270/Add.1 (2006) at 33, para 61, online: <www.wto.org/english/tratop_e/serv_e/transport_e/quasar_partb_e.pdf>.
32 Havel & Sanchez, "Lex Aviatica", *supra* note 6 at 662.
33 Michael Milde, *International Air Law and ICAO*, 2nd ed. (Utrecht: Eleven International Publishing, 2012) at 91.
34 Havel, "Open Skies", *supra* note 1 at 165. See also Pablo Mendes de Leon, "A New Phase in Alliance Building: The Air France/KLM Venture as a Case Study" (2004) 53 Z.L.W. 359 at 362.

that American Airlines be granted additional market access rights between points in the US and Buenos Aires.[35]

This flexible articulation carries considerable implications for liberalizing external restrictions. Since states can decide whether or not to challenge the ownership and control of a foreign carrier, legal reform is not necessary for liberalization. In other words, State A can be silent about sizeable foreign investment in the national air carriers of State B. Thus, one possibility is *de facto* liberalization that does not necessarily require revision of air services agreements. Many Latin American governments appear to have followed this practice. For instance, although LAN Chile owned an 80 percent share in LAN Argentina in 2006,[36] there was no meaningful opposition from the other Latin American states.

Nevertheless, there have been various attempts to *de jure* liberalize the long-established substantial ownership and effective control restrictions through different levels of reforms, namely, multilateral/plurilateral regulatory reform, regional reform, bilateral preferential concessions, and unilateral (and voluntary) relaxation. (See section 4.3 Options for Liberalization of Ownership and Control Restrictions.)

Clearly, there are barriers to such reform. ICAO has summarized the rationale for the nationality clause, namely: 1) the "balance of benefits" policy for the airlines involved, 2) preventing "free riders", 3) identifying the country responsible for safety and security oversight, and 4) national defense considerations.[37]

It would be fair to say that the argument of security and national defense is not convincing anymore.[38] Most countries now rely on their military for national security and defense without needing their national airlines for that purpose.[39] In addition, ensuring safety and security oversight can be achieved by the "effective regulatory control" test rather than the "effective economic control" test. It is important to distinguish the two concepts. While "effective regulatory control" ensures optimal compliance with safety,

---

35 Mendes de Leon, *ibid.* at 362.
36 Aviation Strategy, "LAN Airlines: Discovered by the money managers" (November 2006), online: <https://www.aviationstrategy.aero/newsletter/articles/1458/show>.
37 ICAO, *Liberalization of Air Carrier Ownership and Control*, ICAO Doc ATconf/6-WP/12 (10 December 2013) at 1, para. 1.2., online: <www.icao.int/Meetings/atconf6/Documents/WorkingPapers/ATConf6-wp012_en.pdf>.
38 Milde, *supra* note 33 at 92; But some national defense agencies strongly support the nationality clause. The view of the U.S. Department of Defense, for example, is that the US Civil Reserve Air Fleet (CRAF) program, a wartime readiness program established in 1952, still "ensure(s) quantifiable, accessible, and reliable commercial airlift capability to augment Department of Defense (DOD) airlift." See United States Transportation Command, *Civil Airlift Programs*, USTRANSCOM Instruction 24-9 (13 October 2011); See also Havel *supra* note 1 at 48 (noting the DOD's concern that "[i]f a U.S. carriers were bought by foreign investors, it could no longer be relied on to honor its CRAF commitments."). Havel, however, noted that "[I]n the maritime equivalent of CRAF (the Voluntary Intermodal Sealift Agreement, VISA), the Department of Defense already allows participation by foreign-owned commercial ships that qualify as 'U.S. citizens' under maritime law.". See *ibid*.
39 Braun, *supra* note 2 at 357.

security, and other important regulatory matters,[40] "effective economic control" is about who manages the airline in question. (See section 4.3.1 Multilateral Approach for a more detailed explanation.)

Preventing "free riders" is an important consideration. The following hypothetical situation proposed by Havel and Sanchez is useful for understanding the reciprocal and exclusive nature of ownership and control restrictions in air services agreements:

> If the United States, pursuing market access privileges for its airlines in East Asia, exchanges liberal reciprocal concessions with, for example, South Korea, it would not want investors from a more restrictive state, such as neighboring Japan, to "free ride" these market access privileges by either acquiring or establishing an air carrier in South Korea. Japan's incentive to offer new market concessions to US carriers would be correspondingly diminished in such a scenario.[41]

"Balance of benefit" policies are the strongest barrier to this reform. Many states still prefer implementing a "balance of benefit" policy for the airlines involved, referring to a policy of calculating economic details such that neither party receives a bigger benefit from the agreed international air service.[42] It is obvious that a rigorous insistence on a "balance of benefits" is opposed to free competition in the market.[43]

In addition, it is noteworthy that some labor groups, especially US airline employees, have strongly opposed liberalizing foreign ownership rules because they believe that this could decrease the quality of working conditions and reduce the workforce.[44] Compelling as these arguments may be, the economic disadvantages resulting from the protectionist effects of ownership and control restrictions cannot be disregarded. From an airline's perspective, foreign capital flow is interrupted and normally permissible forms of corporate restructuring (such as mergers) are prohibited by the ownership and control restrictions.[45] From a consumer's perspective, it is perfectly reasonable to ask why "who can perform

---

40   Alan Khee-Jin Tan, "Toward a Single Aviation Market in ASEAN: Regulatory Reform and Industry Challenges" 2013 Economic Research Institute for ASEAN and East Asia (ERIA) Discussion Paper 2013-22 (October 2013) at 19, online: <www.eria.org/publications/discussion_papers/toward-a-single-aviation-market-in-asean-regulatory-reform-and-industry-challenges.html>. [Tan, "SAM in ASEAN"].
41   See Havel & Sanchez, "Lex Aviatica", *supra* note 6 at 649.
42   Milde, *supra* note 33 at 114-115.
43   *Ibid.* at 115.
44   See *e.g.* Patel, *supra* note12 at 515.
45   Havel & Sanchez, "Lex Aviatica", *supra* note 6 at 649.

transport services most efficiently is secondary" and why "what matters is whether [that person] is a foreigner or a national."[46]

In the following section, the national law and policy of the Northeast Asian states with regard to ownership and control restrictions will be examined. After introducing the relevant legislation in these three countries, I will review past precedents dealing with ownership and control tests to understand how each of these governments has interpreted the restrictions, and in particular, effective control inquiries.

4.2 National Law and Policy on Ownership and Control Restrictions in Northeast Asia

4.2.1   Overview

Using the matrix discussed in section 4.1.1 Overview, the three countries in Northeast Asia have rigid legislation involving Subdivision A (substantial ownership restriction in their domestic laws). China permits a maximum of 49 percent foreign ownership (up to 25 percent for one person); Japan, a maximum of 1/3 foreign voting rights; and Korea, no more than 50 percent foreign ownership. The three countries do not have detailed criteria for examining Subdivision B (effective control restriction by domestic law) in their national laws. Nonetheless, past precedents provide ample evidence for deducing each nation's policy on effective control, which will be discussed in the following sections.

However, there is not enough information publicly available to determine how flexibly (or rigidly) the three countries interpret Subdivision C (substantial ownership restriction by air services agreements) and Subdivision D (effective control restriction by air services agreements). One way to look at this is to ask whether they have officially invoked the nationality clause and revoked the permit of foreign airlines whose ownership and control structures are dubious. For example, most AirAsia's joint ventures are majority owned by local investors with minimal expertise in the aviation industry.

---

46   Jürgen Basedow, "Verkehrsrecht und Verkehrspolitik als Europäische Aufgabe" in Gerd Aberle ed., *Europaische Verkehrspolitik* (Tübingen, Paul Siebeck: 1987) 1 at 7 (cited in Havel & Sanchez, "Lex Aviatica", *supra* note 6 at 649) [Havel's translation].

Table 4.3 The Ownership and Control Structure of AirAsia LCC Joint Ventures

Country/Territory	Joint Venture Airline	Local Shareholder/s	Foreign Shareholder/s
Indonesia	Indonesia AirAsia	Pin Harris – 20% and Sendjaja Windjaja – 31%	AirAsia Investment Limited (wholly-owned subsidiary of AirAsia Berhad) – 49%
Indonesia	Indonesia AirAsia X	PT Kirana Anugerah Perkasa (PTKAP) – 51%	AirAsia X Berhad – 49%
Thailand	Thai AirAsia X	Tassapon Bijleveld – 41% and Julpas Krueso-pon – 10%	AirAsia Berhad – 49%;
Japan	Japan AirAsia (Scheduled to launch services in 2015)	Octave Japan Infrastructure Fund – 19%; Rakuten Inc. – 18%; Noevir Holdings Co. Ltd. – 9% and Alpen – 5%	AirAsia Investment Limited (wholly-owned subsidiary of AirAsia Berhad) – 49%
India	India AirAsia	Tata Sons – 30%; Telstra Tradeplace – 21%	AirAsia Investment Limited (wholly-owned subsidiary of AirAsia Berhad) – 49%
Philippines	Philippine AirAsia	F&S Holdings – 16%; TNR Holdings – 16%; Alfredo Yao – 13% and Michael Romero – 16%	AirAsia Investment Limited (wholly-owned subsidiary of AirAsia Berhad) – 40%;
Philippines	AirAsia Zest	AirAsia Inc. (Philippine AirAsia) – 49% and Alfredo Yao – 51%	

Thus, questions have been raised about whether these joint ventures are effectively controlled by local investors or by the holding company in Malaysia. For obvious reasons, it would be quite hard to determine whether airline companies have confidential agreements vesting actual and full control to foreign interests. Based on AirAsia Berhad's corporate filings and that of its associates, it is standard procedure to execute in all its JVs the following: (1) a shareholders' agreement setting out the parties' respective rights and obligations;[47] (2) another agreement in which AirAsia Berhad binds itself to provide technical, operational, and commercial support on an arms-length basis to the JV carrier to ensure commercial, operational, branding, and service-level uniformity throughout existing AirAsia Berhad operations;[48] and (3) a brand license agreement, which permits the JV carrier to use

---

47 See *e.g.* AirAsia, "Prospectus 2004" (11 March 2004) at 159, online: <www.airasia.com/iwov-resources/my/common/pdf/AirAsia/IR/AirAsia_Prospectus_Local_English_20101029.pdf>.
48 See Bursa Malaysia Announcement, "AirAsia Japan Joint Venture" (21 July 2011), online: <http://announcements.bursamalaysia.com/EDMS/edmswebh.nsf/all/482576120041BDAA482578D4001D24CD/$File/AirAsia%20Japan%20Joint%20Venture.pdf>. See also Ellis Taylor, "AirAsia to invest $14.7m

"AirAsia" as a "trade name for business operation, access to market knowledge, and customer services."[49]

It must also be noted that all JVs entered into by AirAsia Berhad are considered its associates. As stated in its financial disclosures, associates are corporations wherein AirAsia Berhad exercises significant influence but not control.[50] Significant influence is defined in the disclosure as "the power to participate in the financial and operating policy decisions of the associates but not the power to exercise control over those policies."[51] Despite this language, it is doubtful that AirAsia Berhad actually lacks the power to make crucial policy decisions.[52]

Although most of AirAsia Berhad's business partners and CEOs appointed to the JVs are nationals of the country where the JV carrier was organized, their lack of previous experience in the airline industry is public knowledge.[53] For instance, Marianne Hontiveros, the CEO of Philippine AirAsia, previously worked for Tony Fernandes when the latter was still the vice president of Warner Music Southeast Asia.[54] The two other major shareholders, Romero and Cojuangco, were co-owners of the Philippine Patriots basketball team.[55] These facts raise a doubt that these executives are merely pawns of AirAsia Berhad, with the management team in Malaysia actually running the show.[56]

AirAsia's joint ventures are operating in China (*e.g.* Thai AirAsia flies between Guangzhou and Bangkok based on the China-Thailand air services agreement), Japan (*e.g.*

---

in Indian joint venture" *Flightglobal* (19 April 2013), online: <www.flightglobal.com/news/articles/airasiato-invest-14.7m-in-indian-joint-venture-384890/>.

49 Asia Aviation Public Company Limited, "Annual Report 2012" at 95, online: <http://aav.listedcompany.com/misc/AR/20140624-aav-ar2012-en-02.pdf>.

50 AirAsia Berhad, "Annual Report 2011 Reports and Financial Statements" at 37, online: <www.airasia.com/iwov-resources/my/common/pdf/AirAsia/IR/annual-report-financials-2011.pdf>.

51 *Ibid.*

52 Jae Woon Lee & Michelle Dy, "Mitigating "Effective Control" Restriction on Joint Venture Airlines in Asia: Philippine AirAsia Case" (2015) 40 Air & Space L. 231 at 251; See also Braun, *supra* note 2 at 353; Similarly, see CAPA, "Jetstar Hong Kong's local investor reflects HK's new attitude, learning from Hong Kong Airlines" (18 June 2013) (noting that "[c]ountries have turned a blind eye to where management control is exercised, so long as on paper there is local ownership. It is quietly accepted that Jetstar Australia exerts considerable, to say the least, influence over Singapore-based Jetstar Asia while AirAsia Berhad (Malaysia) has similar influence over affiliates in countries including Indonesia and Thailand."), online: <http://centreforaviation.com/analysis/jetstar-hong-kongs-local-investor-reflects-hks-new-attitude-learning-from-hong-kong-airlines-114195>.

53 For instance, Tassapon Bijleveld (CEO, Thai AirAsia) and Sendjaja Widjaja (Former CEO, Indonesia AirAsia) have no prior experience in the airline industry. They were in the music industry prior to their stint in AirAsia. See *Bloomberg,* online: <www.bloomberg.com/research/stocks/people/person.asp?personId=25228663&ticker=AIRA:MK>;<www.bloomberg.com/research/stocks/people/person.asp?personId=25228665&ticker=AIRA:MK&previousCapId=6163432&previousTitle=AIRASIA%2520BHD>.

54 See Mary Ann LL. Reyes, "Fernandes, 'Tonyboy' team up for AirAsia Phils", *The Philippine Star* (17 December 2010), online: <www.philstar.com/business/639510/fernandes-tonyboy-team-airasia-phils>.

55 *Ibid.*

56 Lee & Dy, *supra* note 52 at 251.

Thai AirAsia X flies between Tokyo-Narita and Bangkok based on the Japan-Thailand air services agreement), and Korea (*e.g.* AirAsia Zest flies between Seoul-Incheon and Manila based on the Korea-Philippines air services agreement).

Given the ownership and control structure of AirAsia's joint ventures, it would seem that China, Japan, and Korea have sufficient legal grounds to argue that those joint venture airlines do not meet the designation criteria set forth in the relevant air services agreements. However, none of them have moved to revoke the joint ventures' operations on the grounds of effective control, at least according to publicly available sources.

This fact suggests that the three countries do not proactively go into effective control restriction by way of air services agreements (Subdivision D).[57] Indeed, ownership and control restrictions are generally used as "a source of leverage" during negotiations for air services agreement whilst market access restrictions had long been the norm.[58] A classic example is that the US required a grant of additional market access rights in exchange for allowing Aerolineas Argentinas to continue its services between the US and Argentina after a Spanish company became a majority shareholder of Aerolineas Argentinas.[59]

4.2.2   China

The history of national legislation about ownership and control in China reveals a general trend of gradual relaxation of such restrictions. However, the traditional 51:49 structure remains unchanged. Also, it is noteworthy that China's position has varied according to whether the airline in question is a *passenger* airline or a *cargo* airline.

From the early 1990s, China started to draw foreign investors' attention arising from its policy of opening up. Accordingly, the Civil Aviation Authority of China (CAAC) and the Ministry of Foreign Trade and Economic Cooperation (MOFTEC) promulgated the Circular on Relevant Policies on Foreign Investment in the Civil Aviation Industry in 1994.[60] The Circular limited a foreign investor's contribution to an airline to 35 percent

---

57   Havel and Sanchez provide a convincing explanation of this. See Havel & Sanchez, "Lex Aviatica", *supra* note 6 at 653 (stating that "[H]istorically, there was no compelling incentive [to enforce the nationality clauses in bilateral air services agreements]. States engaged in country-to-country negotiation of market access rights naturally sought the most generous concessions for their own airlines within a system that seeks trade equipoise between the national carriers. To suspend the nationality clause would require the state requesting a waiver to deliver greater access rights or even changes in regulatory policy--and to accept the cascading effects of non-enforcement on its other treaty relationships if foreign ownership of its airlines actually ensued. The tightly wound aero-politics of the bilateral system have had little tolerance for such experiments.").
58   *Ibid.* at 654.
59   Mendes de Leon, *supra* note 34 at 362.
60   Zang Hongliang & Meng Qingfen, *Civil Aviation Law in the People's Republic of China* (The Hague: Eleven International Publishing, 2010) at 38.

and the foreign representative's voting rights on the board of directors to 25 percent.⁶¹ Subsequently, Hainan Airlines announced a $25 million investment from American Aviation and became China's first carrier to utilize foreign investment in 1995.⁶²

Later, the Regulation of the People's Republic of China on the Nationality Registration of Civil Aircraft (State Council Order No. 232) in 1997 formalized these ownership and control restrictions as national law. Article 2 of the Regulation is as follows:

> Article 2
> The following civil aircraft shall enter into nationality registration pursuant to these Regulations:
> (1) civil aircraft of state institutions of the People's Republic of China;
> (2) civil aircraft of a corporate enterprise established in accordance with the laws of the People's Republic of China; the registered capital of the corporate enterprise constitutes contributions from foreign businesses, the percentage of foreign businesses in the registered capital or paid-up capital of the said corporate enterprise does not exceed 35 percent, the right to vote of their representatives on the board of directors and the shareholders' conference (shareholders' meeting) does not exceed 35 percent, and a Chinese citizen serves as the chairman of the board of directors of the said corporate enterprise;
> (3) other civil aircraft the registration of which is approved by the competent department of civil aviation under the State Council.⁶³

Thus, the caps on foreign shares and voting rights were officially set at 35 percent by the 1997 Regulation of the People's Republic of China on the Nationality Registration of Civil Aircraft. A more substantial change was made in 2002 through the Regulation on Foreign Investment in the Civil Aviation Industry (CAAC Order No. 110), effective as of 1 August 2002. Article 6 of the Regulation provides the following:

> A foreign-invested public air transport enterprise shall be controlled by the Chinese party or parties, and the contribution of any foreign investor (including its connected enterprises) shall not exceed 25 percent.⁶⁴

---

61 *Ibid.* at 38-39.
62 Jane Pan, "ANALYSIS: The role of foreign investment in Chinese airlines" *Flightglobal* (21 Nov 2012), online: <www.flightglobal.com/news/articles/analysis-the-role-of-foreign-investment-in-chinese-379324/>.
63 *Regulations of the Nationality Registration of Civil Aircraft (1997)* (Asian Legal Information Institute), online: <www.asianlii.org/cn/legis/cen/laws/rotnroca596/>.
64 Hongliang & Qingfen, *supra* note 60 at 121; see different versions of the translation by Asian Legal Information Institute (stating that "[W]here foreign investors invest in public air transport enterprises, the Chinese party shall take the holding position"), online: <www.asianlii.org/cn/legis/cen/laws/pofiica525/>. and by Juan Antonio Fernandez & Leila Fernandez-Stembridge, *China's State Owned Enterprise Reforms:*

The above provision is understood to have increased the cap on foreign investment from 35 percent to 49 percent.[65] Although the number 49 does not actually appear in the provision, the Chinese phrase *xiangduikonggu* "相对控股" (which means "relative controlling shares") implies that the shareholding percentage of the Chinese party has to be greater than any of its foreign partner(s).[66] There is also a specific mention of the numeric restriction of 25 percent for any single investor. Thus, although foreign investors can own up to 49 per cent in sum, no single investor can own more than 25 percent.

Some commentators argued that China's decision to restructure its aviation market in a way that gave foreign investors greater access had to do with the country's admission to the World Trade Organization (WTO) in 2001.[67] Although China did not undertake any specific commitment to liberalizing its air transport industry as a condition of membership in the WTO,[68] it is reasonable to conjecture that foreign investment became more common in China after it joined the WTO.

In practice, China's relaxation of ownership and control restrictions shows two completely different pictures. In the cargo market, China has actively embraced liberalization. For instance, Jade Cargo International became China's first air cargo joint venture, bringing in investment from Shenzhen Airlines (51 percent), Lufthansa Cargo (25 percent) and German Investment and Development (24 percent) in 2004.[69] Grandstar Cargo was another joint venture, with stakes held by Sinotrans, China's logistic company (51 percent), Korean Air (25 percent) and two Korean investment companies, Hana Capital (13 percent) and Shinhan Capital (11 percent).[70] Interestingly, China has allowed foreigners to be appointed as CEOs at both joint ventures. Mr. Frank Naeve, a German citizen, was a CEO for Jade Cargo, and Mr. Kwang-Sa Lee, a Korean citizen, was a CEO for Grandstar Cargo.

In contrast to its remarkably liberal approach to cargo airlines, China has been highly protective in the passenger market. On the surface, most passenger airlines have showed little interest in furthering their financial ties with foreign investors.[71] More accurately, however, the Chinese government appears to have actively blocked foreign investment in

---

An Industrial and CEO Approach (New York: Routledge, 2007) at 56 (stating that "[F]or foreign investment in public air transport enterprises, Chinese side should take the controlling stake on a comparative basis").

65 Alan Williams, *Contemporary Issues Shaping China's Civil Aviation Policy: Balancing International with Domestic Priorities* (Burlington, VT: Ashgate, 2009) at 85.

66 Zane Gresham, "China Moves to Increase Private and International Participation in Airports and Aviation" *Morrison & Foerster* (29 June 2004), online: <www.mofo.com/resources/publications/2004/06/china-moves-to-increase-private-and-internationa>.

67 See *e.g.* Gresham, *ibid.*

68 See WTO, Press Release, "WTO successfully concludes negotiations on China's entry" (17 September 2001), online: <www.wto.org/english/news_e/pres01_e/pr243_e.htm>.

69 See CAPA, Profiles, "Jade Cargo International," online: <http://centreforaviation.com/profiles/airlines/jade-cargo-international-ji>.

70 Geoffrey Thomas, "Korean Air, Sinotrans ink JV cargo carrier agreement" *ATW* (19 September 2006), online: <http://atwonline.com/news/korean-air-sinotrans-ink-jv-cargo-carrier-agreement>.

71 Pan, *supra* note 62.

Chinese passenger airlines in line with its policy of protecting the big three airlines (see above section 3.2.2.1).

For instance, when China Eastern announced that it would sell a 26 percent stake to Singapore Airlines and Temasek Holdings (a Singapore state-owned investment company) in 2007, China National Aviation Holding (Air China's parent company) proposed a counter offer that was 32 percent higher than that of Singapore Airlines at the completion stage, which ultimately blocked the deal.[72] An exception was made for the cross ownership of Air China and Hong Kong's Cathay Pacific. Air China has a 30 percent stake in Cathay Pacific, and Cathay Pacific holds a roughly 20 percent stake in Air China.[73] It can be assumed that the special relationship between China and Hong Kong made this flexible approach possible.

4.2.3 Japan

Japan's domestic legislation regarding ownership appears to be protective. However, it has recently liberalized its policy on assessing effective control without legislative reform. Article 4 and Article 101 of the Civil Aeronautics Act (Act No. 231 of 1952) provide the following:

> Article 4 (Requirement for Registration)
> (1) Any aircraft owned by any person who falls under any of the following items shall not be eligible for registration.
> (i) Any person who does not have Japanese nationality
> (ii) Any foreign state or public entity or its equivalent in any foreign state
> (iii) Any juridical person or body established in accordance with the laws and ordinances of any foreign state
> (iv) Any juridical person of which the representative is any one of those listed in the preceding three items or of which more than one-third of the officers are such persons or more than one-third of voting rights are held by such persons
> (2) Any aircraft which has the registration of any foreign state shall not be eligible for registration.[74]

---

72 Ibid.
73 See Joanne Chiu, "Cathay Pacific, Air China, to Inject $321.4 Million into Cargo Joint Venture" *The Wall Street Journal* (26 June 2014), online: <www.wsj.com/articles/cathay-pacific-air-china-to-inject-321-4m-into-air-cargo-joint-venture-1403783543>.
74 *Civil Aeronautics Act (Act No. 231 of 1952)*, online: <www.cas.go.jp/jp/seisaku/hourei/data/caa.pdf>.

Article 101 (Licensing Standards)

(1) The Minister of Land, Infrastructure, Transport and Tourism shall, when there has been an application under the preceding article, examine whether it conforms to each of the following: ...

(v) Any applicant shall not fall under any of the following categories:

(a) Any person listed in any item of Article 4 paragraph (1)...[75]

Thus, foreigners cannot hold more than one-third of the voting rights in a Japanese air carrier.[76] If the total holdings by foreigners exceed one-third of the voting rights, the aircraft in question is automatically unregistered[77] or the license of the air transport service is invalidated.[78] These ownership and control provisions have never been changed since their enactment in 1952.

However, the Civil Aeronautics Act does not put restrictions on non-voting shares. It is the Foreign Exchange and Foreign Trade Act (1949) that restricts total foreign ownership of Japanese airlines.[79] Under the Foreign Exchange and Foreign Trade Act and associated ordinances, the civil aviation industry falls into specified business sectors that require advance notice and careful examination for foreign investment. In brief, if foreigners own more than half of the total shares of an airline, these strict restrictions apply.[80]

The ownership structure of the first AirAsia Japan (a joint venture between All Nippon Airways and AirAsia that operated from August 2012 to October 2013) offers an eloquent illustration of these restrictions. While ANA held 67 percent and Air Asia 33 percent of voting shares, ANA held 51 percent and AirAsia 49 percent of the total capital.[81] Thus, the Japanese can be said to follow the US model of splitting shares into voting and non-voting stock, placing stricter requirements on voting stock.

---

75 Ibid.
76 Kazuhide Yamazaki, "Airline Ownership and Control Requirement: Changes in the Air – A Legal View from Japan" (2006) 31 Air & Space L. 50 at 52.
77 See Article 8 (Deletion Registration): "(1) Any owner of a registered aircraft shall apply for deletion of the registration in the following cases within a period not exceeding 15 days thereafter: (i) When the registered aircraft has been lost or dismantled (except dismantling for the purpose of repair, alteration, transportation, or custody) (ii) When the registered aircraft has been missing for more than 2 months; (iii) When the registered aircraft has become ineligible for registration pursuant to the provision of Article 4.", online: <www.cas.go.jp/jp/seisaku/hourei/data/caa.pdf>.
78 See Article 120 (Invalidation of License): "In the case where any domestic air carrier has come to fall under any of the categories listed in item of Article 4 paragraph (1) or any holding company of a domestic air carrier as a corporation has come to fall under any of the categories listed in item (iv) of the said paragraph, the license pertaining to the domestic air carrier under Article 100 paragraph (1) shall become invalid", online: <www.cas.go.jp/jp/seisaku/hourei/data/caa.pdf>.
79 Yamazaki, supra note 76 at 53. The relevant provisions are 26 and 27 of the Foreign Exchange and Foreign Trade Act (1949). A rough translation can be found at <www.cas.go.jp/jp/seisaku/hourei/data/FTA.pdf>.
80 Yamazaki, ibid. at 53.
81 AirAsia, Press Release, "ANA and AirAsia to form 'AirAsia Japan'" (21 July 2011), online: <www.airasia.com/my/en/press-releases/ana-and-airasia-form-airasia-japan.page>.

Interestingly, Japanese domestic law (Article 129 of the Civil Aeronautics Act) reconfirms Subdivision C (substantial ownership restriction by air services agreements) and Subdivision D (effective control restriction by air services agreements).[82] Thus, any change in the foreign carrier's ownership and control structure carries the risk that the carrier's service into Japan will be suspended under Japanese domestic law. However, similar to the nationality clause in air services agreements, revocation is not automatic since the government is permitted, but not obligated, to suspend the service of the foreign carrier in question.

More significantly, Japan has taken a flexible approach on Subdivision B (effective control restriction by domestic law). The first AirAsia Japan originally raised the question of how the Japanese government would interpret "control" since AirAsia was effectively trying to run AirAsia Japan despite its minority share.[83] More obvious examples are Spring Airlines Japan and the second Air Asia Japan.

Spring Airlines Japan, an LCC joint venture airline in Japan, commenced operations in July 2014. Spring Airlines owns 33 percent of Spring Airlines Japan, and the rest of the shares are owned by various Japanese investors in the private-equity, travel, and IT industries.[84] Clearly, since none of the investors are Japanese airlines, it is uncertain that Spring Airlines Japan is effectively controlled by the Japanese non-airline investors rather than Spring Airlines. In addition, although local investors are not fully disclosed (except JTB, Japan's largest travel agency), Spring Airlines appears to be the largest investor.

AirAsia Japan is expected to begin operations in 2016. This second AirAsia Japan is a joint venture between AirAsia (49 percent share but 33 percent voting rights) and various Japanese investors (Octave Japan Infrastructure Fund 19 percent, Rakuten 18 percent, Noevir Holding 9 percent, and Alpen 5 percent).[85] Like Spring Airlines Japan, none of the investors are Japanese airlines, and AirAsia is the largest shareholder in AirAsia Japan.

---

82 See Article 129-5 (Suspension of Services and Revocation of License): "The Minister of Land, Infrastructure, Transport and Tourism may, when any foreign international air carrier falls under any of the following cases, order the foreign international air carrier to suspend its services for a certain period or revoke the license. (i) When any foreign international air carrier has violated the provisions of this Act, any disposition under relevant laws and regulations, or any conditions attached to any license or approval under relevant laws and regulations; (ii) When the substantial ownership of shares or equity of any foreign international air carrier or the substantial control of air transport services operated by any foreign international air carrier is no longer vested in the state to which the said foreign international air carrier belongs or its nationals", online: <www.cas.go.jp/jp/seisaku/hourei/data/caa.pdf>.
83 CAPA, "Japan's expanding LCCs drive growth but need cultivating; Spring Airlines and AirAsia re-entry loom" (5 April 2014), online: <http://centreforaviation.com/analysis/japans-expanding-lccs-drive-growth-but-need-cultivating-spring-airlines-and-airasia-re-entry-loom-160039>.
84 Joanne Chiu, "Japan Approves Spring Air's Low-Cost Venture" *The Wall Street Journal* (27 December 2013), online: <www.wsj.com/articles/SB10001424052702303799404579283503425437022>.
85 Gaurav Raghuvanshi, "AirAsia Finds Partners for Return to Japan" *The Wall Street Journal* (1 July 2014), online: <www.wsj.com/articles/airasia-finds-partners-for-return-to-japan-1404202254>.

In response to an inquiry about whether the Japanese partners are willing to accept the AirAsia business model, an AirAsia spokeswoman emphasized that "we are the only airline in this partnership so yes, we expect the relationship to be completely different this time," recalling the company's experience with the first AirAsia Japan.[86]

With this specially designed ownership structure and its experience in the first AirAsia, it is conceivable that AirAsia would try to control the new AirAsia Japan. In fact, AirAsia would be strategically better off with partners that are "more passive and will let them [AirAsia] run the airline and apply their model."[87]

The fact that the Japanese government granted Spring Airlines Japan and the second AirAsia Japan operating licenses as Japanese domestic carriers shows that Japan is not too strict about Subdivision B (effective control restriction by domestic law). At the same time, it is worth noting that Japan has not necessarily given up the effective control test. While Japan is currently taking a flexible stance on effective control, it could still raise concerns about the control structure of those JVs.

4.2.4 Korea

Korean legislation on ownership restrictions adheres to the traditional 51:49 structure. However, unlike Japan, Korea has taken a strict approach to effective control inquiries. Articles 6 and 114 of the Korea Aviation Act outline the legal principles of ownership and control as shown below:

> Article 6 (Restrictions on Registration of Aircraft)
> (1) No aircraft may be registered that is owned or leased by a person who falls under any of the following sub-paragraphs. However, this shall not apply when a national or juridical person of the Republic of Korea has leased, or is otherwise entitled to use, that aircraft.
> 1. a person who is not a citizen of the Republic of Korea;
> 2. a foreign government or foreign public organization;
> 3. a foreign corporation or organization;
> 4. a corporation in which a share equal to or exceeding 50% is held by a person who falls under any of subparagraphs 1 through 3, or a corporation whose operations are effectively controlled by such a person.

---

86 See *ibid*.
87 Brenden Sobie (CAPA) in Gaurav Raghuvanshi, "AirAsia Finds Partners for Return to Japan" *The Wall Street Journal* (1 July 2014), online: <www.wsj.com/articles/airasia-finds-partners-for-return-to-japan-1404202254>.

5. a corporation whose representative is a foreigner, or half or more of whose officers are foreigners.

(2) No aircraft having a foreign nationality may be registered

Article 114 (Disqualification, etc. for License)
(1) The Minister of Land, Transport and Maritime Affairs shall not grant a license for domestic or international air transportation business to a person who falls under any of the following subparagraphs:
1. a person who falls under any of the subparagraphs of Article 6 (1);[88]

Thus, foreign investment in Korean air carriers cannot exceed 50 percent while similarly the number of foreign board members cannot exceed 50 percent. Like Japan, Korean domestic law (Article 150 of the Aviation Act) reconfirms Subdivision C (substantial ownership restriction by air services agreements) and Subdivision D (effective control restriction by air services agreements).[89]

Korea has applied the effective control restrictions more strictly than Japan. In 2008, the Korean government rejected a joint venture to be called Tiger Incheon that Tiger Airways (originally set up by Singapore Airlines) sought to form with a Korean local partner, Incheon Metropolitan City (in which Tiger would have had a 49 percent stake and Incheon a 51 percent stake).[90]

The government's rationale for rejecting this joint venture was that Tiger Incheon would have been effectively controlled by Tiger Airways (i.e. nationals of Singapore) given that the Korean local shareholders and board of directors did not have any experience in aviation. Indeed, the decision was in line with a petition that Korean LCCs (namely, Air Busan, Yeongnam Air (now defunct), Jeju Air, and Jin Air had filed with the Korean Ministry of Transport.[91] The CAPA report harshly criticized the decision: "The request from several vested interests – worded in clear aviation nationalism overtones – was

---

88 *The Aviation Act* (The Korean Ministry Government Legislation).
89 See Article 150 (Revocation, etc. of Permission): "1) If a foreign international air transportation businessman falls under any of the following subparagraphs, the Minister of Land, Transport and Maritime Affairs may revoke the permission, or order him to suspend the business with a period not exceeding six months fixed: Provided, That if he falls under subparagraph 1 or 21, the Minister of Land, Transport and Maritime Affairs shall revoke the permission: ... (18) Where the substantial ownership or effective control belongs no longer to the country in which the foreign international air carrier holds the nationality, or nationals of such country; However, in case air services agreement that Korea signed with a country (including association of nations or economic union) determines otherwise, the air services agreement prevails."
90 See CAPA, "Korea steps back into the dark. Airline protectionism flourishes in Seoul" (28 August 2008), online: <http://centreforaviation.com/analysis/korea-steps-back-into-the-dark-airline-protectionism-flourishes-in-seoul-3619>.
91 See *e.g.* Xiaowen Fu, Tae Hoon Oum & Anming Zhang "Air Transport Liberalization and Its Impacts on Airline Competition and Air Passenger Traffic" (2010) 49:4 Transportation Journal. 24 at 36-37.

designed solely to protect local airlines from added competition."[92] However, the decision was technically in compliance with Korean domestic law, which examines not only majority ownership but also the question of effective control of the airline in question.

Ownership and control restrictions are deeply entrenched in the national laws of most jurisdictions (Subdivision A and Subdivision B), and Northeast Asia is no exception. However, there have been various efforts to liberalize ownership and control restrictions, particularly the external restrictions (Subdivision C and Subdivision D).

4.3 Options for Liberalizing Ownership and Control Restrictions

As the global airline industry became privatized and deregulated in the 1980s and 1990s, the industry became more competitive and new air carriers entered a market that had previously been restricted to a small number of players. Indeed, privatization significantly challenged the rationale for ownership and control restrictions in the airline industry, as Andrew Harrington explains:

> In the period prior to the 1980's, flag carriers were in most cases wholly State-owned. As such it was commonplace for them to enjoy a high level of protectionism (in some cases a legislative prohibition on competition) and state support (in the form of subsidies, interest free loans and other fiscal incentives). As the 1980s and 1990's arrived and privatization or corporatization was implemented as part of an economy wide policy of economic rationalism, these flag carriers were able to rely less and less on that state support and protection.[93]

Not only private investments from domestic investors but furthermore transnational investments became common in the airline industry. In order to address regulatory and market changes, ICAO started to discuss the liberalization of ownership and control restrictions in international fora.

4.3.1 The Multilateral Approach

As an international organization, ICAO has been reluctant to push for reforming national law and policy in regard to ownership and control restrictions (Subdivision A and Subdi-

---

92 CAPA, "Korea steps back into the dark. Airline protectionism flourishes in Seoul" (28 August 2008), online: <http://centreforaviation.com/analysis/korea-steps-back-into-the-dark-airline-protectionism-flourishes-in-seoul-3619>.
93 Andrew Harrington, "Foreign Ownership and the Future of the National Airline" (2013) 38 Ann. Air & Sp. L. 123 at 130-131.

vision B). Instead, ICAO has focused on relaxing ownership and control restrictions in air services agreements (Subdivision C and Subdivision D).

The Fifth ICAO Air Transport Conference in 2003[94] proposed regulatory reform of the issue of air carrier ownership and control and made recommendations about air transportation liberalization. Specifically, the 2003 Conference called upon members to consider replacing the traditional criteria of "substantial ownership and effective control" with "principal place of business and effective regulatory control" in their respective agreements.[95] ICAO defined "principal place of business" and "effective regulatory control" as below:

> Evidence of principal place of business is predicated upon: the airline is established and incorporated in the territory of the designating Party in accordance with relevant national laws and regulations, has a substantial amount of its operations and capital investment in physical facilities in the territory of the designating Party, pays income tax, registers and bases its aircraft there, and employs a significant number of nationals in managerial, technical and operational positions.[96]
>
> Evidence of effective regulatory control is predicated upon but is not limited to: the airline holds a valid operating licence or permit issued by the licensing authority such as an Air Operator Certificate (AOC), meets the criteria of the designating Party for the operation of international air services, such as proof of financial health, ability to meet public interest requirements, obligations for assurance of service; and the designating Party has and maintains safety and security oversight programmes in compliance with ICAO standards.[97]

In fact, on a multilateral level, the idea of using regulatory reform to replace the "substantial ownership" restriction with the "principal place of business" condition first attracted attention in MALIAT, which was adopted in 2001. While MALIAT maintains the effective control requirement, it does not require that an airline be substantially owned either by the state designating it or the citizens thereof.[98] Instead, it replaces this with the "principal

---

94 The ICAO has held six Air Transport Conferences in 1977, 1980, 1985, 1994, 2003 and 2013.
95 Paul Dempsey, *Public international air law* (Montreal: Institute of Air and Space Law, 2008) at 563. [Dempsey, "Air Law"].
96 ICAO, *Consolidated Conclusions, Model Clauses, Recommendations and Declaration*. ICAO Doc. ATConf/5 (31 March 2003, REVISED 10 July 2003) at 5, online: <www.icao.int/Meetings/ATConf5/Documents/atconf5_conclusions_en.pdf>.
97 *Ibid*.
98 See MALIAT Article 3(2): "2. On receipt of such a designation, and of applications from the designated airline, in the form and manner prescribed for operating authorizations and technical permissions, each Party shall grant appropriate authorizations and permissions with minimum procedural delay, provided that: a. effective control of that airline is vested in the designating Party, its nationals, or both; b. the airline

place of business and incorporation" criterion. As previously discussed (see section 3.4.4), however, MALIAT does not have practical impact due to its low acceptance.

However, the ambitious recommendations made by the 2003 Conference were largely ignored by states. For instance, provisions for principal place of business were found in only 6 percent of sampled bilateral air services agreements (100 air services agreements involving 50 parties) when WTO conducted the study in 2006.[99] Although more recent statistics are not publicly available, it is difficult to say that "principal place of business and effective regulatory control" has replaced the traditional criteria of "substantial ownership and effective control."

The Sixth ICAO Air Transport Conference in 2013 once again took the initiative. It suggested that the organization explore the option of developing an international agreement to relax ownership and control requirements for airline designation.[100]

Generally speaking, two options were suggested. The first option is a "waiver of the nationality clause" on the basis of reciprocity. In this formula, parties to the agreement would waive the application of the nationality clause in existing air services agreements with respect to designated airlines and investors' nationalities.[101]

In fact, this formula has its origins in the International Air Transport Association (IATA)'s "Agenda for Freedom" initiative.[102] In 2009, seven states (Chile, Malaysia, Panama, Singapore, Switzerland, the United Arab Emirates and the US) took coordinated action by signing a "Statement of Policy Principles Regarding the Implementation of Bilateral Air Services Agreements"[103] through the platform of the IATA's "Agenda for Freedom" initiative. The Statement of Policy aims to liberalize key aspects of regulatory practice in international air transport, including airline ownership and control, by waiving the nationality clause "on the basis of reciprocity."[104]

---

is incorporated in and has its principal place of business in the territory of the Party designating the airline; c. the airline is qualified to meet the conditions prescribed under the laws, regulations, and rules normally applied to the operation of international air transportation by the Party considering the application or applications; and d. the Party designating the airline is in compliance with the provisions set forth in Article 6 (Safety) and Article 7 (Aviation Security)".

99 WTO, Council for Trade in Services, *Quantitative Air Services Agreements Review (QUASAR): Part B: PRELIMINARY RESULTS*, S/C/W/270/Add.1 (2006) at 33, para 61, online: WTO <www.wto.org/english/tratop_e/serv_e/transport_e/quasar_partb_e.pdf>.

100 See ICAO, *Liberalization of Air Carrier Ownership and Control*, ICAO Doc ATconf/6-WP/12 (10 December 2012), online: <www.icao.int/Meetings/atconf6/Documents/WorkingPapers/ATConf6-wp012_en.pdf>.

101 *Ibid.* at 4 para 3.5.

102 *Ibid.* at 4 para 2.3.

103 *Statement of Policy Principles regarding the Implementation of Bilateral Air Services Agreements*, Done at Montebello, Québec, Canada on 16 November 2009, online: <https://www.iata.org/policy/liberalization/agenda-freedom/Documents/policy-principles-endorsement.pdf>.

104 ICAO, *Liberalization of Air Carrier Ownership and Control*, ICAO Doc ATconf/6-WP/12 (10 December 2012) at 4 para 2.3, online: <www.icao.int/Meetings/atconf6/Documents/WorkingPapers/ATConf6-wp012_en.pdf>.

The second way to develop a multilateral international agreement is to accept and apply relatively relaxed criteria for airline designation, such as the "principal place of business and effective regulatory control."[105]

Although the 2013 Conference recommended that "ICAO should initiate work on the development of an international agreement to liberalize air carrier ownership and control,"[106] there is a long way to go before a new multilateral agreement that would liberalize the ownership and control restrictions can be made. And even if a new multilateral agreement that either waives the application of the nationality clause or accepts relaxed criteria for airline designation is eventually adopted, it is unlikely that such an agreement would be ratified by a large number of states. As discussed in section 1.2 Multilateral Air Law Treaties, in the history of the ICAO, multilateral economic treaties related to air transport have never received support from most states.

Nevertheless, the ICAO's multilateral approach has had one meaningful contribution. As a result of these efforts, more states have become less obsessed with strict restrictions on substantial ownership and effective control and have begun adopting principal place of business and effective regulatory control in their bilateral air services agreements.[107]

4.3.2   The Regional Approach

Arguably, the regional approach has produced the most remarkable achievements over the past two decades. In essence, the regional method of reforming ownership and control restrictions is the adoption of "community carriers." Chapter 2: Comparative Analysis of Regional Liberalization Models shows that the EU, ASEAN, and the League of Arab States have adopted the concept of a community carrier in their respective regions.

Community carriers have liberalized, though not completely, the internal restrictions on ownership and control (Subdivision A and Subdivision B). Community member states grant an air carrier an operating license when that air carrier is majority owned and effectively controlled by community member states or their nationals. Thus, it is a paradigm shift from "national" ownership and control to "community" ownership and control.

---

105 *Ibid.* at 4 para 3.5.
106 ICAO, *Report on Agenda Item 2.2* (summary report of the Air Transport Conference), ICAO ATConf/6-WP/104 (22 March 2013) at para 2.2.4, online: <www.icao.int/Meetings/atconf6/Documents/FinalReport/ATConf6_wp104-2-2.pdf>.
107 See *e.g.* ICAO, *Liberalizing Air Carrier Ownership and Control*, ICAO A35-WP/156 (17 September 2004) (Presented by Singapore) at para 2.2 (noting that "[I]n line with ICAO's recommendation endorsed at the Fifth Worldwide Air Transport Conference, Singapore initiated proposals to move away from the "substantial ownership" and "effective control" criterion, by amending the airline designation clause in a number of our ASAs to one based on "principal place of business" and "effective control". To date, Singapore has managed to liberalise airline designation provisions for more than 20 percent of our ASAs."), online: <www.icao.int/Meetings/AMC/MA/Assembly percent2035th percent20Session/wp156_en.pdf>.

The community carrier concept allows majority ownership to be spread out among community interests as long as effective regulatory control remains with the country in which the airline is based. Thus, the state only requires "effective regulatory control" rather than traditional "effective economic control." In other words, not only is substantial national ownership given up, but effective economic control as well. EU Regulation 2407/92 on the licensing of air carriers is the first to prescribe that, so long as an air carrier meets safety requirements (issues involving "effective regulatory control") and is majority-owned and effectively controlled by EU member states and/or their nationals (issues involving "effective economic control"), EU member states may grant the air carrier an operating license.

As indicted in the previous section, effective control can be divided into effective *economic* control and effective *regulatory* control. In the interest of liberalization, effective economic control need not reside with the designating state or its nationals, as long as effective regulatory control (encompassing safety, security, and other technical matters) remains with the designating state.

Liberalizing the external restrictions (Subdivision C and Subdivision D) through the regional approach would be more difficult because it requires the consent of third countries outside of the grouping. Among several regional groups, only the EU has consistently demanded that the nationality clause be replaced with a community clause.[108] The European Commission officially received authorization from the Council of the European Union to enter into so-called "horizontal agreements" with non-EU states on 29 March 2005.[109] Since then, these horizontal agreements have led non-EU states to recognize the EU "community carrier" designation clause instead of the traditional nationality clause in all the bilateral air services agreements between EU member states and non-EU states.[110]

---

108 See EU Commission, *Bilateral Air Services Agreements brought into legal conformity since the Court of Justice of the EU judgments of 5 November 2002* (Updated 30 January 2013), online: <http://ec.europa.eu/transport/modes/air/international_aviation/external_aviation_policy/doc/table_-_asa_brought_into_legal_conformity_since_ecj_judgments-_january_2013.pdf>..

109 See EU Commission, *Commission Decision on approving the standard clauses for inclusion in bilateral air service agreements between Member States and third countries jointly laid down by the Commission and the Member States,* COM(2005)943 (29 March 2005), online: <http://ec.europa.eu/transport/modes/air/international_aviation/doc/standard_clauses_en.pdf>; see also Brian F. Havel & Gabriel S. Sanchez, *The Principles and Practices of International Aviation Law* (New York: Cambridge University Press, 2014) at 97-98. [Havel & Sanchez, "Aviation Law"].

110 Alan Khee-Jin Tan, "Singapore' New Air Services Agreements with the E.U. and The U.K.: Implications for liberalization in Asia" (2008) 73 J. Air L. & Com. 351 at 354. [Tan, "Singapore's Agreements"].

4.3.3 The Bilateral Approach

The bilateral approach is the most effective way to liberalize the external ownership and control restrictions (Subdivision C and Subdivision D) as most air services agreements are *bilateral* treaties.

Bilateral preferential concessions can relax the ownership and control restrictions on an exceptional basis. The US has widely adopted this approach. While maintaining the prohibition on foreign nationals owning more than 25 percent of a corporation's voting equity under domestic law, the first EU-US Open Skies aviation agreement (2007) permits EU nationals to own up to 49.9 percent of total equity and holds open the possibility that they could be allowed to own more than 50 percent of total equity.[111]

In fact, the US DOT has shown a willingness to ease this restriction either on the basis of reciprocity or where US interests are not jeopardized by a higher percentage of foreign ownership.[112] Havel and Sanchez note that since the late 1990s at least, the US has selectively waived the nationality clause in cases in which the airlines of partner states have been acquired by non-nationals.[113]

As noted, provisions for principal place of business were found in only 6 percent of sampled bilateral air services agreements (100 air services agreements involving 50 parties) in a 2006 WTO review.[114] Although a comprehensive review of publicly available sources has not been conducted more recently, some states are making an effort to liberalize the ownership and control restrictions in their air services agreements.

In particular, Brazil, Chile, Columbia, Egypt, Indonesia, Switzerland, and Vietnam reported at the 2013 ICAO World Air Transport Conference that they are in the process of replacing traditional substantial ownership and control restrictions with "principal place of business and effective regulatory control" in their air services agreements.[115] However,

---

111 See *U.S.-EU Air Transport Agreement of April 30, 2007*, Annex 4 Concerning Additional Matters Related To Ownership, Investment and Control, online: <www.state.gov/e/eb/rls/othr/ata/e/eu/114768.htm>.
112 Antigoni Lykotrafiti, "Consolidation and Rationalization in the Transatlantic Air Transport Market –Prospects and Challenges for Competition and Consumer Welfare" (2011) 76 J. Air L. & Com. 661 at 672.
113 Havel & Sanchez, "Lex Aviatica", *supra* note 6 at 655; See also WTO, Council for Trade in Services, *Quantitative Air Services Agreements Review (QUASAR): Part B: PRELIMINARY RESULTS*, S/C/W/270/Add.1 (2006) at 34, para 68 (noting that "[T]he effective control prerequisite, are often waived in practice. Aerolineas Argentinas, for instance, was never denied the right to fly although it had two successive Spanish majority owners. The same was true for Sabena when it was owned by Air France and then by Swissair."), online: <<www.wto.org/english/tratop_e/serv_e/transport_e/quasar_partb_e.pdf>.
114 WTO, *ibid.* at 33, para 61.
115 See ICAO, *Differences Between Carrier Ownership and Control Principles in Designation Clauses in Air Services Agreements and National Laws Regulating the Subject*, ICAO Doc ATConf/6-WP/94 (7 March 2013) (Presented by Brazil), online: <www.icao.int/Meetings/atconf6/Documents/WorkingPapers/ATConf.6.WP.94.2.en.pdf>; ICAO, *Proposal for the Liberalization of Air Carrier Ownership and Control*, ICAO Doc ATConf/6-WP/29 (13 February 2013) (Presented by Chile), online: <www.icao.int/Meetings/atconf6/Documents/WorkingPapers/ATConf6-wp029_en.pdf>; ICAO, *Market Access Restrictions*, ICAO Doc ATConf/6-WP/59 (19 February 2013), online: <www.icao.int/Meetings/atconf6/Documents/Work-

it should be noted that this replacement is not a simple process because their bilateral partners must agree with the change.

4.3.4 The Unilateral Approach

By its nature, the unilateral approach entails liberalizing ownership and control restrictions by way of domestic law and policy (Subdivision A and Subdivision B). Among others, Australia, Chile, Columbia, and New Zealand have substantially liberalized ownership restrictions through their domestic legislation.

In 1999, the Australian Government amended the Australian Foreign Investment Review Board guidelines to permit foreign persons (including foreign airlines) to acquire up to 100 percent of equity in Australian domestic airlines.[116] An Australian domestic airline refers to "an Australian-domiciled airline that does not have internationally scheduled services departing from Australia."[117] For international services, the traditional 51:49 structure still applies.[118] An important point here is that "what Australia offers is a right for foreign nationals to establish commercial airlines within its territory for the sole purpose of serving domestic routes," not cabotage rights to foreign carriers.[119] At the same

---

ingPapers/ATConf6-wp059_en.pdf>; ICAO, *Egyptian Experience in the Liberalization of Air Carrier Ownership*, ICAO Doc ATConf/6-WP/41 (19 February 2013) (Presented by Egypt), online: <www.icao.int/Meetings/atconf6/Documents/WorkingPapers/ATConf6-wp041_en.pdf>; ICAO, *Air Carrier Ownership and Control Principle*, ICAO Doc ATConf/6-WP/84 (4 March 2013) (Presented by Indonesia), online: <www.icao.int/Meetings/atconf6/Documents/WorkingPapers/ATConf6-wp084_en.pdf>; ICAO, *Air Carrier Ownership and Control Clauses in Bilateral Air Services Agreements*, ICAO Doc ATConf/6-WP/49 (14 February 2013) (Presented by Ireland), online: <www.icao.int/Meetings/atconf6/Documents/WorkingPapers/ATConf6-wp049_en.pdf>; and ICAO, *Vietnam's Air Transport Market, Legislations and Regulations and Policy During 2003-2013*, ICAO Doc ATConf6-IP/22 (17 March 2013) (Presented by Viet Nam), online: <www.icao.int/Meetings/atconf6/Documents/WorkingPapers/ATConf6-ip022_en.pdf>.

116 See Harrington, *supra* note 93 at 134.
117 *Ibid.*
118 The Australian Foreign Investment Review Board (FIRB), "Civil Aviation", online: <www.firb.gov.au/content/other_investment/sensitive/aviation.asp?NavID=51>. It is worth noting that Australia treats Qantas differently. FIRB noted that "[F]oreign persons (including foreign airlines) can generally expect approval to acquire up to 49 per cent of the equity in an Australian international carrier (other than Qantas) individually or in aggregate provided the proposal is not contrary to the national interest. In the case of Qantas, total foreign ownership is restricted to a maximum of 49 per cent in aggregate, with individual holdings limited to 25 per cent and aggregate ownership by foreign airlines limited to 35 per cent. In addition, a number of national interest criteria must be satisfied, relating to the nationality of Board members and operational location of the enterprise."
119 Havel & Sanchez, "Aviation Law", *supra* note 109 at 85 (noting that "[B]y requiring foreign-owned carriers to have a substantial legal and commercial presence within its territory, Australia is able to exert the same regulatory control over the airline's operations that it does not over its "indigenous" air carriers such as Qantas. If, however, Australia were to concede cabotage access under its Air Services Agreements, its regulatory control over foreign airlines utilizing those privileges might be compromised."

time, these airlines cannot operate international routes since in that case the restrictions in the relevant air services agreements would kick in.

Chile has worked to eliminate the nationality requirements since 1979, and, as a consequence, the nationality of a Chilean air carrier is determined by its principal place of business rather than the nationality of its owners.[120] Colombia abolished its foreign ownership limit (up to 40 percent) in 1991 and has allowed unlimited foreign investment in its airlines since 1991.[121] In 1988, New Zealand removed the foreign ownership restriction for domestic airlines.

The unilateral approach of these states is highly exceptional compared to the vast majority of states, which have maintained strict ownership restrictions in their national law. In addition, the impact of the unilateral approach is not significant because it only affects domestic services. Nonetheless, these exceptional cases imply that the assumption that internal restrictions must be maintained on ownership, an assumption influenced by two World Wars, has begun to weaken.

Similarly, states have started to relax inquiries into effective control. This trend has been noticed in many Asian states. Indeed, the Philippines, Indonesia, Thailand, Malaysia, Singapore, Japan, and India appear to be relaxing the effective control test when permitting the operation of a joint venture LCC between an experienced foreign air carrier and local stakeholders with little, if any, aviation experience (for more, see section 4.4.3 Joint Ventures).

It is fundamentally important that this trend is not based on legislative reform. In other words, although legal restrictions have not changed *per se*, some governments have unilaterally turned a blind eye to the effective control test so long as there is local ownership on paper.[122]

Overall, regulatory changes to liberalize the ownership and control restrictions are occurring on multilateral, regional, bilateral, and national levels. In spite of this new trend, however, the level of liberalization led by states is simply not enough for airlines seeking more and better business opportunities. Thus, airlines are making their own efforts to liberalize the industry.

---

120 ICAO, *Proposal for the Liberalization of Air Carrier Ownership and Control*, ICAO Doc ATConf/6-WP/29 (13 February 2013) (Presented by Chile), online: <www.icao.int/Meetings/atconf6/Documents/Working-Papers/ATConf6-wp029_en.pdf>.
121 Jose Ignacio Garcia-Arboleda, "Transnational Airlines in Latin America Facing the Fear of Nationality" (2012) 37 Air & Space L. 93 at 104.
122 CAPA, "Jetstar Hong Kong's local investor reflects HK's new attitude, learning from Hong Kong Airlines" (18 June 2013), online: <http://centreforaviation.com/analysis/jetstar-hong-kongs-local-investor-reflects-hks-new-attitude-learning-from-hong-kong-airlines-114195>.

4.4 Airlines' Response to Ownership and Control Restrictions

4.4.1 Overview (Merger vs. Alliance)

The greatest impact of ownership and control restrictions is the fact that it limits the right of establishment in the airline industry. Havel and Sanchez define the right of establishment as follows:

> In the context of aviation, a right of establishment would allow foreign investors not only to take majority ownership and control of domestic carriers, but also to set up new airlines or subsidiaries of foreign airlines in a domestic market as well as (if compatible with bilateral air services agreements) to be designated to serve international routes.[123]

Indeed, even though a cross-border merger is normally an option in other industries, this structural change is not allowed in the airline industry. The prohibition on cross-border mergers is one of the key reasons that airlines form alliances. (Airlines' motivations for alliances will be extensively discussed in Chapter 5: Airline Alliances in Northeast Asia).

However, mergers and alliances are distinctly different. From a legal perspective, a merger leads to a single entity, while an alliance does not affect legal ownership, with each partner company remaining independent.[124] From a business perspective, although both mergers and alliances have the same goal (achieving maximum efficiency), mergers achieve efficiency more quickly since they allow full consolidation, while the level of integration in alliances is inherently limited.[125]

Joint ventures fall somewhere between mergers and alliances. However, it is necessary to underline the difference between "incorporated" joint ventures and "unincorporated" joint ventures. While an incorporated joint venture forms a separate (legally incorporated) company, an unincorporated joint venture does not create a new single entity. (This will be further examined in 4.4.3 Joint Ventures).

Figure 4.1 shows where mergers and joint ventures are located based on level of integration. In the section below, cross-border mergers and incorporated joint ventures are discussed with a focus on how they circumvent ownership and control restrictions.

---

123 Havel & Sanchez, "Aviation Law", *supra* note 109 at 53.
124 Kostas Iatrou & Lida Mantzavinou, "Chapter 13 The Impact of Liberalization on Cross-border Airline Mergers and Alliances" in Peter Forsyth *et al* eds., *Liberalization in Aviation: Competition, Cooperation and Public Policy* (Farnham: Ashgate, 2013) 233 at 239.
125 *Ibid.* at 238-239.

Figure 4.1   Spectrum of Airline Integration (from Merger to Alliance)

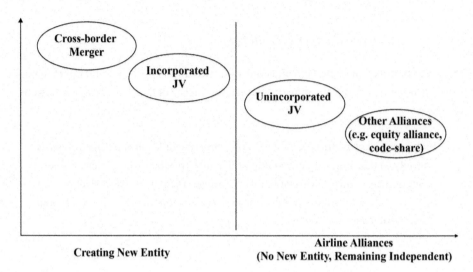

4.4.2   Cross-Border Merger through Holding Company

Generally, a holding company is a company that is formed for two main purposes: to hold investment in subsidiaries and to enjoy tax benefits.[126] However, holding companies have also been used in the airline industry to circumvent the substantial ownership and effective control restrictions.

Until the Air France-KLM merger of 2004, it was assumed that ownership and control restrictions forbade cross-border mergers. But in 2003, Air France and KLM created a "complicated structure designed to match the commercial interests of the two companies with traditional nationality (ownership and control) requirements."[127] This arrangement was approved by the European Commission in 2004, and the holding company, called "Air France-KLM S.A." was established. This merger was possible because the EU had already established the common market and "compatibility with the common market" had been a deciding factor in the EU merger regulations.[128]

---

126   Richard Boykin, "Holing Company Regimes – Introduction" in *International Tax Review: Holding Company Regimes* (London: Euromoney Institutional Investor PLC, 2005) at 3.
127   Mendes de Leon, *supra* note 34 at 374.
128   *Council Regulation (EEC) No 4064/89 of 21 December 1989 on the control of concentrations between undertakings* (now, *Council Regulation (EC) No 139/2004 of 20 January 2004 on the control of concentrations between undertakings*) (the EC Merger Regulation). "Article 6 Examination of the notification and initiation of proceedings – 1. The Commission shall examine the notification as soon as it is received. ... (b) Where it finds that the concentration notified, although falling within the scope of this Regulation, does not raise

Technically, the Air France-KLM arrangement of 2004 is not a complete merger since there is a safeguard provision that instantly increases the Dutch government's capital and voting rights in the company to 50.1 percent if KLM's traffic rights are challenged by third-party states under the Netherlands' bilateral air services agreements.[129] That said, this arrangement was "the first merger in [the aviation] sector between two national airlines with different cultures."[130]

The current ownership structure of Air France-KLM is rather simple. Private shareholders own 81.4 percent (with former Air France shareholders holding 37 percent and former KLM shareholders holding 21 percent), while the French government only owns 18.6 percent.[131] However, it is worth reviewing how Air France and KLM sought to circumvent the substantial ownership and effective control restrictions in 2004. Pablo Mendes de Leon summarizes the structure of the undertaking in 2004 as follows:

- The holding company (Air France-KLM S.A.)'s shares consist of 81 percent of former Air France shares and 19 percent of former KLM shares.
- Air France-KLM S.A. holds two operating companies: Air France and KLM.
- On the Air France side, ownership and control are 100 percent retained by the French.
- KLM is majority owned by the Dutch (the Dutch government and two Dutch foundations) and 49 percent owned by Air France-KLM S.A.
- The principal place of business of KLM remains in Amstelveen, Holland.
- The parties set up a Strategic Management Committee (SMC), which is responsible for the overall group strategy and makes binding recommendations to Air France and KLM.
- The SMC will consist of four representatives from Air France and four from KLM, with the chairman, who casts the deciding vote, from Air France.[132]

---

serious doubts as to its compatibility with the common market, it shall decide not to oppose it and shall declare that it is compatible with the common market."
129 Brian Havel & Gabriel Sanchez, "Restoring Global Aviation's "Cosmopolitan Mentalité"" (2011) 29 B.U. Int'l L.J. 1 at 30. [Havel & Sanchez, "Cosmopolitan Mentalité"].
130 Jean-Cyril Spinetta, *Chairman's Message* in Air France – KLM, *Reference Document 2004-05* (2005) at 3.
131 Mark Toner & Edward Willis, "Foreign Ownership and Control of International Airlines: A New Agenda for Reform" (2012) 24 Air and Space Law at note 9.
132 Mendes de Leon, *supra* note 34 at 374-375.

Figure 4.2 Corporate Structure of Air France-KLM S.A. in 2004[133]

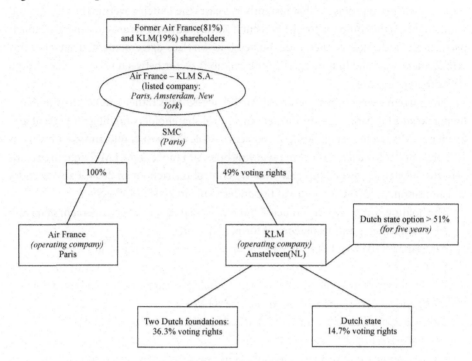

Evidently, the question of who effectively controls KLM remains, at best, unclear. The role and governing structure of SMC make it doubtful that KLM is actually controlled by the Dutch. However, this cross-border merger through a holding company has been operating successfully without being seriously challenged by third party states.

Based on publicly available sources, the only time that a cross-border merger has been meaningfully challenged by a third party state was when India challenged Swiss International Air Lines (SWISS) and Austrian Airlines (both owned by Germany's Lufthansa Group).[134] India's Civil Aviation Ministry raised concerns that the two airlines violated substantial ownership and effective control clauses under existing bilateral air services agreements.[135] However, India ultimately did not take further action as it had threatened,

---

133 Ibid. at 376.
134 CAPA, "India to investigate SWISS and Austrian ownership concerns" (17 November 2011), online: <http://centreforaviation.com/news/india-to-investigate-swiss-and-austrian-ownership-concerns-129137>.
135 Ibid.

4   OWNERSHIP AND CONTROL ISSUES IN NORTHEAST ASIA

such as by revoking SWISS and Austrian's operating rights.[136] Both SWISS and Austrian Airlines currently fly to India.[137]

LATAM Airlines Group S.A. was created through a similar process. In June 2012, the merger between Chilean carrier LAN and Brazilian carrier TAM was completed, creating a mega carrier that is expected to control more than 40 percent of the Latin American air passenger market.[138] In order to circumvent ownership and control restrictions, a rather complicated corporate structure was invented (see Figure 4.3).

Figure 4.3   Corporate Structure of the LATAM Group[139]

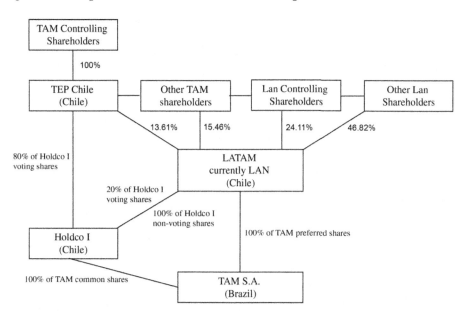

Essentially, TEP Chile is a holding company with a substantial investment in Brazil's TAM and Chile's LATAM. Although the corporate structure of LATAM has similarities with that of Air France-KLM, LATAM in addition had to deal with Brazil's onerous domestic legal restrictions on ownership (80 percent of voting shares must be held by Brazilians).

---

136   Ibid.
137   See SWISS homepage, online: <www.swiss.com/cn/EN/book/where-we-fly/route-network>; Austrian Airlines' homepage, online: <www.austrian.com/?sc_lang=en&cc=AT>.
138   Aaron Karp, "LAN/TAM complete merger under LATAM Airlines Group" *ATW* (22 June 2012), online: <http://atwonline.com/news/lantam-complete-merger-under-latam-airlines-group>.
139   US Securities and Exchange Commission, *Offer to Exchange each Common Share, Preferred Share and American Depositary Share of TAM S.A. for 0.90 of a Common Share of LAN AIRLINES S.A. Represented by American Depositary Shares or Brazilian Depositary Shares* (10 May 2012) at 30, online: <www.sec.gov/Archives/edgar/data/1530924/000119312512224036/d287027d424b3.htm>.

Even if LATAM's corporate structure formally complies with the 80 percent restriction, it is still doubtful whether overall management of TAM is exclusively entrusted to Brazilians, the "effective control" requirement in Brazil.[140]

Avianca Holdings S.A. is another cross-border merger (Avianca and TACA Airlines) that utilized a holding company to circumvent ownership and control restrictions. Avianca is one of the oldest airlines, founded in 1919, and the flag carrier of Colombia.[141] TACA (Transportes Aereos del Continente Americano) was the national carrier of El Salvador until it became Avianca El Salvador.[142]

The complicated corporate structure (see Figure 4.4) essentially allows Avianca Holdings in Panama to control many subsidiaries including TACA Peru (incorporated in Peru) and Tampa Cargo (incorporated in Colombia).[143] Thus, the question can be raised about whether TACA Peru is actually Peruvian under the traditional ownership and control restrictions.[144]

---

140 Braun, *supra* note 2 at 356.
141 See CAPA, Profiles, "Avianca", online: <http://centreforaviation.com/profiles/airlines/avianca-av>.
142 See CAPA, Profiles, "Avianca El Salvador," online: <http://centreforaviation.com/profiles/airlines/avianca-el-salvador-ta>.
143 See Garcia-Arboleda, *supra* note 121 at 101-102.
144 *Ibid.* at102.

Figure 4.4 Corporate Structure of Avianca Holdings S.A.[145]

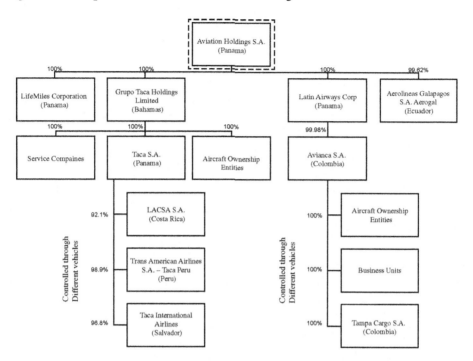

Overall, these cross-border airline mergers were only possible because they took place in regions where regional cooperation, liberalization, and integration were already in progress. In other words, "effective control" inquiries were not *strictly* conducted, or even if they were, not strictly enforced. It is doubtful that the same mergers would have been possible if a totally foreign carrier (*e.g.* a US carrier) had proposed similar mergers to the local governments.

It is also important to emphasize that the international community did not express any meaningful opposition to these cross-border mergers.[146] Although questioning the effective control of the partner airline is inherently discretionary rather than obligatory under air services agreements, it is worth noting that states tend to acquiesce in this issue particularly if they involve airlines from friendly or partner states.

---

145 BTGPactual, "Avianca Holdings" Equity Research (16 December 2013), online: <https://www.btg-pactual.com/Research/OpenPdf.aspx?file=19044.pdf>.
146 See *e.g.* Braun, *supra* note 2 at 356.

4.4.3 Joint Ventures

Generally speaking, there are multiple advantages to establishing joint ventures including, but not limited to, cutting costs, sharing risk, expanding the customer base, and gaining entry to emerging economies.[147] In the airline industry, however, ownership and control restrictions remain the principal reason for establishing joint ventures.

Joint ventures can be broadly divided into incorporated joint ventures and unincorporated joint ventures. An incorporated joint venture is a "full-function" joint venture that "is established by the parties with the intent that it should have its own employees, assets, facilities, funding and markets and generally carry on business as an autonomous economic entity."[148] In the aviation industry, many Asian LCC carriers have adopted this business structure. The likes of AirAsia, Lion Air, Jetstar, Spring Airlines, Tigerair, and VietJet have managed to establish a business presence in jurisdictions outside their own through JV arrangements with local investors.

An unincorporated joint venture is a "limited-function" joint venture that "is not an autonomous or independent unit but one which [is] designed to carry out a more specific and limited role under the direct control of its parents."[149] Unincorporated joint ventures in the aviation industry will be separately discussed in Chapter 5: Airline Alliances in Northeast Asia. Examples of these unincorporated joint ventures include American Airlines-Japan Airlines JV and United Airlines-All Nippon Airways (ANA) JV.

As discussed in Chapter 2, the EU aviation market presents a highly exceptional case. The progress made toward liberalization and integration in the region has enabled EU carriers to have subsidiaries in other EU member states. For instance, Lufthansa's (LH) subsidiaries include Swiss International Air Lines (SWISS), based in Zurich and Geneva but wholly owned by LH; Austrian Airlines, based in Vienna but wholly owned by LH; and Air Dolomiti, a regional Italian airline that is wholly owned by LH.[150] In addition, the EU's horizontal agreements help these carriers effectively deal with ownership and control restrictions in their international operations in non-EU member states.

From a commercial perspective, the more remarkable fact is that unlimited seventh freedom is allowed for EU carriers after the implementation of the third package in 1992.[151] Thus, it is not necessary for air carriers to establish a new airline in other countries within

---

147 See Ian Hewitt, *Joint Ventures*, 4th ed. (London: Sweet and Maxwell Limited, 2008) at 6-7.
148 *Ibid.* at 97.
149 *Ibid.* at 98; See also Ronald Charles Wolf, *Effective International Joint Venture Management* (New York: M. E. Sharpe, 2000) at 163-164 (noting that "[T]he unincorporated joint venture is formed by contract, normally a very detailed one, that elaborates what will be rights and obligations of each of the participants. It is a joint venture based solely on contractual clauses.").
150 CAPA, Profiles, "SWISS", online: <http://centreforaviation.com/profiles/airlines/swiss-lx>; "Austrian Airlines", online: <http://centreforaviation.com/profiles/airlines/austrian-airlines-os>; and "Air Dolomiti", online: <http://centreforaviation.com/profiles/airlines/air-dolomiti-en>.
151 See above Chapter 2, section 2.2.1 Overview.

the EU. Rather, the air carrier itself can operate the routes it wishes to fly while using the seventh freedom. This explains how Ryanair, an Irish carrier, can operate a network covering 40 bases, with some 155 destinations over 1,100 routes in 26 countries (mostly within Europe).[152]

In Asia, both the wholly owned subsidiary strategy and the business opportunities based on unlimited seventh freedom rights are forbidden by law. Under the circumstances, many incorporated joint ventures with local interests were developed in Asia so as to circumvent ownership and control restrictions. In doing so, most airlines chose local investors who were not airline companies or had no prior business experience in the airline industry. Alan Tan explains how the above business model is permissible and why foreign carriers prefer a non-airline company as a partner in the context of ASEAN:

> [T]he related requirement of local "effective control" has taken on a much looser meaning. Most ASEAN member states gloss over the requirement and appear satisfied when their national is appointed as CEO. Whether effective control truly resides locally could be questionable since many of the joint venture airlines are run as integrated operations alongside their parent foreign carriers, using established common brands or identities as well as combined internet booking platforms.[153]

Indeed, joint venture airlines whose local shareholders are not airline companies have been established in many Asian states. Table 4.4 lists Asian joint venture airlines whose local shareholders have minimal business experience in the airline industry:

Table 4.4   Joint Venture Airlines Whose Local Shareholders Are Not Airline Companies

Country/Territory	Joint Venture Airline	Local Shareholder(s)	Foreign Shareholder(s)
Indonesia	Indonesia AirAsia	Pin Harris (20%) and Sendjaja Windjaja (31%)	AAIL (wholly-owned subsidiary of AirAsia Berhad) (49%)
Indonesia	Indonesia AirAsia X	PT Kirana Anugerah Perkasa (PTKAP) (51%)	AirAsia X Berhad (49%)
Thailand	Thai Lion Air	2 Thai businessmen (names undisclosed) (51%)	Lion Air Group (49%)

---

152 CAPA, Profiles, "Ryanair", online: <http://centreforaviation.com/profiles/airlines/ryanair-fr>.
153 Alan Khee-Jin Tan, *Assessing the Prospects for an E.U.-ASEAN Air Transport Agreement*, Discussion Paper No 2015-02, International Transport Forum (Paris: OECD, 2015) at 14.

Country/Territory	Joint Venture Airline	Local Shareholder(s)	Foreign Shareholder(s)
Thailand	Thai AirAsia X	Tassapon Bijleveld (41%) and Julpas Kruesopon (10%)	AirAsia Berhad (49%)
Singapore	Jetstar Asia	Westbrook Investments Pte. Ltd. (51%)	Qantas Airways (49%)
Hong Kong	Jetstar Hong Kong[a]	Shun Tak Holdings (51%)	Qantas Airways (24.5%) and China Eastern Airlines (24.5%)
Japan	Spring Airlines Japan	Various Japanese non-airline related investors (undisclosed) (67%)	Spring Airlines (33%)
Japan	Japan AirAsia[b]	Octave Japan Infrastructure Fund (19%); Rakuten Inc. (18%); Noevir Holdings Co. Ltd. (9%) and Alpen (5%)	AAIL (wholly-owned subsidiary of AirAsia Berhad) (49%)
India	India AirAsia	Tata Sons (30%); Telstra Tradeplace (21%)	AAIL (wholly-owned subsidiary of AirAsia Berhad) (49%)
India	Vistara	Tata Sons (51%)	Singapore Airlines (49%)

a. Its application for an operating license with the Hong Kong SAR government was rejected on 25 June 2015 (discussed below). As of the time of writing, Jetstar Hong Kong is considering its next course of action. See Sijia Jiang, "Jetstar Bid for Hong Kong Licence Rejected" *South China Morning Post* (26 June 2015), online: <www.scmp.com/business/companies/article/1826650/jetstar-bid-hong-kong-licence-rejected>.

b. It is scheduled to begin service in 2015.

Table 4.4 enumerates the joint venture LCCs whose local shareholders hail from various industries outside of aviation such as music recording, entertainment, aerospace, leasing, hospitality, land and water transportation, consumer products, tourism, agriculture, and trading, among others.

There is reason to believe that foreign carriers prefer having non-airline companies as partners instead of other airlines because of the concern that the two airline partners could fail to cooperate well on critical managerial or operational decisions. For instance, ANA and AirAsia failed to harmonize their views on management policy with the first AirAsia Japan. Having only one airline shareholder in the joint venture ensures that the operational standards and commercial strategies are identical across all joint venture airlines in different territories. Otherwise, it can be harder to maximize the advantages that an interconnected network can offer.

Nevertheless, it is important to reiterate that governments still have the right to inquire about effective control. The fact that the governments in question approved the aforementioned JVs (between investor-foreign carriers and non-airline local companies) certainly does not mean that they have given up effective control.

Hence, investor-foreign carriers still need to be careful about the JV structure. This is the main reason why foreign carriers sometimes opt to partner with local air carriers or their subsidiaries. It is relatively easy for such JVs to pass the effective control test since the majority of their shares are owned by a local airline staffed by personnel who would understand the aviation business. Table 4.5 lists Asian joint venture airlines whose local shareholders are airline companies or their subsidiaries.

Table 4.5 Joint Venture Airlines Owned by Airline Companies or Their Subsidiaries

Country/Territory	Joint Venture Airline	Local Shareholder/s	Foreign Shareholder/s
Thailand	NokScoot	Nok Mangkang Co. Ltd. (wholly-owned subsidiary of Nok Airlines) (49%) and Pueannammitr Co. Ltd. (2%)	Scoot Pte. Ltd. (49%)
Thailand	Thai AirAsia	Asia Aviation (55%)	AirAsia Investment Limited (wholly-owned subsidiary of AirAsia Berhad) (45%)
Thailand	Thai Vietjet Air	Kan Air (Somphong Sooksanguan) (51%)	Vietjet (49%)
Philippines	Philippine AirAsia	F&S Holdings (16%); TNR Holdings (16%); Alfredo Yao (13%) and Michael Romero (16%)	AirAsia Investment Limited (wholly-owned subsidiary of AirAsia Berhad) (40%)
Philippines	AirAsia Zest	AirAsia Inc. (Philippine AirAsia) (49%) and Alfredo Yao (51%)	-
Malaysia	Malindo Air	National Aerospace and Defence Industries (51%)	Lion Air (49%)
Vietnam	Jetstar Pacific	Vietnam Airlines (69%) and Saigon Tourist Travel Services (1%)	Qantas Airways (30%)
Japan	Jetstar Japan	Japan Airlines (45.7%); Mitsubishi Corporation (4.3%) and Century Tokyo Leasing (4.3%)	Qantas Airways (45.7%)
Taiwan	Tigerair Taiwan	China Airlines (90%)	Tigerair (10%)

In contrast, when foreign carriers collaborate with local majority shareholders who do not have aviation experience, it is doubtful that the local majority shareholders really manage and control the airline, which is a highly sophisticated business. Indeed, it is likely that the foreign carriers have *de facto* control of the airline in question. Again, this business strategy is only possible if the local government relaxes effective control inquiries (Subdivision B).

Despite the general trend toward gradually relaxing effective control restrictions, an external variable must be noted. In its application to the regulatory authorities for an air operator's license, Jetstar Hong Kong has had to revise its bid more than once to convince Hong Kong regulators that the company's leadership and governance at the board level rest with local shareholders and not with Qantas (the parent group of Jetstar).[154] The public hearing by the Hong Kong authorities regarding the evaluation of Jetstar Hong Kong ended on 14 February 2015.

On 25 June 2015, the Hong Kong Air Transport Licensing Authority delivered its decision rejecting Jetstar Hong Kong's license application. This decision was quite surprising since the language of Hong Kong's Basic Law is ostensibly less protective than that of other states. While remaining silent on substantial ownership and effective control restrictions, Hong Kong's domestic law only requires that a Hong Kong carrier be incorporated and have Hong Kong as its principal place of business.[155] (See above in section 4.3.1 The Multilateral Approach for a discussion of the principal place of business).

However, in the Jetstar Hong Kong decision, the Hong Kong Air Transport Licensing Authority interpreted the meaning of "principal place of business" as being nearly the same as "effective control." In this decision, the Authority stated that the following would satisfy the requirement of "principal place of business" in Hong Kong:

> The airline has to have independent control and management in Hong Kong, free from directions or decisions made elsewhere. The nerve centre has to be in Hong Kong. By nerve centre, the Panel looks at where and by whom the decisions regarding the key operations of an airline are made.[156]

Thus, the Hong Kong Air Transport Licensing Authority concluded that Jetstar Hong Kong's nerve center is not in Hong Kong[157] and that Jetstar Hong Kong cannot make its decisions independently from that of the two foreign shareholders (Qantas Airways and China Eastern Airlines, which have 24.5% shares, respectively).[158]

A much more important question is whether this decision will have an impact on other parts of Asia. Alan Tan noted that "the very public acrimony over Jetstar Hong Kong may actually restore the primacy of the local control requirement that has become all but for-

---

154 Siva Govindasamy, "Jetstar counts the cost of prolonged delay in Hong Kong take-off" *Reuters* (17 November 2014), online: <www.reuters.com/article/2014/11/17/airlines-hong-kong-jetstar-idUSL4N0SQ1J220141117>.
155 *Decision on Principal Place of Business With Regard To Application For Licence by Jetstar Hong Kong Airways Limited Before the Air Transport Licencing Authority*, 2015 § 177.
156 *Ibid.* § 208.
157 *Ibid.* § 240.
158 *Ibid.* § 279.

gotten in much of Asia."[159] The CAPA report also noted that "at worst, it sends a hopeful message to those who would seek to protect the status quo."[160] No doubt, how other states react to the ruling will show whether Asian states had inadvertently overlooked the control requirement or had intentionally relaxed inquiries into effective control.

Overall, both cross-border mergers through holding companies and incorporated joint ventures have managed to establish new companies that either effectively control foreign carriers or operate as new airlines in foreign markets. Although these new entities appear to comply with ownership restrictions, the question of effective control remains.

4.5   Conclusion

The object of this chapter has been to provide an analytical perspective on ownership and control restrictions in Northeast Asia. Although rigid ownership restrictions are still in place in the region according to domestic laws and air services agreements, I have drawn attention to the fairly flexible policy approaches that are taken on the issue of control restrictions. This liberalization of policy will contribute to the discussion of Northeast Asian open skies.

Toward the end of this chapter, I briefly touched on the relationship between legal barriers (ownership and control restrictions) and airline alliances. In short, cross-border mergers and incorporated joint ventures are airlines' direct response to the ownership and control restrictions. This approach can be described as "step-down" (from forbidden merger to merger-like integration). In the next chapter (Chapter 5: Airline Alliances in Northeast Asia), airline alliances will be reviewed as a "step-up" approach (from low-level alliances to high-level alliances). In particular, Chapter 5 will focus on the impact of airline alliances on Northeast Asian open skies.

---

159 Alan Khee-Jin Tan, "Jetstar Hong Kong's arrival puts airline control rules in the spotlight" *South China Morning Post* (15 February 2015), online: <www.scmp.com/comment/article/1493619/jetstar-hong-kongs-arrival-puts-airline-control-rules-spotlight>.

160 CAPA, "Jetstar Hong Kong licence application rejected: Hong Kong becomes an island of protectionism in Asia" (29 June 2015), online: <http://centreforaviation.com/analysis/jetstar-hong-kong-licence-application-rejected-hong-kong-becomes-an-island-of-protectionism-in-asia-206546>.

5 Airline Alliances in Northeast Asia

5.1   Conceptual Analysis of Airline Alliances

Chapter 5 begins with two fundamental questions: what are airline alliances and why do airlines form these alliances? The term "alliance" is used very loosely in the aviation industry.[1] Indeed, airline alliances can refer to any kind of inter-airline cooperation. Thus, a more accurate question is why airlines cooperate. After investigating the factors that motivate airline alliances, I will discuss the various types of airline alliances that can be categorized based on the level of integration.

5.1.1   Motivating Factors for Airline Alliances

Broadly speaking, legal barriers and economic incentives are the two primary reasons why airlines form alliances. As discussed in Chapters 3 and 4, legal barriers refer to the restrictions on market access and on ownership and control that are entrenched in air services agreements and domestic laws. The economic reasons for alliances can generally be divided into three categories: increasing revenue, cutting costs, and reducing competition. That said, airlines rarely form alliances for one reason alone. In other words, airline alliances are typically driven by a combination of factors.

5.1.1.1   Circumventing Legal Barriers

One simple but crucial fact about the airline industry is that airlines cannot determine their markets (that is, their routes) solely on a commercial basis. From a commercial perspective, for instance, Air China would like to offer at least a few flights from Beijing to Seoul and then on to Jeju Island. Many Chinese tourists want to visit both Seoul and Jeju, and the Seoul-Jeju route is one of the most popular air routes in the world.[2] Thus, Air China would take not only Chinese passengers originating from Beijing but also Korean passengers originating in Seoul to Jeju if it could. Alternatively, Air China would want to establish a Korean subsidiary that could operate between Seoul and Jeju or take over a small Korean LCC.

---

1 Stephen Shaw, *Airline Marketing and Management*, 7th ed. (Farnham: Ashgate, 2011) at 126.
2 Chris Kitching, "Busiest flight routes in the world revealed with number one carrying SEVEN MILLION passengers a year" *Main Online* (8 August 2014), online: <www.dailymail.co.uk/travel/travel_news/article-2719733/Busiest-flight-routes-world-revealed.html>.

However, as discussed in Chapter 3, the market access restrictions resulting from protective air services agreements limit even basic third and four freedom traffic, not to mention the cabotage restriction, which prevents an airline from operating domestic routes in other countries (such as Air China for the Seoul-Jeju route in the example above). Similarly, in Chapter 4, we saw how internal and external restrictions on ownership and control prevent airlines from establishing wholly- or majority-owned subsidiaries or acquiring local airlines in foreign markets.

Given these legal challenges, commercial arrangements between airlines (that is, airline alliances) are a practical option and indeed a wise choice. Airline alliances can help to overcome the constraints that hinder the ability of individual airlines to enter and expand into foreign markets.[3] For instance, Air China could *virtually* enter and expand into the Korean market through a code-sharing agreement[4] with Korea's Asiana Airlines, which can operate between Seoul and Jeju without legal restrictions. (Both airlines are in the same global alliance, Star Alliance. The issue is discussed further in section 5.1.2.2 Non-equity Alliance.)

Nevertheless, it is important to note that airline alliances are not completely free from legal barriers. Market access and ownership and control restrictions are not the only provisions in air services agreements relating to airline alliances. Normally, there is a separate and specific provision regarding airline alliances in air services agreements. The relevant provision typically refers to "cooperative arrangements," "code-sharing," or "commercial opportunities." Some states prefer to address code-sharing in the annex (route schedule) to the air services agreement.[5] While an open skies agreement provides open opportunities for code-sharing,[6] a protective air services agreement places tight restrictions on it. Under a protective air services agreement, code-sharing is allowed only on certain routes.

Even under an open skies agreement, national air carriers are required to submit their cooperative service agreements with other carriers to the relevant government authorities for review before (or after) they implement those agreements.[7] The authorities review these

---

3   Kostas Iatrou & Mauro Oretti, *Airline Choices for the Future: From Alliances to Mergers* (Burlington: Ashgate, 2007) at 5.
4   See Chapter 1, section 1.6.1 Rationale for Airline Alliances.
5   See ICAO, *Template Air Services Agreement* (28 September 2009) at 59, online: <www.icao.int/Meetings/AMC/MA/ICAN2009/templateairservicesagreements.pdf>.
6   See *e.g.* US Department of State, *Current Model Open Skies Agreement Text*, online: <www.state.gov/e/eb/rls/othr/ata/114866.htm>. Article 8 Commercial Opportunities – "7. In operating or holding out the authorized services under this Agreement, any airline of one Party may enter into cooperative marketing arrangements such as blocked-space, codesharing, or leasing arrangements, with a. an airline or airlines of either Party; b. an airline or airlines of a third country; [and c. a surface transportation provider of any country;] provided that all participants in such arrangements (i) hold the appropriate authority and (ii) meet the requirements normally applied to such arrangements."
7   See US Department of Transportation, *Alliances and Codeshares,* (updated 18 February 2015), online: <www.dot.gov/policy/aviation-policy/competition-data-analysis/alliance-codeshares>. and 49 US Code § 41720 – Joint Venture Agreements, online: <www.law.cornell.edu/uscode/text/49/41720>.

cooperative agreements to ensure that they are in line with the relevant air services agreements. They also examine the cooperative agreements to ensure that they are not harmful to the public or anti-competitive. (This will be discussed in section 5.2 Competition Law Analysis of Airline Alliances.)

5.1.1.2   Increasing Revenue

Airline alliances play a key role in increasing revenue in airlines' existing markets through the extra traffic generated by foreign alliance partners. For instance, the alliance between KLM and Northwest, the first "modern airline alliance,"[8] increased KLM's traffic by 150,000 passengers and its revenue by USD 100 million while increasing Northwest's traffic by 200,000 passengers and its revenue by USD 125-175 million in 1994, the first year of full cooperation.[9] This growth in revenue was largely due to the increase in the airlines' load factors. Taking advantage of Northwest's hubs in Boston, Detroit, and Minneapolis and KLM's hub in Amsterdam, KLM could codeshare with Northwest on routes between Northwest's three hubs and 88 US cities while Northwest could codeshare with KLM on routes between Amsterdam and 30 cities in Europe and the Middle East.[10] These new routes greatly increased traffic into each other's network.

Airline alliances can also enable airlines to expand into new markets, thus boosting their airlines ticket sales. For instance, although Singapore Airlines does not directly fly to Sapporo in Japan from its home market (Singapore), it can still sell tickets to passengers who want to go from Singapore to Sapporo by suggesting two connected flights on separate airlines: one with Singapore Airlines from Singapore to Tokyo-Narita and the other with ANA (Singapore's alliance partner) from Tokyo-Narita to Sapporo.

Another substantial economic incentive for alliances (and in particular, global alliances such as Star Alliance, Skyteam and Oneworld) are the benefits of their marketing activities, which ultimately increase passenger and cargo traffic, thereby increasing revenue. Generally, alliances' marketing advantages stem from their members' scale of operations and the breadth of their networks.[11]

---

8   Shaw, *supra* note 1 at 125.
9   US Government Accountability Office (US GAO), *International Aviation: Airline Alliances Produce Benefits, But Effect on* Competition is Uncertain (GAO/REC-95-99, April 1995) at 27-28, online: <www.gao.gov/products/RCED-95-99>.
10 *Ibid.* at 29.
11 Rigas Doganis, *The Airline Business in the 21st Century* (London: Routledge, 2001) at 72.

5.1.1.3 Cutting Costs

Achieving greater economies of scale,[12] economies of scope[13] and economies of density[14] has been cited as a motive for forming airline alliances.[15] Although some commentators argue that airline alliances yield economies of scale and economies of density only in limited circumstances,[16] economies of scope are regarded as a highly significant benefit that can be easily enjoyed through alliances.[17] The synergies that can be achieved through economies of scope include shared labor and shared capital equipment.[18]

Indeed, the synergies arising from airline alliances allow alliance members to reduce costs by weeding out redundant operations. Given that the airline industry is very capital-intensive with high fixed costs, cost management is crucial for airlines. The cost structure of an airline is traditionally divided into operating and non-operating (or fixed) costs,[19] with the fixed costs generally representing more than 50 percent of the airline's total costs,[20] which include aircraft financing (lease and loan payments) and airport facility rental charges.

Alliance partners can share facilities (*e.g.* sales offices and passenger lounges) as well as labor (*e.g.* ground handlers and check-in agents). Swissair and Austrian were the first alliance partners to successfully establish joint ticketing and sales offices in many parts of the world, thereby reducing the number of offices and staff required.[21]

In addition, alliances can help members cut their costs by enabling them to share purchases in many areas including aircraft, fuel, and amenities. For instance, Star Alliance

---

12 Economies of scale are "advantages gained when average unit costs decrease with an increase in the quantity being produced", Bijan Vasigh, Ken Fleming & Thomas Tacker, *Introduction to Air Transport Economics – From Theory to Applications* (Hampshire Ashgate: 2008) at 89.
13 Economies of scope refers to "the situation in which the company can reduce its unit costs by leveraging efficiencies through sharing resources for multiple projects or production lines", *ibid*.
14 "Economies of density are achieved through the consolidation of operations", *ibid*. at 90.
15 See *e.g.* Paul Dempsey & Laurence Gesell, *Airline Management Strategies for the 21st Century*, 3rd ed. (Chandler: Coast Aire Publications, 2012) at 644.
16 See Birgit Kleymann & Hannu Seristö, *Managing Strategic Airline Alliances* (Burlington: Ashgate, 2004) at 5-7 (noting that "[I]n the airline case, there are still limited possibilities for reaping scale economies from alliancing: some of the fixed costs (especially aircraft and personnel related) are still very airline specific and many cannot be fully spread over alliance partners due to the regulatory environment in which an airline operates, which in many cases includes very tight and restrictive labour contracts... In an alliance, this type of economies [economies of density] can only be realized if the coordination and feed between partners is optimized or if one airline gives up the route and leaves its operation to its partner. This type of cooperation therefore requires high degrees of partner integration, which in turn are costly to establish and maintain.").
17 *Ibid*. at 8.
18 Vasigh *et al*, *supra* note 12 at 90.
19 See *e.g.* Rogéria de Arantes Gomes Eller & Michelle Moreira, "The Main Cost-related Factors in Airlines Management" (2014) 8 Journal of Transport Literature 8 at 11.
20 Vasigh *et al*, *supra* note 12 at 92.
21 Doganis, *supra* note 11 at 77.

members are reported to generally enjoy a 5 to 7 percent discount on prices through joint purchasing or procurement.[22]

5.1.1.4 Reducing Competition

This factor is the most controversial characteristic of airline alliances. Essentially, alliances enhance member airlines' ability to exercise market power and reduce the level of competition as airlines that previously competed on a route decide to cooperate instead.[23]

It is important to note that not all forms of airline alliances fall into this category. Generally, alliance members remain competitors until the middle stage of cooperation, such as code-sharing.[24] Since a high degree of alliance cooperation has the potential to become anti-competitive, governmental intervention is required. (This will be fully examined in section 5.2 Competition Law Analysis of Airline Alliances.)

5.1.2   Spectrum of Airline Alliances

The two main methods of forming airline alliances are the bilateral approach and the multilateral approach. What began with bilateral code-sharing progressed to bilateral joint ventures and then to multilateral branded global alliances and multilateral joint ventures within global alliances.[25]

As much as global alliances play a pivotal role for many international air carriers, bilateral inter-carrier agreements, which reflect the needs of the individual airline rather than the alliance as a whole, are another key factor in airline operations. As mentioned earlier, bilateral inter-carrier agreements are the foundation of the multilateral alliances mentioned above.

---

22 *Ibid.* at 78.
23 Iatrou & Oretti, *supra* note 3 at 5.
24 See Figure 1.6 Spectrum of Alliance Cooperation in section 1.6.2 Antitrust Immunity.
25 CAPA, *Airlines in Transition report, Part 1: The natural history of airline alliances* (16 April 2013), online: <http://centreforaviation.com/analysis/capa-airlines-in-transition-report-part-1-the-natural-history-of-airline-alliances-105278>.

Table 5.1 Global Branded Airline Alliances

	Star Alliance	Skyteam	Oneworld
Members* as of 2016	27	20	15
Founding members (founding year)	Air Canada, Lufthansa, SAS, Thai Airways, and United Airlines (1996)	Delta, Air France, Aeroméxico, and Korean Air (2000)	American Airlines, British Airways, Cathay Pacific, Canadian Airlines, and Qantas (1999)
Member Airlines	- Adria Airways - Aegean Airlines - Air Canada - Air China - Air India - Air New Zealand - ANA - Asiana Airlines - Austrian - Avianca - Brussels Airlines - Copa Airlines - Croatia Airlines - Egypt Air - Ethiopian Airlines - EVA Air - LOT Polish Airlines - Lufthansa - Scandinavian Airlines - Shenzhen Airlines - Singapore Airlines - South African Airways - Swiss - TAP Portugal - Thai - Turkish Airlines - United	- Aeroflot - Aerolíneas Argentinas - Aeromexico - Air Europa - Air France - Alitalia - China Airlines - China Eastern - China Southern - Czech Airlines - Delta Air Lines - Garuda Indonesia - Kenya Airways - KLM - Korean Air - Middle East Airlines - Saudia - TAROM - Vietnam Airlines - XiamenAir	- Air Berlin - American Airlines - British Airways - Cathay Pacific - Finnair - Iberia - Japan Airlines - LAN - TAM - Malaysia Airlines - Qantas - Qatar Airways - Royal Jordanian - S7 Airlines - SriLankan Airlines

Once an airline joins one of the global alliances, that airline "exclusively" belongs to the alliance. In other words, dual membership is not allowed. However, it is still within an airline's discretion to make a bilateral inter-carrier agreement with an airline that is not a member of the alliance or even an airline that is a member of a different alliance. Each global alliance has a rule on non-member relationships that restricts an airline in one alliance from developing codeshares with a partner in a major rival alliance.[26] Reportedly, Star Alliance restricts activity the most, Oneworld is the most liberal of all the alliances, and Skyteam is in between, having recently relaxed its prohibition on cooperation with airlines from other alliances.[27]

Given the various types of airline alliances, several commentators have proposed ways of categorizing them. For instance, Paul Dempsey and Laurence Gesell divide airline alliances into "marketing alliances" and "equity alliances";[28] Angela Cheng-Fui Lu divides them into "merger & acquisition model," "investor model," and "strategic and tactical alliances";[29] Rigas Doganis into "commercial alliances" and "strategic alliances";[30] and Kostas Iatrou and Mauro Oretti into "marketing alliances" and "strategic alliances."[31] However, since the terms "commercial," "strategic," and "marketing" lack clear definitions, the aforementioned distinctions are inevitably arbitrary. When employed by different commentators, the same terms (*e.g.* marketing alliances and strategic alliances) do not necessarily fall into the same classifications.[32]

A more objective method of categorization is to ask whether or not airline cooperation involves equity (that is, financial investment). Thus, the categories used here are "equity alliances" and "non-equity alliances." In a nutshell, equity alliances involve airlines owning shares in other airlines. While most equity alliances are based on an investor-and-receiver relationship,[33] some equity alliances are based on cross-ownership (*e.g.* Air China-Cathay Pacific: Air China has a 30% stake in Cathay Pacific while Cathay Pacific holds a roughly 20% stake in Air China).

5.1.2.1   Equity Alliances

Paul Dempsey and Laurence Gesell drew an analogy in which they compared equity alliances to marriages:

---

26   Benét J. Wilson, "What the Korean Air-American Air DFW Codeshare Means for the SkyTeam Alliance", *Airways News* (9 February 2015), online: <http://airwaysnews.com/blog/2015/02/09/what-the-korean-air-american-air-dfw-codeshare-means-for-the-skyteam-alliance/>.
27   *Ibid.*
28   See Paul Dempsey & Laurence Gesell, *Airline Management Strategies for the 21st Century*, 3rd ed. (Chandler: Coast Aire Publications, 2012) at Chapter 14 Alliances.
29   See Angela Cheng-Fui Lu, *International Airline Alliances* (The Hague: Kluwer Law International, 2003) at 56-63.
30   See Doganis, *supra* note 11 at Chapter 4 Alliance.
31   See Iatrou & Oretti, *supra* note 3 at Chapter 3: Once Rivals, Now Partners: How?
32   For example, although Iatrou and Oretti's definition of "strategic alliances" includes equity alliances, Doganis' definition does not.
33   Paul Dempsey & Laurence Gesell, *Airline Management Strategies for the 21st Century*, 3rd ed. (Chandler: Coast Aire Publications, 2012) at 672-685.

A marketing alliance [non-equity alliance] is the equivalent of dating: if the relationship sours, the parties are free (within specified contractual limits) to break it off. An equity investment is the equivalent of marriage: if the relation sours, the investor cannot easily extricate himself from his investment. In dating, one cannot easily extricate himself from his investment. In dating, one can afford to be less discriminate in the appearance or health of one's partner. Selecting a marital partner, however, is a more serious endeavor. For example, one would not typically seek out a marital partner with a terminal illness.[34]

Indeed, just like marriage, the equity alliance has been used as a "symbolic reassurance that an alliance is solid and long-term."[35] However, the marriage analogy does not adequately reflect current trends in airline alliances.[36] The swift evolution of alliances has shown airlines that they can work together without equity investments.[37]

Today, the equity alliance *per se* is not necessarily an indication of truly integrated inter-airline cooperation. Nonetheless, equity alliances are very often accompanied by a high degree of integrated non-equity alliances (regardless of whether they are labeled, for example, a marketing alliance, commercial alliance, or strategic alliance). Although these alliances involve the same partners, they are separate contracts (the former is an investment contract and the latter is a commercial contract, such as code-share agreement). Indeed, current equity alliances are "a part of strategy to strengthen and expand market access".[38]

Abu Dhabi-based Etihad has been referred to as the airline that makes the most effective use of equity alliances. As of 2015, Etihad has eight equity alliance members: Air Serbia (the national airline of Serbia), Air Seychelles (the national airline of the Seychelles), Etihad Regional (formerly Darwin Airline, a Swiss regional airline), Air Berlin (Germany's second largest carrier after Lufthansa), Jet Airways (a major Indian carrier), Virgin Australia (Australia's second largest carrier after Qantas) and Aer Lingus (an Irish carrier). Most recently, Alitalia (the largest carrier in Italy) became an Etihad equity alliance member when the Etihad-Alitalia deal received the approval of the European Commission in November 2014.[39] The stake holdings of Etihad can be displayed as follows:

---

34   Paul Dempsey & Laurence Gesell, *Airline Management Strategies for the 21st Century*, 2nd ed. (Chandler: Coast Aire Publications, 2006) at 646.
35   Iatrou & Oretti, *supra* note 3 at 78.
36   In fact, the authors of the analogy (Dempsey & Gesell) noted in 2006 that "[T]hese alliances are shifting swiftly; as a result, any commentary upon the subject may soon become obsolete. The authors therefore urge the reader to look beyond the immediate facts to discern the broader trends and public policy observations" in Paul Dempsey & Laurence Gesell, *Airline Management Strategies for the 21st Century*, 2nd ed. (Chandler: Coast Aire Publications, 2006) at 622.
37   Iatrou & Oretti, *supra* note 3 at 79.
38   *Ibid*. at 78.
39   European Commission, Press Release, "Mergers: Commission approves Etihad's acquisition of joint control over Alitalia, subject to conditions" (14 November 2014), online: <http://europa.eu/rapid/press-release_IP-

Figure 5.1 Etihad Equity Alliance[40]

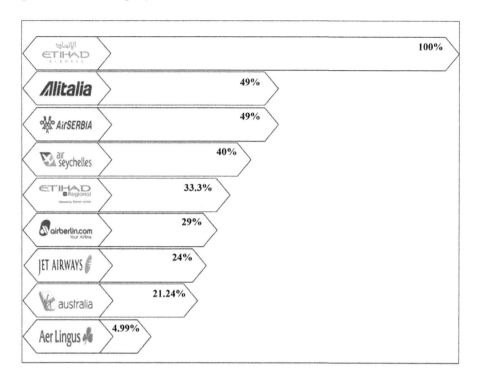

A convincing rationale for equity alliances lies in the ownership and control restrictions. Just as with cross-border mergers and incorporated joint ventures, an equity alliance can be a smart response to legal barriers for an airline. By making a sizeable investment in foreign carriers (though these typically must be below 50% to satisfy the nationality requirements in the air services agreements), a foreign investor airline can gain *de facto* control of the carriers in question.

In fact, regulators in Europe are in the process of investigating whether Etihad effectively controls the European carriers in which it has equity stakes.[41] In response to the allegation

---

14-1766_en.htm>; see also CAPA, "Alitalia and Etihad complete deal as Emirates and Qatar add seats. Record growth for Italy-Gulf" (2 January 2015), online: <http://centreforaviation.com/analysis/alitalia-and-etihad-complete-deal-as-emirates-and-qatar-add-seats-record-growth-for-italy-gulf-203443>.

40   CAPA, "Etihad & Alitalia agree and affirm their partnership vision. Protectionist voices will become louder" (9 August 2014), online: <http://centreforaviation.com/analysis/etihad--alitalia-agree-and-affirm-their-partnership-vision-protectionist-voices-will-become-louder-181662>.

41   In March 2014, the Swiss civil aviation authority launched an investigation into Etihad Regional's ownership and control structure by stating that "we will examine whether the so-called ownership-and-control conditions are met and if the company is still in Swiss hands" in CAPA, "Airline ownership & control. Why might Europe uphold something its officials call "stupid"?" (28 May 2014), online: <http://centreforaviation.com/analysis/airline-ownership--control-why-might-europe-uphold-something-its-officials-call-

that "Etihad is using the investment to buy control,"[42] Etihad argues that the real motivations for equity alliances are good network integration and opportunities to cut costs.[43] CAPA's analysis touches on the practical role of Etihad's equity investment:

> Etihad's increased European footprint has been achieved through commercial codeshare arrangements; equity investments are not in themselves a part of this. However, in the case of airlines that were struggling financially, Etihad's investment has been very important in keeping the partner solvent and thereby in maintaining the viability of the codeshare agreement... [T]he investment means codeshares can be more readily locked in.[44]

Therefore, regardless of the original purpose of the equity alliances, code-sharing agreements between Etihad and its equity alliance partners—which are separate commercial agreements—have played a more important role in the development of Etihad. In fact, code-sharing has been the jewel of the crown in airline alliances as discussed in the following section.

5.1.2.2 Non-equity Alliances

There is a wide spectrum of non-equity alliances (referred to simply as "alliances" in this section). Although it is difficult to fit the manifold varieties of specific airline cooperation into neat categories, the spectrum of alliances can be roughly captured as shown below:

---

stupid-170148>.; The EU has also opened an inquiry into the control of several European airlines including Airberlin and Etihad Regional. See Tom Fairless & Daniel Michaels, "EU Probes Ownership of Virgin, Four Other Airlines" *The Wall Street Journal* (4 April 2014), online: <www.wsj.com/articles/SB10001424052702303847804579481071621614740>.

42   CAPA, "Etihad raises its Europe profile with codeshares and equity, expanding indirect connections" (23 June 2014), online: <http://centreforaviation.com/analysis/etihad-raises-its-europe-profile-with-codeshares-and-equity-expanding-indirect-connections-173845>.

43   "Etihad: Flying against Convention" *The Economist* (28 June 2014).

44   CAPA, "Etihad raises its Europe profile with codeshares and equity, expanding indirect connections" (23 June 2014), online: <http://centreforaviation.com/analysis/etihad-raises-its-europe-profile-with-codeshares-and-equity-expanding-indirect-connections-173845>.

Figure 5.2 Spectrum of Non-equity Airline Alliances

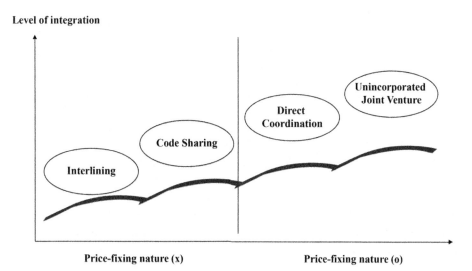

The starting point of an alliance is interlining. From the consumer's perspective, interlining is buying "a single ticket for an itinerary on two or more independent airlines."[45] From the airline's perspective, interline agreements are agreements between airlines with regard to the sale, endorsement, and acceptance of each other's tickets.[46] In essence, interlining is a simple process of linking two separate flights on two different airlines for the convenience of the traveling customer.

While interlining is normally cheaper than the sum of available fares on the individual segments, fares for code-shared flights are typically cheaper than for interline flights.[47] This is because, under an interlining relationship, each airline would set its fares to maximize profit on its own segment regardless of how this might affect demand for the other airline's segment.[48] In other words, interlining does not require a special partnership between the air carriers. A real partnership begins with code-sharing.

In a code-sharing relationship, there is one operating carrier and one or more marketing carriers. The operating carrier is the one that actually operates the aircraft, while the marketing carrier just assigns its airline code onto the flight without operating the aircraft.

---

45 Brian Pearce, "The Economic Benefits Generated by Alliance and Joint Ventures" IATA Economics Briefing (28 November 2011) at 4, online: <https://www.iata.org/whatwedo/Documents/economics/Economics%20of%20JVs_Jan2012L.pdf>.
46 Paul Dempsey & Laurence Gesell, *Airline Management Strategies for the 21st Century*, 2nd ed. (Chandler: Coast Aire Publications, 2006) at 61.
47 Pearce, *supra* note 45 at 4-5.
48 *Ibid.* at 5.

Code-sharing enables airlines to offer consumers more convenient service through coordinated scheduling, close proximity of gates for connecting passengers, access to lounges, and frequent flier programs.[49] For code-sharing, the way a partner airline is chosen changes fundamentally. While almost any airline can be an interlining partner, airlines become highly selective when they look for code-sharing partners.

Some airlines are not fully satisfied with a simple code-sharing relationship as they hope to directly coordinate market-related matters, including prices. At this stage, alliances start to entail price-fixing. Although this type of alliance violates competition law, in principle, it is allowed if the competition authorities grant antitrust immunity. (This will be discussed in the next section.)

Furthermore, some carriers launch highly integrated joint ventures (unincorporated joint ventures) in specific markets. Unincorporated joint ventures are the most intensive form of alliance. While still operating as two independent legal entities, the airlines cooperate as closely as possible. This form of cooperation is effectively "a close substitute to a merger because it typically involves full coordination of the major airline functions on the affected routes, including scheduling, pricing, revenue management, marketing, and sales."[50] Due to the scope of business activities, unincorporated joint ventures are subject to competition law.

5.2   Competition Law Analysis of Airline Alliances

5.2.1   General Principles

First and foremost, it is worth noting that the terms "competition law" and "antitrust law" can be used interchangeably, meaning that there is no substantial difference between the two terms. In general, competition law is a more generic term, since antitrust law typically refers to a set of US federal and state laws covering competition law issues.[51]

---

49   Ibid.
50   The European Commission and the United States Department of Transportation, *Transatlantic Airline Alliances: Competitive Issues and Regulatory Approaches* (16 November 2010) at 8, online: <http://ec.europa.eu/competition/sectors/transport/reports/joint_alliance_report.pdf>.
51   To track how the term 'antitrust law' was made, see Richard Whish, *Competition Law*, 2nd ed. (London: Butterworths, 1989) at 21 (noting that "[I]n the late nineteenth century there was much popular dissatisfaction with railroad companies which, with a monopoly in the carriage of goods, were able to charge prices disproportionate to the value of the service they provided and greatly in excess of what their customers could charge for their own produce. Meanwhile many industries were rife with anti-competitive practices which were privately profitable but injurious to the public at large. In particular trusts were formed, pioneered in large measure by John Rockefeller, whereby the stocks held in competing companies were transferred to the trustees who then managed the affairs of the industry in question. As the trustees had legal control, they could eliminate competitive pressure between the companies concerned. It was because of this particular

Competition law is a relatively new discipline of law. Although the US established an antitrust law regime in the 19th century, many states did not enact competition laws until the late 20th century. Since 2000, competition law has grown at a phenomenal rate. In 2001, there were only about 80 systems of competition law in the world, but by 2012, more than 120 systems could be found on every continent and in every type of economy.[52] In 2008 alone, competition laws came into force in the gigantic economies of China and India.[53] Today, several other states are deliberating the idea of adopting their own systems.

Due to the diverse levels of economic development and widely varying legal cultures in states with competition laws, it would be rash to presume that all these systems are identical in their goals and concerns.[54] Generally, however, competition law consists of "rules that are intended to protect the process of competition in order to maximize consumer welfare."[55] Although the term "competition" has a wide variety of connotations, this explanation by the UK Competition Commission is especially cogent:

> Competition is a process of rivalry as firms seek to win customers' business. It creates incentives for firms to meet the existing and future needs of customers as effectively and efficiently as possible—by cutting prices, increasing output, improving quality or variety, or introducing new and better products, often through innovation; supplying the products customers want rewards firms with a greater share of sales.[56]

Essentially, competition law seeks to promote rivalry among firms (that is, competitors). Nonetheless, the ultimate goal of competition law is not protecting the competitive process itself but rather protecting the interests of consumers.[57] The importance of setting clear goals cannot be overemphasized, especially when exploring antitrust immunity, which will be discussed in the next section.

Above all, competition law prohibits anti-competitive agreements (agreements that have the object or effect of restricting competition). Anti-competitive agreements can be

---

form of co-operation that the term 'antitrust' was coined, but it has since acquired a more general usage to connote any action taken against anti-competitive behavior.").

52 Compare Richard Whish, *Competition Law*, 4th ed. (London: Butterworths, 2001) at 1 and Richard Whish & David Bailey, *Competition Law*, 7th ed. (New York: Oxford University Press, 2012) at 1.
53 Richard Whish, *Competition Law*, 6th ed. (New York: Oxford University Press, 2009) at 1.
54 See Eleanor Fox, "Chapter 22: The Kaleidoscope of Antitrust and Its Significance in the World Economy: Respecting Differences" in Barry Hawk, ed., *International Antitrust Law & Policy* (New York: Juris Publishing, 2002) at 597.
55 Whish, *supra* note 53 at 1.
56 The UK Competition Commission, *Guidelines for market investigations: Their role, procedures, assessment and remedies* (April 2013) at 7, <online: <https://www.gov.uk/government/uploads/system/uploads/attachment_data/file/284390/cc3_revised.pdf>.
57 Whish, *supra* note 53 at 19.

divided into horizontal agreements (agreements between competitors) and vertical agreements (agreements between companies at different levels of the market).

Horizontal agreements include agreements that directly or indirectly relate to prices, agreements to restrict output or capacity, and dividing up the market. An agreement among competitors to fix prices is a classic horizontal agreement that is strictly prohibited in every country that has competition laws.

Vertical agreements involve setting prices that suppliers can charge their own customers, forcing customers to buy products they do not want, and preventing customers from dealing with other competitors. It is generally thought that horizontal agreements are more likely to interfere with competition than vertical agreements.[58]

Airline alliances generally take the form of inter-carrier agreements, which quite often are agreements between competitors. Thus, most airline alliances can be seen as illegal horizontal agreements, at least on the surface. For instance, Korean Air and Japan Airlines are competitors in the Korea-Japan market. Nevertheless, Korean Air and Japan Airlines share lounges at Gimpo Airport and Haneda Airport. Japan Airlines passengers can use Korean Air's lounge at Gimpo Airport, and Korean Air passengers can use Japan Airlines' lounge at Haneda Airport. In so doing, the two airlines do not need to rent a lounge facility in the other airline's country and can therefore cut costs. When costs increase for an airline, it tends to charge passengers more for their tickets. Thus, the fact that the two airlines can cut their costs is, at least in theory, beneficial to passengers.

Similarly, Korean Air and Japan Airlines have widely utilized a codeshare agreement. As noted, although they belong to different global alliances (Korean Air is a founding member of Skyteam and Japan Airlines is a member of Oneworld), airlines are allowed to make bilateral codeshare agreements with airlines in different alliances. Korean Air and Japan Airlines codeshare on thin routes where demand is still limited to no more than one daily flight for a narrow-body aircraft, such as Incheon to Niigata, Komatsu, Shizuoka, and Kagoshima, and thick routes with more schedules, such as Incheon to Narita and Gimpo to Haneda. Overall, passengers can benefit from the improved connectivity and more non-stop services provided by the codeshare agreement.

In other words, the crucial question is not whether an agreement is in place between competitors. Rather, it is whether that agreement has the object or effect of restricting competition. Thus, when an airline alliance is assessed by competition law, the details of that alliance must be carefully reviewed.

Generally, interlining and low-level alliances (*e.g.* sharing facilities) do not have the effect of restricting competition. It can be problematic to generalize too much about codesharing. In fact, code-sharing requires a careful analysis of competition law since the details

---

58   Whish, *supra* note 53 at 3.

of code-sharing can vary. The European competition authorities summarized their findings about code-sharing agreements as follows:

Table 5.2 Categories of Code-sharing Agreements[59]

"Does the code-sharing agreement (CSA) fall under competition law or not?"

"no, it generally does not"	"yes, almost always"	"it may"
1st category	2nd category	3rd category
– agreement between non-competitors – airlines cannot independently carry out the air transport services made possible by the CSA	– the object of the CSA is to restrict competition by means of price fixing, output limitation, market sharing or customer sharing – the CSA is part of a fully-fledged alliance	– CSAs that belong to neither the first nor the second category – requires an assessment of the circumstances and the restrictive effects of the CSA in question

Table 5.2 suggests that direct coordination and unincorporated joint ventures clearly fall under competition law (the 2nd category above). Direct coordination and unincorporated joint ventures are, in principle, illegal horizontal agreements that have the effect of restricting competition. Hence, they should be prevented. However, if the benefits that an airline alliance provides consumers outweigh its anti-competitive effects, the competition authorities may make an exception, which is known as antitrust immunity. Once again, the goal of competition law is not protecting the competitive process but promoting the interests of consumers.

At the same time, the peculiarities of the airline industry vis-à-vis competition law must be emphasized. The first peculiarity is the prohibition on cross-border mergers due to ownership and control restrictions found in domestic law and bilateral air services agreements. Since cross-border mergers are not allowed in the airline industry (unlike most other industries), governments have been much more tolerant of cooperation between airlines.

The second peculiarity has to do with the high entry barriers and small number of market players (that is, airlines) for which the airline industry is well-known, especially in relation to the "efficiencies" argument. To borrow Richard Whish's system of categorization, efficiencies in the context of competition law can be divided into "allocative efficiency," "productive efficiency," and "dynamic efficiency."[60] With regard to a competition law analysis of airline alliances, productive efficiency is the most relevant. Airlines typically argue that alliances can increase productive efficiency by reducing costs, providing new

---

59 European Competition Authorities, "Code-sharing Agreements in Scheduled Passenger Air Transport – The European Competition Authorities' Perspective" (2006) 2 European Competition Journal 263 at 273.
60 See Whish, *supra* note 53 at 4-5.

schedules, and improving service quality. (For a detailed discussion of these arguments, see section 5.2.2.3 Challenges to Antitrust Immunity).

Just as efficiencies are an important justification for regulating mergers,[61] they have also been referred to in many airline antitrust immunity decisions.[62] In the view of government agencies, some form of airline cooperation must be tolerated because efficiencies cannot otherwise be created in the high-cost and few-player environment of the airline industry.

5.2.2 Antitrust Immunity

5.2.2.1 Origin

The US has played a pioneering role in antitrust law. The history of antitrust law in the US began in 1890 with the Sherman Act, the country's first antitrust statue. The Clayton Act and the Federal Trade Commission Act, which were both enacted in 1914, also form the basis of US antitrust law. Since air carriers are explicitly exempt from the Federal Trade Commission Act, the Sherman Act and the Clayton Act are the only relevant laws for antitrust issues involving airlines.[63]

Section 1 of the Sherman Act defines the fundamental principle of competition law: "[E]very contract, combination in the form of trust or otherwise, or conspiracy, in restraint of trade or commerce among the several States, or with foreign nations, is declared to be illegal."[64] Since this message has been echoed in many other jurisdictions, the Sherman Act is considered the "mother of all competition laws."[65]

The US has also helped pioneer the system of antitrust immunity for airlines. The origin of aviation antitrust immunity is found in the US Civil Aeronautics Act of 1938. In brief, with the approval of the US Civil Aeronautics Board (CAB), an inter-carrier agreement

---

61 See *e.g.* US Department of Justice & Federal Trade Commission, *Horizontal Merger Guidelines* (19 August 2010) at 29, online: <https://www.ftc.gov/sites/default/files/attachments/merger-review/100819hmg.pdf>. DOJ and FTC further noted that "a primary benefit of mergers to the economy is their potential to generate significant efficiencies and thus enhance the merged firm's ability and incentive to compete, which may result in lower prices, improved quality, enhanced service, or new products. For example, merger-generated efficiencies may enhance competition by permitting two ineffective competitors to form a more effective competitor, *e.g.*, by combining complementary assets.".
62 See *e.g.* US DOT, *Joint Application of Alitalia-Linee Aeree Italiane-S.p.A., Czech Airlines, Detla Air Lines, Inc., KLM Royal Dutch Airlines, Northwest Airlines, Inc., and Société Air France for Approval of and Antitrust Immunity for Alliance Agreements under 49 U.S.C. ss. 41308 and 41309*, Dkt No DOT-OST-2005-19214-0195, Order 2005-12-12, Order to Show Cause (22 December 2005).
63 H.S. Rutger Jan toe Laer, "Kick-starting Cross-border Alliances: Approval and Clearance; the past, the present and the future" (2007) 32 Air & Space L. 287 at 300.
64 15 US Code § 1 – Trusts, etc., in restraint of trade illegal; penalty.
65 toe Laer, *supra* note 63 at 300.

can be granted antitrust immunity according to Sections 412 and 414 of the Civil Aeronautics Act.[66]

It is important to emphasize that the CAB process of granting antitrust immunity was fairly simple. Essentially, 1) agreements between air carriers affecting air transportation had to be filed with the CAB; 2) the CAB was directed to approve all agreements except those that it found to be adverse to the public interest; and 3) the CAB's approval conferred *automatic* immunity from the antitrust laws.[67] This practice continued until 1978 when the US adopted the Airline Deregulation Act. Under the Airline Deregulation Act, antitrust immunity was no longer automatic and required more thorough investigation by the CAB.[68]

The CAB's jurisdiction over antitrust immunity was transferred to the US Department of Transportation (DOT) in 1985. At the DOT, granting antitrust immunity involves a two-step analysis: the first step is approving the alliance agreement and the second is granting antitrust immunity.[69] Accordingly, the DOT may approve alliance agreements:
1. if it finds that the alliance agreements are not adverse to the public interest;
2. if the agreements are necessary to meet a serious transportation need or to achieve important public benefits; and
3. if that need or those benefits cannot be met or achieved by reasonably available alternatives that are materially less anticompetitive.[70]

---

66 Section 412 of the Civil Aeronautics Act: "(a) Every air carrier shall file with the Authority a true copy, or, if oral, a true and complete memorandum, of every contract of agreement (whether enforceable by provisions for liquidated damages, penalties, bonds, or otherwise) affecting air transportation and in force on the effective date of this section or hereafter entered into, or any modification or cancelation thereof, between such air carrier and any other air carrier, foreign air carrier, or other carrier for pooling or apportioning earnings, losses, traffic, service, or equipment, or relating to the establishment of transportation rates, fares, charges, or classifications, or for preserving and improving safety, economy, and efficiency of operation, or for controlling, regulating, preventing, or otherwise eliminating destructive, oppressive, or wasteful competition, or for regulating stops, schedules, and character of service, or for other cooperative working arrangements. (b) The Authority shall by order disapprove any such contract or agreement, whether or not previously approved by it, that it finds to be adverse to the public interest, or in violation of this Act, and shall by order approve any such contact or agreement, or any modification or cancelation thereof, that it does not find to be adverse to the public interest, or in violation of this Act."; Section 414 of the Civil Aeronautics Act: "Any person affected by any order made under sections 408, 409, or 412 of this Act shall be, and is hereby, *relieved from the operations of the "antitrust law"*, as designated in section 1 of the Act entitled "An Act to supplement existing laws against unlawful restraints and monopolies, and for other purposes", approved October 15, 1914 [Clayton Act], and of all other restraints or prohibitions made by, or imposed under, authority of law, insofar as may be necessary to enable such person to do anything authorized, approved, or required by such order." [emphasis added].
67 Paul Dempsey & William E. Thoms, *Law and Economic Regulation in Transportation* (New York: Quorum Books, 1986) at 243-244.
68 *Ibid*. 245.
69 EU Commission & US DOT, *supra* note 50 at 13.
70 *Ibid*.

The second step for granting antitrust immunity requires two more questions as to whether:
1. The parties to such an agreement would not otherwise go forward without it; and
2. DOT finds that the public interest requires a grant of antitrust immunity.[71]

The DOT granted its first antitrust immunity to the KLM-Northwest alliance in 1993. Two facts are particularly important in this case of antitrust immunity.

First is the fact that KLM and Northwest originally wanted a merger. Due to US domestic law on ownership and control, however, a non-merger alliance remained the only viable alternative for far-reaching inter-carrier cooperation that would allow KLM and Northwest to enjoy the advantages of a merger without actually becoming a single enterprise.[72]

Second is the fact that antitrust immunity for the KLM-Northwest alliance was part of the US's first open skies agreement, which it negotiated with the Netherlands in 1992.[73] (This will be separately discussed below in section 5.2.2.2 Correlation with Open Skies Agreements.)

Interestingly, when antitrust immunity was granted to KLM and Northwest by the US DOT, the Netherlands did not even have competition legislation in place, not to mention legislation for antitrust immunity.[74] This illustrates how the US introduced antitrust laws and a system of antitrust immunity much earlier than other states.

Indeed, competition law is still new in many states, and there are a fair number of states that have enacted competition law without establishing a system of antitrust immunity. This is mainly because antitrust immunity is by definition an "exception" to the principles of competition law. In part, some governments do not have the capacity to assess how consumers can be benefited by giving airline alliances antitrust immunity.

For airlines, commercial advantages provide an incentive to seek antitrust immunity. Antitrust immunity effectively allows partner airlines to fix prices for interline itineraries within the alliance, therefore inducing alliance partners to maximize joint profits.[75]

For governments, the key question is whether granting antitrust immunity to an airline alliance is necessary to bring about airline cooperation, which is beneficial for consumers.[76] (See section 5.2.2.4 for a discussion about whether antitrust immunity always works for

---

71 Ibid.
72 toe Laer, *supra* note 63 at 289-290.
73 Paul Mifsud, "Metal Neutrality and the Nation-Bound Airline Industry" (2011) 36 Air & Space L.117 at 121.
74 toe Laer, *supra* note 63 at 288.
75 Volodymyr Bilotkach & Kai Hüschelrath, "Chapter 14 Economic Effects of Antitrust Immunity for Airline Alliances: Identification and Measurement" in Peter Forsyth *et al* eds., *Liberalization in Aviation: Competition, Cooperation and Public Policy* (Farnham: Ashgate, 2013) 247 at 251. [Bilotkach & Hüschelrath, "Economic Effects of Antitrust Immunity"].
76 Volodymyr Bilotkach & Kai Hüschelrath, "Antitrust Immunity for Airline Alliances" (2011) 7 Journal of Competition Law and Economics. 335 at 343.

the benefit of consumers.) But in addition to economic motivations, the US has also employed antitrust immunity for policy reasons.

5.2.2.2 Correlation with Open Skies Agreements

The US pioneered the system of antitrust immunity for airline alliances, and it has applied that system aggressively for its policy goal of advocating an open skies regime. As discussed in Chapter 1, the US has been at the vanguard of the "free market" approach to international air transportation since the inception of air travel. Although the US has conservative restrictions in place for ownership and domestic cabotage, it has consistently advocated liberalizing international market access, both bilaterally and multilaterally.

When the US first openly advocated its open skies policy, however, the prevailing view in the rest of the world was that the ultimate purpose of this policy was to secure a greater market share by flooding international markets with strong US airlines.[77] Indeed, at the time, the US aviation market was by far the most active in the world. Even into the 1980s, air traffic inside the US was equal to that of the rest of the world put together.[78]

The US was fully aware of the hostility felt by other countries and the challenge it faced in advocating an open skies regime. The US's concerns and its response to this challenge were alluded to in the 1995 Statement of United States International Air Transportation Policy:

> We recognize that considerable time and effort will be required to achieve an open aviation regime worldwide. We can get there by making a concerted effort to eliminate the obstacles to that regime and by taking a more strategic and long-term approach to our overall international aviation policies.[79]

One example of this "strategic and long-term approach" was the divide-and-conquer strategy. This refers to the strategy of breaking up an existing power structure into smaller sections that have less power on their own and then overpowering these individual sections one at a time. Although the term has been used in the military, political, and economic arenas, it was specifically used to describe the US's approach to aviation diplomacy vis-à-vis the states of the EU.[80]

---

77 Christer Jönsson, "Sphere of Flying: The Politics of International Aviation" (1981) 35 International Organization. 273 at 289.
78 Anthony Sampson, *Empires of the Sky: The Politics and Cartels of World Airlines* (London: Hodder and Stroughton, 1984) at 145-146.
79 US, Department of Transportation, *Statement of United States International Air Transportation Policy* (60 Fed. Reg. 21,841) (3 May 1995).
80 See *e.g.* Paul Dempsey, "The Evolution of Air Transport Agreements" (2008) 33 Ann. Air & Sp. L. 127 at 153. [Dempsey, "Air Transport Agreements"].

This divide-and-conquer strategy is also called the strategy of encirclement. Brian Havel defines the encirclement strategy as "using a model liberal aviation agreement that the United States, in effect, would 'export' on a country-by-country basis and use as a lure to entice larger geographical neighbors (fearful of loss of traffic, for example, over the EU's porous borders) into similar liberalized relationships."[81]

The US government saw liberal bilateral agreements as a means of putting pressure on recalcitrant governments in Europe.[82] Obviously, the US's divide-and-conquer strategy is based on a series of open skies agreements. However, granting antitrust immunity was the other component of this strategy.

Indeed, approval for antitrust immunity has been the reward that the US DOT offers in exchange for liberalizing markets through bilateral open skies air transport agreements. In fact, the US-Netherlands open skies agreement and the order granting antitrust immunity for joint activities between KLM and Northwest that was issued shortly thereafter became the template for future US aviation policy.[83] The Memorandum of Consultation between the US and the Netherlands (the essential document for the US-Netherlands open skies agreement), which was signed on 4 September 1992, specifically declares that:

> [It is the intent of the Parties] to give sympathetic consideration, in the context of the Open Skies agreement, to the concept of commercial cooperation and integration of commercial operations between airlines of the United States and the Netherlands through commercial agreements... and to provide fair and expeditious consideration to any such agreements or arrangements filed for approval and antitrust immunity.[84]

Setting aside the diplomatic motivations for the US' use of antitrust immunity, there are eminently logical reasons why antitrust immunity and open skies agreements should go hand in hand. Under protectionist air services agreements, the number of airlines that can operate the agreed service is limited (normally to one or two airlines on each side), and the capacity and frequency (caps on the number of passengers and amount of cargo carried and the number of flights flown) are predetermined. Thus, as illustrated in Figure 5.3, antitrust immunity for airline alliances in a market governed by a protectionist air services

---

81 Brian Havel, *Beyond Open Skies: A New Regime for International Aviation* (Alphen aan den Rijn, Kluwer Law International: 2009) at 30-32. [Havel, "Open Skies"].
82 Sampson, *supra* note 78 at 145.
83 Warren L. Dean, Jr. & Jeffrey N. Shane, "Alliances, Immunity, and the Future of Aviation" (2010) 22 Air & Space Lawyer. 17 at 17.
84 Cited in H.S. Rutger Jan toe Laer, "Kick-starting Cross-border Alliances: Approval and Clearance; the past, the present and the future" (2007) 32 Air & Space L. 287 at 291.

agreement would effectively reduce the number of market players and likely allow the airlines in the alliance to occupy a dominant position in that market.[85]

Figure 5.3   Conceptual Description of Market Change by Antitrust Immunity under a Protectionist Air Services Agreement

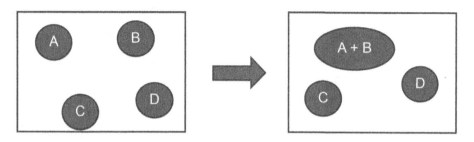

Antitrust immunity for airline alliances can be pro-competitive given an open skies agreement under which market entry barriers for new entrants have already been removed (see above section 3.1.2.1 Carrier Designation). Also, airlines in the said market should be able to choose what capacity to offer without government approval or intervention (that is, free determination; see section 3.1.2.3 Capacity and Frequency).

In a nutshell, market access restrictions (both direct and indirect) must be removed in a market in which antitrust immunity has been granted to an airline alliance, as shown in Figure 5.4. Hence, it is not at all unusual that indirect market access issues such as slot issues are also discussed when a competition agency grants antitrust immunity to an airline alliance.[86]

---

85 "Dominant position" is an important concept in competition law. Since companies in a dominant position have a major influence on the market, most competition laws strictly prohibit such companies from abusing that position. For instance, Article 82 of the EU Treaty stipulates: "Any abuse by one more undertakings of a dominant position within the common market or in a substantial part of it shall be prohibited as incompatible with the common market in so far as it may affect trade between Member States." In one of the first Article 82 cases, *Hoffmann-La Roche* (Judgment of the Court of 13 February 1979. – Hoffmann-La Roche & Co. AG v Commission of the European Communities. – Dominant position. – Case 85/76) the European Court of Justice gave the definition of market dominance, which is still used: "[the dominant position] relates to a position of economic strength enjoyed by an undertaking, which enables it to prevent effective competition being maintained on the relevant market by affording it the power to behave to an appreciable extent independently of its competitors, its customers and ultimately of the consumers. Such a position does not preclude some competition, which it does where there is a monopoly or quasi-monopoly, but enables the undertaking, which profits by it, if not to determine, at least to have an appreciable influence on the conditions under which that competition will develop, and in any case to act largely in disregard of it so long as such conduct does not operate to its detriment".

86 See *e.g.* European Commission, *Commission Decision of 14.07.2010 relating to a proceeding under Article 101 of the Treaty on the Functioning of the European Union and Article 53 of the EEA Agreement* (Case COMP/39.596 – BA/AA/IB).

Figure 5.4 Conceptual Description of Market Change by Antitrust Immunity under an Open Skies Agreement

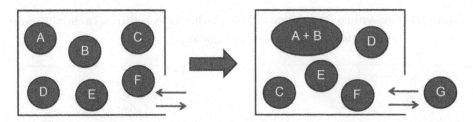

5.2.2.3 Challenges to Antitrust Immunity

At this juncture, it is important to recall that competition law is a *national* law.[87] As a result, antitrust immunity functions differently from state to state. In other words, the responsible institution, the granting process, and, most importantly, the permitted scope of activity are different. As a result, the privileges of airline alliances on the identical international routes can be treated differently in different jurisdictions.

For instance, Delta Air Lines and Korean Air received antitrust immunity from the US government and the Korean government (the responsible institution and the process of granting antitrust immunity in Korea will be discussed below in section 5.3.2.3 Korea) in 2002. However, the scope of the antitrust immunity they received was different. While the US DOT allowed the two airlines to coordinate in any business area including pricing, the Korean government only allowed the two airlines to coordinate in specific areas such as scheduling and marketing. In particular, Delta and Korean Air cannot coordinate prices in any case under the antitrust immunity granted by the Korean government.

Indeed, the fact that states have not established uniform international standards for antitrust immunity for airline alliances was raised at the Sixth ICAO Air Transport Conference in 2013.[88] Although it was proposed that the ICAO establish a working group to discuss coordinating antitrust immunity for airline alliances, the proposal did not receive meaningful support from member states.[89] In fact, many of the 1,100 total delegates from 131 states seemed to be unfamiliar with the concept of antitrust immunity.[90]

---

87 The EU is a highly exceptional case. Since the EU is an economic union, with a common market and common economic policies and institutions, its competition law applies to the entire EU market.
88 See ICAO, *Antitrust Immunity for Airlines Alliances*, ICAO Doc ATConf/6-WP/85 (4 March 2013) (Presented by Republic of Korea), online: <www.icao.int/Meetings/atconf6/Documents/WorkingPapers/ATConf6-wp85_en.pdf>.
89 See ICAO, *Report on Agenda Item 2.4* (summary report of the Air Transport Conference), ICAO Doc ATConf/6-WP/104 (22 March 2013), online: <www.icao.int/Meetings/atconf6/Documents/FinalReport/ATConf6_wp104-2-4_en.pdf>.
90 Author's note (ICAO Headquarter, Montreal, 20 March 2013).

Thus far, the only meaningful effort to harmonize the different approaches has been made by the US and the EU. According to Annex 2 of the EU-US Air Transport Agreement 2008, the EU Commission and US DOT must cooperate with respect to competition issues in the air transport industry. In a joint report (*Transatlantic Airline Alliances: Competitive Issues and Regulatory Approaches*), the two authorities recognize "the importance of continuous cooperation on remedies with the view to avoiding, where possible, conflicting or unnecessarily duplicative remedies in the case of parallel reviews of the same transaction."[91]

In fact, calls to coordinate national competition laws with respect to transactions in international markets have received wide support due to the high likelihood of inconsistent results.[92] In reality, however, it is not easy to achieve substantial convergence in this area. Although soft harmonization has occurred (knowledge-sharing, for example), substantive changes are less likely in mature competition jurisdictions since each jurisdiction has selected an approach that is suitable for itself.[93]

While this "external" challenge (that is, different results from different national competition bodies) should not be overlooked, the "internal" challenge is a more significant problem. The internal challenge refers to discontent about antitrust immunity within the country in question. Since antitrust immunity represents a legal exception to the principles of competition law, it is only natural that the competition authority would want to see the justifications for antitrust immunity prior to and subsequent to granting it.

Airlines that seek antitrust immunity typically argue that an immunized alliance would enhance competition and achieve efficiencies.[94] For instance, member airlines of Oneworld stated that:

---

91 EU Commission & US DOT, *supra* note 50 at 24.
92 Fox, *supra* note 54 at 602.
93 *Ibid*.
94 See *e.g.* US DOT, Joint Application of Virgin Atlantic Airways, Ltd., Delta Air Lines, Inc., *and Société Air France, Koninklijke Luchtvaart Maatschappij N.V., and Alitalia Compagnia Aerea Italiana S.P.A.* under 49 U.S.C. §§ 41308 and 41309 for approval of and antitrust immunity for alliance agreements, Docket DOT-OST-2013-0068, Shaw Cause Order (30 August 2013); U.S.-Japan Alliance Case, Dkt No DOT-OST-2010-0059-0180, Order 2010-10-4, Show Cause Order (6 October 2010); US DOT, *Joint Application of Air Canada, The Austrian Group, British Midland Airways Ltd, Continental Airlines, Inc., Deutsche Lufthansa AG, Polskie Linie Lotnicze LOT S.A., Scandinavian Airlines System, Swiss international Air Lines Ltd., TAP Air Portugal, and United Air Lines, Inc.* to Amend Order 2007-2-16 under 49 U.S.C. ss. 41308 and 41309 so as to Approve and Confer Antitrust Immunity, Dkt No DOTOST-2008-0234-0253, Order 2009-7-10, Final Order (10 July 2009); US DOT, *Joint Application of American Airlines, Inc., British Airways PLC, Finnair OYJ, Iberia Líneas Aéreas de España, S.A., and Royal Jordanian Airlines Under 49 U.S.C. ss. 41308-41309 for approval of and antitrust immunity for alliance agreements*, Dkt No DOT-OST-2008-0252- 3390, Order 2010-2-8, Show Cause Order (13 February 2010); US DOT, *Joint Application of Alitalia-Linee Aeree Italiane-S.p.A., Czech Airlines, Delta Airlines, Inc., KLM Royal Dutch Airlines, Northwest Arilines, Inc, and Société Air France for Approval of and Antitrust Immunity for Alliance Agreements under 49 U.S.C. ss. 41308 and 41309*, Dkt No DOT-OST-2007-28644-0174, Order 2008-4-17, Show Cause Order (9 April 2008).

With its own immunized alliance and joint venture, oneworld could provide the traveling and shipping public with a wide range of valuable benefits, including: lower fares on more itineraries between city-pairs; accelerated introduction of new routes; additional flights on existing routes; improved schedules; reduced travel and connection times, and product and service enhancements that can provide full reciprocal access to their networks. The proposed alliance, if approved, would also allow the alliance partners to improve efficiency, reduce costs, and strengthen their networks to better meet the demands of global customers.[95]

The consideration of immunity for an alliance can be divided into two parts. One is collaboration to provide seamless services on markets between smaller cities, requiring an interline trip that crosses the networks of the alliance partners (for instance, Osaka to Denver can be operated by ANA on the Osaka-LA route and by United Airlines on the LA-Denver route). The other is for non-stop travel between the alliance partners' hub cities, where overlapping services allow the trip to be taken with either airline (for instance, Tokyo-LA).[96] Although there are factors that will lower fares and increase service for interline passengers, the effect of overlapping hub-to-hub services can potentially be anti-competitive, particularly if there are few or no options on other airlines.[97]

Indeed, the competition authorities must conduct a robust economic analysis of whether competitive alternatives are available in the said market (that is, on each route). For instance, if indirect options are available with other airlines or if there is strong competition from sixth freedom carriers in the market (such as the EU-ASEAN market, in which there is fierce competition for both sides' carriers posed by Middle Eastern and Turkish carriers), it would be straightforward to grant immunity for airline alliances from both ends.[98]

But compared to trans-continental routes, there are natural limitations on alternatives in the trans-Atlantic and trans-Pacific markets. Some remedial measures have been developed to prevent hub-to-hub services from having an anti-competitive effect, one of which is a "carve-out." A carve-out prohibits collaboration in hub-to-hub price setting when granting antitrust immunity, while allowing cooperation in other markets.[99] For

---

95 US DOT, *Joint Application of American Airlines, Inc., British Airways PLC, Finnair OYJ, Iberia Líneas Aéreas de España, S.A., and Royal Jordanian Airlines Under 49 U.S.C. ss. 41308-41309 for approval of and antitrust immunity for alliance agreements*, Dkt No DOT-OST-2008-0252- 3390, Order 2010-2-8, Show Cause Order (13 February 2010), online: <www.mainjustice.com/files/2010/02/DOT-BA-AA-Approval.pdf>.
96 Pearce, *supra* note 45 at 2.
97 *Ibid.*
98 Alan Khee-Jin Tan, *Assessing the Prospects for an E.U.-ASEAN Air Transport Agreement*, Discussion Paper No 2015-02, International Transport Forum (Paris: OECD, 2015) at 10, online: <www.internationaltransportforum.org/jtrc/DiscussionPapers/DP201502.pdf>. [Tan, "E.U.-ASEAN"].
99 Jan K. Brueckner & Stef Proost, "Carve-outs under airline antitrust immunity" (2010) 28 International Journal of Industrial Organization. 657 at 658.

example, when the DOT granted immunity to the United-Lufthansa alliance in 1996, it carved out the two non-stop overlaps between their major hubs (Frankfurt-Chicago, Frankfurt-Washington, DC).[100]

Slot concession is another remedial measure. As a slot is an element of indirect market access (see section 3.1.3.1 Airport Capacity), a combination of a slot shortage and cooperation among carriers has the potential to impede competition. For example, a trans-Atlantic JV between British Airways, American Airlines and other Oneworld members was required to give up some slots at London Heathrow Airport and New York JFK Airport.[101]

Despite these remedial measures, a fundamental question remains. Put simply, it is not always clear that antitrust immunity has been directly beneficial for the consumer. Indeed, some respected aviation economists have raised questions about the effects of antitrust immunity. Bilotkach and Hüschelrath asserted that "[A] significant part of the efficiencies realized by airline cooperation are not immunity-specific, as they can in fact be realized by interline or code-share agreements already."[102] Gillespie and Richard questioned that "[T]he evidence in fact shows that, within the major alliances, antitrust immunized arrangements have not allowed the JV partners to reduce fares... below those sold under non-immunized arrangements."[103]

These misgivings are particularly strong in the US because of the divergence between the Department of Justice (DOJ) (the principal body responsible for antitrust law) and the DOT (the body exceptionally endowed with the authority for antitrust immunity for airline alliances). After assessing nearly 40 applications for antitrust immunity and subsequently granting it to most of the applicants,[104] the DOT was criticized for its lax approach by the DOJ and certain members of Congress, who felt that it had led to reduced competition.[105] It is in this context that metal neutrality, a new requirement for antitrust immunity, was developed.

---

100 William Gillespie & Oliver M. Richard, *Antitrust Immunity and International Airline Alliances*, Economic Analysis Group Discussion Paper, Antitrust Division, US Department of Justice, (EAG 11-1)(February 2011) at 16, online: <www.justice.gov/atr/public/eag/267513.pdf>.
101 European Commission, Press Release, "Antitrust: British Airways, American Airlines and Iberia commitments to ensure competition on transatlantic passenger air transport markets made legally binding" (14 July 2010), online: <http://europa.eu/rapid/press-release_IP-10-936_en.htm>.
102 Bilotkach & Hüschelrath, "Economic Effects of Antitrust Immunity", *supra* note 75 at 272.
103 William Gillespie & Oliver M. Richard "Antitrust Immunity Grants to Joint Venture Agreements: Evidence from International Airline Alliances" (2012) 78 Antitrust Law Journal. 443.
104 There were three cases in which the DOT denied an application for ATI. See Norie Hata "JAL/Delta alliance could have trouble receiving ATI approval, experts say" *Financial Times* (4 January 2010), online: <www.ft.com/intl/cms/s/2/68f45a0e-f979-11de-8085-00144feab49a.html#axzz2ZBsyV8rp>.
105 CAPA, "CAPA Airlines in Transition report, Part 1: The natural history of airline alliances" (16 April 2013), online: <http://centreforaviation.com/analysis/capa-airlines-in-transition-report-part-1-the-natural-history-of-airline-alliances-105278>.

5.2.3 Metal Neutrality: New Requirement for Antitrust Immunity

It is worth emphasizing that when the DOT granted its first antitrust immunity to an airline alliance (KLM-Northwest in January 1993), it was a metal neutral alliance. As previously noted, metal neutrality means that the alliance partners are indifferent to which operates the "metal" (that is, the aircraft) when they jointly operate market services. Metal neutral operations essentially "allow hitherto competing players on a particular route to co-operate and engage in joint marketing and revenue-sharing."[106]

Because KLM and Northwest's original objective was a merger that was prohibited by US domestic law (ownership and control restrictions), the carriers tried to achieve maximum integration, closely approximating a merger.[107] The result was metal neutrality, which implies merger-like integration.

The DOT notes the benefits of metal neutrality as follow: "(1) reduction in fares through elimination or reduction of double marginalization on routes; (2) maintaining and expanding nonstop service; (3) an increased network with enhanced online service; (4) better access to lower fares; (5) frequent flyer program cooperation; and (6) reduced costs from consolidation and other efficiencies."[108]

Metal neutrality was available to alliances that received antitrust immunity from the US DOT. Interestingly, however, airline alliance partners did not take advantage of operating as though the partners were one airline.[109] Indeed, airlines in an alliance continued to operate separately rather than jointly within a framework of loose cooperation, meaning that antitrust immunity was only providing "a comfort zone" for discussing pricing and schedule.[110]

Meanwhile, the DOJ questioned whether antitrust immunity benefits consumers, arguing that non-immunized alliances provide the same public benefits through code-sharing, joint marketing programs, and operational cooperation.[111] Considering the fact that no alliance had achieved the merger-like joint venture except the original KLM-

---

106 Tan, "E.U.-ASEAN", *supra* note 98 at 9.
107 toe Laer, *supra* note 63 at 289-290.
108 Although the benefits were originally specified by the applicants, the DOT stated that "[W]e tentatively find that these, and other, benefits are likely to accrue to consumers if both applications are approved." See US DOT, U.S.-Japan Alliance Case, Dkt No DOT-OST-2010-0059-0180, Order 2010-10-4, Show Cause Order (6 October 2010) at 13.
109 Mifsud, *supra* note 73 at 122.
110 *Ibid.*
111 See US DOJ, *Comments of the Department of Justice on the Show Cause Order*, to US DOT, *Joint Application of Air Canada, The Austrian Group, British Midland Airways Ltd, Continental Airlines, Inc., Deutsche Lufthansa AG, Polskie Linie Lotniecze LOT S.A., Scandinavian Airlines System, Swiss International Air Lines Ltd., TAP Air Portugal, and United Air Lines, Inc. to Amend Order 2007-2-16 under 49 U.S.C. ss. 41308 and 41309 so as to Approve and Confer Antitrust Immunity*, Dkt No DOT-OST-2008-0234-0193, Order 2009-4-5, Show Cause Order (7 April 2009).

Northwest alliance and the strong challenge from the DOJ, the DOT tightened its position (that is, the requirement of metal neutrality.)

In 2006, the DOT denied a request for antitrust immunity from Delta Air Lines and Air France due to insufficient information about their planned integration. However, after the two airlines demonstrated their plans to integrate using the concept of metal neutrality, the DOT approved a second application in 2008.[112] Also, recent developments, including antitrust immunity for Star Alliance in July 2009[113] and for Oneworld in July 2010,[114] show that the DOT is now insisting on binding agreements that require the sharing of revenue between marketing carrier and operating carrier.

Previously, the requirement of metal neutrality for antitrust immunity was an important consideration mainly in the transatlantic market. However, recent developments show that antitrust immunity and metal neutrality are also affecting the trans-Pacific market, and specifically Northeast Asia.

After examining how airline alliances are regulated and how antitrust immunity is given to airline alliances in Northeast Asia (section 5.3 Airline Alliances and Competition Law in Northeast Asia), I will discuss metal neutral joint ventures in the context of Northeast Asian open skies (section 5.4 Metal Neutral Joint Ventures in the Trans-Pacific Market and section 5.5 Impact of Metal Neutral Joint Ventures in Northeast Asia).

5.3   AIRLINE ALLIANCES AND COMPETITION LAW IN NORTHEAST ASIA

5.3.1   *Airline Alliances in the Northeast Asian Market*

In the Northeast Asian market, airline alliances have not advanced beyond code-sharing. No antitrust immunity has been granted to alliances among Northeast Asian air carriers, so all kinds of coordination are prohibited. Hence, unincorporated joint ventures are not permitted at present. This contrasts with the joint ventures that have been set up between Northeast Asian carriers and American carriers in the trans-Pacific market. (This will be

---

112   CAPA, "CAPA Airlines in Transition report, Part 1: The natural history of airline alliances" (16 April 2013), online: <http://centreforaviation.com/analysis/capa-airlines-in-transition-report-part-1-the-natural-history-of-airline-alliances-105278>.

113   US DOT, *Joint Application of Air Canada, The Austrian Group, British Midland Airways Ltd, Continental Airlines, Inc., Deutsche Lufthansa AG, Polskie Linie Lotnicze LOT S.A., Scandinavian Airlines System, Swiss international Air Lines Ltd., TAP Air Portugal, and United Air Lines, Inc. to Amend Order 2007-2-16 under 49 U.S.C. ss. 41308 and 41309 so as to Approve and Confer Antitrust Immunity*, Dkt No DOT-OST-2008-0234-0253, Order 2009-7-10, Final Order (10 July 2009).

114   US DOT, *Joint Application of American Airlines, Inc., British Airways PLC, Finnair OYJ, Iberia Líneas Aéreas de España, S.A., and Royal Jordanian Airlines Under 49 U.S.C. ss. 41308- 41309 for approval of and antitrust immunity for alliance agreements*, Dkt No DOT-OST-2008-0252-3406, Order 2010-7-8 Final Order (20 July 2010).

discussed in section 5.4 Metal Neutral Joint Ventures in the Trans-Pacific (Northeast Asia-US) Market.)

As previously noted, airline alliances can be broadly categorized into two types: multilateral branded global alliances and bilateral inter-carrier agreements. The Northeast Asian carriers in multilateral branded global alliances are listed in Table 5.3:

Table 5.3   Member Airlines in Global Alliances (China, Japan and Korea)

	Star Alliance	Skyteam	Oneworld
China	Air China Shenzhen Airlines	China Southern China Eastern Xiamen Air	
Japan	ANA		Japan Airlines
Korea	Asiana Airlines	Korean Air	

Just as cooperation among global alliance members is crucial in the modern airline industry, bilateral inter-carrier agreements are another key factor in airline operations. While multilateral branded global alliance members tend to cooperate for the interest of the alliance members as a whole, bilateral inter-carrier agreements reflect the specific needs of the two individual airlines.

Although carriers are not allowed to have dual membership in the global alliances, they still have the prerogative to make bilateral inter-carrier agreements with airlines that are not members of their alliance or even with airlines that are members of a different alliance. For instance, Korean Air, a member of Skyteam, and Japan Airlines, a member of Oneworld, have widely used code-sharing agreements. Both China Eastern and China Southern, members of Skyteam, exercise broad commercial agreements with Japan Airlines. Also, Asiana Airlines, a member of Star Alliance, enjoys a code-sharing relationship with China Southern. The relationships between airline alliances in each market are summarized in the three tables below.

Table 5.4   Airline Alliances in the China–Japan Market

Chinese Carriers	Japanese Carriers	
	Japan Airlines (Oneworld)	ANA (Star Alliance)
Air China (Star Alliance)		Code-sharing
China Southern (Skyteam)	Code-sharing	
China Eastern (Skyteam)	Code-sharing	
Shenzhen Airlines (Star Alliance)		Code-sharing
Shandong Airlines		Code-sharing

Table 5.5 Airline Alliances in the Japan–Korea Market

Korean Carriers	Japanese Carriers	
	Japan Airlines (Oneworld)	ANA (Star Alliance)
Korean Air (Skyteam)	Code-sharing	
Asiana Airline (Star Alliance)		Code-sharing

Table 5.6 Airline Alliances in the China–Korea Market

Chinese Carriers	Korean Carriers	
	Korean Air (Skyteam)	Asiana (Star Alliance)
Air China (Star Alliance)		Code-sharing
China Southern (Skyteam)	Code-sharing	Code-sharing
China Eastern (Skyteam)	Code-sharing	
Shenzhen Airlines (Star Alliance)		Code-sharing
Xiamen Airlines (Skyteam)	Code-sharing	
Shandong Airlines		Code-sharing
Shanghai Airlines	Code-sharing	

Two important developments are expected in the near future. The first development will be new alliances between new airlines. With LCCs booming in Northeast Asia, we are likely to see an alliance between LCCs. China's Spring Airlines and Korea's Eastar Jet used to have an inter-carrier agreement, though this is now defunct. There will obviously be cooperation between Spring Airlines and a joint venture between that airline and Japanese investors called Spring Airlines Japan. The second development will be more integrated alliances between existing airlines. This change will likely require antitrust immunity. Thus, it is necessary to briefly review the competition laws relating to airlines alliances in China, Japan and Korea.

5.3.2 *Competition Law Regimes Relating to Airline Alliances in Northeast Asia*

The competition laws in the three states in Northeast Asia are at different stages of development. In addition, the states do not have uniform systems of antitrust immunity for aviation. While China only recently enacted competition laws and does not have antitrust immunity on the surface, Japan has well-established competition laws and a concrete system for antitrust immunity for airline alliances. Although Korea does not have explicit provisions for antitrust immunity, it has granted antitrust immunity in the past. Table 5.7 provides a snapshot of how airline alliances are handled by competition law in Northeast Asia.

Table 5.7   Competition Law Regimes Relating to Airline Alliances in Northeast Asia

	China	Japan	Korea
Is there a national competition law?	o	o	o
Are there explicit ATI provisions in the national law?	x	o	x
Has the government granted ATI in practice to airlines?	x	o	o
Has the government granted ATI allowing metal neutrality?	x	o	x

5.3.2.1   China

Today, competition law is a "universal regulatory impulse in developing and globalizing economies."[115] Despite this, the law is at different stages in different economies. This contrast is evident when we compare the two biggest economies in the world: the US and China. While US antitrust law was first established in 1890, China did not enact its first comprehensive competition law, the Antimonopoly Act, until 2007, with the law taking effect in 2008.

Though many jurisdictions have adopted competition laws in the 21st century, none of these laws has received the same level of interest as China's Antimonopoly Act.[116] Several factors for this include the sheer scale of China's markets, the vast amounts of foreign investment in China, and the tension resulting from the integration of free market competition with China's socialist economy.[117]

Another reason for this global attention is related to the law's surprisingly long history. Though the law was added to China's national legislative plan in 1994, it took thirteen years before it was finally promulgated.[118] During this preparatory period, key Chinese government agencies including the Ministry of Commerce, the National Development and Reform Commission, and the State Administration for Industry and Commerce received numerous comments and support from international organizations and competition law agencies in major jurisdictions.[119]

Despite the years spent drafting the Antimonopoly Act and the substantial support it received, China will need more time to enhance this competition law. Indeed, the law is

---

115   Salil K. Mehra & Meng Yanbei, "Against Antitrust Functionalism: Reconsidering China's Antimonopoly Law" (2009) 49 Virginia Journal of International Law. 379 at 385.
116   H. Stephen Harris Jr, "The Making of an Antitrust Law: The Pending Anti-Monopoly Law of the People's Republic of China" (2006) 7 Chicago Journal of International Law. 169 at 169.
117   Ibid.
118   Mehra & Yanbei, *supra* note 115 at 397.
119   Harris, *supra* note 116 at 176.

viewed as "an ongoing process of Chinese reform in competition law."[120] There are many aspects of the law that need improvement. One particular criticism is that it fails to provide answers to key questions, such as whom to regulate, what to regulate, and who will regulate.[121] Indeed, antitrust enforcement in China is still at a formative stage.[122]

The three Chinese antitrust regulators have yet to complete the process of building their capabilities. These regulators are the Ministry of Commerce (MOFCOM, responsible for merger control), the State Administration for Industry and Commerce (SAIC, responsible for non-merger enforcement, and in particular non-price-related conduct), and the National Development and Reform Commission (NDRC, responsible for price-related non-merger conduct).[123] In the meantime, the NDRC announced China's first ever prosecution of an international price-fixing cartel in January 2013, signaling that the country means to more vigorously enforce its regulations against price-fixing.[124]

The same institutional ambiguity applies to the question of which governmental agencies in China have jurisdiction over airline antitrust issues.[125] Since the NDRC is given broad competence over all matters relating to price-fixing, monopolies, and general anti-competitive conduct, the NDRC can take the lead in dealing with airline antitrust cases.[126] Another relevant agency is the Ministry of Commerce (MOFCOM), which also has broad jurisdiction over matters relating to consumer protection, market competition, and bilateral and multilateral trade agreements.[127] At the same time, because the Civil Aviation Authority of China (CAAC) is the agency responsible for air transport matters, China's antitrust regulators will eventually seek the views of the CAAC.[128]

With regard to antitrust immunity, the most relevant provision is Article 15 of the Antimonopoly Act.[129] This provision states that an agreement among business operators

---

120 Mehra & Yanbei, *supra* note 115 at 386.
121 *Ibid.* at 402.
122 "Lessons from Four Years of Antitrust Enforcement in China" *Jones Day* (September 2012), online: <www.jonesday.com/lessons_from_four_years/>.
123 *Ibid.*
124 "Antitrust Alert: China Takes First Enforcement Action against International Price Fixing Cartel" Jones Day (January 2013), online: <www.jonesday.com/antitrust-alert--china-takes-first-enforcement-action-against-international-price-fixing-cartel-01-06-2013/>.
125 Alan Khee-Jin Tan, "Antitrust Immunity for Trans-Pacific Airline Alliance Agreements: Singapore and China as 'Beyond' Markets" 38 Air & Space L. 275 at 285. [Tan, "Antitrust Immunity"].
126 *Ibid.* at 286.
127 *Ibid.* at 287.
128 *Ibid.*
129 Article 15 of Anti-monopoly Law of the People's Republic of China "An agreement among business operators shall be exempted from application of articles 13 and 14 if it can be proven to be in any of the following circumstances: (1) for the purpose of improving technologies, researching and developing new products; (2) for the purpose of upgrading product quality, reducing cost, improving efficiency, unifying product specifications or standards, or carrying out professional labor division; (3) for the purpose of enhancing operational efficiency and reinforcing the competitiveness of small and medium-sized business operators; (4) for the purpose of achieving public interests such as conserving energy, protecting the environment and

for the purpose of improving efficiency can be exempted from the law's regulations.[130] However, it is not clear whether airline alliances are eligible for this exemption, and no explanation is provided about how the exemption process would apply in practice.

As of 2015, China has never granted antitrust immunity to an airline alliance. Although Japan Airlines/American Airlines and ANA/United Airlines have asked the NDRC to approve their metal neutral joint ventures, the agency has yet to issue a decision.[131] The main reasons that there have been few developments could be that the NDRC has no airline expertise.[132]

If the NDRC (or any other competition agency) decides to review antitrust immunity for the Japan Airlines/American Airlines and ANA/United Airlines alliances (or any other airline alliance) in the future, it will likely seek the views of the Civil Aviation Authority of China (CAAC).[133] As previously discussed (see section 5.2.2.2 Correlation with Open Skies Agreements), governments need to coordinate their policies about antitrust immunity for airline alliances and open skies agreements. Thus, the CAAC's input on important aero-political considerations would play a critical role in granting antitrust immunity.[134]

5.3.2.2   Japan

Japan has a relatively long history of competition law. The first Antimonopoly Act (formally called the Act Concerning Prohibition of Private Monopoly and Maintenance of Fair Trade) was passed in 1947.[135] This act provided for the establishment of the Japan Fair Trade Commission (JFTC). However, the Antimonopoly Act of 1947 was not produced independently by Japanese society; rather, it was imposed on it by the US during its occupation of the country.[136] Kenji Suzuki describes Japan's understanding of competition in the 19th century as follows:

---

relieving the victims of a disaster and so on; (5) for the purpose of mitigating serious decrease in sales volume or obviously excessive production during economic recessions; (6) for the purpose of safeguarding the justifiable interests in the foreign trade or foreign economic cooperation; or (7) other circumstances as stipulated by laws and the State Council. Where a monopoly agreement is in any of the circumstances stipulated in Items 1 through 5 and is exempt from Articles 13 and 14 of this Law, the business operators must additionally prove that the agreement can enable consumers to share the interests derived from the agreement, and will not severely restrict the competition in relevant market, online, Ministry of Commerce, People's Republic of China <http://english.mofcom.gov.cn/aarticle/policyrelease/announcement/200712/20071205277972.html>.

130 See *ibid*. Article 15, paragraph 2 of Anti-monopoly Law of the People's Republic of China.
131 Alan Khee-Jin Tan, "Aeropolitical Brand Battles in Asia" (Presentation to the International Air Transport Association (IATA) Legal Symposium, Seoul, Korea, 26 February 2015) [unpublished].
132 *Ibid*.
133 Tan, "Antitrust Immunity", *supra* note 125 at 286.
134 *Ibid*. at 286-287.
135 Kenji Suzuki, *Competition Law Reform in Britain and Japan* (London: Routledge, 2002) at 19.
136 *Ibid*. at 18.

Traditionally, the concept of "fair competition" was not the norm in the Japanese market. There is a story about public officials in the mid-nineteenth century who had difficulty even in translating the word "competition" into Japanese, since it was neither "battle" nor "cooperation."[137]

After the Second World War, Japanese policy makers wished to pursue a command-and-control economy that disregarded the value of competition.[138] In contrast, the view of the US (the occupying forces) was that Japan's economy had been largely under the control of a few great business organizations (known as *zaibatsu* in Japanese) which had received preferential treatment from the government. This monopoly-oriented economy, the US believed, should be changed.[139] Eventually, the proposal made by the US occupying forces was adopted.[140]

Over the past seven decades, this competition law has been localized. Since the original Antimonopoly Act of 1947, which was modeled on the US antitrust law system, was too stringent for Japan, Japan substantially amended the Act in 1953.[141] Since then, the Antimonopoly Act has been gradually strengthened, including a revision in 1977 that increased the administrative fines and guidelines issued by the JFTC.[142]

Japan's Aviation Act contains explicit provisions about antitrust immunity for airline alliances. The relevant provisions are Article 110 (Exception from Application of the Act concerning Prohibition of Private Monopolization and Maintenance of Fair Trade), Article 111 (Approval of Agreement), Article 111-2 2 (Order for Alteration of Agreement and Revocation of Approval for Agreement) and Article 111-3 (Relationship with Fair Trade Commission).[143]

---

137 *Ibid.*
138 See Harry First, "Antitrust In Japan: The Original Intent" (2000) 9 Pacific Rim Law and Policy Journal 1 at 16 (noting that "[F]air and free competition alone cannot be the sole solution [to] Japan's economic problems]... Planned and fairly strict state control of the economy [will be] required in the process of Japan's economic democratization").
139 See Harry First, "Antitrust In Japan: The Original Intent" (2000) 9 Pacific Rim Law and Policy Journal 1 at 21-29.
140 Suzuki, *supra* note 135 at 19.
141 See *ibid.* at 21 (noting the following important amendments: "First, Article 4, which provided per se illegality of cartels and other inter-firm agreements, was abandoned. The new legislation prohibited inter-firm agreements only if those agreements caused substantial restraint of market competition in a particular field of trade...Second, Article 8, which provided per se illegality of dominant market position, was also abandoned. In relation to this, the prohibition of mergers and acquisitions (M&As) was removed on condition that they should not restrain competition in any specific market (Articles 10–16)... Third, the 1953 amendment introduced the exemption of resale price maintenance control, which had been entirely prohibited in the original Act.").
142 Mitsuo Matsushita, *International Trade and Competition Law in Japan* (Oxford: Oxford University Press, 1993) at 85.
143 A rough translation can be found at <www.cas.go.jp/jp/seisaku/hourei/data/caa.pdf>.

Essentially, antitrust immunity can be granted to airline alliances if it offers benefits to consumers and if it is necessary for the alliance. One interesting part is the relationship between the Ministry of Land, Infrastructure, Transport, and Tourism (the MLIT) and the JFTC. While the MLIT is the body responsible for granting antitrust immunity, it must consult with the JFTC before granting it. In addition, the JFTC monitors whether alliance activities meet the requirements for immunity and can ask the MLIT to take necessary action (Article 111-3).

In 2010, the Japanese government granted antitrust immunity to two airline alliances, the first time it had done so. These alliances were designated as metal neutral joint ventures. One was for Japan Airlines and American Airlines and the other for ANA and United (these agreements will be reviewed in sections 5.4.2 and 5.4.3). Subsequently, antitrust immunity was granted to ANA and Lufthansa in June 2011 and to JAL and British Airways in May 2012, after which these companies initiated joint ventures. Given that Japan modeled its competition law on the US antitrust law system and that it has a formal system in place to provide airline alliances with antitrust immunity just like the US, it is safe to assume that Japan will continue to be flexible about granting antitrust immunity.

5.3.2.3   Korea

The evolution of Korea's competition law is closely related to Korea's business conglomerates, or *chaebol*. When Korea's Economic Planning Board (EPB, now defunct) drafted the Fair Trade Law in 1964, strong opposition from big business blocked the enactment of the bill.[144] Although the Price Stabilization and Fair Trade Act (PSFT Act) was enacted in 1975, it was effectively toothless due to the lack of a culture of competition law and experience with enforcement.[145]

The real history of Korean competition law began in 1980. In October of that year, the Korean Constitution was revised to include a provision about competition that states, "Abuse of monopoly shall be appropriately regulated and corrected."[146] In December of the same year, the Monopoly Regulation and Fair Trade Act (MRFT Act) was enacted, coming into force in April 1981. Later, the Korea Fair Trade Commission (KFTC) was founded under the MRFT Act.

Youngjin Jung and Seung Wha Chang offer a succinct summary of the background of the MRFT Act:

---

144   Meong-Cho Yang, "Competition Law and Policy of the Republic of Korea" (2009) 54 The Antitrust Bulletin. 621 at 621.
145   Yo Sop Choi, "The Rule of Law in a Market Economy: Globalization of Competition Law in Korea" (2014) 15 European Business Organization Law Review. 419 at 420.
146   *Constitution of the Republic of Korea*, No.9 of 1980, Article 120, § 3.

[T]he Korean government aggressively pursued an intensive growth strategy throughout the 1960's and 1970's. In doing so, it relied heavily on industrial policy while virtually disregarding the notion of competition policy. This strategy succeeded in recording phenomenal economic growth, but at significant political and social costs. The advent of competition law in 1981 was a manifestation of the Korean government's desire to address this problem in its economic policy-making by strengthening market competition.[147]

Since 1981, Korea's competition law and policy have significantly matured, and the KFTC has become a powerful regulatory body.[148]

Korean law does not provide clear-cut provisions for antitrust immunity for airline alliances. This is different from Japan, which provides for explicit exemption from competition law in its Aviation Act. Although Article 121 of the Korea Aviation Act[149] broadly deals with alliance agreements and requires *ex ante* consultation with the KFTC for their approval, there is no explanation about immunity from competition law.

However, *de facto* antitrust immunity for an airline alliance was actually granted for the Delta-Korean Air alliance in 2002.[150] In addition, the Korean government publicly confirmed that "[I]n the Republic of Korea the authority for granting antitrust immunity

---

147 Youngjin Jung & Seung Wha Chang, "Korea's Competition Law and Policies in Perspective" (2006) 26 Nw. J. Int'l L. & Bus. 687 at 722.
148 For the history of the KFTC, see online: <http://eng.ftc.go.kr/about/history.jsp?pageId=0104>.
149 Article 121 (Agreement, etc. pertaining to Transportation) "(1) Where a domestic or international air transportation businessman intends to conclude an agreement on air transportation (hereinafter referred to as the 'transportation agreement'), including any joint operation agreement, with any other air transportation businessman (including any foreign air transportation businessman) or to conclude an agreement on business cooperation or other alliance in regard of flight schedules, fares, public information or sales (hereinafter referred to as the 'alliance agreement'), he shall obtain approval of the Minister of Land, Transport and Maritime Affairs as prescribed by the Ordinance of the Ministry of Land, Transport and Maritime Affairs. The same shall also apply in the case of altering the approved matters: Provided, That where the businessman intends to alter minor matters prescribed by the Ordinance of the Ministry of Land, Transport and Maritime Affairs, he shall in advance file a report thereof with the Minister of Land, Transport and Maritime Affairs as prescribed by the Ordinance of the Ministry of Land, Transport and Maritime Affairs. (2) Neither transportation agreement nor alliance agreement shall include any of the following matters in its contents: 1. Matters relating to the practical restriction of competition among the air transportation businessmen; 2. Matters relating to unjust infringement on customers' benefit or discrimination against a particular customer; and 3. Matters relating to the unjust restriction of gaining new membership in such agreement or of withdrawal from such membership. (3) In approving any alliance agreement referred to in paragraph (1) or any change in such alliance agreement, the Minister of Land, Transport and Maritime Affairs shall do so after a prior consultation with the Fair Trade Commission. (4) Any conclusion or alteration of the transportation agreement or alliance agreement shall take effect upon approval of the Minister of Land, Transport and Maritime Affairs.", online: Ministry of Government Legislation, Republic of Korea <www.moleg.go.kr/english/korLawEng?pstSeq=52736>.
150 This application was submitted for the first time in 2002 and then resubmitted in 2007, 2010 and 2015. See <www.dailyairlinefilings.com/ostpdf78/711.pdf>.

is vested in both the Ministry of Land, Transport, and Marine Affairs and the Korean Fair Trade Commission"[151] at the Sixth ICAO Air Transport Conference in 2013.

Nevertheless, the scope of antitrust immunity allowed by the MLIT and the KFTC is inherently limited under current Korean law. This is because, according to Article 121, Paragraph 2, airline alliances cannot substantially limit the competition among air carriers under any circumstances.[152] Put differently, blanket immunity for airline alliances is not permitted under Korean law. This explains why Korean Air and Delta Airlines only received limited immunity for certain activities.

In other jurisdictions with systems for antitrust immunity, the competition authorities compare how the business activities in question will benefit consumers with how they will limit competition. If they conclude that the benefits an airline alliance provides consumers outweigh its anti-competitive effects, the competition authorities may grant a legal exception.

In Korea, however, this is not the case. In other words, even antitrust immunity does not guarantee unrestricted coordination for pricing between airlines. These strict legal regulations make complete metal neutral joint ventures impossible because price coordination is inevitable in the unincorporated joint venture model. (This will be further discussed in section 5.4.4 Proposed Delta-Korean Air Joint Venture.)

5.4 Metal Neutral Joint Ventures in the Trans-Pacific (Northeast Asia-US) Market

5.4.1 US Policy on Open Skies and Antitrust Immunity in Asia

In section 5.2.2.2 Correlation with Open Skies Agreements, I examined how antitrust immunity and open skies agreements are interconnected. A basic rationale for this correlation is to maintain fair competition. Accordingly, pursuant to U.S. DOT policy, only after an open skies agreement is implemented that provides other airlines with unrestricted access to the market can antitrust immunity be granted to a particular airline alliance.

The other reason is a policy objective that the US has been pursuing since the 1990s. Indeed, the US's divide-and-conquer strategy, which combines open skies agreements with granting antitrust immunity, proved highly successful in the EU.[153] In 1995 alone,

---

151 ICAO, *Antitrust Immunity for Airlines Alliances*, ICAO Doc ATConf/6-WP/85 (4 March 2013) (Presented by Republic of Korea), online: <www.icao.int/Meetings/atconf6/Documents/WorkingPapers/ATConf6-wp85_en.pdf>.
152 See *supra* note 149.
153 Havel, "Open Skies", *supra* note 81 at 32.

the US reached open skies agreements with Belgium, Finland, Denmark, Norway, Sweden, Luxembourg, Austria, Iceland, Switzerland, and the Czech Republic.[154]

After 1992, when the US and the Netherlands reached an open skies agreement and the KLM-Northwest alliance received antitrust immunity, an increasing number of German passengers bound for the US started to fly through Amsterdam Schiphol Airport (using KLM's sixth freedom services) in the Netherlands instead of Frankfurt Airport. Due to the drain of passengers and revenue from Lufthansa's network, Germany signed a transitional agreement toward open skies with the US in 1996.[155]

By 1997, about 40 percent of US-Europe traffic was flying under open skies.[156] France, another major economy in Europe, signed an open skies agreement with the US in 2001. The US's open skies with Germany and France resulted in antitrust immunity for Lufthansa and United and for Delta Airlines and Air France.[157] Clearly, the availability of US antitrust immunity in exchange for open skies had a "honey pot effect" on other European governments and airlines.[158]

The ultimate target of the strategy, the UK, refused to reach a bilateral open skies agreement with the US for several more years. Presumably, since the UK is geographically closer to the US than EU members on the continent—that is, since passengers flying from the UK to the US or vice versa would have to backtrack if they wanted to use European hubs—the US's divide-and-conquer strategy did not have as big an impact on the UK as it did on Germany and France. Eventually, however, open skies came into effect between the US and the UK through the 2007 US–EU Air Transport Agreement, to which the UK is a party.

For the US, the open skies agreement with Germany reached in February 1996 meant the opening of a large aviation market on the European continent. Soon after the agreement, the US started to shift the focus of its international aviation policy to Asia, announcing the US open skies initiative in Asia in the summer of 1996.[159]

In January 1997, Singapore became the first state in Asia to sign an open skies agreement with the US. In the press release about the US-Singapore open skies agreement, US Transportation Secretary Federico Peña made it clear that the US was seeking a series of

---

154 See US Department of State, *Open Skies Partners* (updated on 14 January 2015), online: <www.state.gov/e/eb/rls/othr/ata/114805.htm>. (In chronological order: Netherlands (14 October 1992); Belgium (1 March 1995); Finland (24 March 1995); Denmark (26 April 1995); Norway (26 April 1995); Sweden, (26 April 1995); Luxembourg (6 June 1995); Austria (14 June 1995); Iceland (14 June 1995); Switzerland (15 June 1995); and Czech Republic (8 December 1995)).
155 Dempsey, "Air Transport Agreements", *supra* note 80 at 168-169.
156 Leonard Hill, "Bilateral Ballistics" *Air Transport World* 34:2 (February 1997) 53.
157 Brian F. Havel & Gabriel S. Sanchez, *The Principles and Practices of International Aviation Law* (New York: Cambridge University Press, 2014) at 149. [Havel & Sanchez, "Aviation Law"].
158 *Ibid.*
159 Tae Hoon Oum & Chunyan Yu, *Shaping Air Transport in Asia Pacific* (Burlington: Ashgate, 2000) at 136.

open skies relationships with Asian countries just as it was doing in the EU.[160] In the following month, Taiwan signed an open skies agreement with the US.

A greater impact was exerted by the open skies agreement between the US and Korea in June 1998. In fact, the US's open skies agreement with Korea was directly connected with Japan since the US had consistently associated its Korean aviation policy with its Japanese policy. In 1978, two decades before this open skies agreement was adopted, Korea had become the first Asian country to conclude a relatively liberal bilateral agreement with the US, which explicitly allowed an unlimited number of carriers to be designated in exchange for opening more routes from Seoul to US cities.[161] This agreement was clearly intended to put pressure on Japan, which had been refusing to accept unlimited designations.[162]

Likewise, Korea was a key part of the US plan to reach an open skies agreement with Japan, given its proximity to the country and its relatively liberal attitude on international air transportation issues.[163] Just as the US approached the Netherlands as part of its plan to pressure Germany into signing an open skies agreement, the US's successful open skies agreement with Korea was largely aimed at forcing Japan to change its aviation policy.

While Japan was still resisting the US's open skies proposal, some Japanese experts believed that the US divide-and-conquer strategy would not succeed in Northeast Asia because of the large size of China and Japan, which would prevent the threat of traffic diversion from working as it had in Europe.[164] But contrary to expectations, a significant traffic diversion has occurred through Korea. In particular, Korean Air has been "the quiet achiever in the North America-Asia transfer market,"[165] picking up a large portion of traffic in that market. The CAPA report articulates the comparative advantages of Korean Air as follows:

> Korean Air holds an advantage for its geography (unlike Hong Kong or Taipei), hub airport not being constrained by slots (unlike Beijing, Hong Kong and

---

160 See US Department of Transportation, Press Release, "U.S., Singapore Reach Open Skies Aviation Agreement" (23 January 1997), online: <www.usembassy-israel.org.il/publish/press/trnsport/archive/1997/january/td10124.htm>. (noting that "[T]his agreement initiates what we hope will be a series of open skies relationships with our partners in Asia. Developing a consensus for open aviation markets in Asia, just as we are in Europe, furthers President Clinton's policy of opening aviation markets around the world.").
161 Paul Dempsey, *Law and Foreign Policy in International Aviation* (Dobbs Ferry, Transnational Publishers: 1987) at 68 & 208. [Dempsey, "Foreign Policy"].
162 Melvin A. Brenner, James O. Leet & Elihu Schott, *Airline Deregulation* (Westport: Eno Foundation for Transportation, 1985) at 13.
163 Oum & Yu, *supra* note 159 at 138.
164 *Ibid.* at 129 (the authors' interview with a Japanese airline executive).
165 CAPA, "Korean Air returns to profit in 1Q2014 on the back of yield recovery and cost discipline" (11 June 2014), online: <http://centreforaviation.com/analysis/korean-air-returns-to-profit-in-1q2014-on-the-back-of-yield-recovery-and-cost-discipline-171834>.

Tokyo) and being permitted to cater, albeit in a limited way to the outbound-China sixth-freedom market (unlike Taiwanese carriers).[166]

Indeed, Japanese passengers traveling abroad increasingly used Incheon Airport in Korea instead of Haneda and Narita airports in the 2000s.[167] Subsequently, the US achieved its long-standing goal of open skies with Japan in October 2010, 12 years after signing an open skies agreement with Korea. Although the impact of Korea (that is, the drain of US-bound Japanese passengers to flights departing from Incheon International Airport in Korea) was not the only reason for the agreement, it was a significant factor.

There were two other reasons—distinct from but related to the US's divide-and-conquer strategy—that led Japan to sign an open skies agreement with the US. The first (and more fundamental) reason was national policy reform in Japan. In April 2007, the Japanese government unveiled its "Asia Gateway" plan, which was designed to remove restrictions on foreign air carriers' access to Japanese airports and to have its airports become international hubs, as the name suggests. (See section 3.2.3.1 Policy Transformation through the Asian Gateway Initiative)

Secondly, the US DOT guaranteed it would provide antitrust immunity to Japanese carriers and US partner carriers if Japan signed the open skies agreement. As had happened many times before, antitrust immunity for Japan Airlines and American Airlines ("JL/AA") and for All Nippon Airways, Continental Airlines, and United Air Lines ("NH/CO/UA" or "ANA/United") was an incentive for Japan to reach an open skies agreement with the US. Because the US DOT had made metal neutral joint ventures a new requirement for antitrust immunity in 2008, these two alliances were established as unincorporated joint ventures.

5.4.2   American Airlines-Japan Airlines JV

On 11 December 2009, the US and Japan signed an MOU promising to establish an open skies relationship. Two months later, on 12 February 2010, Japan Airlines (JL) and American Airlines (AA) applied to the US DOT for antitrust immunity.[168] Their application

---

166   Ibid.
167   Patrick M. Cronin, *Taking Off Civil Aviation, Forward Progress and Japan's Third Arrow Reforms* (Washington, DC: Center for a New American Security, 2013) at 13.
168   See US DOT, *Joint Application of American Airlines, Inc. and Japan Airlines International Co., Ltd. under 49 U.S.C. ss. 41308 and 41309 for approval of and antitrust immunity for alliance agreements*, Dkt No DOT-OST-2010-0034-0001 (16 February 2010).

described plans to launch metal neutral joint ventures in the trans-Pacific market, focusing on the US–Japan market.[169]

Interestingly, during this two-month period, there was a bitter fight between two leading US airlines (American Airlines and Delta Air Lines) over who would be partners with Japan Airlines. American Airlines was the original alliance partner with Japan Airlines (both are Oneworld members) and Delta Airlines was the challenger. Indeed, Delta Airlines pulled out all the stops, even offering financial aid, to establish an alliance with JAL when JAL was going through bankruptcy proceedings in January 2010.[170]

In fact, the battle had begun in October 2008 when Delta merged with Northwest Airlines, which had operated a Narita hub for many years, flying from several US gateways to Tokyo before continuing on to about 10 other Asian cities.[171] Although Asia was a minor concern for pre-merger Delta, usually accounting for only two percent of Delta's total passenger revenue,[172] Northwest's strong presence in Asia helped Delta realize the enormous potential of the trans-Pacific market.

Despite considerable efforts by Delta, Japan Airlines eventually chose on 2 February 2010 to keep its ties with American Airlines, which was a major blow for Delta.[173] After Japan Airlines and American Airlines applied for antitrust immunity, the US DOT issued the show cause order on 6 October 2010, which tentatively granted antitrust immunity to the JL/AA alliance.[174]

On 25 October 2010, the US and Japan officially signed an open skies agreement in Tokyo.[175] Soon after, on 10 November 2010, the US DOT released the final order, which officially granted antitrust immunity to the JL/AA as well as the ANA/UA alliances (see below).[176] Both the show cause order and the final order made it clear that the US–Japan

---

169 See US DOT, *U.S.-Japan Alliance Case*, Dkt. No. DOT-OST-2010-0059, Final Order 2010-11-10 (10 November 2010).
170 CAPA, "Delta Air Lines seeks a Tokyo Haneda base. Skymark a potential partner, to shake up alliances?" (2 August 2013), online: <http://centreforaviation.com/analysis/delta-air-lines-seeks-a-tokyo-haneda-base-skymark-a-potential-partner-to-shake-up-alliances-121506>.
171 Jeffrey Ng, "Delta Shifts Focus From Japan as Trans-Pacific Hub" *The Wall Street Journal* (10 February 2014), online: <www.wsj.com/articles/SB10001424052702303874504579375670306517530>.
172 CAPA, "Delta Air to use its Chinese SkyTeam partners to grow, connecting over the main hubs" (15 July 2013), online: <http://centreforaviation.com/analysis/delta-air-to-use-its-chinese-skyteam-partners-grow-in-north-asia-connecting-over-the-main-hubs-118492>.
173 See Mariko Sanchanta & Mike Esterl, "JAL Stays in AMR Alliance, Delta Out" *The Wall Street Journal* (7 February 2010), online: <www.wsj.com/articles/SB10001424052748703615904575053860586727220>.
174 See US DOT, *U.S.-Japan Alliance Case*, Dkt No DOT-OST-2010-0059-0180, Order 2010-10-4, Show Cause Order (6 October 2010).
175 See US Department of State, Press Release, "United States and Japan Sign Open Skies Memorandum of Understanding on Air Transportation" (25 October 2010).
176 See US DOT, *U.S.-Japan Alliance Case*, Dkt. No. DOT-OST-2010-0059, Final Order 2010-11-10 (10 November 2010).

open skies agreement was a precondition for these orders taking effect.[177] Also, the DOT's approval for antitrust immunity specifically stated that the two airlines would have to start metal neutral joint ventures in the trans-Pacific market within eighteen months of the final order being issued.[178]

American Airlines and Japan Airlines also sought antitrust immunity from the Japanese government. Japan Airlines applied to the Ministry of Land, Infrastructure, Transport, and Tourism of Japan (MLIT), seeking antitrust immunity with American Airlines on 18 June 2010,[179] and the MLIT approved the application on 22 October 2010.[180] This was Japan's first ever application for airline antitrust immunity.[181]

Table 5.8 Snapshot of American Airlines and Japan Airlines

	American Airlines	**Japan Airlines**
Global Alliance	Oneworld	Oneworld
Hub Airports	Dallas, Chicago, and Miami	Tokyo (Narita and Haneda)
Fleet	627	162
Destinations	330 destinations in 50 states	80 destinations in 20 states

In April 2011, Japan Airlines and American Airlines commenced their joint venture on the following routes.[182]

---

177 See US DOT, *U.S.-Japan Alliance Case*, Dkt No DOT-OST-2010-0059-0180, Order 2010-10-4, Show Cause Order (6 October 2010) at 1 (stating that "[T]he tentative decisions in this order are conditioned upon the U.S.-Japan Open Skies aviation agreement being applied."); US DOT, *U.S.-Japan Alliance Case*, Dkt. No. OST-2010-0059, Final Order 2010-11-10 (10 November 2010) at 4 (stating that "[O]ur approval and grant of immunity are subject to the condition that the U.S.-Japan Open Skies aviation agreement is applied.") .
178 US DOT, *U.S.-Japan Alliance Case*, Dkt. No. DOT-OST-2010-0059, Final Order 2010-11-10 (10 November 2010).
179 Japan Airlines, Press Release, "Japan Airlines Submits Antitrust Immunity Application for a Tighter Cooperation with American Airlines on the Trans-Pacific Routes to the Ministry of Land, Infrastructure, Transport and Tourism of Japan" (18 June 2010), online: <http://press.jal.co.jp/en/uploads/20100618_-_JAL_submits_ATI_application_to_JCAB_FINAL.pdf>.
180 Japan Airlines, Press Release, "Japan Airlines Welcomes the Approval by the Ministry of Land, Infrastructure, Transport and Tourism of Japan for Antitrust Immunity with American Airlines to Cooperate on Trans-Pacific Routes" (22 October 2010), online: <http://press.jal.co.jp/en/uploads/20101022%20-%20JAL%20receives%20Approval%20from%20MLIT%20for%20ATI%20Application%20with%20American%20American%20Airlines.pdf>.
181 Japan Airlines, Press Release, "Japan Airlines Submits Antitrust Immunity Application for a Tighter Cooperation with American Airlines on the Trans-Pacific Routes to the Ministry of Land, Infrastructure, Transport and Tourism of Japan" (18 June 2010), online: <http://press.jal.co.jp/en/uploads/20100618_-_JAL_submits_ATI_application_to_JCAB_FINAL.pdf>.
182 American Airlines, Press Release, "American Airlines and Japan Airlines Announce Joint Business Benefits for Trans-Pacific" (11 January 2011), online: <http://hub.aa.com/en/nr/pressrelease/japan-airlines-and-american-airlines-announce-joint-business-benefits-for-trans-pacific-consumers>.

Table 5.9 Routes on the Metal Neutral Joint Venture between AA and JAL[183]

Operating Carrier	Route
AA	Narita ↔ Dallas/Fort Worth, New York, Chicago, Los Angeles
	Haneda ↔ New York
JAL	Narita ↔ New York, Chicago, Los Angeles, Vancouver
	Haneda ↔ San Francisco

5.4.3 United Airlines-All Nippon Airways (ANA) JV

Compared to the Japan Airlines-American Airlines joint venture, the path to a joint venture for United Airlines (United) and All Nippon Airways (ANA) was smooth and uneventful. While Japan Airlines was initially unsure about global branded alliances and did not join Oneworld until 2007, ANA was more proactive and joined Star Alliance in 1999. Since then, ANA has maintained a close relationship, including wide code-sharing, with United Airlines, a founding member of Star Alliance.

On 23 December 2009, immediately after the US and Japan signed an MOU for an open skies agreement, ANA, United Airlines, and Continental Airlines applied for antitrust immunity.[184] At that time, United Airlines and Continental Airlines were in the process of discussing a merger. During the DOT's review period, United Airlines' parent company, UAL Corporation (UAL), and Continental announced on 2 May 2010 their intention to merge operations. Although the merger was completed on 1 October 2010, the US DOT considered United and Continental to be separate entities in its order.[185]

On 6 October 2010, the US DOT issued the show cause order, which tentatively granted antitrust immunity to the United-ANA alliance.[186] Shortly after the US and Japan officially signed the open skies agreement in Tokyo,[187] the US DOT issued the final order, granting antitrust immunity to the ANA/UA alliance on 10 November 2010.[188]

The ANA/UA alliance application for antitrust immunity was reviewed in parallel with the JAL/AA application. Indeed, the US DOT granted approval of and antitrust immunity

---

183 *Ibid.*
184 See US DOT, *Joint Application of All Nippon Airways Co., Ltd., Continental Airlines, Inc. and United Air Lines, Inc. under 49 U.S.C. ss.41308 and 41309 for approval and antitrust immunity for alliance agreements,* Dkt No DOTOST-2009-0350-0001 (23 December 2009).
185 See US DOT, *U.S.-Japan Alliance Case,* Dkt. No. DOT-OST-2010-0059, Final Order 2010-11-10 (10 November 2010).
186 See US DOT, *U.S.-Japan Alliance Case,* Dkt No DOT-OST-2010-0059-0180, Order 2010-10-4, Show Cause Order (6 October 2010).
187 See US Department of State, Press Release, "United States and Japan Sign Open Skies Memorandum of Understanding on Air Transportation" (25 October 2010).
188 See US DOT, *U.S.-Japan Alliance Case,* Dkt. No. DOT-OST-2010-0059, Final Order 2010-11-10 (10 November 2010).

for the two separate applications in one consolidated order titled "U.S.-Japan Alliance Case."[189] Furthermore, in reaching this conclusion, the UD DOT opined that the applications influenced each other, noting that "inter-alliance competition would likely be strengthened in US–Asia and US–Japan markets as a result of immunizing the Star applicants and the oneworld applicants."[190]

Table 5.10   Snapshot of United Airlines and All Nippon Airways

	United Airlines	All Nippon Airways
Global Alliance	Star Alliance	Star Alliance
Hub Airports	Chicago, Denver, and LAX	Tokyo (Narita and Haneda)
Fleet	705	211
Destinations	373 destinations in 60 states	72 destinations in 18 states

United Airlines and ANA also sought antitrust immunity from the Ministry of Land, Infrastructure, Transport, and Tourism of Japan (MLIT) which granted it on 22 October 2010.[191] In April 2011, ANA and United started their joint venture,[192] which featured more routes on trans-Pacific routes than the JAL/AA joint venture.

Table 5.11   Routes on the Metal Neutral Joint Venture between United and ANA[193]

Operating Carrier	Route
United	Narita ↔ Los Angeles, San Francisco, Seattle, Houston, Chicago, New York (Newark), Washington, D.C., Honolulu, Denver
	Osaka ↔ San Francisco
ANA	Narita ↔ Los Angeles, San Francisco, Chicago, New York (JFK), Washington, D.C., Honolulu, San Jose, Seattle
	Haneda ↔ Los Angeles, Honolulu

In November 2014, United Airlines and ANA filed a separate application for antitrust immunity to enable the two airlines to create a more comprehensive business network for trans-Pacific air cargo.[194] This joint venture for trans-Pacific cargo (the first of its kind

---

189 Ibid.
190 Ibid. at 2.
191 ANA, Press Release, "ANA, Continental and United Secure Japanese Anti-Trust Immunity for Trans-Pacific Joint Venture" (22 October 2010), online: <www.ana.co.jp/eng/aboutana/press/2010/pdf/101022.pdf>.
192 "United Continental and ANA launch trans-Pacific joint venture" Japan Today (5 April 2011), online: <www.japantoday.com/category/travel/view/united-continental-and-ana-launch-trans-pacific-joint-venture>.
193 ANA, "Expanding Our Network with United Airlines!" online: <www.ana.co.jp/wws/us/e/local/amc/jv/>.
194 "ANA seeks anti-trust immunity for JV" The Business Desk (21 November 2014), online: <www.thebusinessdesk.com/northwest/ana-seeks-anti-trust-immunity-for-jv.html>.

between the US and Asia)[195] hints that cooperation between the two carriers has been going smoothly.

Only a few decades ago, the current dynamic would have been nearly unimaginable. In the 1990s and early 2000s, the aero-political tensions between the US and Japan may well have been higher than between any other trans-Pacific countries. But now the two countries enjoy one of the strongest, and mostly deeply strategic, trans-Pacific partnerships.[196]

5.4.4 Proposed Delta-Korean Air JV

Among the trans-Pacific airline partnerships (that is, between US carriers and Asian carriers), the alliance between Delta Airlines and Korean Air was the first to receive antitrust immunity. In 2002, Delta Airlines and Korean Air filed an application for antitrust immunity with the US DOT as part of the Skyteam joint application for antitrust immunity.

Given that the US and Korea reached an open skies agreement in 1998, antitrust immunity for Delta and Korean Air seemed less relevant to the agreement between the two countries. To be sure, antitrust immunity would not have been possible if the US–Korea open skies agreement had not been in place, but it cannot be seen as a direct incentive for that agreement.

Even though Delta and Korean Air received antitrust immunity, the level of their cooperation did not exceed code-sharing. First of all, the US DOT's policy on antitrust immunity did not include metal neutrality as a condition for the partnership in the early 2000s. In addition, it is unlikely that the Korean Fair Trade Commission would have allowed a highly integrated joint venture because of the strict law (Article 121 of the Korea Aviation Act). As noted earlier, Asia had barely been on Delta's radar prior to its merger with Northwest in 2008.[197] But the situation changed dramatically after the merger and Delta's painful failure to partner with Japan Airlines in 2009.

Korean Air was Delta's obvious choice for the trans-Pacific market. Both the airlines were founding members of Skyteam and both had already received antitrust immunity. Just like Japan, Korea is strategically located for traffic between China and Southeast Asia and North America. Korean Air's map of destinations in the Asia-Pacific region sheds

---

195 ANA, Press Release, "Antitrust Immunity Requested for United-All Nippon Airways Joint Cargo Venture" (21 November 2014), online: <https://www.ana.co.jp/eng/aboutana/press/2014/141121.html>.
196 CAPA, "North Pacific air route development: Part 4. Japan's hub role diminishes; Partnerships remain weak" (26 August 2014), online: <http://centreforaviation.com/analysis/north-pacific-air-route-development-part-4-japans-hub-role-diminishes-partnerships-remain-weak-183391>.
197 CAPA, "Delta Air to use its Chinese SkyTeam partners to grow, connecting over the main hubs" (15 July 2013), online: <http://centreforaviation.com/analysis/delta-air-to-use-its-chinese-skyteam-partners-grow-in-north-asia-connecting-over-the-main-hubs-118492>.

some light on the geographical advantages that Korea and Japan enjoy in the trans-Pacific market.

Figure 5.5   Korean Air Route Map

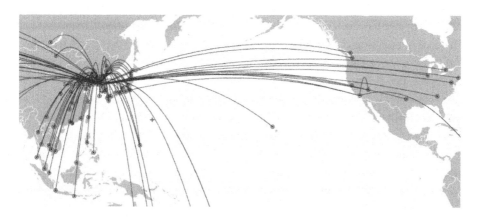

Considering that the two major Japanese carriers are already partners with Delta's competitors (American Airlines and United Airlines), Delta hopes today that a fully immunized metal neutral joint venture with Korean Air will help it compete with the other metal neutral joint ventures.

On the other hand, Korean Air appears to be satisfied with continuing code-sharing with Delta without stepping up their relationship. This is because Korean Air already has an established presence in the US market. Despite Korea's small size, Korean Air is the Asian airline with the most passenger services to the US – to 11 destinations in total (Los Angeles, New York, Atlanta, Chicago, Dallas, Honolulu, Houston, Las Vegas, San Francisco, Seattle, and Washington Dulles).[198] The US market has been a main source of revenue for the airline for over a decade, accounting for about a third of total passenger revenue.[199] The CAPA offers a concise summary of Korean Air's competitiveness on trans-Pacific routes:

> Korean Air has a number of advantages: generally solid geography that often places Seoul on the shortest flight path between Asia and North America, a

---

198   CAPA, "Korean Air seeks new markets after betting the house on N America, seemingly without SkyTeam support" (30 September 2013), online: <http://centreforaviation.com/analysis/korean-air-seeks-new-markets-after-betting-the-house-on-n-america-seemingly-without-skyteam-support-130189>.
199   *Ibid.*

lower cost base than Japanese peers ANA and JAL, early open skies with the US, and relatively extensive access to China as a sixth-freedom source market.[200]

In response to Korean Air's inertia, Delta has eliminated Korean Air flights from earning miles in its frequent flyer programme and cut code-shares between the two. Delta argues that Korean Air has been able to divert China–US traffic to its hub of Incheon to the detriment of non-stop carriers like Delta.[201] Logically, Delta would prefer to have a direct joint venture with a Chinese carrier, but the lack of open skies between the US and China negates this possibility (This will be further discussed below.) Also, a joint venture with a Japanese carrier is no longer a possibility since the two large Japanese carriers (JAL and ANA) already have arrangements with American and United Airlines, respectively.

For Korean Air, a metal neutral joint venture is a new form of airline cooperation and an unfamiliar business model. This contrasts with the rich experience that Delta (and previously Northwest) have had in this kind of cooperation in the trans-Atlantic market. Moreover, Korean Air has little reason to launch a joint venture in the US market, where it is already profitable. There are also regulatory concerns. It is unclear whether the Korean Fair Trade Commission would grant antitrust immunity, and if it did, what the extent of this immunity would be. Since a metal neutral joint venture is beyond the scope of any antitrust immunity that Korean Air has hitherto received, Korean Air must seek new immunity if it decides to initiate a joint venture with Delta.

Despite these challenges, Delta and Korean Air could explore closer cooperation, including the establishment of a joint venture, in the near future. Their direct competitors continue to cooperate more closely together, and Delta's network in the US market is important for Korean Air. As an illustration, Korean Air used to have more than 100 code-sharing routes (domestic US, US-Canada, selected South American service) with Delta until Delta scaled back its codeshare partnership in July 2013.[202]

Meanwhile, Korean Air (KE) and American Airlines (AA) recently agreed to codeshare on flights between Dallas/Fort Worth and Seoul.[203] A media report speculated that Korean Air's limited pact with American Airlines comes against "the backdrop of a seemingly

---

200 CAPA, "North Pacific airline route development: Part 1 – Market growth and the Asian airlines' strategies" (18 August 2014), online: <http://centreforaviation.com/analysis/north-pacific-airline-route-development-part-1---market-growth-and-the-asian-airlines-strategies-182848>.
201 CAPA, "North Pacific air route development: Part 4. Japan's hub role diminishes; Partnerships remain weak" (26 August 2014), online: <http://centreforaviation.com/analysis/north-pacific-air-route-development-part-4-japans-hub-role-diminishes-partnerships-remain-weak-183391>.
202 "Korean Air / DELTA Reduces Codeshare Operation in S13" *Airline Route* (26 August 2013), online: <http://airlineroute.net/2013/08/26/kedl-codeshare-s13/>.
203 Ben Mutzabaugh, "AA, Korean cross alliance lines on Dallas codeshare pact" *USA TODAY* (4 February 2015), online: <www.usatoday.com/story/todayinthesky/2015/02/04/american-korean-air-to-codeshare-on-seoul-dallas-route/22862651/>.

deteriorating relationship between Korean Air and SkyTeam partner Delta."[204] Although the scope of the KE-AA codeshare agreement is limited (only for flights between Dallas/Fort Worth and Seoul), it signals that the joint venture deal between Korean Air and Delta cannot be easily achieved. Thus, it will be interesting to see whether Delta and Korean Air will mend their differences in the near future and eventually establish a joint venture in the trans-Pacific market.

5.4.5 Possibility of a JV between a Chinese Airline and a US Airline

A more interesting scenario in the trans-Pacific market is the possibility of Chinese carriers entering into joint ventures with US alliance partners. In the long run, it is undisputed that the China–US aviation market will be the most lucrative in the world. The US and China represent the world's two largest domestic aviation markets, and Chinese carriers continue to increase their share of the global market. While China's domestic market is currently only half the size of the US domestic market, it is projected to overtake the US market by 2031.[205]

Media reports have confirmed that China Southern Airlines has offered to form a joint venture with Delta. For now, though, China Southern's offer is not tenable because the US DOT only grants antitrust immunity to joint ventures when open skies agreements are already in place.[206]

The ties between Delta and China Eastern are growing stronger as well. According to another media report, Delta and China Eastern are working closely to address a problem bedeviling airlines in both the US and China, namely, the sense that US and Chinese carriers do not benefit enough from the US–China market.[207] According to Delta's calculations, national carriers usually control 85 percent of the air traffic between the US and other nations, but US and Chinese airlines only control about 60 percent of the traffic between the US and China.[208] In other words, 40 percent of total passengers between the two countries use third-country hubs, mostly Incheon, Narita and Hong Kong.

At present, Delta and China Eastern are focusing on lower-level airline cooperation, including reducing connecting times, providing premium customer service and high-quality lounges, and boosting the reliability of transfers.[209] However, their partnership

---

204 Ibid.
205 "China's Power Change and Airline Impacts" *Airline Leader* 15 (October 2012) 28 at 30.
206 CAPA, "U.S.-Japan Airline Alliances Become Lopsided as JAL, ANA Expand while U.S. to Shift to Other Markets" (4 February 2013), online: <http://centreforaviation.com/analysis/us-japan-airline-alliances-become-lopsided-as-jal-ana-expand-while-us-to-shift-to-other-markets-95799>.
207 Susan Carey, "Delta, China Eastern Try to Solve Air Traffic Riddle" *The Wall Street Journal* (19 March 2014), online: <www.wsj.com/articles/SB10001424052702304732804579425363833070996>.
208 Ibid.
209 Ibid.

cannot evolve into joint operations, which would require antitrust immunity, because the US and China do not currently have an open skies agreement. Paul Mifsud predicts that Delta could bring to bear its experience with metal neutral joint ventures if its Chinese partner could persuade its government to adopt an open skies agreement with the US.[210]

Indeed, Mr. Edward Bastian, president of Delta Airlines, said, "[J]oint-venture is the model for international collaboration. Hopefully, with the Chinese, we can get there as well," predicting that the US and China would reach a deal on open skies between 2018 and 2023.[211]

5.5   Impact of Metal Neutral Joint Ventures in Northeast Asia

5.5.1   Analysis of US–China Aviation Market

At this juncture, it is worth reviewing a few facts: 1) the US and Japan already have an open skies agreement; 2) the US and Korea already have an open skies agreement; 3) Japan and Korea already have an open skies agreement; 4) US carriers and Japanese carriers received antitrust immunity after meeting metal neutrality requirements; 5) a US carrier and Korean carrier have received antitrust immunity and are discussing a joint venture; 6) China does not have an open skies agreement with the US, Japan, or Korea; and 7) Chinese carriers cannot form joint ventures with US carriers.

Analyzing the imbalance that China has unwittingly created raises questions about the scope of the US–China aviation market and the implications for that market: how the US–China aviation market is defined; whether the US's close aviation relationship with Japan and Korea affects the US–China aviation market; and whether China should be concerned about the US's close aviation relationship with Japan and Korea. These questions are taken up below.

5.5.1.1   Market Definition: "Relevant Market" in the Context of Competition Law

Market definition is a critical stage in the structural analysis employed in many antitrust cases, including but not limited to cases involving mergers and acquisitions, to help assess actual or potential market power.[212] The US DOJ provides a formal distinction between "market" and "relevant market" in its Merger Guidelines:

---

210 Mifsud, *supra* note 73 at 129.
211 See Jeffrey Ng, "Delta Shifts Focus From Japan as Trans-Pacific Hub" *The Wall Street Journal* (10 February 2014), online: <www.wsj.com/articles/SB10001424052702303874504579375670306517530>.
212 Gregory J. Werden, "The History of Antitrust Market Delineation" (1992) 76 Marq. L. Rev. 123 at 123.

A market is defined as a product or group of products and a geographic area in which it is produced or sold such that a hypothetical profit-maximizing firm, not subject to price regulation, that was the only present and future producer or seller of those products in that area likely would impose at least a "small but significant and non-transitory" increase in price, assuming the terms of sale of all other products are held constant. A relevant market is a group of products and a geographic area that is no bigger than necessary to satisfy this test.[213]

More specifically, the European Commission opined that a relevant market is composed of a relevant product market and a relevant geographic market. The EU Commission defined those concepts as follows:

A relevant product market comprises all those products and/or services which are regarded as interchangeable or substitutable by the consumer by reason of the products' characteristics, their prices and their intended use;
A relevant geographic market comprises the area in which the firms concerned are involved in the supply of products or services and in which the conditions of competition are sufficiently homogeneous.[214]

The EU Commission made it clear that the key concept in identifying the relevant product/service market is *substitutability*. Put simply, whether one product or service can be replaced by another is a prime consideration in determining the relevant market for that product or service. Pertinent questions include what methods customers have for acquiring the desired product; what alternatives they have to that product; and whether those are good alternatives.[215] Thus, substitutability concerns the possibility of a customer switching to alternative products that are already available on the market.[216]

The relevant geographic market, the other component of defining a relevant market, is one in which external enterprises are unable to swiftly begin operations and customers are unable or unwilling to switch suppliers located outside the given area.[217] While the relevant market in the context of competition law is usually defined both in terms of product and geography, these two dimensions are so closely related in the case of air

---

213　US DOJ & FTC, *supra* note 61 at 4.
214　European Commission, *Commission Notice on the Definition of Relevant Market for the Purposes of Community Competition Law,* Official Journal C 372, 09/12/1997, 5,5-6 (1997).
215　Luc Peeperkorn & Vincent Verouden, "The Economics of Competition" in Jonathan Faull & Ali Nikpay eds., *The EU Law of Competition,* 3rd ed. (Oxford: Oxford University Press, 2014) at 1.135.
216　Jakub Kociubiński, "Relevant Market in Commercial Aviation of the European Union" (2011) 1 Wroclaw Review of Law, Administration and Economics 12 at 14.
217　*Ibid.* at 15.

transport that they are rarely discussed separately.[218] Needless to say, the product/service of air transport is transporting passengers or cargo by aircraft from point A to point B.

5.5.1.2   Relevant Market of Passenger Air Transport

With respect to passenger air transport, the relevant market is traditionally defined as each individual route connecting a point of origin to a point of destination (O&D city pair).[219] When the US DOT uses traditional antitrust analysis to define relevant markets and measure concentration, it regards city pairs as relevant markets.[220] This market definition reflects the demand-side perspective, as passengers usually wish to travel a specific route.[221]

The question of whether the traditional demand-side approach to defining the relevant market is still appropriate has been tested by the EU Commission.[222] Essentially, the argument is that network effects (such as competition between airline hubs and between alliances) should be given more consideration in defining the relevant market.[223] However, the EU Commission concluded that network competition was not sufficient to modify its traditional demand-based approach mainly because consumers continue to ask for transport service between two points.[224] In addition, the demand-based O&D city pair approach has been applied in recent EU antitrust and merger cases as well as in EU Court decisions.[225] Thus, it is safe to say that the relevant market for passenger air transport is still defined by the demand-based O&D city pair.

Shippers, too, send their cargo based on the O&D city pair formula. However, the relevant market for the air transport of cargo is different from that of passengers for a number of reasons, including the fact that 1) cargo (except for perishable goods) is less time-sensitive than passengers, 2) physical inconvenience (*e.g.* the number of stops and the length of layovers) is not an important consideration, and 3) multi-modal transportation (*e.g.* combining air transport with trucking, train transport, and ship transport) is well-developed. Thus, the relevant market for the air transport of cargo is much wider than that of transportation of passengers.[226] In a nutshell, in the air transport of cargo, various alterna-

---

218 Hubert de Broca, Marta Mielecka Riga & Anatoly Subocs, "Transport" in Jonathan Faull & Ali Nikpay eds., *The EU Law of Competition*, 3rd ed. (Oxford: Oxford University Press, 2014) at 15.42.
219 See Ben Van Houtte, "Relevant Markets in Air Transport" (1990) 27 Common Market Law Review. 521.
220 See *e.g.* US DOT, *U.S.-Japan Alliance Case*, Dkt No DOT-OST-2010-0059-0180, Order 2010-10-4, Show Cause Order (6 October 2010)
221 Broca, Riga & Subocs, *supra* note 218 at 15.44.
222 See *e.g.* Case No COMP/M.2041 -United Airlines/ US Airways case, Notification of 22.09.2000 pursuant to Article 4 of Council Regulation No 4064/89 (2001).
223 Joos Stragier, Monique Negenman, Maria Jaspers & Rita Wezenbeek, "Transport" in Jonathan Faull & Ali Nikpay eds., *The EU Law of Competition*, 2nd ed. (Oxford: Oxford University Press, 2007) at 14.19.
224 *Ibid.*
225 Broca, Riga & Subocs, *supra* note 218 at 15.44.
226 *Ibid.* at 15.66.

tives can substitute for each individual route connecting a point of origin to a point of destination.

For the air transport of passengers, the alternatives are inherently limited. While cost (airfare) is an important consideration for both passengers and shippers, passengers are uniquely sensitive to total flight duration, convenience of departure/arrival times, the frequency of flights (and therefore flexibility in schedule), frequent flyer programs and corporate promotions, and quality of service (including airline reputation, presence of a flight bed, and so on).[227] The scope of the relevant market can also be affected by the type of passenger (time-sensitive passengers versus price-oriented passengers) and airport substitutability (only one airport in a catchment area versus two or more airports serving the relevant point of origin or point of destination).

Some one-stop flights that can compete with non-stop flights are included in the relevant market for long-haul flights. The European Commission provided specific conditions for being part of the relevant market, in particular a connection time of no longer than 150 minutes:

> With respect to long-haul flights the Commission has found ... that indirect flights constitute a competitive alternative to non-stop services under certain conditions in particular when they are marketed as connecting flights on an origin and destination (O&D) pair in the computer reservation systems, they operate on a daily basis and they only result in a limited increase of traveling time, maximum 150 minutes of waiting time.[228]

Along with the connection time, the direction of flight is obviously crucial to ensure that the total traveling time of a one-stop flight is only marginally longer than the flight time of the non-stop flight. In the case of a joint venture among British Airways, American Airlines, and Iberia Líneas Aéreas de España (*BA/AA/IB* case), the European Commission, which was examining trans-Atlantic routes to and from London, concluded that one-stop services via continental European hubs were only remote substitutes for non-stop services because they required backtracking.[229] Accordingly, it is safe to say that daily one-stop flights that do not substantially deviate from the direction of the non-stop route with less than 150 minutes of connection time can be included in the relevant market of passenger air transport.

---

227 European Commission, *Case No COMP/M.2041 – UNITED AIRLINES / US AIRWAYS* (12 January 2001) at 4, online: <http://ec.europa.eu/competition/mergers/cases/decisions/m2041_en.pdf>.
228 European Commission, *Case No COMP/M.5403 – LUFTHANSA / BMI* (14 May 2009) at 4, online: <http://ec.europa.eu/competition/mergers/cases/decisions/m5403_20090514_20310_en.pdf>.
229 European Commission, *Case COMP/39.596 – BA/AA/IB* (14 July 2010) at 6, online: <http://ec.europa.eu/competition/antitrust/cases/dec_docs/39596/39596_4342_9.pdf>.

5.5.1.3 China–US Market for Passenger Air Transport

Considering that relevant markets in air transport are defined for each individual route, it is essential to know which routes (that is, city pairs) are the major markets in the larger China–US market and to see whether there are one-stop flights that can be included in the relevant market. The largest China–US O&D markets are Shanghai-Los Angeles, Beijing-San Francisco, Shanghai-San Francisco, Beijing-Los Angeles, Beijing-New York (JFK), and Shanghai-New York (JFK).[230] Interestingly, the four largest China–US O&D markets have competitive indirect flights via Korea or Japan, which can be regarded as relevant markets. In other words, the geography of Korea and Japan means that no backtracking and less than 150 minutes of connection time are required for passengers traveling the four largest China–US O&D markets.

Table 5.12 The Largest China–US O&D Markets (2015 Winter Schedule)

Route	US and Chinese Non-Stop Carriers on China–US routes		Korean and Japanese Daily One-Stop Carriers on China–US routes			
	US Carriers	Chinese Carriers	Korean Carriers		Japanese Carriers	
	American/United/Delta	Air China/China Eastern	Korean Air (via Seoul)	Asiana Airlines (via Seoul)	Japan Airlines (via Tokyo either individually or jointly with American Airlines)	ANA (via Tokyo either individually or jointly with United Airlines)
Shanghai-LA	11h 40m (American Delta & United)	11h 40m (China Eastern)	14h 00m (1h for transfer)	16h 00m (3h for transfer)	13h 40m (1h 35m for transfer)	13h 45m (1h 30m for transfer)
Beijing-SFO	11h 20m (United)	11h 20m (Air China)	14h 35m (1h)	N/A (overnight layover)	15h 05m (2h 50m)	15h 25m (3h 30m)
Shanghai-SFO	11h 05m (United & Delta)	11h 05m (China Eastern)	14h 40m (2h)	13h 55m (1h 40m)	18 h (6 h)	13h 20m (1h 20m)
Beijing-LA	12h (United)	12h (Air China)	14h 50m (2h 10m)	14h 10m (1h 35m)	17h (5h 20m)	15h 30m (3h 40m)

---

230 See US Department of Transportation, *Application of American Airlines, Inc. For an Exemption and Allocation of Frequencies (Los Angeles – Shanghai)* (1 October 2010), online: <http://dailyairlinefilings.com/ost-pdf79/627.pdf>.

Route	US and Chinese Non-Stop Carriers on China–US routes		Korean and Japanese Daily One-Stop Carriers on China–US routes			
	US Carriers	Chinese Carriers	Korean Carriers		Japanese Carriers	
	American/United/Delta	Air China/China Eastern	Korean Air (via Seoul)	Asiana Airlines (via Seoul)	Japan Airlines (via Tokyo either individually or jointly with American Airlines)	ANA (via Tokyo either individually or jointly with United Airlines)
Shanghai-New York	14h 30m (United)	14h 30m (China Eastern)	18h 30m (2h 30m)	N/A (overnight layover)	17h 25m (2h 25m)	18h (2h 45m)
Beijing-New York	13h 30m (United)	13h 30m (Air China)	20h 45m (4h 30m)	N/A (overnight layover)	21h (5h 15m)	18h 30m (3h 20m)

It is likely that more competitive one-stop flights on China–US routes will be arranged in the future. Benefiting from larger combined networks and passenger pools and more attractive pricing, AA/JAL and United/ANA (as well as possibly Delta/KAL) could strengthen their competitiveness in the China–US market to the possible detriment of Chinese carriers.[231] In addition, airlines that are partners in joint ventures can work together to reduce the connection time for Chinese passengers at their hub airports.

All things considered, Korea and Japan are currently and will remain a relevant market in the context of the China–US market, and particularly in the US West Coast market (*e.g.* Los Angeles and San Francisco). Hence, as the US's closer aviation ties with Japan and Korea make one-stop flights via their hub airports more competitive, this will slowly but surely have an impact on the US–China aviation market.

5.5.2   Impact on Chinese Aviation Policy

Generally, in order for the divide-and-conquer strategy to work effectively, two conditions are required: 1) the smaller state that made the open skies agreement and the target state must be in the relevant market, and 2) the smaller state should be able to provide direct substitutes rather than remote substitutes.[232]

For instance, since Germany and the Netherlands are in the relevant market for transatlantic routes to and from Frankfurt, Amsterdam Airport Schiphol is a direct substi-

---

231 Tan, "Antitrust Immunity", *supra* note 125 at 291-292.
232 Jae Woon Lee, "The U.S.'s New Divide-and-Conquer Strategy in Northeast Asia" (2014) 14 Issues in Aviation Law and Policy 83 at 100.

tute. However, for non-stop services between the UK and the US, Schiphol and Frankfurt are only remote substitutes because of their geographical disadvantage. These factors could explain why it took only four years for the US to convince Germany to agree to an open skies agreement after reaching an open skies agreement with the Netherlands, its first in Europe, in 1992, while it took 15 years to do the same with the UK.

Looking at trans-Pacific routes to and from China, it is clear that Korea and Japan are in the relevant market and provide direct substitutes. In these circumstances, China cannot ignore the fact that the US has closer aviation ties with Japan and Korea. Through open skies agreements with Japan and Korea as well as joint ventures with Japanese carriers and Korean carriers involving substitutable one-stop flights, US carriers can capture a larger portion of the US–China air passenger market than they currently do with their limited direct third/fourth freedom flights. Indeed, there is limited capacity under the current US–China bilateral agreement.[233] Not only are the US–Japan and US-Korea markets both enormously important in their own right, both states are also strategically located for the US–China air passenger market.

At the same time, the US's close aviation relationships with Japan and Korea give Chinese carriers an incentive to establish joint ventures with US carriers. Conceivably, US carriers' trans-Pacific joint ventures with Japanese and Korean partners could be part of the US government's plan to use the divide-and-conquer approach to induce China to accept an open skies agreement.

Given the circumstances, China has three possible courses of action. First is doing nothing, taking a wait-and-see approach. On 25 December 2014, CAAC Director General Li Jiaxiang said Air China had become the largest carrier in the China–US market, ending the "domination" of US carriers.[234] Although this claim was based on the number of US destinations while other metrics (such as frequency and capacity) showed that the US's United Airlines remains the largest carrier, it is true that the China–US market is becoming more balanced as Chinese airlines gain market share.[235]

---

233 Tan, "Antitrust Immunity", *supra* note 125 at 294.
234 CAPA, "Air China and United Airlines vie for title of largest carrier between China and the United States" (28 January 2015), online: <http://centreforaviation.com/analysis/air-china-and-united-airlines-vie-for-title-of-largest-carrier-between-china-and-the-united-states-203546>.
235 *Ibid*.

Figure 5.6 Non-stop China–US Seat Capacity Share by Carrier Nationality: 2005-2015[236]

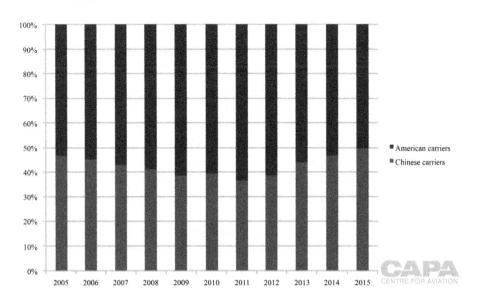

Thus, China could opt not to discuss any trans-Pacific joint ventures while focusing on increasing its market share. China has long been sensitive to foreign carriers having a higher share of traffic, and this imbalance has worked against efforts to expand air service agreements.[237] Now that Chinese airlines' market share is on the rise, the Chinese government may just wait until its carriers, and especially Air China, notice a capacity shortage before agreeing to increase bilateral third/fourth freedom capacity with the US. Even then, it may do so on a piecemeal, incremental basis instead of agreeing to a "big bang" open skies approach that instantly opens up all third/fourth freedom capacity.

China's second option is to consider joint ventures with US carriers. Indeed, Alan Tan argued that Chinese carriers should enter into joint venture agreements with US alliance partners, since this would help to neutralize any competitive advantage provided by alliances between JAL and AA, ANA and UA, and KAL and Delta.[238] He further predicted that consideration of joint venture agreements with US airlines would be the decisive catalyst in changing China's attitude toward open skies with the US.[239]

Interestingly, joint ventures with foreign carriers are booming in China. In 2014 alone, Air China agreed to establish joint ventures with Air Canada, Air New Zealand, and

---

236 Ibid.
237 Ibid.
238 Tan, "Antitrust Immunity", *supra* note 125 at 294-295.
239 Ibid. at 295.

Lufthansa, while China Eastern and Qantas agreed to establish one as well.[240] The details of these new joint ventures are currently under negotiation.[241] However, none of them appear to be metal neutral joint ventures.

If Air China, China's "favorite child," sees an opportunity to establish a metal neutral joint venture with a US carrier (most likely its global alliance partner United Airlines), the CAAC may consider making an open skies agreement with the US in exchange for antitrust immunity for the joint venture. Last but not least, Chinese carriers could reconsider their relationship with Northeast Asian carriers. Northeast Asian carriers have never tried—or even considered the possibility of trying—close cooperation. Presumably, a lack of regional cooperation on a state level has made Northeast Asian airlines reluctant to explore closer relationships.

Because of their geographical location, Japan and Korea are natural gateways for traffic between Asia and North America. However, and for the same geographical reasons, China's major airlines and airports are well positioned to be Asia's gateway to Europe, including connecting traffic originating from or destined for Korea and Japan via its major hubs (Beijing, Shanghai, Guangzhou, and Chengdu).[242] Indeed, Chinese carriers have a stronger service network to Europe than their Japanese and Korean counterparts in terms of destinations, frequency, and number of seats offered.[243]

---

240 See Lufthansa, Press Release, "Lufthansa and Air China strengthen partnership" (7 July 2014), online: <www.lufthansa.com/mediapool/pdf/90/media_649885890.pdf>; Air Canada, Press Release, "Air China and Air Canada to Form Comprehensive Strategic Alliance, Strengthening Canada-China Network" (8 November 2014), online: <www.aircanada.com/cn/zh/news/en/141108.html>; and CAPA, "China Eastern-Qantas & Air China-Air New Zealand JVs show renewed interest from Chinese airlines" (26 November 2014), online: <http://centreforaviation.com/analysis/china-eastern-qantas--air-china-air-new-zealand-jvs-show-renewed-interest-from-chinese-airlines-197782>.

241 Indeed, each joint venture may be different. See CAPA, "Air China-Lufthansa Group JV will control 35% of Europe-China market while easing growth tensions" (8 July 2014) (noting that "JVs by now have forged a well-trodden path of joint pricing (allowing different carriers' flights to be combined more flexibly), schedule coordination (enabling more connections and reducing connection times while also opening new routes), joint marketing and customer experience (such as through loyalty programmes). These are guidelines and not definitive; the Japanese-North American JVs feature higher pricing from Japanese carriers than their North American counterparts, a response to market demand. JVs can also differ in how – and if – they embrace financial performance (revenue or profit)."), online: <http://centreforaviation.com/analysis/air-china-lufthansa-group-jv-will-control-35-of-europe-china-market-while-easing-growth-tensions-176266>.

242 Xiaowen Fu & Tae Hoon Oum, *Dominant Carrier Performance and International Liberalisation: The Case of North East Asia,* Discussion Paper No 2015-03, International Transport Forum (Paris: OECD, 2015) at 17, online: <www.internationaltransportforum.org/jtrc/DiscussionPapers/DP201503.pdf>.

243 *Ibid.* at 11. The authors further argue that "[I]n terms of geographic location and market potential, major Chinese airports such as Guangzhou, Chengdu and Xi'an can serve as Asian gateway hubs to Europe. In fact, China Southern has been making good progress in developing the "Canton route" via Guangzhou airport, which could potentially feed traffic from Southeast Asia, Australia and New Zealand to its European services. Since Guangzhou airport has a large capacity and a fast increasing local market, it is well positioned to compete with other Asian hubs such as Bangkok, Singapore or even Dubai in the long term. China Southern may also be able to capture a share of the traffic originally served by the "Kangaroo routes" linking Australia and New Zealand to Europe."

Table 5.13 Northeast Asian Airline Service to Europe Destinations[244]

2014	Chinese Carriers	Japanese Carriers	Korean Carriers
Number of Destinations in Europe	20	7	12
Weekly Frequency	219	88	82
Weekly Seats	54,801	18,151	23,778
Number of Airlines	4	2	2

Hence, there is a way, albeit not a perfect one, to balance the geographical advantages and disadvantages. This approach, of course, cannot mean "equal" benefits. The gains that Korean and Japanese carriers could receive from the US–China market, the most lucrative country-to-country aviation market in the world, would be bigger than those that Chinese carriers could receive from the Europe-Korea/Japan market. More importantly, there is much less competition on the US–China market while there is strong competition from formidable Middle Eastern carriers in the Europe-Korea/Japan market.

However, it is important to note that the Europe-Japan and the Europe-Korea markets are very sizable. Indeed, in terms of the total number of passengers, the Europe-Japan market was bigger than the US–China market in 2014. Furthermore, the Europe-Korea market is about 60 percent of the US–China market, which is significant given the huge population gap between China (1.4 billion) and Korea (50 million). In other words, it would be possible to offset the geographical advantages that Japan and Korea enjoy in the China–US market if Chinese carriers became more competitive in the Europe-Korea/Japan markets. The numbers of passengers in these markets are detailed in Table 5.14.

Table 5.14 Comparison among China–US, Japan-EU, and Korea-EU Markets[245]

Market		China–US	Japan-Europe	Korea-Europe
Route	A	China→US	Japan→Europe	Korea→Europe
	B	US→China	Europe→Japan	Europe→Korea
Number of passengers who traveled either A or B in 2014		5,537,641	6,258,351	3,320,364

Setting aside rigorous calculations about individual benefits, Chinese carriers could consider (and even suggest) much closer relations with their alliance partners in Korea or Japan. For example, the three Star Alliance members in Northeast Asia (Air China, Asiana Airlines,

---

244 *Ibid.* at 27.
245 The data is based on IATA's Direct Data Solutions, online <www.arccorp.com/dds>.

and ANA) could strengthen their relationship, including a revenue-sharing agreement. In this way, the Star Alliance partners could co-operate internally and compete with other alliance partners subject to the government's review of competition law. Notably, Star Alliance is the only global alliance that includes airlines from all three countries.

A more commercially viable combination is China Southern and Korean Air because of their hub airports (Guangzhou Baiyun International Airport and Incheon International Airport) that are not being constrained by slots and their wide networks (China Southern in India, Southern Europe, Africa, and Oceania and Korean Air in North America). As Skyteam partners, they have already built a relatively solid partnership.

Either way, the development and impact of airline alliances in the Northeast Asian market will change the *status quo*, and China will eventually have to re-evaluate its view of open skies agreements with the US, Japan, and Korea. This re-evaluation will change the dynamic of Northeast Asian open skies.

5.6 CONCLUSION

This chapter has explored various aspects of airline alliances. Analyses not only of aviation law but also of competition law were conducted to ensure a thorough examination of airline alliances. Throughout, a strong case has been made for the important role of airline alliances in the discussion of open skies agreements. Clearly, the ongoing development of airline alliances in the Northeast Asian market has an enormous potential to reshape the discussion of Northeast Asian open skies.

In Chapter 6: Towards Northeast Asian Open Skies: Liberalization by the Airline Industry and States, the final chapter of this research, I will present my key findings and propose institutional, legal, and policy approaches for bringing about Northeast Asian open skies.

6 TOWARDS NORTHEAST ASIAN OPEN SKIES: LIBERALIZATION BY THE AIRLINE INDUSTRY AND STATES

6.1 THEORETICAL FINDINGS

The object of this research has been to explore the central issues underlying Northeast Asian open skies from a multi-dimensional perspective. This research began with two primary goals. The first was to analyze market access and ownership and control restrictions in Northeast Asia and to propose the approaches and steps that need to be taken to achieve Northeast Asian open skies (a specific proposal is provided in section 6.3 Action Plans for Northeast Asian Open Skies). The second was to challenge the orthodox position that intergovernmental agreements are the sole factor determining the degree of air transport liberalization.

The previous chapters contained a comprehensive discussion of market access and ownership and control liberalization through the regional and bilateral approaches with a focus on Northeast Asia. This study also alluded to the emerging role of airlines, arguing that they themselves can have a substantial impact on liberalization. Indeed, airlines have become active reformers of government regulations rather than merely passive subjects of those regulations.

In the broader discourse of regulation, the role of private actors in governance powers has received special attention in recent academic literature, particularly in topics related to transnational private regulation (TPR).[1] Although an in-depth discussion of TPR is beyond the scope of this research, it is worth examining the thrust of TPR arguments in order to better understand the influence of airlines in the context of the broader discussion about the role of non-state actors.

The concept of TPR emerged to express the idea of governance regimes that take the form of coalitions of non-state actors.[2] The view of TPR scholars is that while governance powers were traditionally considered the prerogative of the state, those powers have shifted

---

1 For instance, Journal of Law and Society published a special issue on *The Challenge of Transnational Private Regulation: Conceptual and Constitutional Debates* in March 2011.
2 Colin Scott, Fabrizio Cafaggi & Linda Senden, "The Conceptual and Constitutional Challenge of Transnational Private Regulation" (2011) 38 J.L. & Soc'y 1 at 3.

towards non-governmental bodies, including industry actors.[3] Globalization, market liberalization, and economic integration have been described as powerful drivers of TPR.[4]

TPR differs fundamentally from traditional international regulations mainly because rule making is not based on states' legislation.[5] Indeed, TPR emphasizes the role of the state as a "rule taker" as opposed to a "rule maker."[6] However, this does not mean that TPR disregards formal sources of rules (*e.g.* national legislation and international treaties). Fabrizio Cafaggi, a leading authority on TPR, asserts that "when international treaties are in place, private regulation acts as a complement to specify rules and it tailors them to specific markets and formal or informal delegation take place."[7]

TPR initially developed as regulation of a specific sector.[8] Clearly, the discussion of economic air transport liberalization does not appear to be directly connected to the scope of TPR. Nevertheless, the TPR approach provides a useful framework for understanding the larger picture of how airlines (one example of non-state actors) reform regulations, either directly or indirectly.

There is at least one clear implication of TPR: namely, that the orthodox position that the level of deregulation (or liberalization) is solely determined by intergovernmental agreements is inadequate for understanding the bigger picture of air transport liberalization. Rather, airlines should be seen as key non-state actors that wield enormous power and influence over the process by which regulation regimes are formed.

More concretely, there are three respects in which airlines are involved in reforming regulations. First is the airlines' ability to lobby for the liberalization of air services agreements. Air services negotiations can result in the revision of air services agreements. Although air services negotiations are, by definition, intergovernmental negotiations, they are normally initiated by one or more airlines from one or both states. When airlines feel the need to expand the degree of market access, they urge their respective governments to re-negotiate air services agreements. It is common for airlines in the same state to have conflicting positions. (For instance, one airline could prefer the *status quo*, while others want carriers and capacity to be expanded). However, if none of the national airlines want to expand market access, the air services negotiations are unlikely to succeed.

---

3 *Ibid.* at 1-2.
4 See OECD, *International Regulatory Co-operation: Case Studies, Vol. 3 Transnational Private Regulation and Water Management* (2013) at 10. See also Fabrizio Cafaggi, "New Foundation of Transnational Private Regulation" (2011) 38 J.L. & Soc'y 20 at 24-25.
5 Cafaggi, *ibid.* at 21.
6 *Ibid.*
7 *Ibid.* at 42-43.
8 The environment, financial markets, technical standards, food safety, and e-commerce are some areas in which the systems of TPR play important roles. See OECD, *supra* note 4 at 14.

Figure 6.1 The Influence of Airlines on Liberalizing Air Services Agreements

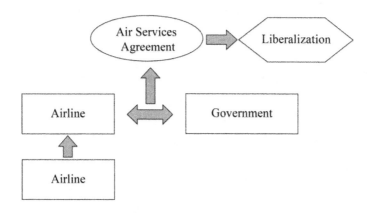

Crudely put, states typically liberalize their markets when it is in the benefit of their national carriers, including the traditional flag carriers and the newer low-cost carriers. Conversely, states generally do not open their markets when their carriers are not interested in liberalization. For public policy makers, the interests of national carriers are often considered part of the national interest.[9]

Although the benefits of air transport liberalization for consumers and the economy as a whole are widely acknowledged,[10] its benefits for national airlines are still the real driver of liberalization, at least in Asia. Although states are becoming less defensive of national airlines in general, air services negotiations continue to be airline-centric.[11] Nonetheless, a fundamentally important point in recent years is that national airlines include not only incumbent carriers but also newly established ones, and particularly low-cost carriers (LCCs).

The success of national LCCs is likely to convince self-interested governments that open skies agreements make their airlines better off. Strictly speaking, most of these LCCs are not state-owned companies (that is, the government holds no share in them). That said, government policy makers tend to regard the interest of carriers owned and operated by their nationals as being within the ambit of the national interest.

As emphasized in previous chapters, the role of LCCs in Northeast Asia cannot be underestimated. LCCs have already been a major driving force for liberalizing market

---

9   See Peter Forsyth, "Chapter 21 Economic Evaluation of Air Services Liberalization: The New Calculus" in Peter Forsyth *et al* eds., *Liberalization in Aviation: Competition, Cooperation and Public Policy* (Farnham: Ashgate, 2013) 403.
10 See Chapter 1, section 1.4.2 Impact of Economic Liberalization in International Air Transport.
11 Forsyth, *supra* note 9 at 403.

access and ownership and control restrictions in Southeast Asia, and they are beginning to do the same in Northeast Asia as well.[12]

Indeed, the second way in which airlines reform regulations is through inventing new business models. Although cross-border mergers through holding companies that have been formed in other parts of the world have yet to appear in Asia, the joint venture LCC model is booming on the continent (see Chapter 2 and Chapter 4).

Admittedly, this new form of business model requires the government's support in the form of mitigating effective control requirements. Despite the existing legal barriers (namely, market access restrictions and ownership and control restrictions), creative airlines have used transnational business models like joint ventures to acquire *de facto* seventh freedom and cabotage rights.

Figure 6.2   Airlines' New Business Model for *de facto* Liberalization

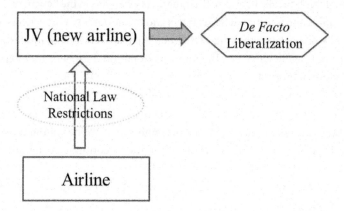

Alliances are the third and perhaps the most powerful way for airlines to reform regulations. An alliance is a private contract between airlines. This private law model of governance has a significant effect on air services negotiations. This is largely because airline alliances can be initiatives by national carriers from *both* state parties to a bilateral air services agreement. While aggressive efforts to liberalize a market by one airline supported by its government can be blocked by the other negotiating partners (the other government and national carriers), a campaign to liberalize the market in support of an integrated airline alliance for the national carriers of both states is likely to be welcomed.

---

12   See Chapter 3, sections 3.2.2.2 Promoting LCCs (For China); 3.2.3.3 Promoting LCCs (For Japan); 3.2.4.2 Promoting LCCs (For Korea); and 3.4.2 The Role of LCCs.

Indeed, Havel and Sanchez argue that "the alliances have shifted the rules of the game for air services negotiations."[13] As discussed in Chapter 5, airlines alliances have had a powerful impact on air services agreements. Antitrust immunity for airline alliances has been a strong incentive for open skies in the trans-Atlantic market and, more recently, the trans-Pacific market. This sequence represents "an alternative account of legal change."[14]

Figure 6.3   How Airline Alliances Affect Liberalization

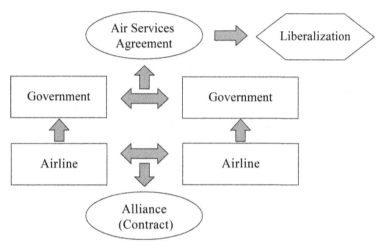

With this new perspective on the role of airlines and particularly of airline alliances, section 6.2 Ongoing Regional Liberalization in Northeast Asia will recap the main arguments and set out the major findings of this research. Section 6.3 Action Plans for Northeast Asian Open Skies, the crux of this chapter, will provide prescriptive analyses of Northeast Asian open skies. More specifically, section 6.3 Action Plans for Northeast Asian Open Skies will propose short-term (2020), mid-term (2025), and long-term (2030) steps for achieving Northeast Asian open skies. Lastly, 6.4 Conclusion will bring this research to an end.

6.2   Ongoing Regional Liberalization in Northeast Asia

These research findings provide several justifications for regional liberalization. Some empirical studies have found that liberalizing air transport has a strongly positive impact on the economy, society, and the individual. Regional liberalization, which typically has

---

13   Brian Havel & Gabriel Sanchez, "Restoring Global Aviation's "Cosmopolitan *Mentalité*"" (2011) 29 B.U. Int'l L.J. 1 at 37.
14   *Ibid.*

closed membership for various reasons (such as a political and economic union, physical proximity, and so on), was the focus of this study, as opposed to global multilateral liberalization and bilateral liberalization.

Various regional liberalization models (namely, the EU SAM, ASEAN SAM, the Australia-New Zealand SAM, APEC's MALIAT, regional agreements in the League of Arab States, regional and sub-regional agreements in Latin America, the Pacific Islands Air Services Agreement, and regional agreements in Africa) were discussed to explicate the similarities and differences of these models. In doing so, I sought to find principles that can be applied to Northeast Asian open skies and the lessons to be learned from these models of liberalization.

The important aero-political finding is that bigger markets with less competitive national airlines (*e.g.* Indonesia in ASEAN, Egypt and Saudi Arabia among the Arab states, Brazil in Latin America, and Nigeria in Africa) are resistant to the trend of regional liberalization because they have more to lose than to gain in their respective regional liberalization groups. Dealing with deeply embedded aero-political complications is a major obstacle to successful regional liberalization.

Northeast Asia is no exception. It is undeniable that China (more precisely, Chinese airlines, and particularly the "Big Three" state-owned airlines) has more to lose than Japan and Korea combined in the context of Northeast Asian open skies. In particular, China is concerned that Northeast Asian open skies that entail generous or unlimited third and fourth freedom rights (thereby resulting in generous or unlimited sixth freedom rights) would enable Japanese and Korean carriers to use Tokyo and Incheon as gateway hubs from China to North America and vice versa, the most lucrative aviation market.

This is why regional liberalization in Northeast Asia remains at a preliminary discussion stage at an intergovernmental level. Although bilateral air services agreements among the three states have been relaxed to some degree, we have yet to see any compromises made or substantial results achieved involving Northeast Asian open skies.

Nevertheless, there are convincing reasons to pursue open skies in Northeast Asia. First and foremost, China, Korea, and Japan rely heavily on each other's markets and influence each other in significant ways; second, aviation blocs are emerging or have already emerged in most regions of the world and these may form competitive threats if the three countries are not united on the issue; third, the three countries already have in place many trilateral consultative mechanisms on various matters; fourth, Northeast Asia is one of the few regions where a stable, developed economy coexists with enormous potential for economic growth; and lastly, national carriers are by and large becoming more competitive and LCCs are growing quickly in Northeast Asia.

In addition, a multi-dimensional perspective is required to predict the future of Northeast Asian open skies. In particular, changes in China–US aviation diplomacy should be taken into consideration. There are encouraging signs that China will become more flexible in its negotiations with the US for the open skies agreement: the China–US market is becoming more balanced; the US is relaxing its visa rules for Chinese nationals; and joint ventures with foreign carriers are booming in China, which could lead to joint ventures between Chinese airlines and US airlines. If China and the US adopt an open skies agreement, Chinese and US carriers will operate many direct flights between China and the US, significantly reducing China's concern about losing passengers transferring at Tokyo or Seoul.

A more important factor is the role of airlines in the discourse of Northeast Asian open skies. From the perspective of traditional public law, regulatory changes in Northeast Asia have been markedly slow. This new perspective on the role of airlines, however, suggests that dynamic liberalization has already started in Northeast Asia. Indeed, Northeast Asian airlines are in the process of reforming regulations. Matched with the findings discussed in section 6.1, airlines' lobbying power, the innovative business model of LCCs, and airline alliances are actively promoting regional liberalization in Northeast Asia.

Airlines' lobbying power, which leads to expanding market access, continues to grow in Northeast Asia. As the number of airlines in Northeast Asia increases, the market share of these new airlines grows. For now, newly established airlines can only fly on routes that are under-utilized under the relevant air services agreements. However, new airlines will eventually hope to fly new routes that can only be opened up by air services negotiations. This will push for liberalization of market access.

While the Northeast Asian market has long been dominated by seven major airlines (namely, Air China, China Eastern, China Southern, Korean Air, Asiana Airlines, Japan Airlines, and All Nippon Airlines), the growth of LCCs is indisputable. Although incumbent airlines continue to check the development of LCCs, the attitude of Northeast Asian governments toward LCCs (and especially their own LCCs) has shifted in their favor. Witnessing the success of LCCs in Southeast Asia, Northeast Asian states hope to develop their own LCCs (that is, LCCs that are majority-owned and effectively controlled by their nationals).

In addition, from a long-term perspective, the development of LCCs does not necessarily conflict with sustainable growth of incumbent carriers. Although the media normally focuses on the market share of each airline, a more important factor for airlines is their actual growth. In other words, as long as the total pie grows, the importance of their market share is secondary. Even when their market share decreases, their total revenue can increase year-on-year, provided that the volume of the total market increases.

But regardless, the age of LCCs will come to Northeast Asia. Table 6.1 provides profiles of the current Northeast Asian LCCs.

Table 6.1 Profiles of Northeast Asian Low-Cost Carriers[15]

Country	Airlines (code)	Fleet Size	Service Starting Date	Key Share-Holder and/or Parent Airline	Main Hub
China	Spring Airline (9C)	41	18 July 2005	Shanghai Spring International Travel Service	Shanghai Hongqiao Airport
	Lucky Air (8L)	26	July 2004	Hainan Airlines Group (HNA)	Kunming Airport
	West Air (PN)	14	14 July 2010	Hainan Airlines Group (HNA)	Chonquig Airport
	Juneyao Airlines (HO)	34	June 2005	Juneyao Group	Shanghai Hongqiao Airport
Japan	Air Do	13	October 2012	ANA, DBJ (Development Bank of Japan)	Tokyo Haneda Airport
	Jetstar Japan (GK)	18	3 July 2012	Quanta, Japan Airlines ANA, First Eastern Investment Group and INCJ	Tokyo Haneda Airport
	Peach (MM)	13	March 2012		Osaka Kansai Airport
	Skymark Airlines (BC)	32	19 September 1998	Shinichi Nishikubo	Tokyo Haneda Airport
	Solaseed Air (6J)	13	July 2011	Miyakoh Holding	Tokyo Haneda Airport
	StarFlyer (7G)	10	16 March 2006	Star Flyer Inc.	Tokyo Haneda Airport
	Vanilla Air (JW)	6	20 December 2013	ANA	Tokyo Nanta Airport
Korea	Air Busan (BX)	12	October 2008	Asiana Airlines	Busan Gimhae Airport
	Eastar Jet (ZE)	8	7 January 2009	Privately owned, not listed	Jeju Airport
	Jeju Air (7C)	15	2 June 20906	Aekyung Group	Jeju Airport
	Jin Air (LJ)	11	July 2008	Korean Air	Jeju Airport
	t'way (TW)	7	September 2010	KDIC, YeaRimDang Publishing	Seoul Gimpo Airport

Close attention should be paid to China's Spring Airlines, the largest LCC in Northeast Asia. With 41 aircraft in 2015, the airline plans to have 100 by 2020.[16] In January 2015,

---

15 Xiaowen Fu & Tae Hoon Oum, *Dominant Carrier Performance and International Liberalisation: The Case of North East Asia*, Discussion Paper No 2015-03, International Transport Forum (Paris: OECD, 2015) at 24.

16 CAPA, "13 Chinese airlines could each have a fleet of over 100 aircraft by 2020" (26 May 2014), online: <http://centreforaviation.com/analysis/13-chinese-airlines-could-each-have-a-fleet-of-over-100-aircraft-by-2020-169778>.

Spring Airlines became the first LCC to be listed in China.[17] In addition, while the operating margins of Northeast Asia's LCCs have generally been in positive territory due to their increasing popularity in the region, Spring Airlines is significantly outperforming its competitors.[18]

Figure 6.4 Selected Northeast Asian LCCs' Operating Margin[19]

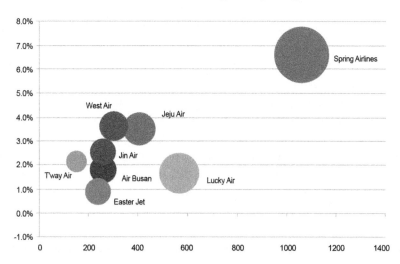

It is worth repeating that the rapid development of national LCCs helped change governments' mindset toward regional liberalization in ASEAN. The success of Malaysia-based AirAsia led to policy changes in Malaysia, which had been much less enthusiastic about regional liberalization.[20] As discussed in section 3.4.2 The Role of LCCs, the relationship between LCCs and liberalization is bi-directional. While the liberalization of market access has facilitated the growth of LCCs, LCCs themselves also promote policy reform and liberalization by pressing regulators to provide access to more international routes.

Furthermore, Spring Airlines is the first Northeast Asian LCC that has successfully managed to establish a business presence outside its own territory through JV arrangements with local investors (that is, Spring Airlines Japan).[21] As discussed in section 2.3.3 Benefits

---

17 CAPA, "Spring Airlines shares increase 44% on trading debut" (22 January 2015), online: <http://centreforaviation.com/news/spring-airlines-shares-increase-44-on-trading-debut-411707>.
18 CAPA, "Asia's LCCs: Airasia leads the pack" Airline Leader 25 (November 2014), online: <www.airlineleader.com/categories/finance/asias-lccs-airasia-leads-the-pack-194771>.
19 *Ibid.*
20 Peter Forsyth, John King & Cherry Lyn Rodolfo, "Open skies in ASEAN" (2006) 12 Journal of Air Transport Management 143 at 150.
21 See Chapter 4, section 4.2.3 Japan.

of the ASEAN SAM, these business models are commonplace in Southeast Asia, pioneered by the likes of AirAsia, Lion Air, Jetstar, Tigerair, and Vietjet.

One interesting hypothesis is about the possibility of Spring Airlines launching a joint venture in Korea. As noted, the Korean government has applied the effective control restriction strictly, rejecting JVs proposed by Tiger Airways (Singapore) and AirAsia (Malaysia).[22] But if Spring Airlines approaches Korea in the context of liberalization discourse, the Korean authorities might reach a different conclusion. For instance, if the Chinese government supports the idea of "Spring Airlines Korea" and promises to liberalize market access between China and Korea, Korea may have to reconsider its position on effective control restriction. As discussed in Chapter 4, the relevant government body can exercise wide discretion in interpreting effective control.

Lastly, airline alliances are becoming a powerful way to reform regulations. As noted, airline alliances with various degrees of density, geography, and membership are appearing in Northeast Asia. While the focus has been on the trans-Pacific market and the Europe-Asia market, Northeast Asian carriers may create more sophisticated kinds of alliances among themselves once they become familiar with advanced forms of alliances. Such new alliance between Northeast Asian airlines will be a tipping point in Northeast Asian open skies.

Despite the role of airlines as a regulation reformer, it must be recognized that it is ultimately public regulation that internalizes and formalizes these non-state actors' involvement in revising regulations from the bottom up. It is clear that liberalization without an institutional and legal framework is unstable. Liberalization led by airlines can complement, but not replace, liberalization implemented through the formal actions of states.

While airline-led liberalization is an important source of air transport liberalization, only state-led liberalization can guarantee stable and concrete changes. Hence, three forms of state-led liberalization—institutional framework, legal reforms and policy liberalization—are needed to make Northeast Asian open skies a reality.

6.3 ACTION PLANS FOR NORTHEAST ASIAN OPEN SKIES

6.3.1 Institutional Framework

Comparative studies of various models for regional liberalization make a convincing case for the importance of institutions. The EU, a regional group with strong institutions, was

---

22 "AirAsia Korea prospects fade as Seoul blocks launch" *ch-aviation* (18 May 2014), online: <www.ch-aviation.com/portal/news/28152-airasia-korea-prospects-fade-as-seoul-blocks-launch>.

able to achieve liberalized market access, relax ownership and control regulations, and make unified external policies. In contrast, the fact that ASEAN does not have strong institutions led to the starkly different outcomes of the EU Single Aviation Market and the ASEAN Single Aviation Market.

In order to make regional liberalization work, there should be either a central organization that coordinates and reconciles the member states' political will or, at the very least, an aviation cooperation group that can devise a master plan for aviation policy. Obviously, China, Japan, and Korea at present have neither a central organization nor an aviation cooperation group.

Historically, there has been little cooperation among China, Japan, and Korea. In terms of high-level cooperation, the ASEAN Plus Three (China, Japan, and Korea) Summit provided a unique opportunity for the leaders of the three countries to meet annually. The 1st Trilateral Summit was held in 1999 during the ASEAN Plus Three Summit. The trilateral meeting formally separated itself from the ASEAN Plus Three process and acquired its own identity in December 2008.[23]

At the 3rd trilateral summit in Jeju, Korea, in May 2010, the three countries adopted the Memorandum on the Establishment of the Trilateral Cooperation Secretariat and decided to set up an office in Korea by the end of 2011. After each of the three governments signed and ratified the Agreement on the Establishment of the Trilateral Cooperation Secretariat in 2010, the Trilateral Cooperation Secretariat (TCS) was officially inaugurated in Seoul in September 2011.[24]

Unfortunately, soon after the TCS was established, relations between China and Japan rapidly chilled mainly due to a territorial dispute between China and Japan over some uninhabited islands (Diaoyu in Chinese and Senkaku in Japanese). The subsequent political tensions kept the trilateral cooperation represented by the TCS from gaining momentum. Thus far, the role of the TCS is limited, and the scope of trilateral cooperation under the TCS remains uncertain.

Notwithstanding the fluctuating political tensions, it is undeniable that the three states regard each other as important economic partners and share the goal of promoting peace and prosperity in the region. These political tensions will not fundamentally reverse the movement towards cooperation. The three states should prepare for a cooling-off period and, in this regard, the role of the TCS should not be underestimated.

---

23 Joel Rathus, "China-Japan-Korea Trilateral Cooperation and the East Asian Community", *East Asia Forum* (15 June 2010), online: <www.eastasiaforum.org/2010/06/15/china-Japan-Korea-trilateral-cooperation-and-the-east-asian-community>.
24 See TCS, "Overview of TCS", online: <www.tcs-asia.org/dnb/user/userpage.php?lpage=1_1_overview>.

The TCS is a regional organization supported by all three governments that is based on a treaty, namely, the Agreement on the Establishment of the Trilateral Cooperation Secretariat.[25] Thus, it provides a legitimate platform for cooperation among the three states.

Under the Agreement on the Establishment on the Trilateral Cooperation Secretariat, the TCS's functions are, *inter alia*, to "explore and identify potential cooperative projects among the Parties, and report those projects to the relevant consultative mechanisms for adoption."[26] Furthermore, the TCS aims to serve in the future as a hub for trilateral cooperation across a broad spectrum of sectors.[27] Thus, as an initial stage, the TCS could discuss regional aviation cooperation given the cumulative impact that air transport has on trilateral cooperation. Moving forward, the TCS could provide an institutional framework for regional liberalization in Northeast Asia.

Another potential institutional platform is the China-Japan-Korea Ministerial Conference on Transport and Logistics, which has been held every two years since 2006.[28] Although its initial focus was maritime transport logistics, the scope of the conference has expanded to cover other modes of transportation including air transportation.

Since the three countries share the common goals of reducing the cost of logistics and enhancing product competitiveness so as to promote their respective economic development,[29] regional liberalization in the cargo market should receive relatively strong support. To make discussion more effective, the conference should take place more frequently (annually at least), and the agenda should cover not just cargo air transport but also passenger air transport.

It is worth recalling that the regular meetings of the ASEAN transport ministers gave birth to the concept of the ASEAN Single Aviation Market, and the Action Plan for ASEAN Air Transport Integration and Liberalization 2005-2015 (Action Plan for ASEAN) and the Roadmap for Integration of the Air Travel Sector (RIATS) were finally adopted at the 10th meeting of the ASEAN transport ministers in 2004.[30]

The Action Plan set the long-term goal of ASEAN regional liberalization, while the RIATS identified specific goals and target dates. These documents laid out the broad policies that led to the eventual adoption of the ASEAN multilateral agreements relating

---

25 See online: Ministry of Foreign Affairs of Japan <www.mofa.go.jp/region/asia-paci/jck/pdfs/jck_sec1012.pdf>.
26 *Agreement on the Establishment of the Trilateral Cooperation Secretariat Among the Governments of Japan, The People's Republic of China and The Republic of Korea*, Article. 3. 1(c).
27 See TCS, "Overview of TCS", online: <www.tcs-asia.org/dnb/user/userpage.php?lpage=1_2_1_overview>.
28 See TCS, "The 5th Trilateral Ministerial Conference on Transport and Logistics was held in Yokohama", online: <http://en.tcs-asia.org/dnb/board/view.php?board_name=2_1_news&view_id=245>.
29 See Northeast Asia Logistics Information Service Network (NEAL-NET), Press Release, "The 4th China-Japan-Korea Ministerial Conference on Transport and Logistics Held in Busan Korea" (19 July 2012), online: <www.nealnet.org/nealnet/web/webAction.do?action=NewsView&newsid=40288a49380db66d01389e8984d10a38>.
30 The ASEAN Secretariat, *ASEAN Documents Series 2004* (Jakarta: ASEAN Secretariat, 2005) at 221-226.

to aviation: namely, the 2009 Multilateral Agreement on Air Services (MAAS),[31] the 2009 Multilateral Agreement for Full Liberalization of Air Freight Services (MAFLAFS),[32] and the 2010 Multilateral Agreement for Full Liberalization of Passenger Air Services (MAFLPAS).[33] In essence, MAAS, MAFLAFS and MAFLPAS are the backbone of the ASEAN Single Aviation Market.

The lesson to be learned from ASEAN is that a robust framework and concrete timeline are necessary for Northeast Asian open skies. The fact that ASEAN used a concrete action plan to push ahead regional liberalization within an institutional framework was instrumental in achieving meaningful results. Needless to say, the action plan for Northeast Asian open skies can only be formulated by a legally binding international treaty, which is to say, an air services agreement of some form or other. In ASEAN regional liberalization, RIATS was successfully incorporated into the above-mentioned formal legal agreements for ASEAN member states to accept.

6.3.2   Legal Reforms

6.3.2.1   Overview

With regard to the format of the legal reform, either the bilateral approach or the trilateral approach is possible because there are only three parties involved. The bilateral approach puts a greater emphasis on bilateral air service agreements among the three countries. In other words, this entails establishing three bilateral open skies agreements between China and Korea, Korea and Japan, and Japan and China. The creation of a regional liberalization regime on a bilateral basis could lead to the formation of Northeast Asian open skies if each of the bilateral agreements were similarly broad and ambitious.

However, the bilateral approach lacks a systematic and coherent approach. If one bilateral agreement is less broad than the other two bilateral agreements, there would no longer be symmetry. Indeed, this is the current situation in Northeast Asia (that is, three separate and asymmetric bilateral air services agreements).

The trilateral approach involves a centralized regional approach. This would require a new air services agreement to which all three states are parties. The trilateral approach would be more effective than the bilateral approach for phasing in gradual changes.

---

31 *ASEAN Multilateral Agreement on Air Services*, done at Manila, Philippines, 20 May 2009, online: <www.asean.org/communities/asean-economic-community/item/asean-multilateral-agreement-on-air-services-manila-20-may-2009-2>.
32 *ASEAN Multilateral Agreement on the Full Liberalisation of Air Freight Services*, done at Manila, Philippines, 20 May 2009, online: <http://cil.nus.edu.sg/2009/2009-asean-multilateral-agreement-on-the-full-liberalisation-of-air-freight-services-signed-on-20-may-2009-in-manila-the-philippines-by-the-transport-ministers/>.
33 *ASEAN Multilateral Agreement on Full Liberalisation of Passenger Air Services*, done at Bandar Seri Begawan, Brunei Darussalam, 12 November 2010, online: <http://cil.nus.edu.sg/2010/2010-asean-multilateral-agreement-on-full-liberalisation-of-passenger-air-services/>.

In ASEAN, the 2009 Multilateral Agreement on Air Services (MAAS) provided a step-by-step approach by laying out several implementing protocols that aimed to ease the liberalization of market access in the region. In Northeast Asia, a trilateral agreement on air services (TAAS), as I will call it, could be considered. If adopted, this TAAS would lay out similar implementing protocols that aim to ease the liberalization of market access.

It is worth noting that the ASEAN model of agreements carries the risk of adopting the relevant agreements and then having to wait (often for a substantial amount of time) for a state to ratify them. For instance, although Protocol 5 on Unlimited Third and Fourth Freedom Traffic Rights between ASEAN Capital Cities (one of the six implementing protocols to MAAS) was adopted on 20 May 2009 in Manila, the Philippines (the hosting state for the signing of the agreement) only ratified on 10 February 2016. Indeed, there was a 7-year gap between Singapore, which ratified the protocol first, and the Philippines, which ratified it the most recently (see Table 6.2).

Table 6.2 Ratification Dates for the Protocol 5 of MAAS[34]

No	State	Date
1	Brunei Darussalam	30 March 2010
2	Cambodia	5 May 2011
3	Indonesia	5 June 2014
4	Lao PDR	17 March 2011
5	Malaysia	23 January 2010
6	Myanmar	1 July 2011
7	Philippines	10 February 2016
8	Singapore	3 July 2009
9	Thailand	13 October 2009
10	Vietnam	22 December 2009

Notably, the Trilateral Agreement on Air Services (TAAS) would involve less risk of delay arising from ratifications since there are only three member states, unlike ASEAN, which consists of ten states. However, all three of the states need to be firmly committed to the policy before they actually adopt the TAAS. In other words, the three states should adopt an agreement that each of them can and will ratify promptly. Otherwise, the TASS could also face a long delay by one member state.

Indeed, a state's policy decisions are the key at the initial stage. The ASEAN MAAS was based on the goals set out in the Action Plan for ASEAN Air Transport Integration

---

34 The ASEAN Secretariat, ASEAN Legal Instruments, Protocol 5 on Unlimited Third and Fourth Freedom Traffic Rights between ASEAN Capital Cities, online: <http://agreement.asean.org/agreement/detail/97.html>.

and Liberalization 2005–2015 and RIATS. Adopting the Action Plan and the RIATS was a policy decision by ASEAN member states based on their calculation of national interests. In other words, the ASEAN states, to greater and lesser degrees, believed that the ASEAN Single Aviation Market would make them all better off.

Thus, the roadmap for Northeast Asian open skies must instill the confidence that Northeast Asian open skies will make states (more specifically, their national carriers and their citizens) better off. While the benefits of Northeast Asian open skies are clear for Korea and Japan (the Chinese market will provide enormous business opportunities for their carriers), China is worried that Northeast Asian open skies will divert more of the direct China–US traffic through Korea or Japan, and vice versa. Indeed, it is no secret that Chinese suspicions about Japanese and Korean sixth freedom operations are the greatest impediment to Northeast Asian open skies.

Taking into consideration China's reasonable concerns, one option to consider would be giving preferential access to Chinese carriers. In this scenario, Chinese carriers would be allowed market access for a certain period before Korean and Japanese carriers could enjoy the same rights. (See the following sections for proposals to give Chinese airlines a head start on liberalization.)

An idealist might object to such preferential treatment based on the noble idea that "all states are equal." But in the real world, aero-political considerations must be acknowledged. That is to say, the Chinese market is much bigger than that of Korea and Japan. In addition, although the principle of equality under international law is firmly recognized regardless of a state's size, population, or political importance, this equality does not mean that all states are equal in power, wealth, and capability.[35]

Moreover, preferential relaxation of market access was used in the Canada-US open skies agreement of 1995 and, more recently, in the Memorandum of Understanding to the Air Services Agreement between China and Korea in 2006 with regard to the fifth freedom.[36] In addition, it is worth noting that preferential relaxation of market access was discussed at the 1st International Symposium on Liberalizing Air Transport in Northeast Asia in 2006, the first meeting at which the three states entered into negotiations about regional liberalization.[37]

Tae Hoon Oum, the keynote speaker at the symposium, held up the Canada-US open skies agreement of 1995 as a template for the preferential relaxation of market access and suggested negotiations focusing on sharing and distributing gains and losses for all parties

---

35 Christopher C. Joyner, *International Law in the 21st Century* (Lanham: Rowman & Littlefield, 2005) at 51.
36 See Chapter 3, section 3.3.3 Korea-China.
37 See Tae Hoon Oum, "Air Transport Network Developments and Challenges to East Asian Airlines and Policy Makers" (Presentation material presented to the 1st International Symposium on Liberalizing Air Transport in Northeast Asia, 9 June 2006) [unpublished].

in Northeast Asia.[38] He added that creating a "positive-sum game" (that is, mutually beneficial gains) is the key to Northeast Asian open skies.[39]

Although the annual trilateral symposiums ended in 2010 without producing solid results due to the disparities of the three countries' positions, it is important to recall that the symposium originally began as a forum for government authorities and academics from the three countries to meet together and engage in comprehensive and practical discussion.[40]

Above is the background of the following proposal for Northeast Asian open skies, which includes short-term (2020), mid-term (2025), and long term (2030) stages. During the development of this proposal, careful consideration was given to the following questions: what is needed; what the barriers are; what factors are changing, both internally and externally; what can be done; and what cannot be done.

Specifically, I suggest adopting the Trilateral Agreement on Air Services (TAAS), which consists of one mother treaty and four implementing protocols (see Table 6.3). The details of each protocol, including the timeline, are explained in the following sections.

Table 6.3 Implementing Protocols to the TAAS

Protocol	Scope
Protocol 1	On Unlimited Third and Fourth Freedom Traffic Rights between the three states – Passenger Services
Protocol 2	On Unlimited Third and Fourth Freedom Traffic Rights between the three states – Cargo Services
Protocol 3	On Unlimited Fifth Freedom Traffic Rights between and beyond the three states – Passenger Services
Protocol 4	On Unlimited Fifth Freedom Traffic Rights between and beyond the three states – Cargo Services

The TAAS should be the basic framework for trilateral air transport liberalization. However, the TAAS *per se* does not have to contain details about market access liberalization. Just as the ASEAN's MAAS consists of "[the] Agreement (MAAS), its Annexes and its Implementing Protocols and any amendments thereto"[41] and leaves all the crucial details to protocols,[42] the TAAS can have one symbolic article dealing with market access exchange

---

38   Ibid.
39   Ibid.
40   J.H. Park, *A Study on the Effects of Air Transport Liberalization on Air Transport Markets, Department of Logistics Management.* (PhD Thesis, University of Incheon, 2011) [unpublished].
41   *ASEAN Multilateral Agreement on Air Services*, done at Manila, Philippines, 20 May 2009, Article 1, paragraph 11., online: <http://cil.nus.edu.sg/rp/pdf/2009%20ASEAN%20Multilateral%20Agreement%20on%20Air%20Services-pdf.pdf>.
42   See *ibid.*

and leave all the crucial details to protocols. The real value of the TASS will be formalizing a trilateral agreement on air services.

Three important principles must be applied in the TAAS and the protocols. First, the TAAS and each implementing protocol must be legally separate and independent treaties. This means that states have to ratify the protocols separately while or after ratifying the original TAAS. This step-by-step scheme allows Northeast Asian governments and airlines to adopt regional liberalization gradually, similar to ASEAN's step-by-step approach. Second, the TAAS and each protocol will be effective only when all three states have ratified them. In other words, the TAAS must be a truly *trilateral* agreement rather than a supplement to existing bilateral air services agreements. Lastly, a related but separate principle is that the TAAS and the protocols must supersede the previous bilateral air services agreements.

6.3.2.2 Roadmap for Northeast Asian Open Skies by 2020

Protocol 1 to the TASS would introduce unlimited third and fourth freedoms for passenger air transport between all cities in the three states. At the same time, China would be allowed to opt out of three cities—most likely, Beijing, Shanghai, and Guangzhou. The basic goal, then, would be to liberalize all secondary Chinese cities, all Korean cities, and all Japanese cities.

Table 6.4   Protocol 1 to the TAAS

Protocol	Scope	Deadline
Protocol 1 to the TAAS	Unlimited third and fourth freedoms between all cities in the three states with three opt-out choices for China – Passenger Services	2020 (All three states should ratify by 2020)

This degree of liberalization is both necessary and feasible. The needs of Northeast Asian carriers and consumer demand both call for this change. There are also factors favoring the success of Protocol 1. First of all, China's airport capacity and airspace shortage problems will be much improved by 2020,[43] especially with the new airport in Beijing and reform of the government's airspace control.[44] Secondly, the visa application process will either be

---

43 See Guillaume Dupont, "China Airports Build: Too Many Too Fast?" *New Airport Insider* (14 January 2014), online: <http://dcdesigntech.com/new-airport-insider/china-airports-build-too-many-too-fast/> (noting that "[A]s part of the Chinese government 5-year plan, China is building many airports. A plan that includes the construction of 82 new civil airports and the expansion of 101 existing Chinese airports, totaling more than 230 airports by the end of 2015 with an estimated 80% of China's population living at less than 100 km of an airport.").

44 See "Chinese aviation's on-time rate dropped to 68% in 2014" *China Travel News* (9 March 2015), online: <www.chinatravelnews.com/article/print/89870>. (noting that "[T]he National Air Traffic Committee will launch a national low-altitude airspace control reform in 2015. CAAC will boost its efforts to set up air

substantially simplified or waived altogether for Chinese tourists, which will give another boost to Chinese tourists who want to visit Korea and Japan. Third, the competitiveness of Chinese airlines, which has been considered a major barrier to reaching any open skies agreement,[45] will have improved over this time period. Last but not least, Northeast Asian LCCs have significant potential to move the liberalization agenda forward.

Most LCCs in Northeast Asia will look to grow quickly. It has been observed that many Northeast Asian LCCs focus on domestic markets for a time but soon shift to neighboring markets.[46] The partner Northeast Asian states are obvious targets because of enormous demand, short flight times, and low operating cost. This, of course, requires more liberal air services agreements among the three states. At the very least, LCCs would want unlimited third and fourth freedoms even if there are some opt-outs at an initial stage of market access liberalization.

At the same time, it should be noted that China will need additional time to fully adapt to the increase of capacity. More importantly, the central pillar of China's international aviation policy, protecting the "Big Three" airlines, must be taken into consideration. Although the level of protectionism will have diminished somewhat by 2020, it will not have disappeared entirely. Thus, recognition should be given to the geographical market allocation of China's three primary hubs—Beijing to Air China, Shanghai to China Eastern, and Guangzhou to China Southern—in order to soften the three airlines' resistance to Protocol 1. In brief, Protocol 1 to the TAAS should provide China with three opt-out choices.

However, these opt-outs should not continue indefinitely. For a more balanced approach, there should be a mandatory link between Protocol 1 and Protocol 3 on unlimited fifth freedom operations. That is, when Protocol 3 to the TAAS takes effect, the opt-outs in Protocol 1 should expire. (For more discussion, see the next section on Protocol 3.)

A critic may object that China could reject Protocol 1 because its unlimited third and fourth freedoms, even excluding the three major Chinese cities, would effectively create unlimited sixth freedom benefits for Korean and Japanese carriers in the China–US market. However, it is worth repeating that the bilateral air services agreement between China and Japan already allows unlimited third and fourth freedom flights except to Beijing, Shanghai, and Tokyo (thus, Guangzhou is included). Although China's concern about the sixth freedom is understandable, the high demand for traffic within Northeast Asia (thus, third

---

traffic institutions, consolidate industry resources, explore large-scale air traffic control models, develop civil aviation development for the 13th Five-Year Plan and launch experimental integrated aviation reform projects in the industry.").

45   Bin Li, "Open China's Skies or Not? – From the Perspective of a Chinese Scholar" (2010) 9 Issues in Aviation Law and Policy. 209 at 212.
46   Fu & Oum, *supra* note 15 at 24.

and fourth freedom traffic) must be fully recognized. In addition, China may take advantage of unlimited sixth freedom opportunities in the context of the Northeast Asia-Europe market. (See section 5.5.2 Impact on Chinese Aviation Policy.)

Turning to Protocol 2 to the TAAS, it is important to note that there will be stronger momentum for the cargo side than the passenger side. In many regional models, cargo service has been easier to liberalize than passenger service. Indeed, cargo air transport is less complex than passenger air transport, with nationalism playing a less significant role, and it provides speedy and efficient access to supply chains that reduce logistical costs. In short, it helps exports.

Protocol 2 to the TAAS would introduce unlimited third and fourth freedoms for cargo air transport between all cities in the three states. Protocol 2 is likely to be ratified by the three states earlier than Protocol 1. While passenger air services have been closely associated with traditional aero-political calculations, cargo air services are less affected by these calculations. Accordingly, the opt-out choices do not need to be incorporated in Protocol 2.

Table 6.5   Protocol 2 to the TAAS

Protocol	Scope	Deadline
Protocol 2 to the TAAS	Unlimited third and fourth freedom flights – Cargo Services	2020 (All three states should ratify by 2020)

The fact that there is wide discussion of bilateral FTAs and a trilateral FTA among China, Japan, and Korea (see section 3.4.3 Developing a China-Japan–Korea Free Trade Agreement) cannot be underestimated. In the process of discussing Northeast Asian open skies, Chinese commentators have suggested a link between FTAs and air services agreements for cargo air transport, e.g. "a liberalized bilateral ASA may be signed after the conclusion of the bilateral FTA"[47] and "there is a need for the integration of air transportation after the economic integration comes to a high degree of the free trade area."[48]

All in all, it is likely that efforts to liberalize the cargo sector in Northeast Asia will bear fruit in the near future, leading to the successful implementation of Protocol 2 to the TAAS.

---

47   Zheng Xingwu, "China's Approaches to Aviation Market Liberalization in Northeast Asia: An Academic Viewpoint" in Yeon Myung Kim and Sungwon Lee, eds., *Negotiating Strategies for Creating a Liberalized Air Transport Bloc in Northeast Asia* (Honolulu, HI; The Korea Transport Institute & East-West Center, 2009) 295 at 343.

48   Fang Liu, "Comments in Part III: Negotiating Strategies for Coping with the Key Barriers to Liberalization of Northeast Asian Aviation Markets" in Yeon Myung Kim and Sungwon Lee, eds., *Negotiating Strategies for Creating a Liberalized Air Transport Bloc in Northeast Asia* (Honolulu, HI; The Korea Transport Institute & East-West Center, 2009) 423 at 425.

6.3.2.3 Roadmap for Northeast Asian Open Skies by 2025

Protocol 3 of the TAAS would provide unlimited fifth freedom traffic rights for passenger air transport between and beyond the three states. However, Chinese carriers would enjoy a head start on this liberalization. More specifically, designated Chinese airlines would be entitled to operate unlimited fifth freedom traffic rights on passenger service through Korean points and Japanese points. Designated Korean airlines and Japanese airlines, however, would have to wait five years after Chinese carriers commence operations. Then, they could enjoy the same unlimited fifth freedom traffic rights through Chinese points.

The fifth freedom traffic rights described above entail not only *internal* fifth freedom flights (that is, operations that cover only Chinese, Korean, and Japanese cities without touching any external points, such as a Beijing-Seoul-Tokyo route by a Chinese airline) but also *external* fifth freedom flights (that is, operations involving points external to the three states, such as a Beijing-Seoul-LA route by a Chinese airline).[49] Of course, the external fifth freedom flights must be allowed by the air services agreements with the relevant third countries. In other words, the above Beijing-Seoul-LA route by a Chinese airline would be permitted by Protocol 3 to the TAAS, but the China–US air services agreement would need to separately permit traffic rights for the Chinese carrier between Seoul and LA.

Table 6.6 Protocol 3 to the TAAS

Protocol	Scope		Deadline
	Internal 5th freedom	External 5th freedom	
Protocol 3 to the TAAS	Unlimited fifth freedoms for Chinese carriers via Korea and Japan (for five years) – Passenger Services	Unlimited fifth freedoms for Chinese carriers via Korea and Japan for external points outside the three countries (for five years) – Passenger Services	2025 (All three states should ratify by 2025)
	Korean airlines and Japanese airlines could only enjoy the same unlimited fifth freedom traffic rights through Chinese points five years after the use of fifth freedom traffic rights by Chinese airlines		

This change would likely be fiercely resisted by Korean and Japanese legacy carriers flying to North America. Unlimited fifth freedom would mean that Chinese carriers could take Korean passengers from Seoul to Los Angeles (on a flight originating and terminating in Beijing) or take Japanese passengers from Tokyo to New York (on a flight originating and terminating in Shanghai) without capacity restrictions. Korean and Japanese LCCs would also be affected by Chinese fifth freedom operations between the Korea and Japan market

---

49 For a detailed explanation of internal and external fifth freedoms, see Alan Khee-Jin Tan "The 2010 ASEAN – China Air Transport Agreement: Much Ado over Fifth Freedom Rights?" (2014) 14 Issues in Aviation Law and Policy. 19 at 21-30.

(*e.g.* a Guangzhou – Busan – Osaka operation). It would effectively mean that Chinese carriers could operate unlimited fifth freedom flights between Seoul and Tokyo.

Despite the expected resistance, preferential access for Chinese carriers is necessary to overcome the Chinese aero-political imbalance connected with Northeast Asian open skies. The potential of Northeast Asian open skies will eventually convince the parties concerned of the need for preferential access.

However, China's opt-out of three cities—most likely, Beijing, Shanghai, and Guangzhou—under Protocol 1 should expire with the implementation of Protocol 3. Otherwise, the whole trilateral liberalization picture would be substantially imbalanced. With the opt-outs, Chinese carriers could fly Seoul-Tokyo routes without capacity limits on their fifth freedom market while Korean carriers and Japanese carriers would still face capacity limits on their third and fourth freedom markets (*e.g.* Seoul-Beijing and Seoul-Shanghai (for Korean carriers); Tokyo-Beijing and Tokyo-Shanghai (for Japanese carriers)).

Hence, it is necessary that the opt-out choices under Protocol 1 should be automatically lifted when Protocol 3 takes effect (that is, when it is ratified by the three states). In brief, the second stage of liberalization (with a deadline of 2025) would provide unlimited third and fourth freedoms (with no exceptions) on passenger services while giving Chinese carriers preferential relaxation of the fifth freedom market access.

Turning to the cargo side, Protocol 4 to the TAAS would provide unlimited fifth freedom traffic rights on cargo services between and beyond the three states.

Table 6.7   Protocol 4 to the TAAS

Protocol	Scope	Deadline
Protocol 4 to the TAAS	Unlimited fifth freedoms – Cargo Services	2025 (All three states should ratify by 2025)

Protocol 4 to the TAAS could be implemented without significant difficulties. By 2025, bilateral FTAs and a trilateral FTA among China, Japan, and Korea will likely be in place, creating the need for liberalized air services agreements for cargo air transport. In essence, Protocol 4 will provide more efficient access to global and regional supply chains that can reduce logistical costs.

It is also worth noting that there has been an attempt to develop a new multilateral agreement specifically for air cargo services. ICAO suggested developing a specific international agreement to facilitate further liberalization of all cargo services at the ICAO Sixth Worldwide Air Transport Conference in 2013,[50] and the Conference made the following official recommendation:

---

50   ICAO Secretariat, *Liberalization of Air Cargo Services*, ICAO Doc ATConf/6-WP/14 (13 December 2012) at 2 para 2.5, online: <www.icao.int/Meetings/atconf6/Documents/WorkingPapers/ATConf6-wp014_en.pdf>,

ICAO should take the lead in the development of a specific international agreement to facilitate further liberalization of air cargo services, taking into account past experiences and achievements, views of States on existing arrangements, and suggestions made during the Conference.[51]

During the discussion at the Conference, the International Air Cargo Association (TIACA) argued that the fifth freedom is key to viable route structures for a cargo airline's network since very few products fly round trip (the third and fourth freedoms) the way passengers do.[52] Indeed, air cargo traffic is inherently one-way, unlike passenger traffic, which tends to involve round trips (bi-directional).[53]

If the new multilateral all-cargo agreement involving unlimited third, fourth, and fifth freedom operations is adopted and ratified by the three Northeast Asian states over the next ten years by 2025, there is no reason not to ratify Protocol 4 to the TAAS.

6.3.2.4 Roadmap for Northeast Asian Open Skies by 2030

The third stage of liberalization (with a deadline of 2030) would complete the transition to Northeast Asian open skies by allowing unlimited third, fourth, and fifth freedoms for passenger and cargo services on an equal and unconditional basis. By this stage, five years after 2025, when Chinese airlines began to enjoy fifth freedom traffic rights, Korean and Japanese airlines could enjoy the same unlimited fifth freedom traffic rights through Chinese points. This means the TAAS and all four protocols would be implemented by 2030.

Table 6.8   Roadmap for Northeast Asian Open Skies by 2030

Scope	Deadline
Unlimited third, fourth and fifth freedom flights – Passenger and Cargo Services	2030

This optimistic outlook is supported by the following factors. First, it is likely that China and the US will have adopted an open skies agreement by 2030. For instance, Mr. Edward

---

(noting that 78% of responding states (48 of 61) generally supported the idea of the ICAO leadership developing the agreement in a recent survey of ICAO member states).

51   ICAO, *the Report on Agenda Item 2.1*(summary report of the Air Transport Conference), ICAO Doc ATConf/6-WP/104 (22 March 2013) at para 2.1.8.C.

52   ICAO, *Needed: Rapid Liberalization of Air Cargo Services Through a New Multilateral Approach*, ICAO Doc ATConf/6-WP/96 (7 March 2013) (Presented by The International Air Cargo Association (TIACA)) at 3 para 3.1., online: <www.icao.int/Meetings/atconf6/Documents/WorkingPapers/ATConf.6.WP.96.2.en.pdf>.

53   ICAO, *Liberalization of Air Cargo Services*, ATConf/6-WP/14 (13 December 2012) (Presented by ICAO Secretariat) at 2 para 1.3, online: <www.icao.int/Meetings/atconf6/Documents/WorkingPapers/ATConf6-wp014_en.pdf>.

Bastian, president of Delta Airlines, once predicted that the US and China would reach a deal on open skies by 2023.[54] Although Bastian's view can be interpreted as a rather "hopeful" view since US carriers like Delta have wanted an open skies agreement with China for many years, China will definitely be more flexible in its negotiations with the US for an open skies agreement over the next fifteen years.

If China and the US adopt an open skies agreement, Chinese and US carriers will operate many direct flights between China and the US. As a consequence, China's concerns about losing passengers transferring at Seoul or Tokyo will be significantly reduced.

Another important factor is that China's domestic market, which is currently only half the size of the US domestic market, will overtake the US domestic market by 2030.[55] In other words, China will become the world's largest passenger market by 2030. This growth will subsequently lead Chinese airlines to improve their management ability and service quality. Thus, by 2030, Chinese airlines will have become so competitive that "protecting the major carriers at this stage [will be] akin to 'treating Giants as Babies.'"[56]

One thought-provoking possibility is that Chinese carriers may eventually want more open skies just as Gulf carriers do. CAPA hinted at the potential of sixth freedom traffic for Chinese carriers as follows:

> In addition to their home market, Chinese carriers have been growing sixth freedom traffic from China to other parts of Asia, a far more populous catchment area than the US carriers can target beyond the US. Air China even looks at US-China-India traffic flows, and with time Chinese carriers will be much stronger sixth freedom players.[57]

Returning to Northeast Asian open skies, since we have already considered the question of what *can* be done, we should also consider the question of what *cannot* be done. Indeed, it is premature to discuss liberalizing market access beyond the fifth freedom in the context of Northeast Asian open skies. Liberalization of the seventh, eighth, and ninth freedoms (much more liberalized freedoms) would be hard to predict at this stage. Accordingly, a genuine single aviation market in Northeast Asia can only be imagined in the distant future.

---

54 See Jeffrey Ng, "Delta Shifts Focus From Japan as Trans-Pacific Hub" *The Wall Street Journal* (10 February 2014), online: <www.wsj.com/articles/SB10001424052702303874504579375670306517530>.
55 See "China's Power Change and Airline Impacts" *Airline Leader* 15 (October 2012) 28 at 30; See also "Is it time for China-US Open Skies?" *Global Travel Industry News* (9 April 2015), online: <www.eturbonews.com/57422/it-time-china-us-open-skies>.
56 Fu & Oum, *supra* note 15 at 29.
57 CAPA "Chinese airlines overtake US carriers across the Pacific. The big dilemma: US-China open skies?" (4 May 2015), online<https://centreforaviation.com/analysis/chinese-airlines-overtake-us-carriers-across-the-pacific-time-for-us-china-open-skies-222454>.

Neither will legal reform of ownership and control restrictions be feasible for the foreseeable future. Although the community carrier concept, as found in other single aviation markets, can be taken into consideration, any proposal that requires domestic legislative changes would face severe difficulties. Nevertheless, it is worth considering the possibility of a Northeast Asian community carrier.

The ASEAN model of the community carrier concept[58] allows majority ownership to be spread out among community interests as long as effective regulatory control remains with the country in which the airline is based. The success of Northeast Asian community carriers would ideally take the form of new regional LCCs owned by nationals of the three countries. For instance, the ownership of a hypothetical LCC that might be called Air Northeast Asia could consist of a 33 percent Chinese stake, a 33 percent Japanese stake, and a 34 percent Korean stake.

The success of Northeast Asian community carriers could contribute significantly to Northeast Asian open skies. However, the concept of Northeast Asian community carrier is complicated by domestic legislation about ownership restriction that requires nationals to hold a majority share in airlines. Thus, policy liberalization, rather than legal reforms, would be a more realistic way of relaxing ownership and control restrictions.

6.3.3 Policy Liberalization

Throughout this research, the importance of policy liberalization has been emphasized. Although this research principally deals with the architecture of international treaties and domestic laws with respect to economic air transport in Northeast Asia, there are considerable policy aspects that affect the law.

To be sure, the term "policy" is used in diverse disciplines with significantly or subtly different meanings. While surveying various legal theories about policy, Mauro Zamboni concluded that "the vast majority of contemporary legal scholars and practitioners tend to conceive of policies in a similar way: political standards that can penetrate and have a (direct and indirect) relevancy for the making and applying of legal categories and concepts."[59] In short, policy affects legal actors both when they are making laws and when they are applying them.[60] The application of a law is the use of that law in a particular situation.

In the context of Northeast Asian open skies, the application of ownership restrictions is a simple process since the relevant law is mathematical (*e.g.* no more than 50 percent

---

58 See Chapter 2, section 2.3.2.2 Ownership and Control for the explanation about Article 3(2)(a)(ii) of MAAS.
59 Mauro Zamboni, *The Policy of Law – A Legal Theoretical Framework* (Oxford: Hart Publishing, 2007) at 117.
60 *Ibid.* at 119.

foreign ownership). Hence, liberalizing ownership restrictions entails legislative reform that either entirely removes the limit on foreign ownership or increases that limit by reducing the minimum share that must be owned by nationals. Numerical restrictions on foreign ownership can be replaced by the "principal place of business" formula, an approach that has been endorsed by the ICAO and adopted by some more liberal states (*e.g.*, Chile and Singapore).

However, legislative reform of ownership restrictions is and will be a difficult task in the vast majority of states, including those in Northeast Asia. This inertia is largely due to economic protectionism and partly due to outdated security concerns. Even relatively small-scale changes often face major hurdles.

A classic example of this difficulty is the impasse in the second-stage open skies agreement between the EU and US. The EU and US reached a second-stage open skies agreement in March 2010 that allows further liberalization of airline ownership and control subject to legislative changes in the US.[61] That is, when the US changes its legislation to allow EU investors majority ownership of US airlines by increasing the limit on foreign ownership beyond the current level of 25 percent of voting equity, the EU will reciprocally allow US investors to have majority ownership in EU airlines.[62] However, though this reform has been in the hands of US Congress for the past five years,[63] it has yet to take any action.

Although China and Korea have relaxed foreign ownership restrictions in the past (China and Korea have increased the cap on foreign investment from 35 percent to 49 percent in 2002[64] and from 20 percent to 49 percent in 1998,[65] respectively), it is highly unlikely that they will reform the 51/49 ownership structure (that is, majority ownership by nationals) in the foreseeable future. As discussed in section 4.1.3 External (Air Services Agreement) Restrictions, any change in the 51/49 structure could affect the rights of all airlines from all three states to fly to destinations outside those three states.

---

61 See European Union Press Release, "FAQs on the Second Stage EU-US "Open Skies" Agreement and Existing First Stage Air Services Agreement" (March 25, 2010), online: <http://europa.eu/rapid/press-release_MEMO-10-103_en.htm?locale=en>.

62 See European Union Press Release "Breakthrough in EU–US second-stage Open Skies negotiations: Vice-President Kallas welcomes draft agreement" (March 25, 2010), online: <http://europa.eu/rapid/press-release_IP-10-371_en.htm?locale=en>.

63 See *Protocol To Amend the Air Transport Agreement Between the United States of America and the European Community and Its Member States*, signed on 25 and 30 April 2007, Article 6 (Art 21(3) of the original Agreement), online: <www.state.gov/documents/organization/143930.pdf>.

64 Alan Williams, *Contemporary Issues Shaping China's Civil Aviation Policy: Balancing International with Domestic Priorities* (Burlington, VT: Ashgate, 2009) at 85.

65 Chia-Jui Hsu & Yu-Chun Chang, "The Influences of Airline Ownership Rules on Aviation Policies and Carriers' Strategies" (2005) 5 Proceedings of the Eastern Asia Society for Transportation Studies 557 at 558, online: <www.easts.info/on-line/proceedings_05/557.pdf>.

In contrast with the application of ownership restrictions, the application of control restrictions makes space for policy, which plays a key role in the application of the law. A policy, to borrow the words of Roy Brooks, is "a community's values, culture or expectations."[66] Thus, a nation's values, culture, and expectations can influence the application of control restrictions, even if they have not been solidified into new laws. In other words, liberalizing control restrictions does not necessarily require legal reform. Even without legal reform, policy liberalization can effectively contribute to Northeast Asian open skies.

There are indications of policy liberalization in Northeast Asia. Granting the application of China's Spring Airlines Japan was a telltale sign that control restrictions are being relaxed in the region. Down the road, we may see new joint venture airlines, which could conceivably include "Spring Airlines Korea" (from China), "Jin Air Japan" (from Korea), and "Vanilla Air China" (from Japan). In time, AirAsia-type pan-regional airlines with subsidiaries in other states could emerge, the first being Spring Airlines. As noted, this business model is widely used in Southeast Asia. More Northeast Asian airlines will pursue the benefits of integrated operations.

The joint ventures between Northeast Asian airlines and investors in other Northeast Asian countries will show whether and to what extent airline-led liberalization and national policy-led liberalization will succeed in Northeast Asia. If the liberalization efforts turn out to be successful, we may see a pan-Northeast Asian carrier in the near future.

This *de facto* liberalization can come to Northeast Asia if governments adopt more liberal policies. In sum, ownership and control restrictions, the main hurdle for Northeast Asian open skies along with restrictions on market access, should be relaxed by policy liberalization.

6.4 Conclusion

Liberalization has become an unassailable doctrine in international air transport over the past two decades. However, international air transport is still beset by two major legal impediments: market access and ownership and control restrictions. Amid these legal restrictions, airlines of the past carried on their business within the exact scope that governments explicitly permitted. Such airlines were simple entities that governments tightly regulated and strictly controlled.

Because of the nationalism that is deeply rooted in airlines, the relationship between governments and national airlines was a special one. This close bond was strengthened by the fact that airlines tended to be state-owned and that there were few national airlines, and sometimes only one. But as the global airline industry was privatized and deregulated

---

66   Roy L. Brooks. "The Use of Policy in Judicial Reasoning" (2002) 13 Stan. L. & Pol'y Rev. 33 at 36.

in the 1980s and 1990s, the industry became more competitive. In the 2000s, competition increased between full-service carriers, while new air carriers—most of them LCCs—entered a market that had previously been restricted to a small number of players. Today's airlines strive to survive in a much more competitive market.

Northeast Asia, which once was an extremely protective market, is slowly becoming liberalized. The increased competition resulting from this liberalization has made Northeast Asian airlines more competitive. Moreover, the number of airlines in Northeast Asia has increased significantly, mainly because of LCCs. In fact, the most significant development in the post-liberalization period has been the emergence and growth of LCCs in many parts of the world, and Northeast Asia was no exception.

In this era of greater competition, Northeast Asian airlines are no longer (and should not be) the passive subjects of government regulation. They are (and should be) active regulation reformers. Indeed, change is already in the air. With their strong lobbying power, innovative business models, and airline alliances, airlines are actively promoting liberalization in Northeast Asia. In this sense, airlines have already begun the push for Northeast Asian open skies.

Although airline-led liberalization is fundamentally important, only the actions of states can guarantee stable and concrete changes. The most important prerequisite is for the three states to recognize that Northeast Asian open skies are already on the way. Along with this recognition, the states should focus on what they can do to benefit their airlines and consumers. In this regard, the three pivots of state-led liberalization—institutional framework, legal reforms, and policy liberalization—can make Northeast Asian open skies a reality.

A robust institutional framework is necessary for the success of Northeast Asian open skies. The Trilateral Cooperation Secretariat (TCS) is an ideal platform for the initial discussion. Alternatively, the China-Japan-Korea Ministerial Conference on Transport and Logistics could provide a framework for regional liberalization in Northeast Asia. Currently, neither is an adequately robust institution, but both of these frameworks have great potential for building capacity.

Legal reforms are the key to Northeast Asian open skies. The proposal offered in this chapter for short-term (2020), mid-term (2025), and long term (2030) stages of liberalization by the TAAS and its implementing protocols offer a feasible target. Taking into account aero-political considerations and changes in direct and indirect market access elements, the goals of this proposal are modest and realistic, incorporating aero-political concessions such as according China the right to exclude its three largest cities.

Policy liberalization has already started through the mitigation of control restrictions in Northeast Asia. It must continue. Airline-led liberalization can flourish as states support them through policy liberalization. Equally importantly, policy liberalization lays the groundwork for governmental legal reforms.

This research ends with the key messages I have sought to deliver throughout. Change has begun, liberalization is inevitable, and progress is achievable. Airlines have already started moving toward Northeast Asian open skies; now states need to make this goal a reality. (end)

Bibliography

A Treaties and Other International Agreements

Agreement between the Government of the United Kingdom of Great Britain and Northern Ireland and the Government of the United States of America concerning Air Services, done at Bermuda on 23 July 1977

Agreement between the Government of the United States of America and the Government of the United Kingdom of Great Britain and Northern Ireland, signed at Bermuda on 11 February 1946

Agreement for the Liberalization of Air Transport between the Arab States in Damascus, Syria in 2004

Agreement on Sub-regional Air Services (Fortaleza Agreement) of the Southern Common Market (MERCOSUR) in 1996

Agreement on the Establishment of the Trilateral Cooperation Secretariat Among the Governments of Japan, The People's Republic of China and The Republic of Korea in 2010

Air Service Agreement between the Government of the United States of America and the Government of the United Kingdom of Great Britain and Northern Ireland, signed at Bermuda on 11 February 1946

Air Transport Agreement between the European Communities and Its Member States,, and the United States of America, done at Brussels and Washington, D.C., 25 and 30 April 2007

Air Transport Agreement between the Governments of the Member States of the Association of Southeast Asian Nations and the Government of the People's Republic of China on 12 November 2010

Air Transport Agreement of the Association of Caribbean States in 2004

ANNEX on Air Transport Services of Annex 1B General Agreement on Trade in Services

ASEAN Multilateral Agreement on Air Services, done at Manila, Philippines on 20 May 2009

ASEAN Multilateral Agreement on Full Liberalisation of Passenger Air Services, done at Bandar Seri Begawan, Brunei Darussalam on 12 November 2010

ASEAN Multilateral Agreement on the Full Liberalisation of Air Freight Services, done at Manila, Philippines on 20 May 2009;

Australia-New Zealand Single Aviation Market Arrangements, signed in Canberra, on 19 September 1996

Convention for the Suppression of Unlawful Acts against the Safety of Civil Aviation signed at Montreal on 23 September 1971

Convention for the Suppression of Unlawful Seizure of Aircraft signed at the Hague on 16 December 1970

Convention for the Unification of Certain Rules for International Carriage by Air done at Montreal on 28 May 1999

Convention for the Unification of Certain Rules Relating to International Carriage by Air Signed at Warsaw on 12 October 1929

Convention on Compensation for Damage Caused by Aircraft to Third Parties on 2 May 2009

Convention on Compensation for Damage to Third Parties, Resulting from Acts of Unlawful Interference Involving Aircraft Done at Montreal on 2 May 2009

Convention on Damage Caused by Foreign Aircraft to Third Parties on the Surface singed at Rome on 7 October 1952

Convention on International Civil Aviation signed at Chicago on 7 December 1944

Convention on Offences and Certain Other Acts Committed on Board Aircraft singed at Tokyo on 14 September 1963

Convention on the Marking of Plastic Explosives for the Purpose of Detection done at Montreal on 1 March 1991

Decision on Integration of Air Transport of the Andean Community in 1991

Decision Relating to the Implementation of the Yamoussoukro Declaration Concerning the Liberalisation of Access to Air Transport Markets in Africa, done in Yamoussoukro on 14 November 1999

General Agreement on Trade in Services on 15 April 1994

International Air Services Transit Agreement, signed at Chicago on 7 December 1944

International Air Transport Agreement, signed at Chicago on 7 December 1944

MAAS Protocol 1 on Unlimited Third and Fourth Freedom Traffic Rights within the ASEAN Sub-Region, done at Manila, Philippines, on 20 May 2009

MAAS Protocol 2 on Unlimited Fifth Freedom Traffic Rights within the ASEAN Sub-Region, done at Manila, Philippines, on 20 May 2009

MAAS Protocol 3 on Unlimited Third and Fourth Freedom Traffic Rights between the ASEAN Sub-Regions, done at Manila, Philippines, on 20 May 2009

MAAS Protocol 4 on Unlimited Fifth Freedom Traffic Rights between the ASEAN Sub-Regions, done at Manila, Philippines, on 20 May 2009

MAAS Protocol 5 on Unlimited Third and Fourth Freedom Traffic Rights between ASEAN Capital Cities, done at Manila, Philippines, on 20 May 2009

MAAS Protocol 6 on Unlimited Fifth Freedom Traffic Rights between ASEAN Capital Cities, done at Manila, Philippines, on 20 May 2009

MAFLAFS Protocol 1 on Unlimited Third, Fourth and Fifth Freedom Traffic Rights Among Designated Points in ASEAN, done at Manila, Philippines, on 20 May 2009

MAFLAFS Protocol 2 on Unlimited Third, Fourth and Fifth Freedom Traffic Rights Among All Points with International Airports in ASEAN, done at Manila, Philippines, on 20 May 2009

MAFLPAS Protocol 1 on Unlimited Third and Fourth Freedom Traffic Rights between Any Points in Contracting Parties, done at Bandar Seri Begawan, Brunei Darussalam, on 12 November 2010

MAFLPAS Protocol 2 on Unlimited Fifth Freedom Traffic Rights between Any Points in Contracting Parties, done at Bandar Seri Begawan, Brunei Darussalam, on 12 November 2010

Memorandum of Understanding on Open Skies between Australia and New Zealand, signed at Melbourne, on 20 November 2000

Memorandum of Understanding to the Air Services Agreement between China and Korea in 2006

Multilateral Open Skies Agreement for Member States of the Latin American Civil Aviation Commission (LACAC Agreement) at Punta Cana, Dominican Republic in 2010

Pacific Islands Air Services Agreement, done at Auckland on 16 May 2003

Protocol for the Suppression of Unlawful Acts of Violence at Airports Serving International Civil Aviation, Supplementary to the Convention for the Suppression of Unlawful Acts against the Safety of Civil Aviation done at Montreal on 23 September 1971 Singed at Montreal on 24 February 1988

Protocol to Amend the Air Transport Agreement between the United States of America and the European Community and Its Member States, signed on April 25 and 30, 2007, done on 25 March 2010

Protocol to Amend the Convention for the Unification of Certain Rules Relating to International Carriage by Air (Warsaw Convention) at the Hague on 28 September 1955

Protocol to Amend the Convention on Damage Caused by Foreign Aircraft to Third Parties on the Surface signed at Rome on 7 October 1952 Singed at Montreal on 23 September 1978

Protocol to the Multilateral Agreement on the Liberalization of International Air Transportation, done at Washington D.C. on 1 May 2001

Statement of Policy Principles regarding the Implementation of Bilateral Air Services Agreements, Done at Montebello, Québec, Canada on 16 November 2009

Treaty Establishing the European Economic Community, done at Rome on 25 March 1957

Treaty of Lisbon Amending the Treaty on European Union and the Treaty Establishing the European Community, signed at Lisbon on 13 December 2007

B   LEGISLATION

49 U.S.C. Subtitle VII – Aviation Programs

China, Antimonopoly Act of the People's Republic (2007)

China, Regulation of the People's Republic of China on the Nationality Registration of Civil Aircraft (State Council Order No. 232) (1997)

China, Regulation on Foreign Investment in the Civil Aviation Industry (CAAC Order No. 110) (2002)

EC, Council Regulation (EC) No 549/2004 of the European Parliament and of the Council of 10 March 2004 laying down the framework for the creation of the single European sky (the framework Regulation) [2004]

EC, Council Regulation (EC) No. 550/2004 on the provision of air navigation services for the Single European Sky [2004]

EC, Council Regulation (EC) No. 551/2004 on the organisation and use of the airspace in the Single European Sky [2004]

EC, Council Regulation (EC) No. 552/2004 on the interoperability of the European Air Traffic Management network [2004]

EC, Council Regulation (EEC) No 4064/89 of 21 December 1989 on the control of concentrations between undertakings (now, Council Regulation (EC) No 139/2004 of 20 January 2004 on the control of concentrations between undertakings) [2004]

EC, Council Regulation 2342/90 on fares for scheduled air services [1990]

EC, Council Regulation 2343/90 on access for air carriers to scheduled intra-Community air service routes and on the sharing of passenger capacity between air carriers on scheduled air services between Member States [1990]

EC, Council Regulation 2344/90 amending Regulation 3976/87 on the application of Article 85(3) of the Treaty to certain categories of agreements and concerted practices in the air transport sector [1990]

EC, Council Regulation 2407/92 on licensing of air carriers [1992]

EC, Council Regulation 2408/92 on access for Community air carriers to intra-Community air routes [1992]

EC, Council Regulation 2409/92 on fares and rates for air services [1992]

EC, Council Regulation 2410/92 amending Council Regulation 3875/87 laying down the procedure for the application of the rules on competition to undertakings in the air transport sector [1992];

EC, Council Regulation 2411/92 amending Council Regulation 3976/87 on the application of Article 85(3) of the Treaty to certain categories of agreements and concerted practices in the air transport sector [1992]

EC, Council Regulation 3975/87 laying down the procedure for the application of the rules on competition to undertakings in the air transport sector [1987]

EC, Council Regulation 3976/87 on the application of Article 85(3) of the EC Treaty to certain categories of agreements and concerted practices in the air transport sector [1987]

EC, Council Regulation 87/602 on the sharing of passenger capacity between air carriers on scheduled air services between Member States and on access for air carriers to scheduled air service routes between Member States [1987]

Japan, Act Concerning Prohibition of Private Monopoly and Maintenance of Fair Trade (1947)

Japan, Civil Aeronautics Act (1952)

Japan, Foreign Exchange and Foreign Trade Act (1949)

Korea, Aviation Act (1961)

Korea, Constitution of the Republic of Korea, No.9 (1980)

Korea, Monopoly Regulation and Fair Trade Act (1980)

U.S., Airline Deregulation Act of 1978

U.S., Civil Aeronautics Act of 1938

C   Cases

Ministere Public v. Asjes, C-209-213/84 [1986] E.C.R. I-1425

Commission of the European Communities v. United Kingdom of Great Britain and Northern Ireland, C-466/98, [2002] E.C.R. I-09427

Commission of the European Communities v. Kingdom of Denmark, C-467/98, [2002] E.C.R. I-09519

Commission of the European Communities v. Kingdom of Sweden, C-468/98, [2002] E.C.R. I-09575

Commission of the European Communities v. République de Finlande, C-469/98, [2002] E.C.R. I-09627

Commission of the European Communities v. Kingdom of Belgium, C-471/98, [2002] E.C.R. I-09681

Commission of the European Communities v. Grand Duchy of Luxemburg, C-472/98, [2002] E.C.R. I-09741

Commission of the European Communities v. Republic of Austria, C-475/98, [2002] E.C.R. I-09797

Commission of the European Communities v. Federal Republic of Germany, C-476/98, [2002] E.C.R. I-09855

Decision on Principal Place of Business With Regard To Application For Licence by Jetstar Hong Kong Airways Limited Before the Air Transport Licencing Authority, 2015

Metropolitan Cebu Water District (MCWD) v. Margarita A. Adala, [2007] (the Philippines Supreme Court Decision)

Hoffmann-La Roche (Judgment of the Court of 13 February 1979. – *Hoffmann-La Roche & Co. AG v. Commission of the European Communities*. – Dominant position. – Case 85/76)

D Administrative Orders, Decisions and Documents

ASEAN Secretariat, ASEAN Documents Series 2004 (Jakarta: ASEAN Secretariat, 2005)

ASEAN, ASEAN Economic Community Blueprint Blueprint (Jakarta: ASEAN Secretariat, 2008)

EC, Communication from the Commission to the council and the european parliament – The creation of the single European sky, COM (1999) 614

EC, Council Directive 87/601 on fares for scheduled air services between Member States [1987]

EC, EU Commission, Commission Decision on approving the standard clauses for inclusion in bilateral air service agreements between Member States and third countries jointly laid down by the Commission and the Member States, COM (2005) 943

EC, EU Commission, Communication from the Commission on relations between the Community and third countries in the field of air transport, COM (2003) 94

EC, EU Commission, Communication from the Commission on the consequences of the Court judgements of 5 November 2002 for European air transport policy, COM (2002) 649

EC, EU Commission, Contribution of the European Communities to the development of air transport services (Luxembourg: EC, 1979) EC Bulletin, Supplement 5

EC, European Commission, Bilateral Air Services Agreements brought into legal conformity since the Court of Justice of the EU judgments of 5 November 2002 (Updated 30 January 2013)

EC, European Commission, Case COMP/39.596 – BA/AA/IB (14 July 2010)

EC, European Commission, Case No COMP/M.2041 – UNITED AIRLINES / US AIRWAYS (12 January 2001)

EC, European Commission, Case No COMP/M.2041 -United Airlines/ US Airways case, Notification of 22.09.2000 pursuant to Article 4 of Council Regulation No 4064/89 (2001)

EC, European Commission, Case No COMP/M.5403 – LUFTHANSA / BMI (14 May 2009)

EC, European Commission, Commission Decision of 14.07.2010 relating to a proceeding under Article 101 of the Treaty on the Functioning of the European Union and Article 53 of the EEA Agreement (Case COMP/39.596 – BA/AA/IB)

EC, European Commission, Commission Notice on the Definition of Relevant Market for the Purposes of Community Competition Law, Official Journal C 372, 09/12/1997, 5, 5-6 (1997)

EC, European Parliament legislative resolution of 12 March 2014 on the proposal for a regulation of the European Parliament and of the Council amending Regulation (EC) No 216/2008 in the field of aerodromes, air traffic management and air navigation services

European Commission & US DOT, Transatlantic Airline Alliances: Competitive Issues and Regulatory Approaches (16 November 2010)

US Transportation Command, Civil Airlift Programs, USTRANSCOM Instruction 24-9 (13 October 2011)

US DOJ, Comments of the Department of Justice on the Show Cause Order, to US DOT, Joint Application of Air Canada, The Austrian Group, British Midland Airways Ltd, Continental Airlines, Inc., Deutsche Lufthansa AG, Polskie Linie Lotnicze LOT S.A., Scandinavian Airlines System, Swiss International Air Lines Ltd., TAP Air Portugal, and United Air Lines, Inc. to Amend Order 2007-2-16 under 49 U.S.C. ss. 41308 and 41309 so as to Approve and Confer Antitrust Immunity, Dkt No DOT-OST-2008-0234-0193, Order 2009-4-5, Show Cause Order (7 April 2009)

US DOT, Acquisition of Northwest Airlines by Wings Holdings, Inc. (Order 89-9-51)

US DOT, Application of American Airlines, Inc. For an Exemption and Allocation of Frequencies (Los Angeles – Shanghai) (1 October 2010)

US DOT, DHL AIRWAYS, INC. n/k/a ASTAR AIR CARGO, INC. (Docket OST-2002-13089) (10 May 2004)

US DOT, Joint Application of Air Canada, The Austrian Group, British Midland Airways Ltd, Continental Airlines, Inc., Deutsche Lufthansa AG, Polskie Linie Lotniecze LOT S.A., Scandinavian Airlines System, Swiss international Air Lines Ltd., TAP Air Portugal, and United Air Lines, Inc. to Amend Order 2007-2-16 under 49 U.S.C. ss. 41308 and 41309 so as to Approve and Confer Antitrust Immunity, Dkt No DOT-OST-2008-0234-0253, Order 2009-7-10, Final Order (10 July 2009)

US DOT, Joint Application of Alitalia-Linee Aeree Italiane-S.p.A., Czech Airlines, Detla Air Lines, Inc.,KLM Royal Dutch Airlines, Northwest Airlines, Inc., and Société Air France for Approval of and Antitrust Immunity for Alliance Agreements under 49 U.S.C. ss. 41308 and 41309, Dkt No DOT-OST-2005-19214-0195, Order 2005-12-12, Order to Show Cause (22 December 2005)

US DOT, Joint Application of Alitalia-Linee Aeree Italiane-S.p.A., Czech Airlines, Delta Airlines, Inc., KLM Royal Dutch Airlines, Northwest Arilines, Inc, and Société Air France for Approval of and Antitrust Immunity for Alliance Agreements under 49 U.S.C. ss. 41308 and 41309, Dkt No DOT-OST-2007-28644-0174, Order 2008-4-17, Show Cause Order (9 April 2008)

US DOT, Joint Application of All Nippon Airways Co., Ltd., Continental Airlines, Inc. and United Air Lines, Inc. under 49 U.S.C. ss.41308 and 41309 for approval and antitrust immunity for alliance agreements, Dkt No DOTOST-2009-0350-0001 (23 December 2009)

US DOT, Joint Application of American Airlines, Inc. and Japan Airlines International Co., Ltd. under 49 U.S.C. ss. 41308 and 41309 for approval of and antitrust immunity for alliance agreements, Dkt No DOT-OST-2010-0034-0001 (16 February 2010)

US DOT, Joint Application of American Airlines, Inc., British Airways PLC, Finnair OYJ, Iberia Líneas Aéreas de España, S.A., and Royal Jordanian Airlines Under 49 U.S.C. ss. 41308-41309 for approval of and antitrust immunity for alliance agreements, Dkt No DOT-OST-2008-0252- 3390, Order 2010-2-8, Show Cause Order (13 February 2010)

US DOT, Joint Application of American Airlines, Inc., British Airways PLC, Finnair OYJ, Iberia Líneas Aéreas de España, S.A., and Royal Jordanian Airlines Under 49 U.S.C. ss. 41308- 41309 for approval of and antitrust immunity for alliance agreements, Dkt No DOT-OST-2008-0252-3406, Order 2010-7-8 Final Order (20 July 2010)

US DOT, Joint Application of Delta Air Lines, INC. Korean Air Lines CO., LTD., Societe Air France, Alitalia-Linee Aeree Italiane-S.p.A. Czech Airlines under 49 U.S.C. §§ 41308 and 41309 for approval of and antitrust immunity for alliances agreements, Dkt OST-2002-11842 ORDER GRANTING APPROVAL AND ANTITRUST IMMUNITY FOR ALLIANCE AGREEMENTS Final Order (27 June 2002)

US DOT, Joint Application of Virgin Atlantic Airways, Ltd., Delta Air Lines, Inc., and Société Air France, Koninklijke Luchtvaart Maatschappij N.V., and Alitalia Compagnia Aerea Italiana S.P.A. under 49 U.S.C. §§ 41308 and 41309 for approval of and antitrust immunity for alliance agreements, Docket DOT-OST-2013-0068, Shaw Cause Order (30 August 2013)

US DOT, Order 92-8-13 (In the Matter of Defining "Open Skies"), Docket 48130 U.S. Model Open Skies Agreement Text

US DOT, Statement of United States International Air Transportation Policy (60 Fed. Reg. 21,841) (3 May 1995)

US DOT, U.S.-Japan Alliance Case, Dkt No DOT-OST-2010-0059-0180, Order 2010-10-4, Show Cause Order (6 October 2010)

US DOT, U.S.-Japan Alliance Case, Dkt. No. DOT-OST-2010–0059, Final Order 2010–11–10 (10 November 2010)

US GAO (General Accounting Office), Airline Competition Impact of Changing Foreign Investment and Control Limits on U.S. Airlines Foreign Investment in U.S. Airlines, GAO/RCED-93-7 (1992)

US GAO, International Aviation: Airline Alliances Produce Benefits, But Effect on Competition is Uncertain, GAO/RCED-95-99 (Apr. 1995)

US Securities and Exchange Commission, FORM F-1 REGISTRATION STATEMENT UNDER THE SECURITIES ACT OF 1933: AVIANCA HOLDINGS S.A. (19 September 2013)

US Securities and Exchange Commission, Offer to Exchange each Common Share, Preferred Share and American Depositary Share of TAM S.A. for 0.90 of a Common Share of LAN AIRLINES S.A. Represented by American Depositary Shares or Brazilian Depositary Shares (10 May 2012)

E   International Civil Aviation Organization Documents

ICAO Secretariat, "Overview of Trends and Developments in International Air Transport" (24 March 2009)

ICAO Secretariat, "Regulatory and Industry Overview" (20 September 2013)

ICAO Secretariat, "Trans Tasman Single Aviation Market" (2007)

ICAO, "Regional/Plurilateral Agreements and Arrangements for Liberalization" (updated 22 July 2009)

ICAO, "Status of the International Air Transport Services Regulation in the Latin American and Caribbean States" (4 September 2004) (Presented by the Latin American Civil Aviation Commission)

ICAO, Africa's Strategy for Market Access and Catalyst for Air Transport Growth, ICAO Doc. ATConf/6-WP/35 (18 February 2013) (Presented by Members of the African Civil Aviation Commission (AFCAC))

ICAO, Air Carrier Ownership and Control Clauses in Bilateral Air Services Agreements, ICAO Doc ATConf/6-WP/49 (14 February 2013) (Presented by Ireland)

ICAO, Air Carrier Ownership and Control Principle, ICAO Doc ATConf/6-WP/84 (4 March 2013) (Presented by Indonesia)

ICAO, Antitrust Immunity for Airlines Alliances, ICAO Doc ATConf/6-WP/85 (4 March 2013) (Presented by Republic of Korea)

ICAO, Consolidated Conclusions, Model Clauses, Recommendations and Declaration, ICAO Doc. ATConf/5 (31 March 2003, REVISED 10 July 2003)

ICAO, Developments in the Liberalization of International Air Transport Services in the Latin American Region, ICAO Doc ATConf/6-IP/6 (5 March 2013) (Presented by LACAC)

ICAO, Differences Between Carrier Ownership and Control Principles in Designation Clauses in Air Services Agreements and National Laws Regulating the Subject, ICAO Doc ATConf/6-WP/94 (7 March 2013) (Presented by Brazil)

ICAO, Egyptian Experience in the Liberalization of Air Carrier Ownership, ICAO Doc ATConf/6-WP/41 (19 February 2013) (Presented by Egypt)

ICAO, Evolution of the Liberalization of the Services of Air Transport in the Services of Air Transport in the State Members of the Latin American Civil Aviation Commission – LACAC, ICAO Doc A36-WP/282 (21 September 2007) (Presented by the Latin American Civil Aviation Commission)

ICAO, Expanding Market Access For International Air Transport, ICAO Doc ATConf/6-WP/13 (13 December 2012) (Presented by ICAO Secretariat)

ICAO, Expansion of Market Access for International Air Transport in a Proactive, Progressive, Orderly and Safeguarded Manner, ICAO Doc ATConf/6-WP/97 (6 March 2013) (Presented by China)

ICAO, FIJI'S Position on Multilateral Air Service Agreements: Pacific Islands Air Services Agreement (PIASA), ICAO Doc. ATConf/5-WP/45 (23 January 2003) (Presented by Fiji)

ICAO, ICAO Template Air Services Agreement (28 September 2009)

ICAO, Liberalization of Air Cargo Services, ICAO ATConf/6-WP/14 (13 December 2012) (Presented by ICAO Secretariat)

ICAO, Liberalization of Air Carrier Ownership and Control, ICAO Doc ATconf/6-WP/12 (10 December 2012)

ICAO, Liberalization of Market Access, ICAO ATConf/6-WP/60 (14 February 2013) (Presented by United States of America)

ICAO, Liberalizing Air Carrier Ownership and Control, ICAO A35-WP/156 (17 September 2004)

ICAO, Manual on the Regulation of International Air Transport, ICAO Doc. 9626 (2nd ed. 2004)

ICAO, Market Access Restrictions, ICAO Doc ATConf/6-WP/59 (19 February 2013)

ICAO, Needed: Rapid Liberalization of Air Cargo Services Through a New Multilateral Approach, ICAO Doc ATConf/6-WP/96 (7 March 2013) (Presented by The International Air Cargo Association (TIACA))

ICAO, Night Flight Restriction, ICAO Doc. ATConf/6-WP/8 (10 December 2012)

ICAO, Policy and Guidance Material on the Economic Regulation of International Air Transport, 2008, ICAO Doc 9587

ICAO, Proposal for the Liberalization of Air Carrier Ownership and Control, ICAO Doc ATConf/6-WP/29 (13 February 2013) (Presented by Chile)

ICAO, Regulatory Implications of the Allocation of Flight Departure and Arrival Slots at International Airports, ICAO Circular 283 (2001)

ICAO, Relaxing the Rules for Airline Designation, ICAO Doc. ATConf/6-WP/46 (13 March 2013) (Presented by Members of the African Civil Aviation Commission (AFCAC))

ICAO, Report on Agenda Item 2.1(summary report of the Air Transport Conference), ICAO ATConf/6-WP/104 (22 March 2013)

ICAO, Report on Agenda Item 2.2 (summary report of the Air Transport Conference), ICAO ATConf/6-WP/104 (22 March 2013)

ICAO, Report on Agenda Item 2.4 (summary report of the Air Transport Conference), ICAO Doc ATConf/6-WP/104 (22 March 2013)

ICAO, Slot Allocation, ICAO Doc. ATConf/6-WP/11 (10 December 2012)

ICAO, Template Air Services Agreement (28 September 2009)

ICAO, The Multilateral Agreement on the Liberalization of International Air Transportation: A Basis for the Future Economic Regulation of Air Services, ICAO Doc ATConf/6-WP/34 (12 February 2013) (Presented by New Zealand)

ICAO, Vietnam's Air Transport Market, Legislations and Regulations and Policy During 2003-2013, ICAO Doc ATConf/6-IP/22 (17 March 2013) (Presented by Viet Nam)

F   BOOKS

Aust, Anthony, *Modern treaty law and practice,* 2nd ed. (Cambridge: Cambridge University Press, 2007)

Bennett, A. LeRoy, *International Organizations: Principles and Issues*, 6th ed. (Englewood Cliffs: Prentice Hall, 1995)

Black's Law Dictionary, 9th ed

Bonin, Jason R., *International Air Transport Liberalization in East Asia: A Regional Approach to Reform* (Ph.D Thesis, National University of Singapore, 2013)

Brenner, Melvin A., Leet, James O. & Schott, Elihu, *Airline Deregulation* (Westport: Eno Foundation for Transportation, 1985)

Checkel, Jeffrey T. & Katzenstein, Peter J., eds., *European Identity*, (Cambridge: Cambridge University Press, 2009)

Czerny, Achim, Forsyth, Peter, Gillen, David, and Niemeier, Hans-Martin, eds., *Airport Slots: International Experiences and Options for Reform* (Burlington: Ashgate, 2008)

Dempsey, Paul Stephen & Gesell, Laurence, *Airline Management Strategies for the 21st Century*, 3rd ed. (Chandler: Coast Aire Publications, 2012)

Dempsey, Paul Stephen & Gesell, Laurence, *Airline Management Strategies for the 21st Century*, 2nd ed. (Chandler: Coast Aire Publications, 2006)

Dempsey, Paul Stephen & Milde, Michael, *International air carrier liability: the Montreal Convention of 1999* (Montreal: McGill University, Centre for Research of Air & Space Law, 2005)

Dempsey, Paul Stephen, *Law and Foreign Policy in International Aviation* (Dobbs Ferry, Transnational Publishers: 1987)

Dempsey, Paul Stephen, *Public international air law* (Montreal: Institute of Air and Space Law, 2008)

Dempsey, Paul, & Thoms, William E., *Law and Economic Regulation in Transportation* (New York: Quorum Books, 1986)

Diederiks-Verschoor, Isabella H.Ph, *An Introduction to Air Law*, 9th ed. revised by Pablo Mendes de Leon (Alphen aan den Rijn: Kluwer Law International, 2012)

Doganis, Rigas, *The Airline Business in the 21st Century* (London: Routledge, 2001)

Dworkin, Ronald, *Taking Rights Seriously* (London : Duckworth, 1981)

Fernandez, Juan Antonio & Fernandez-Stembridge, Leila, *China's State Owned Enterprise Reforms: An Industrial and CEO Approach* (New York: Routledge, 2007)

Goh, Jeffrey, *European Air Transport Law and Competition* (Chichester: John Wiley & Sons, 1997)

Goh, Jeffrey, *The Single Aviation Market of Australia and New Zealand* (London: Cavendish Publishing Limited, 2001)

Goode, Walter, *Dictionary of Trade Policy Terms*, 5th ed. (Cambridge: Cambridge University Press, 2007)

Guzman, Andrew T., *How International Law Works* (Oxford: Oxford University Press, 2008)

Haanappel, Peter P.C., *The Law and Policy of Air Space and Outer Space: A Comparative Approach* (Alphen aan den Rijn: Kluwer Law International, 2009)

Havel, Brian F. & Sanchez, Gabriel S., *The Principles and Practices of International Aviation Law* (New York: Cambridge University Press, 2014)

Havel, Brian F., *Beyond Open Skies: A New Regime for International Aviation* (Alphen aan den Rijn, Kluwer Law International: 2009)

Hewitt, Ian, *Joint Ventures*, 4th ed. (London: Sweet and Maxwell Limited, 2008)

Iatrou, Kostas & Oretti, Mauro, *Airline Choices for the Future: From Alliances to Mergers* (Burlington: Ashgate, 2007)

Johnson, D.H.N., *Rights in Air Space* (Manchester: Manchester University Press, 1965)

Joyner, Christopher C., *International Law in the 21st Century* (Lanham: Rowman & Littlefield, 2005)

Lelieur, Isabelle, *Law and Policy of Substantial Ownership and Effective Control of Airlines: Prospects for Change* (Aldershot & Burlington, Vermont: Ashgate, 2003)

Li, Jiaxiang, *Route to Fly* (Beijing: China Machine Press, 2007)

Lu, Angela Cheng-Fui, *International Airline Alliances* (The Hague: Kluwer Law International, 2003)

Macedo, Bruno, *A Potential Open Sky Agreement Between the EU and MERCOSUR Based on the EU-US Agreement* (Master Thesis, Universidade do Porto, 2008)

Matsushita, Mitsuo, *International Trade and Competition Law in Japan* (Oxford: Oxford University Press, 1993)

Mendes de Leon, Pablo, *Cabotage in Air Transport Regulation* (London: Martinus Nijhoff, 1992)

Milde, Michael, *International Air Law and ICAO*, 2d ed. (Utrecht: Eleven International Publishing, 2012)

Moussis, Nicholas, *Access to European Union: law, economics, policies*, 16th ed. (Rixensart: European Study Service, 2007)

Odekon, M, *Encyclopedia of World Poverty* (Sage Publications, 2006)

Oum, Tae Hoon & Yu, Chunyan, *Shaping Air Transport in Asia Pacific* (Burlington: Ashgate, 2000)

Oxford Advanced American Dictionary

Paris, Michael, *From the Wright Brothers to Top Gun: Aviation, Nationalism, and Popular Cinema* (Manchester: Manchester University Press, 1995)

Park, J.H., *A Study on the Effects of Air Transport Liberalization on Air Transport Markets* (PhD Thesis, Department of Logistics Management, University of Incheon, 2011)

Proceedings of the International Conference on Civil Aviation, Chicago, 1 November – 7 December 1944 (Washington, D.C.: United States Government Printing Office, 1948)

Sampson, Anthony, *Empires of the Sky: the Politics, and Cartels of World Airlines* (London: Hodder and Stroughton, 1984)

Schlumberger, Charles E., *Open Skies for Africa Implementing the Yamoussoukro Decision* (Washington D.C.: The World Bank, 2010)

Shaw, Stephen, *Airline Marketing and Management*, 7th ed. (Farnham: Ashgate, 2011)

Staniland, Martin, *A Europe of the air?: The Airline Industry and European Integration* (Lanham: Rowman & Littlefield, 2008)

Suzuki, Kenji, *Competition Law Reform in Britain and Japan* (London: Routledge, 2002)

Vasigh, Bijan, Fleming, Ken & Tacker, Thomas, *Introduction to Air Transport Economics – From Theory to Applications* (Hampshire Ashgate: 2008)

Vlasic, Ivan A., ed., *Explorations in aerospace law, selected essays by John Cobb Cooper, 1946-1966* (Montreal: McGill University Press, 1968)

Von Den Steinen, Erwin, *National Interest and International Aviation* (Alphen aan den Rijn: Kluwer Law International, 2006)

Wassenbergh, Henri, *Principles and Practices in Air Transport Regulation* (Paris: Institut du Transport Aérien, 1993)

Whish, Richard & Bailey, David, *Competition Law*, 7th ed. (New York: Oxford University Press, 2012)

Whish, Richard, *Competition Law*, 2nd ed. (London: Butterworths, 1989)

Whish, Richard, *Competition Law*, 4th ed. (London: Butterworths, 2001)

Whish, Richard, *Competition Law*, 6th ed. (New York: Oxford University Press, 2009)

Williams, Alan, *Contemporary Issues Shaping China's Civil Aviation Policy: Balancing International with Domestic Priorities* (Burlington, VT: Ashgate, 2009)

Wolf, Ronald Charles, *Effective International Joint Venture Management* (New York: M. E. Sharpe, 2000)

Young, Edward M., *Aerial Nationalism: A History of Aviation in Thailand* (Washington: Smithsonian Institution Press, 1995)

Zaidi, Wasim, *Breaking the Shackles: Foreign Ownership and Control in the Airline Industry* (LL.M Thesis, McGill University Institute of Air and Space Law, 2008)

Zamboni, Mauro, *The Policy of Law – A Legal Theoretical Framework* (Oxford: Hart Publishing, 2007)

Zang, Hongliang & Meng, Qingfen, *Civil Aviation Law in the People's Republic of China* (The Hague: Eleven International Publishing, 2010)

G   Articles and Book Chapters

Baur, Jahannes, "EU-Russia Aviation Relations and the Issue of Siberian Overflights" (2010) 35 Air & Space L. 225

Bilotkach, Volodymyr & Hüschelrath, Kai, "Antitrust Immunity for Airline Alliances" (2011) 7 Journal of Competition Law and Economics. 335

Bilotkach, Volodymyr & Hüschelrath, Kai, "Chapter 14 Economic Effects of Antitrust Immunity for Airline Alliances: Identification and Measurement" in Peter Forsyth et al eds., *Liberalization in Aviation: Competition, Cooperation and Public Policy* (Farnham: Ashgate, 2013)

Bilotkach, Volodymyr, "Price Effects of Airline Consolidation: Evidence from a Sample of Transatlantic Markets" (2007) 33 Empirical Economics. 427

Bonin, Jason R., "Regionalism in International Civil Aviation: A Re-evaluation of the Economic Regulation of International Air Transport in the Context of Economic Integration" (2008) 12 Singapore Year Book of International Law 113

Boykin, Richard, "Holing Company Regimes – Introduction" in *International Tax Review: Holding Company Regimes* (London: Euromoney Institutional Investor PLC, 2005)

Braun, Lucas, "Liberalization or Bust: A Double Step Approach to Relaxing the Foreign Ownership and Control Restrictions in the Brazilian Aviation Industry" (2014) 39 Air & Space L. 343

Breyer, Stephen, "Regulation and Deregulation in the United States: Airlines, Telecommunications and Antitrust". in Giandomenico Majone, ed., *Deregulation or Re-regulation?* (London: Pinter Publishers, 1990) 7

Brooks, Roy L., "The Use of Policy in Judicial Reasoning" (2002) 13 Stan. L. & Pol'y Rev. 33

Brueckner, Jan K. & Proost, Stef, "Carve-outs under airline antitrust immunity" (2010) 28 International Journal of Industrial Organization. 657

Brueckner, Jan K., "International Airfares in the Age of Alliances: the Effects of Codesharing and Antitrust Immunity" (2003) 85 Review of Economic and Statistics 105

Cafaggi, Fabrizio, "New Foundation of Transnational Private Regulation" (2011) 38 J.L. & Soc'y 20

Cameron, Fraser, "The European Integration Model: What Relevance for Asia?" in G. John Ikenberry, ed., *Regional Integration and Institutionalization Comparing Asia and Europe* (Kyoto: Shoukadoh Publishers, 2012)

Choi, Yo Sop, "The Rule of Law in a Market Economy: Globalization of Competition Law in Korea" (2014) 15 European Business Organization Law Review. 419

Chung, Yi-Shih & Wu, Cheng-Lung, "Chapter 12 Air Market Opening between Taiwan and China: Impact on Airport and Airline Network Developments in Neighboring Asia Pacific Countries" in David Timothy Duval, ed., *Air Transport in the Asia Pacific* (Burlington: Ashgate, 2014) 199

Constantine Alexandrakis, "Foreign Investment in U.S. Airlines: Restrictive Law is Ripe for Change" (1993-1994) 4 U. Miami Bus. L. Rev. 71

Crespo, Daniel Calleja & Fenoulhet, Timothy, "Chapter 1 The Single European Sky (SES): 'Building Europe in the Sky'" in Pablo Mendes de Leon & Daniel Calleja Crespo, eds., *Achieving the Single European Sky: Goals and Challenges* (Alphen aan den Rijn: Kluwer Law International, 2011) 1

Daft, Jost & Albers, Sascha, "A profitability analysis of low-cost long-haul flight operations" (2012) 19 Journal of Air Transport Management 49

De Broca, Hubert, Riga, Marta Mielecka & Subocs, Anatoly. "Transport" in Jonathan Faull & Ali Nikpay eds., *The EU Law of Competition*, 3rd ed. (Oxford : Oxford University Press, 2014)

Dean, Warren L. Jr., & Shane, Jeffrey N., "Alliances, Immunity, and the Future of Aviation" (2010) 22 Air & Space Lawyer. 17

Dempsey, Paul Stephen, "The Evolution of Air Transport Agreements" (2008) 33 Ann. Air & Sp. L. 127

Devall, James L., "The U.S.-EU Agreement – A Path to a Global Aviation Agreement" (2008) Issues in Aviation Law and Policy

Dresner, Martin, "Chapter 23 US Bilateral Air Transport Policy" in Peter Forsyth et al ed., Liberalization in Aviation: Competition, Cooperation and Public Policy (Farnham: Ashgate, 2013) 429

Dubey, Sangita & Gendron, François, "The U.S.-Canada Open Skies Agreement: Three Years Later" (1999) 18:3 Travel-Log

Eller, Rogéria de Arantes Gomes & Moreira, Michelle, "The Main Cost-related Factors in Airlines Management" (2014) 8 Journal of Transport Literature 8

European Competition Authorities, "Code-sharing Agreements in Scheduled Passenger Air Transport – The European Competition Authorities' Perspective" (2006) 2 European Competition Journal 263

Ewing-Chow, Michael, "Multilateral or Regional – WTO "and/or" FTAs? An Academic's View of the Trenches" in C L Lim & Margaret Liang eds., *Economic Diplomacy* (Singapore: World Scientific Publishing, 2011) 257

Fang, Liu, "Comments in Part III: Negotiating Strategies for Coping with the Key Barriers to Liberalization of Northeast Asian Aviation Markets" in Yeon Myung Kim and Sungwon Lee, eds., *Negotiating Strategies for Creating a Liberalized Air Transport Bloc in Northeast Asia* (Honolulu, HI; The Korea Transport Institute & East-West Center, 2009) 423

Findlay, Christopher, Forsyth, Peter, and King, John, "Developments in Pacific Islands' Air Transport" in Satish Chand ed., *Pacific Islands Regional Integration and Governance* (Canberra: Asia Pacific Press, 2005)

Fiorilli, Francesco, "International Air Transport Economic Regulation: Globalization vs Protection of National Interest" (2011) 10:3 Aviation and Space Journal

First, Harry, "Antitrust In Japan: The Original Intent" (2000) 9 Pacific Rim Law and Policy Journal 1

Forsyth, Peter, "Chapter 21 Economic Evaluation of Air Services Liberalization: The New Calculus" in Peter Forsyth et al ed., *Liberalization in Aviation: Competition, Cooperation and Public Policy* (Farnham: Ashgate, 2013) 403

Forsyth, Peter, King, John & Rodolfo, Cherry Lyn, "Open skies in ASEAN" (2006) 12 Journal of Air Transport Management 143

Fox, Eleanor, "Chapter 22: The Kaleidoscope of Antitrust and Its Significance in the World Economy: Respecting Differences" in Barry Hawk, ed., *International Antitrust Law & Policy* (New York: Juris Publishing, 2002)

Fu, Xiaowen, Oum, Tae Hoon & Zhang, Anming, "Air Transport Liberalization and Its Impacts on Airline Competition and Air Passenger Traffic" (2010) 49:4 Transportation Journal. 24

Fujita, Katsutoshi, "Some Considerations for the Modernization of the Rome Convention, in case of Unlawful Interference" (2008) 23 Korean J. Air & Sp. L. 59.

Garcia-Arboleda, Jose Ignacio, "Transnational Airlines in Latin America Facing the Fear of Nationality" (2012) 37 Air & Space L. 93

Giavazzi, Francesco & Tabellini, Guido, "Economic and Political Liberalizations" (2005) 52 Journal of Monetary Economics 1297

Gillen, D., Harris, R. and Oum, T., "Measuring the Economic Effects of Bilateral Liberalization on Air Transport" (2002) 38 Transportation Research Part E 155

Gillespie, William & Richard, Oliver M., "Antitrust Immunity Grants to Joint Venture Agreements: Evidence from International Airline Alliances" (2012) 78 Antitrust Law Journal. 443

Gjerset, James E., "Crippling United States Airlines: Archaic Interpretations of the Federal Aviation Act's Restriction on Foreign Capital Investments" (1991) 7 American University Journal of International Law and Policy. 173

Haanappel, Peter P.C., "Airline Ownership and Control and Some Related Matters" (2001) 26 Air & Space L. 90

Haanappel, Peter P.C., "Multilateralism and Economic Bloc Forming in International Air Transport" (1994) 19 Ann. Air & Sp. L. 279

Haanappel, Peter P.C., "The Transformation of Sovereignty in the Air" in Chia-Jui Cheng ed., *The Use of Air and Outer Space Cooperation and Competition* (The Hague: Kluwer Law International, 1998) 13

Haanappel, Peter, "Bilateral Air Transport Agreements – 1913-1980" (1980) 5 International Trade Law Journal. 241

Harrington, Andrew, "Foreign Ownership and the Future of the National Airline" (2013) 38 Ann. Air & Sp. L. 123

Harris, H. Stephen Jr, "The Making of an Antitrust Law: The Pending Anti-Monopoly Law of the People's Republic of China" (2006) 7 Chicago Journal of International Law. 169

Havel, Brian & Sanchez, Gabriel, "Restoring Global Aviation's "Cosmopolitan *Mentalité*"" (2011) 29 B.U. Int'l L.J. 1

Havel, Brian & Sanchez, Gabriel, "The Emerging *Lex Aviatica*" (2011) 42 Geo. Int'l L.J. 639

Hilf, Mailhard & Salomn, Tim Rene, "Running in Circles: Regionalism in World Trade and How It will lead back to Multilateralism" in Ulrich Fastenrath, ed., *From Bilateralism to Community Interest: Essays in Honour of Bruno Simma* (Oxford: Oxford University Press, 2011) 257

Hill, Leonard, "Bilateral Ballistics" *Air Transport World* 34:2 (February 1997) 53

Hsu, Chia-Jui & Chang, Yu-Chun, "The Influences of Airline Ownership Rules on Aviation Policies and Carriers' Strategies" (2005) 5 Proceedings of the Eastern Asia Society for Transportation Studies. 557

Iatrou, Kostas & Mantzavinou, Lida, "Chapter 13 The Impact of Liberalization on Cross-border Airline Mergers and Alliances" in Peter Forsyth *et al* eds., *Liberalization in Aviation: Competition, Cooperation and Public Policy* (Farnham: Ashgate, 2013) 233

Jönsson, Christer, "Sphere of Flying: The Politics of International Aviation" (1981) 35 International Organization. 273

Jung, Youngjin & Chang, Seung Wha, "Korea's Competition Law and Policies in Perspective" (2006) 26 Nw. J. Int'l L. & Bus. 687

Keum, Hieyeon, "Globalization and Inter-City Cooperation in Northeast Asia" (2000) 18 East Asia. 97

Kim, Yeon Myung & Lee, Sean Seungho, "Chapter 9 Air Transport in Korea and Northeast Asia" in *The Impacts and benefits of structural reforms in the transport, energy and telecommunications sector* (Singapore: Asia-Pacific Economic Cooperation, 2011) 219

Kim, Yeon Myung & Lee, Sean Seungho, "Korea's Approaches to Aviation Market Liberalization in Northeast Asia" in Yeon Myung Kim & Sungwon Lee, eds., *Negotiating Strategies for Creating a Liberalized Air Transport Bloc in Northeast Asia* (Honolulu, HI; The Korea Transport Institute & East-West Center, 2009) 393

Kincaid, Ian & Tretheway, Michael, "Chapter 19 Economic Impact of Aviation Liberalization" in Peter Forsyth et al ed., *Liberalization in Aviation: Competition, Cooperation and Public Policy* (Farnham: Ashgate, 2013) 345

Kociubiński, Jakub, "Relevant Market in Commercial Aviation of the European Union" (2011) 1 Wroclaw Review of Law, Administration and Economics 12

Lee, Jae Woon & Dy, Michelle, "Mitigating "Effective Control" Restriction on Joint Venture Airlines in Asia: Philippine AirAsia Case" (2015) 40 Air & Space L. 231

Lee, Jae Woon, "Chapter 13 Regional Liberalization in Northeast Asia (China, South Korea, and Japan)" in David Timothy Duval, ed., *Air Transport in the Asia Pacific* (Burlington: Ashgate, 2014) 217

Lee, Jae Woon, "Revisiting Freedom of Overflight in International Air Law: Minimum Multilateralism in International Air Transport" (2013) 38 Air & Space L. 351

Lee, Jae Woon, "The Regime of Compensable Damage in the Modernized Rome Conventions: a Comparison between Article 3 of the General Risks Convention of 2009 and Article 17 of the Montreal Convention of 1999" (2010) 35 Ann. Air & Sp. L. 213

Lee, Jae Woon, "The U.S.'s New Divide-and-Conquer Strategy in Northeast Asia" (2014) 14 Issues in Aviation Law and Policy 83

Li, Bin, "Open China's Skies or Not? – From the Perspective of a Chinese Scholar" (2010) 9 Issues of Aviation Law and Policy 209

Lykotrafiti, Antigoni, "Consolidation and Rationalization in the Transatlantic Air Transport Market –Prospects and Challenges for Competition and Consumer Welfare" (2011) 76 J. Air L. & Com. 661

McGonigle, Sean, "Assessing the APEC Multilateral Agreement After 5 Years of Inactivity" (2013) 38 Ann. Air & Sp. L. 429

McGonigle, Sean, "Past its Use-By Date: Regulation 868 Concerning Subsidy and State Aid in International Air Services" (2013) 38 Air & Space L. 1

Mehra, Salil K. & Yanbei, Meng "Against Antitrust Functionalism: Reconsidering China's Antimonopoly Law" (2009) 49 Virginia Journal of International Law. 379

Mendelsohn, Allan I., "The USA and the EU- Aviation Relations: An Impasse or an Opportunity?" (2004) 29 Air & Space L. 263

Mendes de Leon, Pablo, "A New Phase in Alliance Building: The Air France/KLM Venture as a Case Study" (2004) 53 Z.L.W. 359

Mifsud, Paul, "Metal Neutrality and the Nation-Bound Airline Industry" (2011) 36 Air & Space L.117

Milde, Michael, "Some question marks about the price of 'Russian air'" (2000) 49 Z.L.W. 147

Oum, Tae Hoon & Lee, Yeong Heok, "The Northeast Asian Air Transport Network: Is There a Possibility of Creating Open Skies in the Region?" (2002) 8 Journal of Air Transport Management. 325

Patel, Bimal, "A Flight Plan Towards Financial Stability – The History and Future of Foreign Ownership Restrictions in the United States Aviation Industry" (2008) 73 J. Air L. & Com. 487

Peeperkorn, Luc & Verouden, Vincent, "The Economics of Competition" in Jonathan Faull & Ali Nikpay eds., *The EU Law of Competition*, 3rd ed. (Oxford : Oxford University Press, 2014)

Picciotto, Sol, "Introduction: What Rules for the World Economy?" in Sol Picciotto & Ruth Mayne, ed., *Regulating International Business: Beyond Liberalization* (New York: St. Martin's Press, 1999)

Saraswati, Batari & Hanaoka, Shinya, "Aviation Policy in Indonesia and Its Relation to ASEAN Single Aviation Market" (2013) 9 Proceedings of the Eastern Asia Society for Transportation Studies. 2

Schilde, Kaija E, "Who are the Europeans? European Identity Outside of European Integration" (2014) 52 Journal of Common Market Studies. 650

Schlumberger, Charles E., "Africa's Long Path to Liberalizing Air Services – Status Quo of the Implementation of the Yamoussoukro Decision" (2008) 33 Ann. Air & Sp. L. 194

Scott, Colin, Cafaggi, Fabrizio & Senden, Linda, "The Conceptual and Constitutional Challenge of Transnational Private Regulation" (2011) 38 J.L. & Soc'y 1

Stragier, Joos, Negenman, Monique, Jaspers, Maria & Wezenbeek, Rita, "Transport" in Jonathan Faull & Ali Nikpay eds., *The EU Law of Competition*, 2nd ed. (Oxford : Oxford University Press, 2007)

Tan, Alan Khee-Jin, "Antitrust Immunity for Trans-Pacific Airline Alliance Agreements: Singapore and China as 'Beyond' Markets" (2013) 38 Air & Space L. 275

Tan, Alan Khee-Jin, "Aviation Policy in the Philippines and the Impact of the Proposed Southeast Asian Single Aviation Market" (2009) 34 Air and Space L. 285

Tan, Alan Khee-Jin, "Chapter 15 The Future of Multilateral Liberalization of Air Transport in Asia" in David Duval, ed., *Air Transport in the Asia Pacific* (Burlington: Ashgate, 2014) 259

Tan, Alan Khee-Jin, "India's Evolving Policy on International Civil Aviation" (2013) 38 Air and Sp. L. 439

Tan, Alan Khee-Jin, "Liberalizing Aviation in the Asia-Pacific Region: The Impact of the EU Horizontal Mandate" (2006) 31 Air & Sp. L. 432

Tan, Alan Khee-Jin, "Prospects for a Single Aviation Market in Southeast Asia" (2009) 34 Ann. Air & Sp. L. 253

Tan, Alan Khee-Jin, "Singapore' New Air Services Agreements with the E.U. and The U.K.: Implications for liberalization in Asia" (2008) 73 J. Air L. & Com. 351

Tan, Alan Khee-Jin, "The 2004 Damascus Agreement: Liberalizing Market Access and Ownership Rules for Arab Air Carriers" (2010) 35 Ann. Air & Sp. L. 1

Tan, Alan Khee-Jin, "The 2010 ASEAN–China Air Transport Agreement: Placing the Cart before the Horse?" (2012) 37 Air & Space L. 35

Tan, Alan Khee-Jin, "The 2010 ASEAN–China Air Transport Agreement: Much Ado over Fifth Freedom Rights?" (2014) 14 Issues in Aviation and Policy 19

Tan, Alan Khee-Jin, "The ASEAN Multilateral Agreement on Air Services: En Route to Open Skies?" (2010) 16 Journal of Air Transport Management 289

Toe Laer, H.S. Rutger Jan, "Kick-starting Cross-border Alliances: Approval and Clearance; the past, the present and the future" (2007) 32 Air & Space L. 287

Toe Laer, H.S. Rutger Jan, "The ECJ Decisions: 'Blessing in Disguise'?" (2006) 31 Air & Space L. 19

Tompkins George N. Jr., "Some Thought to Ponder when Considering Whether to Adopt the New Aviation General Risks and Unlawful Interference Convention Proposed by ICAO"(2008) 33 Air & Space L. 81

Toner, Mark & Willis, Edward, "Foreign Ownership and Control of International Airlines: A New Agenda for Reform" (2012) 24 Air and Space Law. 1

Van Fenema, Peter, "EU Horizontal Agreements: Community Designation and the 'Free Rider' Clause" (2006) 31 Air & Space L. 172

Van Houtte, Ben, "Relevant Markets in Air Transport" (1990) 27 Common Market Law Review. 521

Wallace, Claire & Stromsnes, Kristin, "Introduction: European Identities" (2008) 9 Perspectives on European Politics and Society 378

Warden, Jacob A., "Open Skies" at a Crossroads: How the United States and European Union Should Use the ECJ Transport Cases to Reconstruct the Transatlantic Aviation Regime" Northwestern Journal of International Law & Business Vol 24 Issue 1 (2003) 227

Wassenbergh, Henri A., "The Future of International Air Transport Law: A Philosophy of Law and the Need for Reform of the Economic Regulation of International Air Transport in the 21st Century" (1995) 20 Ann. Air & Sp. L. 405

Wensveen, John G. & Leick, Ryan, "The long-haul low-cost carrier: A unique business model" (2009) 15 Journal of Air Transport Management 127

Werden, Gregory J., "The History of Antitrust Market Delineation" (1992) 76 Marq. L. Rev. 123

Whalen, W. Tom, "A Panel Data Analysis of Code Sharing, Antitrust Immunity and Open Skies Treaties in International Aviation Market" (2007) 30 Review of Industrial Organization. 39

Wu, Zhouhong, Comment to "Implementation the Process of the European Common Air Transport Market and the Common Air Transport Policy" by Kenneth Button (2003) 90

Yamazaki, Kazuhide, "Airline Ownership and Control Requirement: Changes in the Air – A Legal View from Japan" (2006) 31 Air & Space L. 50

Yang, Meong-Cho, "Competition Law and Policy of the Republic of Korea" (2009) 54 The Antitrust Bulletin. 621

Yu, Gong, "U.S. – E.U. Open Skies Deal and Its Implication for the Liberalization of International Air Transport Services: A Chinese Perspective" (2009) 2 Journal of East Asia and International Law. 129

Zhang, Anming & Chen, Hongmin, "Evolutions of China's Air Transport Development and Policy towards International Liberalization" (2003) 42:3 Transportation Journal 31

Zhang, Anming, "Northeast Asia's Unified, Concerted Approaches to the Inter-continental and Sub-continental Air Services Linkages" in Yeon Myung Kim & Sungwon Lee, eds., *Negotiating Strategies for Creating a Liberalized Air Transport Bloc in Northeast Asia* (Honolulu, HI; The Korea Transport Institute & East-West Center, 2009) 461

Zheng, Xingwu, "China's Approaches to Aviation Market Liberalization in Northeast Asia: An Academic Viewpoint" in Yeon Myung Kim & Sungwon Lee, eds., *Negotiating Strategies for Creating a Liberalized Air Transport Bloc in Northeast Asia* (Ilsan: Korea Transport Institute, 2009) 295

H   Reports

"Antitrust Alert: China Takes First Enforcement Action against International Price Fixing Cartel" Jones Day (January 2013)

"Lessons from Four Years of Antitrust Enforcement in China" Jones Day (September 2012)

Air France – KLM, "Reference Document 2004-05" (2005)

AirAsia Berhad, "Annual Report 2011 Reports and Financial Statements" (1 January 2011)

AirAsia, "Prospectus 2004" (11 March 2004)

Arab Air Carrier Organization (AACO), "AACO / IATA Declaration Aeropolitical Forum, Abu Dhabi" (16 January 2012)

Arab Air Carriers Organization, "Agenda Item 9: Air Transport, Air Transport Relations between the Arab World & the European Union" (the First Meeting of Directors General of Civil Aviation – Middle East Region, DGCA-MID/1-WP/31) (22 February 2011)

Asia Aviation Public Company Limited, "Annual Report 2012" (1 January 2012)

Association of Caribbean States, "20 Years Promoting Cooperation in the Greater Caribbean" (April 2014)

Aviation Strategy, "LAN Airlines: Discovered by the money managers" (November 2006)

CAPA, "Air China-Lufthansa Group JV will control 35% of Europe-China market while easing growth tensions" (8 July 2014)

CAPA, "Air China and United Airlines vie for title of largest carrier between China and the United States" (28 January 2015)

CAPA, "Air Pacific's trouble in paradise" (19 June 2009)

CAPA, "Airline ownership & control. Why might Europe uphold something its officials call "stupid"?" (28 May 2014)

CAPA, "Airlines in Transition report, Part 1: The natural history of airline alliances" (16 April 2013)

CAPA, "Alitalia and Etihad complete deal as Emirates and Qatar add seats. Record growth for Italy-Gulf" (2 January 2015)

CAPA, "Asia's LCCs: Airasia leads the pack" Airline Leader 25 (November 2014)

CAPA, "Asia leads the field in airport construction but privatisation opportunities are few" *Airline Leader* 25 (November 2014)

CAPA, "Calm before the Big Bang – Japan Airlines on track to report first profit in three years" (11 February 2008)

CAPA, "China's aviation reforms and a rush of airline start-ups boost growth prospects; and fleets recycle" (3 January 2015)

CAPA, "China's territorial disputes with Japan and the Philippines see traffic dips" (21 September 2012)

CAPA, "China–Japan traffic bottoms out but faces massive challenge; Spring Airlines to launch new routes" (17 January 2013)

CAPA, "China Eastern-Qantas & Air China-Air New Zealand JVs show renewed interest from Chinese airlines" (26 November 2014)

CAPA, "China Eastern, Delta and Hainan Airlines' new routes accelerate US-China aviation development" (23 February 2015)

CAPA, "China's looming airspace squeeze" (21 April 2011)

CAPA, "China's Power Change and Airline Impacts" *Airline Leader* 15 (October 2012) 28;

CAPA, "Chinese airlines overtake US carriers across the Pacific. The big dilemma: US-China open skies?" (4 May 2015)

CAPA, "Chinese airlines pioneer new international strategies: JVs to overcome internal limitations" (12 March 2014),

CAPA, "Chinese carriers in for the long haul but face stumbling blocks along the way" (26 December 2012)

CAPA, "Competition in Southeast Asia's low-cost airline sector heats up as capacity surges" (5 September 2013)

CAPA, "Delta Air Lines seeks a Tokyo Haneda base. Skymark a potential partner, to shake up alliances?" (2 August 2013)

CAPA, "Delta Air to use its Chinese SkyTeam partners to grow, connecting over the main hubs" (15 July 2013)

CAPA, "Etihad & Alitalia agree and affirm their partnership vision. Protectionist voices will become louder" (9 August 2014)

CAPA, "Etihad raises its Europe profile with codeshares and equity, expanding indirect connections" (23 June 2014)

CAPA, "For Northeast Asia's airlines, previously slow to adapt, 2015 spells opportunity" *Airline Leader* 26 (February 2015)

CAPA, "Foreign LCCs line up for JVs in South Korea as aviation market changes" (21 January 2013)

CAPA, "India to investigate SWISS and Austrian ownership concerns" (17 November 2011)

CAPA, "Jakarta Halim Airport re-opening frees Soekarno-Hatta slots for Citilink, Garuda, AirAsia, Lion Air" (12 January 2014)

CAPA, "Japan's expanding LCCs drive growth but need cultivating; Spring Airlines and AirAsia re-entry loom" (5 April 2014)

CAPA, "Japan and China expand bilateral air services agreement" (9 August 2012)

CAPA, "Japan awards international Tokyo Haneda Airport slots, but Narita Airport remains the main hub", (9 October 2013)

CAPA, "Japan relaxes Chinese visas to stimulate visitor & airline growth, following Southeast Asia success" (13 January 2015)

CAPA, "Jeju Air: 2014 is first year where Korean Govt has really supported LCC development" (13 October 2014)

CAPA, "Jetstar Hong Kong licence application rejected: Hong Kong becomes an island of protectionism in Asia" (29 June 2015)

CAPA, "Jetstar Hong Kong's local investor reflects HK's new attitude, learning from Hong Kong Airlines" (18 June 2013);CAPA, "Korea steps back into the dark. Airline protectionism flourishes in Seoul" (28 August 2008)

CAPA, "Korean Air returns to profit in 1Q2014 on the back of yield recovery and cost discipline" (11 June 2014)

CAPA, "Korean Air seeks new markets after betting the house on N America, seemingly without SkyTeam support" (30 September 2013)

CAPA, "LCCs help Japanese domestic market grow for first time in six years, but market situation still dire" (8 August 2013)

CAPA, "Lion's Malindo Air to compete vs AirAsia, Jetstar & Tigerair on world's top international LCC route" (12 October 2014)

CAPA, "New runways for Tokyo Haneda and Narita airports would allow Japan to catch up to other Asian hubs" (19 June 2014)

CAPA, "North Asia's aviation gradually breaks with tradition but a legacy mindset persists" *Airline Leader* 25 (November 2014)

CAPA, "North Asian LCC, Round 1: Inertia prevails over innovation in 2013" *Airline Leader* 18 (Aug-Sep 2013) 36;

CAPA, "North Pacific air route development: Part 4. Japan's hub role diminishes; Partnerships remain weak" (26 August 2014)

CAPA, "Outbound Chinese tourists to surpass 100 million in 2014. Northeast Asian airlines first to benefit" (16 July 2014)

CAPA, "Southeast Asia low-cost airline fleet to expand by almost 20% in 2014. Are more deferrals needed?" (11 March 2014)

CAPA, "Spring Airlines shares increase 44% on trading debut" (22 January 2015)

CAPA, "Tokyo Narita Outlook Part 1: once a mega hub, international and transit passengers decline" (23 March 2015)

CAPA, "U.S.-Japan Airline Alliances Become Lopsided as JAL, ANA Expand while U.S. to Shift to Other Markets" (4 February 2013)

CAPA, "Virgin Australia CEO John Borghetti interview: dual-brand strategies, Asia & being a modern airline" (4 December 2014)

CAPA, Consulting's 2008 report, Ian Thomas, David Stone, Alan Khee-Jin Tan, Andrew Drysdale, & Phil McDermott, *Developing ASEAN's Single Aviation Market and Regional Air Services Arrangements with Dialogue Partners* (Final Report, June 2008, REPSF II Project No. 07/003)

Centre for Aviation (CAPA), "13 Chinese airlines could each have a fleet of over 100 aircraft by 2020" (26 May 2014)

Centre for International Law, "ASEAN Integration Through Law Plenary 1 – General Architecture of ASEAN" (4 July 2013)

Centre for International Law, "AVIATION, Lifting-The-Barriers Roundtables" (Preliminary paper presented to the 2013 Network ASEAN Forum, August 2013)

China, "Chinese Paper on Transportation Industry on Implementation of the Recommendations on More Competitive Air Service" (Paper presented to the 22nd APEC Transportation Working Group Meeting, 1-5 September 2003)

Cronin, Patrick M., "Taking Off Civil Aviation, Forward Progress and Japan's Third Arrow Reforms" (Washington D.C.: Center for a New American Security, 2013)

EU Member States, "European Experience of Air Transport Liberalization" (2003 February)

EU Member States, "The European Union's Commitment to Cooperation with the World Aviation Community"

European Commission and the United States Department of Transportation, "Transatlantic Airline Alliances: Competitive Issues and Regulatory Approaches" (16 November 2010)

European Commission, "Report from the Commission to the European Parliament and the Council on the Implementation of the Single Sky legislation: time to deliver" (Brussels: EC, 2011)

FlightStats, "On-time Performance Report – June 2013" (15 August 2013)

Fu, Xiaowen & Oum, Tae Hoon, "Dominant Carrier Performance and International Liberalisation: The Case of North East Asia", Discussion Paper No 2015-03, International Transport Forum (Paris: OECD, 2015)

Gillespie, William & Richard, Oliver M., "Antitrust Immunity and International Airline Alliances", Economic Analysis Group Discussion Paper, Antitrust Division, US Department of Justice, (EAG 11-1) (February 2011)

Gresham, Zane, "China Moves to Increase Private and International Participation in Airports and Aviation" Morrison & Foerster (29 June 2004)

Holden, Michel, "Stages of Economic Integration: From Autarky to Economic Union" (13 February 2003, PRB 02-49E)

IATA "Liberalization of Air Transport and the GATS" IATA Discussion Paper to WTO (October 1999)

IATA, "Economics Briefing the Economic Benefits Generated by Alliances and Joint Venture" (2011)

International Chamber of Commerce (ICC) Committee on Air Transport, "Policy Statement: The Need for Greater Liberalization of International Air Transport" (1 December 2005)

Intervistas-ga2, "The Economic Impact of Air Service Liberalization" (2006)

Japan, The Council for the Asian Gateway Initiative, "Asian Gateway Initiative" (16 May 2007)

Mendes De Leon, Pablo, "Competition in International Markets: A Comparative Analysis" Paper to Organisation for Economic Co-operation and Development (OECD) (13 June 2014)

National Institute for Research Advancement, "Proposal for Promotion of the Realization of the BESETO Corridor Vision – Toward sustained development in the Northeast Asia Region" (March 2007)

OAG, "May FACTS" (2013)

OECD, "Background Document" (OECD Workshop on Regulatory Reform in International Air Cargo Transportation, Paris) (5-6 July 1999)

OECD, "International Regulatory Co-operation: Case Studies, Vol. 3 Transnational Private Regulation and Water Management" (2013)

OECD, "Liberalisation of International Air Cargo Transport" (2002)

Pearce, Brian "The Economic Benefits Generated by Alliance and Joint Ventures" IATA Economics Briefing (28 November 2011)

Piermartini, Roberta and Rousova, Linda, "Liberalization of Air Transport Services and Passenger Traffic", Staff Working Paper ERSD-2008-06, World Trade Organization (2008)

Rathus, Joel, "China-Japan–Korea Trilateral Cooperation and the East Asian Community", *East Asia Forum* (15 June 2010)

Steer Davies Gleave, "Competition Impact of Airline Code-Share Agreements" (London: Steer Davies Gleave, 2007)

Tan, Alan Khee-Jin, "Assessing the Prospects for an E.U.-ASEAN Air Transport Agreement", Discussion Paper No 2015-02, International Transport Forum (Paris: OECD, 2015)

Tan, Alan Khee-Jin, "Toward a Single Aviation Market in ASEAN: Regulatory Reform and Industry Challenges" 2013 Economic Research Institute for ASEAN and East Asia (ERIA) Discussion Paper 2013-22 (October 2013)

The Pacific Islands Forum Secretariat, "The Pacific Islands Air Services Agreement (PIASA): Phased Development of a Single Aviation Market in the Pacific" (February 2003)

Tong, Sarah Y. & Chong, Catherine Siew Keng, "China-ASEAN Free Trade Area in 2010: A Regional Perspective" 2010 East Asia Institute, National University of Singapore, Background Brief No. 519 (12 April 2010)

Trilateral Cooperation Secretariat (TCS), "2013 Trilateral Statistics – Trade" (March 2014)

U.K., Authority of the House of Lords, ""Open Skies" or Open Markets? The Effect of the European Court of Justice (ECJ) Judgments on Aviation Relations Between the European Union (EU) and the United States of America (USA)" (London: The Stationary Office, 2003)

U.K., Civil Aviation Authority, "Ownership and Control Liberalisation: A Discussion Paper" (London: The Stationery Office, 2006)

U.K., UK Competition Commission, "Guidelines for market investigations: Their role, procedures, assessment and remedies" (April 2013)

U.S., US Congress, Office of Technology Assessment, "Airport and Air Traffic Control System (1982)" (Washington, D.C.: U.S. Government Printing Office, 1982)

U.S., US Department of Justice & Federal Trade Commission, "Horizontal Merger Guidelines" (19 August 2010)

United Nations Conference on Trade and Development, "Air Transport Services: the Positive Agenda for Developing Countries" (16 April 1999)

United Nations, "Economic and Social Commission for Western Asia (ESCWA) Study on Air Transport in the Arab World" (2007)

UNWTO (World Tourism Organization) & World Travel & Tourism Council (WTTC), "The Impact of Visa Facilitation in ASEAN Member States" (January 2014)

UNWTO (World Tourism Organization), "Visa Openness Report 2014" (November 2014)

World Bank, "Pacific Islands Overview" (updated 1 October 2014)

World Tourism Organization (UNWTO) & World Travel & Tourism Council (WTTC), "The Impact of Visa Facilitation in APEC Economies" (Madrid: Centro Español de Derechos Reprográfico, 2013)

WTO, Council for Trade in Services, "Quantitative Air Services Agreements Review (QUASAR): Part B: PRELIMINARY RESULTS" S/C/W/270/Add.1 (2006)

Yang, Xiuyun & Yu, Hong, "China's airports : recent development and future challenges" (Singapore : East Asian Institute, National University of Singapore, 2010)

I   Speeches, Addresses, and Presentations

Calleja, Daniel, "Aviation in the European Union – an Overview" (EU-Latin America Civil Aviation Summit Rio de Janeiro, 24-26 May 2010)

Choi, Jeong-Ho, "Keynote address to the 52th Conference of the Korea Society of Air & Space Law and Policy" (Seoul, 23 May 2014)

Hutt, Jonathan, "Spring Airlines International Expansion from China into North Asia" (Presentation material to the CAPA LCCs & New Age Airlines, Seoul, 4 September 2013)

IATA (Speech at Arab Air Carriers Organization Assembly, Cairo, 20 October 2010)

Kim, Sang-Do "Strategy for Liberalized Air Transport Market in NE Asia" (Presentation material presented to the 2009 ICAO Legal Seminar in Asia-Pacific Region, Seoul, 2 April 2009)

Lee, Yeong Heok, "Open Sky and Common Aviation Market in Northeast Asia" (Presentation material presented to the 51th International Conference on Law and Policy in Air and Space Field – Enhancing International Cooperation in Air Transport between Korea and China, Seoul, 6 December 2013)

Lee, Yeong Heok, "The Effects of Open Sky and its Prospects in NE Asia" (Presentation to the International Conference on Air Transport, Air Law and Regulation, Singapore, 24-26 May 2010)

Oum, Tae Hoon, "Air Transport Network Developments and Challenges to East Asian Airlines and Policy Makers" (Presentation material presented to the 1st International Symposium on Liberalizing Air Transport in Northeast Asia, Seoul, 9 June 2006)

Oum, Tae Hoon, "Liberalization and Future Developments in Asia-Pacific Air Transport, Networks and Policy" (Presentation material to the 3rd Conference on International Air Transport Cooperation, Seoul, May 2010)

Rifai, Taleb, Keynote Address to the Sixth ICAO Worldwide Air Transport Conference, Montreal, 18 March 2013)

Rogerson, Evan, "Emerging Issues and Challenges of the WTO" (Speech to National University of Singapore Centre for International Law Distinguished Speaker Series, Singapore, 19 June 2013)

Satar, Emirsyah, "The next biggest growth opportunities for Indonesia's airline market" (Address to the 7th Annual Aviation Outlook Asia Conference, Singapore, 29 October 2014)

Shane, Jeffery, "Open Skies Agreements and the European Court of Justice" (Speech presented to the American Bar Association's forum on Air and Space Law, November 2002)

Sobie, Brendan, "LCC Subsidiaries of Legacy Carriers" (Presented to the ICAO/CAAC Symposium on Low Cost Carriers, Beijing, October 2014)

Taguchi, Yoshiro, "Updates on Japan's International Aviation Policy" (Presentation to IATA Schedule Committee, 13 November 2011)

Tan, Alan Khee-Jin, "Aeropolitical Brand Battles in Asia" (Presentation to the International Air Transport Association (IATA) Legal Symposium, Seoul, Korea, 26 February 2015)

Tan, Alan Khee-Jin, "AVIATION, Lifting-The-Barriers Roundtables" (Presentation to the 2013 Network ASEAN Forum, Singapore, August 2013)

J Press Releases

Air Canada, Press Release, "Air China and Air Canada to Form Comprehensive Strategic Alliance, Strengthening Canada-China Network" (8 November 2014), online: <www.air-canada.com/cn/zh/news/en/141108.html>

AirAsia, Press Release, "ANA and AirAsia to form 'AirAsia Japan'" (21 July 2011), online: <www.airasia.com/my/en/press-releases/ana-and-airasia-form-airasia-japan.page>

All Nippon Airways (ANA), Press Release, "ANA, Continental and United Secure Japanese Anti-Trust Immunity for Trans-Pacific Joint Venture" (22 October 2010), online: <www.ana.co.jp/eng/aboutana/press/2010/pdf/101022.pdf>

American Airlines, Press Release, "American Airlines and Japan Airlines Announce Joint Business Benefits for Trans-Pacific" (11 January 2011)

ANA, Press Release, "Antitrust Immunity Requested for United-All Nippon Airways Joint Cargo Venture" (21 November 2014), online: <https://www.ana.co.jp/eng/aboutana/press/2014/141121.html>

Bursa Malaysia Announcement, "AirAsia Japan Joint Venture" (21 July 2011), online: <http://announcements.bursamalaysia.com/EDMS/edmswebh.nsf/all/482576120041BDAA482578D4001D24CD/$File/AirAsia%20Japan%20Joint%20Venture.pdf>

European Commission, Press Release, "Antitrust: British Airways, American Airlines and Iberia commitments to ensure competition on transatlantic passenger air transport markets made legally binding" (14 July 2010), online: <http://europa.eu/rapid/press-release_IP-10-936_en.htm>

European Commission, Press Release, "Breakthrough in EU–US second-stage Open Skies negotiations: Vice-President Kallas welcomes draft agreement" (March 25, 2010), online: <http://europa.eu/rapid/press-release_IP-10-371_en.htm?locale=en>

European Commission, Press Release, "FAQs on the Second Stage EU-US "Open Skies" Agreement and Existing First Stage Air Services Agreement" (March 25, 2010), online: <http://europa.eu/rapid/press-release_MEMO-10-103_en.htm?locale=en>

European Commission, Press Release, "Mergers: Commission approves Etihad's acquisition of joint control over Alitalia, subject to conditions" (14 November 2014), online: <http://europa.eu/rapid/press-release_IP-14-1766_en.htm>

European Commission, Press Release, "New Era for Air Transport: Loyola de Palacio welcomes the mandate given to the European Commission for negotiating an Open Aviation Area with the US", IP/03/806 (5 June 2003), online:<http://europa.eu/rapid/press-release_IP-03-806_en.htm>

Japan Airlines, Press Release, "Japan Airlines Submits Antitrust Immunity Application for a Tighter Cooperation with American Airlines on the Trans-Pacific Routes to the

Ministry of Land, Infrastructure, Transport and Tourism of Japan" (18 June 2010), online: <http://press.jal.co.jp/en/uploads/20100618_-_JAL_submits_ATI_application_to_JCAB_FINAL.pdf>

Japan Airlines, Press Release, "Japan Airlines Welcomes the Approval by the Ministry of Land, Infrastructure, Transport and Tourism of Japan for Antitrust Immunity with American Airlines to Cooperate on Trans-Pacific Routes" (22 October 2010), online: <http://press.jal.co.jp/en/uploads/20101022%20-%20JAL%20receives%20Approval%20from%20MLIT%20for%20ATI%20Application%20with%20American%20American%20Airlines.pdf>

Japan Ministry of Land, Infrastructure, Transport and Tourism, Press Release, "Aeronautical Consultations between Japan and Austria", online: <www.mlit.go.jp/common/001042207.pdf>

Lufthansa, Press Release, "Lufthansa and Air China strengthen partnership" (7 July 2014), online: <www.lufthansa.com/mediapool/pdf/90/media_649885890.pdf>

Northeast Asia Logistics Information Service Network (NEAL-NET), Press Release, "The 4th China-Japan-Korea Ministerial Conference on Transport and Logistics Held in Busan Korea" (19 July 2012), online: <www.nealnet.org/nealnet/web/webAction.do?action=NewsView&newsid=40288a49380db66d01389e8984d10a38>

US Department of State, Press Release No. 510, reprinted in [Oct. 1998] 3 Av. L. Rep. (CCH) 26,016 at 21.117 (Jul. 25, 1946)

US Department of State, Press Release, "United States and Japan Sign Open Skies Memorandum of Understanding on Air Transportation" (25 October 2010)

US Department of Transportation, Press Release, "U.S., Singapore Reach Open Skies Aviation Agreement" (23 January 1997), online: <www.usembassy-israel.org.il/publish/press/trnsport/archive/1997/january/td10124.htm>

WTO, Press Release, "WTO successfully concludes negotiations on China's entry" (17 September 2001), online: <www.wto.org/english/news_e/pres01_e/pr243_e.htm>

K   News Articles

"AirAsia Korea prospects fade as Seoul blocks launch" *ch-aviation* (18 May 2014), online: <www.ch-aviation.com/portal/news/28152-airasia-korea-prospects-fade-as-seoul-blocks-launch>

"ANA seeks anti-trust immunity for JV" *The Business Desk* (21 November 2014), online: <www.thebusinessdesk.com/northwest/ana-seeks-anti-trust-immunity-for-jv.html>

"China's Air Regulator Will Consider Ways to Boost Budget-Carrier Market" *The Wall Street Journal*, (July 29, 2013), online: <http://stream.wsj.com/story/latest-headlines/SS-2-63399/SS-2-288619/>

"China's private airlines facing cross-winds" *Financial Times* (March 22, 2010) <www.ft.com/intl/cms/s/0/6c9e60bc-35d5-11df-aa43-00144feabdc0.html#axzz2eB2aRTYj>

"Chinese aviation's on-time rate dropped to 68% in 2014" *China Travel News* (9 March 2015), online: <www.chinatravelnews.com/article/print/89870>

"Etihad: Flying against Convention" *The Economist* (28 June 2014)

"Foreign visitors to Seoul exceed 10 million in 2013" *The Korea Herald* (23 January 2014), online: <www.koreaherald.com/view.php?ud=20140123000963>

"Is it time for China–US Open Skies?" *Global Travel Industry News* (9 April 2015), online: <www.eturbonews.com/57422/it-time-China–US-open-skies>

"Japan gives up on launching flights to Nanyuan Airport before Olympics." *Kyodo News International* (8 May 2008), online: <www.thefreelibrary.com/Japan+gives+up+on+launching+flights+to+Nanyuan+Airport+before...-a0179075052>

"Korean Air / DELTA Reduces Codeshare Operation in S13" *Airline Route* (26 August 2013), online: <http://airlineroute.net/2013/08/26/kedl-codeshare-s13/>

"United Continental and ANA launch trans-Pacific joint venture" *Japan Today* (5 April 2011), online: <www.japantoday.com/category/travel/view/united-continental-and-ana-launch-trans-pacific-joint-venture>

Anderlini, Jamil, "China's private airlines facing cross-winds" *Financial Times* (22 March 2010)

Boehmer, Jay, "Slots, Visas Stymie U.S.-China Open Skies", *Business Travel News* (11 April 2011), online: <www.businesstravelnews.com/article.aspx?id=20338&ida=Airlines&a=btn>

CAPA, *"Japan and South Korea Reach Historic "Open Skies" Deal"* (3 August 2007), online: <http://centreforaviation.com/analysis/japan-and-south-korea-reach-historic-open-skies-deal-1928>

Carey, Susan, "Delta, China Eastern Try to Solve Air Traffic Riddle" *The Wall Street Journal* (19 March 2014), online: <www.wsj.com/articles/SB10001424052702304732804579425363833070996>

Chiu, Joanne, "Cathay Pacific, Air China, to Inject $321.4 Million into Cargo Joint Venture" *The Wall Street Journal* (26 June 2014), online: <www.wsj.com/articles/cathay-pacific-air-china-to-inject-321-4m-into-air-cargo-joint-venture-1403783543>

Chiu, Joanne, "China's Air Regulator Will Consider Ways to Boost Budget-Carrier Market" *The Wall Street Journal* (29 July 2013), online: <http://online.wsj.com/news/articles/SB10001424127887323854904578634920047272886>

Chiu, Joanne, "Japan Approves Spring Air's Low-Cost Venture" *The Wall Street Journal* (27 December 2013), online: <www.wsj.com/articles/SB10001424052702303799404579283503425437022>

Dupont, Guillaume, "Beijing New Airports" *New Airport Insider* (24 September 2014), online: <http://dcdesigntech.com/new-airport-insider/beijing-new-airports/>

Dupont, Guillaume, "China Airports Build: Too Many Too Fast?" *New Airport Insider* (14 January 2014), online: <http://dcdesigntech.com/new-airport-insider/china-airports-build-too-many-too-fast/>

Fairless, Tom & Michaels, Daniel, "EU Probes Ownership of Virgin, Four Other Airlines" *The Wall Street Journal* (4 April 2014), online: <www.wsj.com/articles/SB10001424052702303847804579481071621614740>

Govindasamy, Siva, "Jetstar counts the cost of prolonged delay in Hong Kong take-off" *Reuters* (17 November 2014), online: <www.reuters.com/article/2014/11/17/airlines-hong-kong-jetstar-idUSL4N0SQ1J220141117>

Hata, Norie "JAL/Delta alliance could have trouble receiving ATI approval, experts say" *Financial Times* (4 January 2010), online: <www.ft.com/intl/cms/s/2/68f45a0e-f979-11de-8085-00144feab49a.html#axzz2ZBsyV8rp>

Jessop, David, "Who will save Caribbean Aviation?" *The Gleaner* (28 April 2013), online: <http://jamaica-gleaner.com/gleaner/20130428/business/business5.html>

Jiang, Sijia, "As public hearing wraps, Jetstar Hong Kong awaits word of its fate" *South China Morning Post* (15 February 2015), online: <www.scmp.com/business/companies/article/1713538/public-hearing-wraps-jetstar-hong-kong-awaits-word-its-fate>

Jung, Kwon-hyun, "Korea-Japan Visa Waiver" *Chosun-ilbo* (7 February 2006), online: <www.chosun.com/national/news/200602/200602060370.html>

Kanter, James & Clark, Nicola, "U.S. and E.U. Agree to Expand Open Skies Accord" *The New York Times* (25 March 2010), online :<www.nytimes.com/2010/03/26/business/global/26skies.html>

Karp, Aaron, "LAN/TAM complete merger under LATAM Airlines Group" *ATW* (22 June 2012), online: <http://atwonline.com/news/lantam-complete-merger-under-latam-airlines-group>

Kitching, Chris, "Busiest flight routes in the world revealed with number one carrying SEVEN MILLION passengers a year" *Main Online* (8 August 2014), online: <www.dailymail.co.uk/travel/travel_news/article-2719733/Busiest-flight-routes-world-revealed.html>.

Lin, Izzie, "China Rolls Out Policies to Boost Budget Airlines" *World Civil Aviation Resource Net* (6 November 2013), online: <www.wcarn.com/news/30/30194.html>

Mutzabaugh, Ben, "AA, Korean cross alliance lines on Dallas codeshare pact" *USA TODAY* (4 February 2015), online: <www.usatoday.com/story/todayinthesky/2015/02/04/american-korean-air-to-codeshare-on-seoul-dallas-route/22862651/>

Ng, Jeffrey, "Delta Shifts Focus From Japan as Trans-Pacific Hub" *The Wall Street Journal* (10 February 2014), online: <www.wsj.com/articles/SB10001424052702303874504579375670306517530>

Olczak, Nicholas, "Japan and China expand bilateral air service" *Business Traveller* (9 August 2012), online: <www.businesstraveller.com/asia-pacific/news/japan-and-china-expand-bilateral-air-service>

Pan, Jane, "ANALYSIS: The role of foreign investment in Chinese airlines" *Flightglobal* (21 Nov 2012), online: <www.flightglobal.com/news/articles/analysis-the-role-of-foreign-investment-in-chinese-379324/>

Park, Kyunghee & Tan, Clement, "China Eastern Sets Up Budget Carrier, Rivals May Follow" *Bloomberg* (2 July 2014), online: <www.bloomberg.com/news/2014-07-02/china-eastern-sets-up-budget-carrier-rivals-may-follow.html>

Park, Kyunghee & Wang, Jasmine "Jakarta 4:30 A.M. Flights Show Budget Carriers Outgrow Airports" *Bloomberg* (4 February 2013), online: <www.bloomberg.com/news/2013-02-03/jakarta-4-30-a-m-flights-show-budget-carriers-outgrow-airports.html>

Parker, Andrew, "Moscow kickback set to squeeze western airlines" *Financial Times* (6 August 2014)

Raghuvanshi, Gaurav, "AirAsia Finds Partners for Return to Japan" *The Wall Street Journal* (1 July 2014), online: <www.wsj.com/articles/airasia-finds-partners-for-return-to-japan-1404202254>

Reyes, Mary Ann LL., "Fernandes, 'Tonyboy' team up for AirAsia Phils", *The Philippine Star* (17 December 2010), online: <www.philstar.com/business/639510/fernandes-tonyboy-team-airasia-phils>

Sanchanta, Mariko & Esterl, Mike, "JAL Stays in AMR Alliance, Delta Out" *The Wall Street Journal* (7 February 2010), online: <www.wsj.com/articles/SB10001424052748703615904575053860586727220>

Tan, Alan Khee-Jin, "Clear take-off on Asean Open Skies" *The Straits Times* (5 April 2013)

Tan, Alan Khee-Jin, "Jetstar Hong Kong's arrival puts airline control rules in the spotlight" *South China Morning Post* (15 February 2015), online: <www.scmp.com/comment/article/1493619/jetstar-hong-kongs-arrival-puts-airline-control-rules-spotlight>

Thomas, Geoffrey, "Korean Air, Sinotrans ink JV cargo carrier agreement" *ATW* (19 September 2006), online: <http://atwonline.com/news/korean-air-sinotrans-ink-jv-cargo-carrier-agreement>

Thompson, Chuck, "China airports world's worst for on-time performance" *CNN* (12 July 2013), online: <http://edition.cnn.com/2013/07/12/travel/china-airport-performance/>

Tiezzi, Shannon, "China–Japan-South Korea Hold FTA Talks Despite Political Tension" *The Diplomat* (5 March 2014)

Walton, John, "New airport for Beijing: "impossible to add even one more flight" to current airport" *Australian Business Traveller* (13 January 2011), online: <www.ausbt.com.au/new-airport-for-beijing-impossible-to-add-even-one-more-flight-to-current-airport>

Wattanapruttipaisan, Thitipha, *Asia Views Regional Insights, Global Outreach Columns & Commentaries Priority integration sectors: performance and challenges Asia Views*, Bangkok Post (29 August 2006), online: <www.asean.org/resources/publications/published-articles/item/asiaviews-regional-insights-global-outreach-columns-commentaries-priority-integration-sectors-performance-and-challenges-asiaviews-edition-33iiiaug2006-2>

Wilson, Benét J., "What the Korean Air-American Air DFW Codeshare Means for the SkyTeam Alliance", *Airways News* (9 February 2015), online: <http://airwaysnews.com/blog/2015/02/09/what-the-korean-air-american-air-dfw-codeshare-means-for-the-skyteam-alliance/>

Zhang, Vanessa, "CAAC Mulls Low-Cost Carrier Terminal at New Beijing Airport" *World Civil Aviation Resource Net* (6 November 2013), online: <www.wcarn.com/news/30/30198.html>

L   Websites

All Nippon Airways, "Expanding Our Network with United Airlines!," online: <www.ana.co.jp/wws/us/e/local/amc/jv/>

Austrian Airlines' homepage, online: <www.austrian.com/?sc_lang=en&cc=AT>

CAPA, Profiles, "Air Dolomiti", online: <http://centreforaviation.com/profiles/airlines/air-dolomiti-en>

CAPA, Profiles, "Avianca El Salvador," online: <http://centreforaviation.com/profiles/airlines/avianca-el-salvador-ta>.

CAPA, Profiles, "Avianca", online: <http://centreforaviation.com/profiles/airlines/avianca-av>

CAPA, Profiles, "Jade Cargo International," online: <http://centreforaviation.com/profiles/airlines/jade-cargo-international-ji>

CAPA, Profiles, "Ryanair", online: <http://centreforaviation.com/profiles/airlines/ryanair-fr>

China Vitae, online: <www.chinavitae.com/biography/Li_Jiaxiang%7C4095>

Civil Aviation Administration of China, "中日民航会谈在武汉举行" (13 March 2007), online: <www.caac.gov.cn/L1/L3/L3_16/L3_16_3/200703/t20070313_1673.html>

Embassy of Japan in Singapore, "Visa Exemption For Nationals Of The Republic Of Korea", online: <www.sg.emb-japan.go.jp/visa_korea.htm>

Eurocontrol, "Single European Sky", online: <https://www.eurocontrol.int/dossiers/single-european-sky>

European Commission, "Bilateral Air Services Agreements brought into legal conformity since the Court of Justice of the EU judgments of 5 November 2002", online: <http://ec.europa.eu/transport/modes/air/international_aviation/external_aviation_policy/doc/table_-_asa_brought_into_legal_conformity_since_ecj_judgments-_january_2013.pdf>

European Commission, "External Aviation Policy", online: <http://ec.europa.eu/transport/modes/air/international_aviation/external_aviation_policy/neighbourhood_en.htm>

European Commission, "Internal Market", online: <http://ec.europa.eu/transport/modes/air/internal_market/index_en.htm>

European Commission, "Market integration", online: <http://ec.europa.eu/transport/modes/air/internal_market/integration_en.htm>

European Union, "EU institutions and other bodies", online: <http://europa.eu/about-eu/institutions-bodies/index_en.htm>

IATA's Direct Data Solutions, online: <www.arccorp.com/dds>

ICAO Asia & Pacific Regional Sub-Office, "APAC Civil/Military Cooperation Lecture/Seminar 2014 OVERVIEW", online: <www.icao.int/APAC/RSO-Beijing/Pages/APAC-Overview.aspx>

ICAO Asia & Pacific Regional Sub-Office, "Strategic Framework for the APAC Regional Sub-Office (RSO)", online: <www.icao.int/APAC/RSO-Beijing/Pages/Strategic.aspx>

Japanese Ministry of Land, Infrastructure, and Transport, "日本・.中国航空関係" (30 July 2012), online: <www.mlit.go.jp/common/000220340.pdf>

Korea-China–Japan Free Trade Agreements, online: <www.fta.go.kr/cnjp/>

Korea Aviation Information Portal, online: <www.airportal.go.kr/knowledge/statistics/index.jsp?pg=01>

Korean Ministry of Land, Infrastructure and Transport, "Aviation Policy," online: <http://english.molit.go.kr/USR/sectoral/>

Korean Ministry of Land, Infrastructure and Transport, "Plan for Advancing Incheon International Airport Authority" (24 August 2012), online: <www.mltm.go.kr/USR/policyTarget/m_24066/dtl.jsp?idx=153>

Korean Ministry of Land, Infrastructure and Transport, "The Aviation Policy Basic Plan" (10 August 2012), online: < www.molit.go.kr/USR/policyData/m_34681/dtl.jsp?search=&srch_dept_nm=&srch_dept_id=&srch_usr_nm=&srch_usr_titl=Y&srch_usr_ctnt=&search_regdate_s=&search_regdate_e=&psize=10&s_category=p_sec_7&p_category=701&lcmspage=1&id=256>

Multilateral Agreement on the Liberalization of International Air Transportation, "Countries", online: <www.maliat.govt.nz/country/>

Prime Minister of Japan and His Cabinet, "Council for Asian Gateway Initiative", online: <http://japan.kantei.go.jp/gateway/index_e.html>

SWISS homepage, online: <www.swiss.com/cn/EN/book/where-we-fly/route-network>

The Australian Foreign Investment Review Board (FIRB), "Civil Aviation", online: <www.firb.gov.au/content/other_investment/sensitive/aviation.asp?NavID=51>.

The Union of South American Nations, online: <www.unasursg.org>

Trilateral Cooperation Secretariat, "Overview of TCS", online: <www.tcs-asia.org/dnb/user/userpage.php?lpage=1_1_overview>.

Trilateral Cooperation Secretariat, online: <www.tcs-asia.org>

US Department of State, "Current Model Open Skies Agreement Text", online: <www.state.gov/e/eb/rls/othr/ata/114866.htm>

US Department of State, "Open Skies Partners" (updated on 14 January 2015), online: <www.state.gov/e/eb/rls/othr/ata/114805.htm>

US Department of Transportation, "Alliances and Codeshares" (updated 18 February 2015), online: <www.dot.gov/policy/aviation-policy/competition-data-analysis/alliance-codeshares>.

INDEX

A
African Civil Aviation Commission (AFCAC), 90
Agenda for Freedom, 171
Airline alliances, 193
Airline Deregulation Act, 25
Airport curfew, 110
Airport slots, 109
Airside, 109
Andean Pact, 83
Antitrust immunity, 39, 208, 209, 210, 211
ASEAN–China Air Transport Agreement, 27
Asian Gateway, 26, 126
Asian Gateway Initiative, 126, 127

B
Bermuda II type, 107
Bermuda type 1 agreement, 7, 23
BESETO, 140
Bilateral air services agreements, 1, 2

C
Cabotage, 5
Capacity, 107
Caribbean Air Transport Agreement, 85, 86
Carrier designation, 104, 105
Carve-out, 214
Chicago Convention, 6
China-Japan–Korea Free Trade Agreement, 95
Civil Aviation Authority of China (CAAC), 116
Code-sharing, 35, 202

Comitè International Technique d'Experts Juridiques Aeriens (CITEJA), 11
Common market, 47
Community carrier, 9, 50, 173
Competition law, 204
Customs union, 46

D
Damascus Agreement, 81, 82
Divide-and-conquer strategy, 210

E
Economic union, 47
Economies of density, 194
Economies of scale, 194
Economies of scope, 194
effective control, 149, 151
Effective regulatory control, 156, 170
Equity alliance, 198, 199, 200
EU-US Air Transport Agreement, 56

F
Fortaleza Agreement, 83
Free trade area, 46
Freedoms of the air, 3
Frequency, 107

G
General Agreement on Trade in Services (GATS), 17

H
Holding Company, 178
Horizontal agreements, 55

I
ICAO air transport conference, 17

Interlining, 202
International Air Services Transit Agreement, 14
International Air Services Transport Agreement, 14

J
Joint ventures, 177, 184, 185, 189

L
Landside, 109
Latin American Civil Aviation Commission (LACAC), 83
Law and economics, 114
Liberalization, 1, 24

M
Market, 104, 240
Market Access, 103
Metal neutrality, 38
Metal Neutrality, 40, 217
Multilateral Agreement for the Full Liberalization of Air Freight Services (MAFLAFS), 66
Multilateral Agreement for the Full Liberalization of Passenger Air Services (MAFLPAS), 65
Multilateral Agreement on Air Services (MAAS), 64

N
National interest, 115

O
One route, one carrier, 116
Open Skies, 3
Open skies agreement, 3
Overflight, 111
Ownership and Control, 147

P
Pacific Islands Air Services Agreement (PIASA), 88
Preferential Treatment, 263
Principal Place of Business, 51, 170
Protectionism, 19

R
Regional Liberalization, 27
Relevant market, 240
Route Designation, 106

S
Shuttle services, 134, 141
Single aviation market (SAM), 45
Single European Act, 49
Substantial ownership, 148, 149
Substitutability, 241

T
Transnational private regulation (TPR), 249
Trilateral Agreement on Air Services (TAAS), 262
Trilateral Cooperation Secretariat (TCS), 10, 259

V
Vertical Mandate, 56
Visa, 112

W
World Trade Organization (WTO), 17

Y
Yamoussoukro Decision, 90

Essential Air and Space Law (Series Editor: Marietta Benkö)

Volume 1: Natalino Ronzitti & Gabriella Venturini (eds.), The Law of Air Warfare – Contemporary Issues, ISBN 978-90-77596-14-2

Volume 2: Marietta Benkö & Kai-Uwe Schrogl (eds.), Space Law: Current Problems and Perspectives for Future Regulations, ISBN 978-90-77596-11-1

Volume 3: Tare Brisibe, Aeronautical Public Correspondence by Satellite, ISBN 978-90-77596-10-4

Volume 4: Michael Milde, International Air Law and ICAO, ISBN 978-90-77596-54-8

Volume 5: Markus Geisler & Marius Boewe, The German Civil Aviation Act, ISBN 978-90-77596-72-2

Volume 6: Ulrich Steppler & Angela Klingmüller, EU Emissions Trading Scheme and Aviation, ISBN 978-90-77596-79-1

Volume 7: Heiko van Schyndel (ed.), Aviation Code of the Russian Federation, ISBN 978-90-77596-80-7

Volume 8: Zang Hongliang & Meng Qingfen, Civil Aviation Law in the People's Republic of China, ISBN 978-90-77596-91-3

Volume 9: Ronald M. Schnitker & Dick van het Kaar, Aviation Accident and Incident Investigation. Concurrence of Technical, ISBN 978-94-90947-01-9

Volume 10: Michael Milde, International Air Law and ICAO, second edition, ISBN 978-90-90947-35-4

Volume 11: Ronald Schnitker & Dick van het Kaar, Safety Assessment of Foreign Aircraft Programme. A European Approach to Enhance Global Aviation Safety, ISBN 978-94-9094-793-4

Volume 12: Marietta Benkö & Engelbert Plescher, Space Law: Reconsidering the Definition/Delimitation Question and the Passage of Spacecraft through Foreign Airspace, ISBN 978-94-6236-076-1

Volume 13: Heiko van Schyndel (ed.), Aviation Code of the Russian Federation, second edition, ISBN 978-94-6236-433-2

Volume 14: Alejandro Piera Valdés, Greenhouse Gas Emissions from International Aviation: Legal and Policy Challenges, ISBN 978-94-6236-467-7

Volume 15: Peter Paul Fitzgerald, A Level Playing Field for "Open Skies": The Need for Consistent Aviation Regulation, ISBN 978-94-6236-625-1

Volume 16: Jae Woon Lee, Regional Liberalization in International Air Transport: Towards Northeast Asian Open Skies, ISBN 978-94-6236-688-6

Volume 17: Tanveer Ahmad, Climate Change Governance in International Civil Aviation. Toward Regulating Emissions Relevant to Climate Change and Global Warming, ISBN 978-94-6236-692-3